THE COMPLETE

WOODWORK

FURNITURE

**INTRODUCTION
TO FURNITURE
MAKING**

**WOODWORKING
& FURNITURE
MAKING**

**THE COMPLETE
BOOK OF
WOODWORK**

INTRODUCTION TO FURNITURE MAKING

John R. Trussell

DRAKE PUBLISHERS INC.
NEW YORK   LONDON

Acknowledgment

The author is pleased to acknowledge the help he has received in assembling the information in this book from the various firms who have assisted him, especially those mentioned by name in the text and to Ridley and Hoopers of Bury St Edmunds. He would like to apologise to firms producing similar products to those referred to who are not mentioned.

He is greatly indebted to Batsfords for the courtesy, help and advice received from Miss Thelma M. Nye who has managed to reduce everything to some semblance of order and see it through to publication. Also he would like to thank Mr B. M. Chester for reading and checking the proofs.

Published in 1976 by
Drake Publishers Inc.
801 Second Avenue
New York, N.Y. 10017

LC: 76-49687

ISBN: 0-8473-1339-5

Book Club Edition

Printed in the United States of America

Contents

Introduction

This book is written for the express purpose of helping those who have acquired a basic knowledge of woodworking techniques and who now want to progress to designing and making their own furniture. It is not its purpose to provide ready made solutions for all problems or to offer completed designs but to present at least some of the possibilities and their advantages and disadvantages and leave it to the reader to choose his own answer. To this end the book is divided into several parts with the writing deliberately kept to a minimum to make reference easy.

The second part is intended as a guide to designing technique. It offers a method of approach to design which can be applied to any problem. By taking a simple example it shows how to get beyond preconceived ideas and find a new solution. It then applies the suggested method to a specific design problem.

The remainder of the parts provide readily accessible material to supplement the designer's own knowledge. He can select the joint which best suits his requirements, find the fitting that does just what he wants and the right finish to complete the job. He will be saved from making some mistakes and will be made aware of new possibilities. He will also be encouraged to tackle more advanced work than he might otherwise do.

It is hoped that it will provide a very welcome reference book for the amateur craftsman both at home and at school.

1 Timber

There are many different materials used in modern furniture manufacture, plastics, metal and cardboard, materials which, a few years ago, would not have been considered. These may provide articles of a functional nature but they lack the beauty and satisfaction which comes from using wood. This beauty remains throughout the life of the piece of furniture. As it ages it develops, through polishing and handling, a patina peculiar to wood. This book is primarily concerned with natural woods although various modern materials are introduced when appropriate.

The cabinet maker must not only know his wood, he must also be in sympathy with it. He must know its strength and its weakness and use it to its best advantage, asking it to do only those things for which it is best suited. He designs in such a way that the wood is favourably displayed not to show off his own clever construction. He will store a board having especially choice grain and colour until just the right job comes along. Rather like a sculptor working in wood lets it suggest the subject rather than the other way round.

The outstanding quality of wood is its great natural beauty. Words cannot describe the appearance of a polished walnut panel with all its gradations of colour. No one can improve on it, it just needs showing to advantage. Similarly an attractively figured oak board is complete in itself. But it takes a craftsman to find it, converting the tree in a particular way and selecting each board with great care. Even here the layman would miss the latent beauty. But the expert sees, beneath the rough sawn face, what the wood will be like when it has been cleaned up and polished. He knows from experience the transformation that will take place as he works on it, until with a final inspection he announces the job finished.

Nor are any two pieces of wood exactly the same, indeed it is common to find one end of a board quite different from the other. Some manufacturers use stain to reduce all the pieces to a uniform colour but the hand craftsman lets the wood speak for itself. Not all woods are equally attractive but possibly because they are cheaper and stable are kept for the hidden parts of furniture, the sides and bottoms of drawers for example.

If wood is to be used intelligently it is necessary to have some knowledge of the way it grows and how it behaves after it has been felled and converted for use. While the tree is growing it

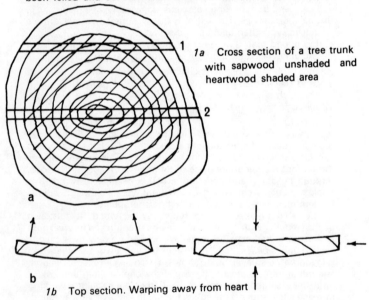

1a Cross section of a tree trunk with sapwood unshaded and heartwood shaded area

1b Top section. Warping away from heart

is full of sap and when it is felled and converted into boards it must be seasoned (dried out) before it is ready for use. This means reducing the moisture content to around 15 per cent. There are two stages in this process, in the first the 'free water' within the cells dries out and no change of shape takes place. In the second stage the cell walls themselves dry out and at this point shrinkage does occur. It would be disastrous if this movement were to happen after the piece of furniture was made.

Figure *1a* shows the cross section of a tree with the sapwood unshaded and the heartwood shaded. A tree grows by adding a ring to its growth each year. This takes place just under the bark and the sap runs freely in this area. Thus the further you are from the heart the more moisture there is to dry out.

The position of two boards is illustrated by pairs of parallel lines on the first illustration. The top one is well away from the heart and the lower one passes through it. The top face of the first board will contain more moisture than the lower face and proportionally through it and so, as it dries out, the top will shrink more than the bottom causing it to warp. The direction of warp or curve is indicated by the arrows and is always away from the heart. The second board will remain flat although it will shrink in width and thickness as it dries out, see figures *1a* and *b*.

Wood shrinks about its width and thickness but the length remains, for all practical purposes, unaltered. The shrinkage will continue until the wood has reached the same state of moisture content as the atmosphere in which it is placed. It can be reduced below this level by artificial means but it will then absorb moisture until a state of equilibrium is reached. Should the local conditions change, and this is happening all the time, the wood will react and expand or contract as the humidity goes up or down. This will continue throughout the life of the timber although the amount of movement becomes less as the timber gets older.

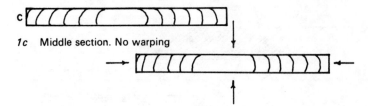

1c Middle section. No warping

The cabinet maker has to design with this twin problem in mind. His material will constantly expand and contract and will also, if he does not prevent it, tend to warp as it does so. This means that if a door is required for a cabinet it is not sufficient to plane up a rectangle of wood to the right size and hang it on hinges. At times it would jam tight and at others be too small, and it would most likely warp and twist as well.

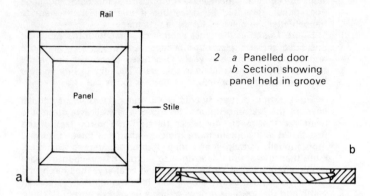

Rail

Panel

Stile

2   a Panelled door
    b Section showing
      panel held in groove

a

b

This problem is overcome by making a panelled door (see *2a* and *b*). The width of the rails and stiles is kept to a minimum and the panel is held unglued in a groove so that it can expand and contract but not warp. The door remains true and any alterations to its outside measurements are too small to be of importance. The method of securing table tops and other problems in this field are dealt with in Part 5.

Wood cells are long and narrow and bound loosely together. A chopper illustrates how easily the bond is broken. Figures *3a* and *b* show two seesaws. In the first the grain is running across the board and it would collapse as soon as it was used while the second would last as long as it was required.

3   a Short grain seesaw

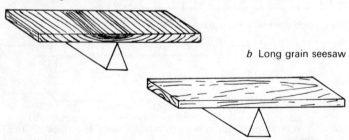

b Long grain seesaw

4 *a* Grain running round a box   *b* Grain running round a box

This means that the grain must 'run round' a box if it is to have any strength, this is illustrated in figure *4a* and *b*. If a mistake is made, as could easily happen if one of the ends was square, it would only require a slight knock for it to shatter. *5a* and *b* show two handles, in (*a*) the shaping is brought down almost to a point which has such little strength that the corners would most likely fall off during making or while gluing. This has been corrected in (*b*) to produce a strong handle.

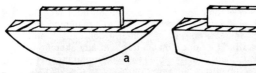

5 *a* Unsuccessful handle   *b* Successful handle

By the same reasoning dovetails and tenons must have the grain running along them as in *6a* and *b*. If they were made with the grain running across they would have no strength at all. This is also apparent in the handles already referred to.

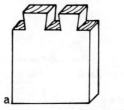

6 *a* Dovetails
   b Tenon

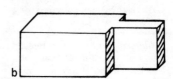

When the grain runs across or obliquely across a piece of wood then it is termed short grained as opposed to one where the

grain runs straight down it. (*7a* and *b*.) Any deviation from the straight means a loss in strength. In order to achieve this maximum strength with a curved member like a chair leg a board is carefully chosen which has a matching curve to the grain. (*8*).

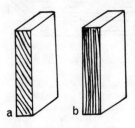

7   *a* Short grain
     b Long grain

8   Grain selected to run in same direction as shape of leg

9   Curved grain in chestnut showing how this curve can be utilised

A selection of timbers

Abura   Not a very interesting timber but suitable for hidden details; e.g. drawer sides, etc.

Agba   Another rather colourless timber similar to above. Slight odour attached to it, unsuitable for food storage.

Ash   The example in the photograph is olive ash. It can vary from this colour to near white.

Beech Red   The red colour comes through steam seasoning. Very hard wearing, tough to work, uniform in colour, takes a good polish.

Beech White   Similar except in colour.

Black Bean   A beautiful wood, rich in colour, polishes well but expensive.

Cedar   Aromatic, hard wood. Makes a scented lining for a linen chest.

Cherry   An attractive wood with a variety in colour and markings.

Chestnut   Similar to oak but without figuring, very attractive grain, useful cabinet wood.

Elm   Not always easy to obtain sound boards.

Limba   A light wood useful for interior fittings.

Mahogany Honduras   Traditional favourite of the cabinet maker.

Mahogany West African   Similar to above but lacks the quality.

Mansonia   Close grained wood which takes a good polish. Colour fades with exposure.

Oak English   A lovely timber to work, finishes cleanly, polishes well.

Oak Brown   If obtainable makes a most attractive wood.

Oak Japanese   Needs careful sorting to exclude sap, samples vary greatly in quality, slight pink cast.

Obeche   Interior fittings if straight grained.

Plum and *Pear*   'Fruit woods' which may become available to the home craftsman. The latter is especially useful for turnery.

Rosewood Indian   Turns nicely to make handles, expensive, polishes well.

Sapele   Attractive colour but inclined to be unstable in use.

Sycamore   Best quality white, used for bureau fitments, as veneer for interior of cocktail cabinets.

Teak   Rather a dull but stable timber.

Walnut English   Difficult to obtain but well worth effort, polishes well, most attractive timber.

Walnut West Africa   Possible alternative for the English variety.

Yew   Soft wood, polishes well, fair number of natural defects, knots, etc., which must be accepted.

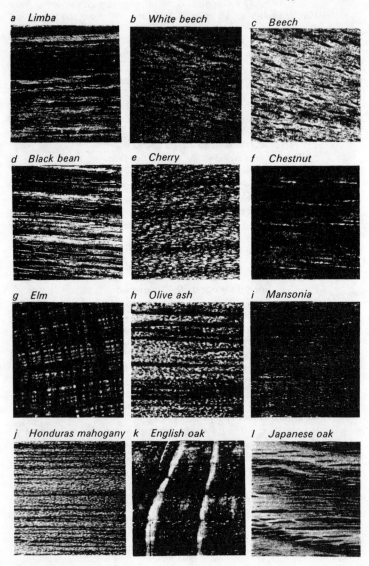

a Limba
b White beech
c Beech
d Black bean
e Cherry
f Chestnut
g Elm
h Olive ash
i Mansonia
j Honduras mahogany
k English oak
l Japanese oak

Timber and how it behaves

Movement of seasoned timber
    L Large
    M Medium
    S Small

Leaflet 47,
Forest Products Research,
Princes Risborough,
Aylesbury,
Buckinghamshire

Steam bending properties
    Radius of curvature in inches

Less than 6	Very good	VG
6 to 10	Good	G
11 to 20	Moderate	M
21 to 30	Poor	P
Exceeding 30	Very poor	VP

Leaflet 45,
Forest Products Research

Resistance to decay
    VR Very Resistant
    R   Resistant
    MR Moderate Resistance
    NR Not Resistant
    P   Perishable

Gradings used in the table of timbers
Price A up to 27s 6d a cube
        B up to 28s to 43s a cube
        C up to 43s 6d to 65s a cube
        D up to 65s 6d and over a cube

William Mallinson & Sons,
130 Hackney Road,
London E.2

Based on Forest Products Research

m —r Different types of woods

m Obeche   *n Rosewood*   *o Sapele*

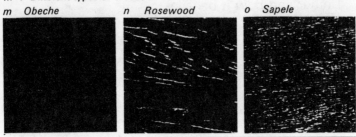

Commonly used hardwoods

Wood	Country of Origin	Price
Abura	West Africa	A
Agba	West Africa	A/B
Ash	England	A/B/C
Beech Red	Europe	A/B
Beech White	England	A/B
Black Bean	Australia	D
Cedar	Central America	C/D
Cherry	Europe	B/C
Chestnut	England	A/B
Elm	England	A/B
Limba	West Africa	B
Mahogany	Honduras	D
Mahogany	West Africa	B
Mansonia	West Africa	B/C
Oak	England	A/D
Oak Brown	England	A/D
Oak	Japan	B/D
Obeche	West Africa	A
Plum	England	—
Rosewood	India	D
Sapele	West Africa	A/B
Sycamore	England	C
Teak	Burma	C/D
Walnut	England	C/D
Walnut	West Africa	B
Yew	England	C

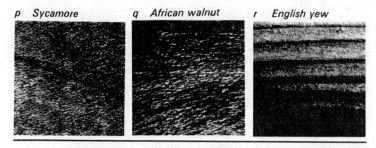

p Sycamore   q African walnut   r English yew

Colour	Movement	Bending	Resistance to decay
Straw/Pink Brown	S	VP	NR
Straw/Light Brown	S	M	R
White/Cream/Brown	M	VG	NR
Pink flecked	L	VG	NR
White flecked	L	VG	NR
Dark Brown to Black	M	VP	R
Light/Medium Brown	S	VP	R
Yellow/Pink Brown	M	VG	MR
Straw/Yellow Brown	S	G	R
Grey/Brown	M	VG	NR
Pale Yellow/Grey	S	—	NR
Pink/Dark Red Brown	S	M	R
Light/Dark Red Brown	S	VP	MR
Grey/Purple Brown	M	G	VR
Yellow Brown	M	VG	VR
Rich Brown	M	—	—
Pink/Yellow Brown	M	VG	—
Cream/Yellow	S	M	NR
Various Brown	—	—	—
Dark Purple	S	—	VR
Red Brown	M	P	MR
White	M	VG	P
Yellow/Brown	S	M	VR
Grey/Dark Brown	M	VG	MR
Yellow Brown/Brown	—	M	MR
Straw Pink/Red	—	G	VR

2 Design

Wood is essentially a beautiful material and if care is taken even the most difficult piece of timber can take on a smooth finish which will show off the infinite variety of markings which are naturally there. The range of wood available allows a great choice of colour and within the timber chosen or even the individual board there is continuous and subtle change which ensures that no two pieces will ever look exactly alike.

The designer with wood as his basic material has this tremendous advantage. His raw material is beautiful and attractive before he starts to do anything and nothing he can do can compete with this natural loveliness. His task, then, is to provide the means for displaying it.

No elaborate shapes are necessary to supply interest, this is there already, provided by the wood itself. All the designer has to do is to make the outline harmonise with the wood and its environment. The hanging book rack or display wants to 'belong' to the wall and not to stick out awkwardly.

He wants his shapes to be interesting and satisfying so that the eye travels easily around. For this purpose a curve is more pleasing than a straight line because a straight line is monotonous. A table top should not be left simply as a rectangle when a very slight curve would transform the shape.

A large amount of furniture is based on the rectangle. There are various formulae for working out certain rectangles which are said to be especially well proportioned. It is not necessary to know or use these formulae to achieve a satisfactory result. One thing that should be remembered is that a square or a near square is not a very happy solution. The eye tends to be 'unsettled' and gets worried in case it isn't exactly equal in length and height. A definite rectangle is much to be preferred.

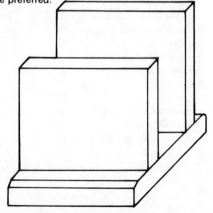

11   Basic book rack

The intending designer should study as much furniture as possible by going to the most reputable shops to see what is being made and by visits to the Design Centre and the Craft Centre. He should make copious sketches and measured drawings (a scale of $\frac{1}{8}$ in. to 1 in. is suitable). In this way he will become familiar with his subject and have a wealth of experience to draw upon.

The problem

To attempt to lay down what is or is not good design seems dangerously arbitrary. A study of the subject merely confirms the view that good design is easily confused with current fashion which varies all too inconsistently. On the other hand there are certain points which can be taken up and illustrated which will help designers to think more clearly about the problems they are trying to solve.

There are two quite different questions which will arise. In one the designer has, within limits, a free hand in choosing a particular shape and in the other he finds that decisions which are outside his control fix the basic shape that he has to start with. There will also be combinations of both.

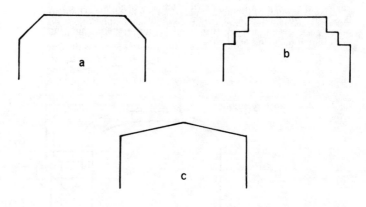

12   a–e A series of different shaped ends

d   e

Look at a simple example of the free shape. Imagine you are designing a letter rack, the size is by no means critical provided the letters are firmly held and there is enough room. The point to be considered is the shape of the partitions. Figure *11* starts with a basic rack with the corners left square and then goes through a series of shapes starting with straight lines and finishing with curves. Figure *12a* is a possibility, it takes away the sharpness of the corner; *12b* is terrible and forces the eye to go up in jerks; *12c* is an improvement on *12a* because it joins the sides and top rather more smoothly; *12d* is similar to *12a* while *12e* is most offensive, the eye is shot off instead of moving smoothly round the corners; figure *13* does all that is required. It is still a simple shape, although made up of two different curves, and it acts as a complete link bridging the sides and also providing a little interest.

Other examples of this first type of problem are provided by a book end, a coffee table top, the end of a small hanging display cabinet, the end of a bookrack (this latter is dealt with in detail later on) and a table lamp. There are some limiting factors but broadly the designer is left to himself to find a shape satisfying both functionally and aesthetically.

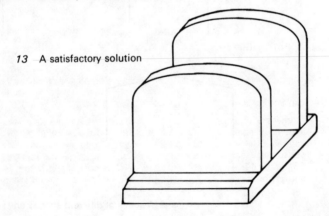

13 A satisfactory solution

18

Assembling facts

Take a piece of paper and jot down all the questions that occur to you about the article you are designing.

What is its function?
What is it to hold and how many of them?
What size are they, how heavy?
Is it to stand on the floor or hang on the wall?
Has it to fit in with any other furniture?
Is it to withstand especially heavy wear?
Is there a price ceiling?

These are just some of the questions that will occur and they will vary with different jobs. Once the list is complete then they should be answered. It is very likely that there will be two or even more answers to a number of the questions. For example, the books could be stored in a bookcase which stands on the floor or it could be secured to the wall. All these various solutions should be written down.

There will probably be certain points which allow no choice at all. Perhaps the article has to fit in with other furniture and it is felt that the same wood should be used. Taking the bookcase example again it could be that it is to be designed to hold a set of encyclopaedias and the internal dimensions are therefore fixed. Again it might have to fit into a recess between a wall and the chimney breast thus deciding the extreme sizes. These essentials should be shown very clearly on the information sheet.

Preliminary sketches

The designer now has in front of him the broad details on which he can set to work. He should make as many different sketches as he can and try to explore all the possibilities.

Imagine that the project is a magazine rack and he has been allowed a relatively free hand. He will find the answers to his various problems in the sections which follow this one. By consulting section twelve he finds that a magazine requires $13\frac{1}{2}$ in. by 11 in. of space. He then starts sketching and figure *14* shows the result of his work. He sees that the rack could stand on a table or shelf, be fastened on the wall or be part of an actual table and the sketches illustrate these three ideas. They are freehand but roughly to scale so that they give a fair idea of what each example would look like.

To make sure that they can be made the drawings should have noted the joints which are intended to be used and section three will supply the answers. While he is doing this the designer should try to visualise himself gluing up the article and go through the motions in his mind just to see that it is feasible.

The sketches should include the wood and finish. Sections 1 and 11 will give all the help that is required here. The finish will be decided by the use to which the job is to be put. If the surface is to have a lot of handling and to resist damp and heat it would be wrong to use wax polish and one of the wood seals would be more suitable.

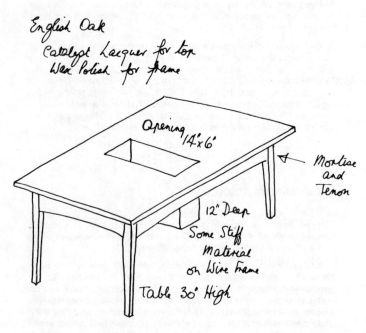

14 Preliminary sketches

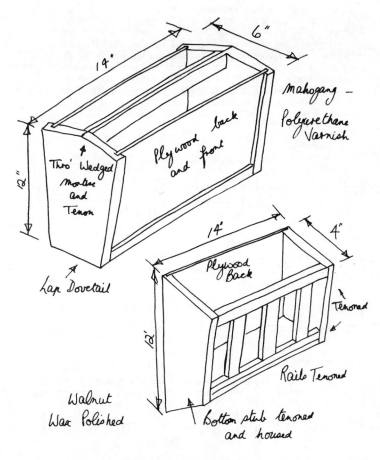

14"

6"

mahogany –

Polyurethane
Varnish

Thro' Wedged
mortise
and
Tenon

12"

Plywood back
and front

Lap Dovetail

14"

4"

Plywood
Back

12"

Tenoned

Rails Tenoned

Walnut
Wax Polished

Bottom stub tenoned
and housed

Exploring the chosen sketch

Choose the sketch that most nearly fulfils the requirements of the
brief and draw it to scale. Do this a number of times varying the
sizes this way and that. In figure *15* this technique has been
applied to a coffee table. The height, length, leg and top shape and
arrangement of stretcher rail have all been varied to see what
effect they have on the appearance.

Figure *15a* shows four different table top shapes; in (*b*) the first table has parallel legs, the second has tapered ones, in the next the rail is curved and the last has a stretcher rail added; row (*c*) shows the effect of angling the legs and repeating the variations in the row above; (*d*) illustrates the same table but the stretcher rail is moved up and down. Notice how these changes affect the whole design as the rectangles formed between the rails and the stretcher rail and the floor alter in proportions;

15 Variations for coffee table

(*e*) gradually decreases the length of the top; (*f*) increases the height. These are only some of the changes that can be made; there are many more, e.g. the amount of overhang of the top, the dimensions of the top, the degree of slope of the legs, the dimensions of the legs, the arrangement of the underframing and so on and so on. All these variations will still be within the brief and the choosing of the right one will determine whether the final solution is a happy one or not.

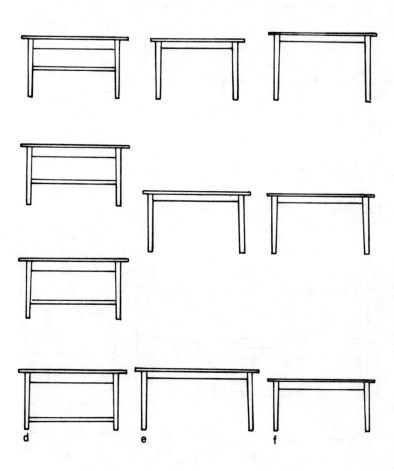

d   e   f

Working drawing

To return to the example of the magazine rack, one of the pre-liminary sketches will be chosen and drawn out to scale and various modifications made. It is now time to prepare a detailed working drawing. This should contain all the information necessary to make it. See figure *16*.

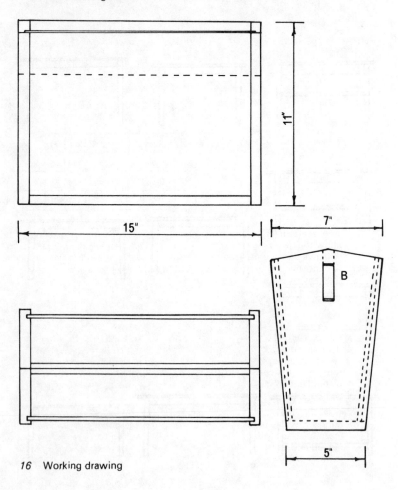

16 Working drawing

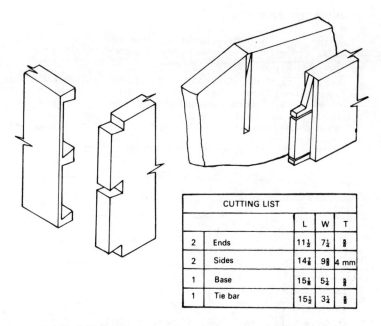

CUTTING LIST				
		L	W	T
2	Ends	$11\frac{1}{2}$	$7\frac{1}{4}$	$\frac{5}{8}$
2	Sides	$14\frac{7}{8}$	$9\frac{5}{8}$	4 mm
1	Base	$15\frac{1}{8}$	$5\frac{1}{4}$	$\frac{5}{8}$
1	Tie bar	$15\frac{1}{2}$	$3\frac{1}{4}$	$\frac{5}{8}$

A scale drawing showing three views will give the sizes and show the general arrangement. Using $\frac{1}{8}$ scale (that is $\frac{1}{8}$ in. to 1 in.) will give a very good idea of what the finished article will look like. Around this should be drawn the joint details. It is at this stage that any mistakes can be corrected. If they are left any later they may be expensive in time as well as in material. It will be noticed there have been some alterations to the sizes as a result of all the scale drawings that were made.

To this working drawing should be added a cutting list. All the pieces of wood required are listed with the use to which they are to be put. Having the use noted will allow the selection of particularly attractive wood for such items as drawer fronts and tops. It is usual to make an allowance on the finished sizes for planing the edges and squaring the ends. This is the list which can be handed to the timber supplier.

If the drawing is more complicated and involves difficult curves it will be necessary to make a full size drawing. A dining room chair is a good illustration of this point. The legs are usually curved and a scaled down drawing would not be accurate enough to work from.

Rectangular shapes

Figure *17* shows a number of outline shapes of pieces of furniture. All are rectangular, in some the base is long compared with the height and in others the reverse is true.

In many cases the outside shape is decided by circumstances. The article must contain a certain number of items of a particular size and it has to match the height of another piece of furniture or it has to fit into a recess. This basic shape may not itself be well proportioned or pleasant to look at. The problem is to know how it can be improved.

17 Outline shapes

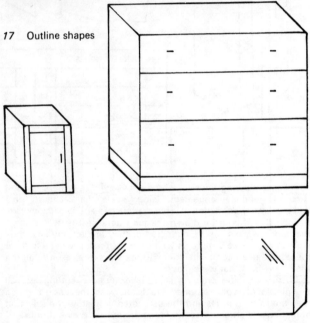

Figure *18* starts by illustrating a square and then two well-proportioned rectangles, one standing on its long side and the other on the short. Both the latter look very much happier than the square.

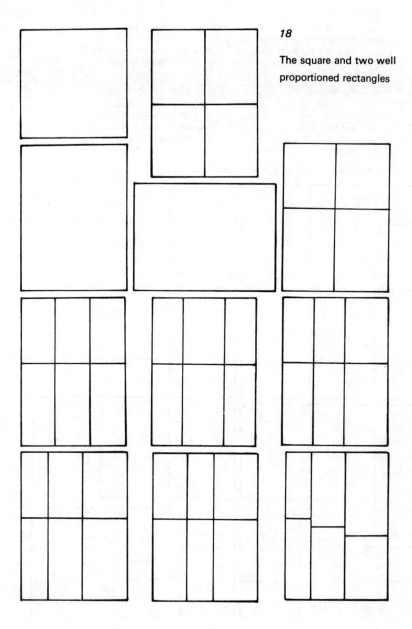

The square and two well
proportioned rectangles

The second and third lines take a rectangle and divide it up to see what effect this has. These eight variations are only a few of the possibilities but they are enough to show that the designer has tremendous scope. He can, by altering the internal arrangement, create his own interest.

Figure *19* applies this to a specific problem. A sideboard is required, the length is dictated by the room and the height has also been stipulated. Once again only eight arrangements are shown but many more are possible. It is not essential to have a symmetrical design like (*b*) or (*d*); there is a whole range of other permutations.

19 *a–h* The rectangle applied to a specific problem

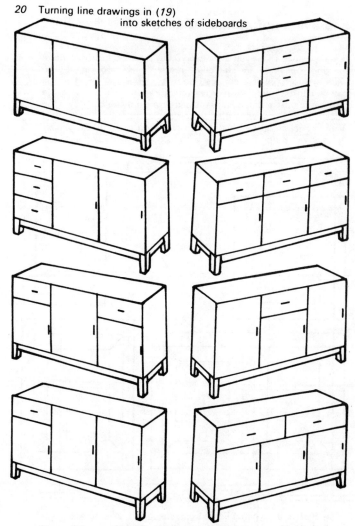

20 Turning line drawings in (*19*) into sketches of sideboards

Figure *20* turns the line drawings into sketches of sideboards to give a better idea of what they would look like. In this way the designer takes an unpromising shape and improves it by the way he arranges the various cupboards and drawers. There is nearly always something that can be done in even the most difficult and unfavourable situation and it is under difficult conditions like this that the designer shows his true worth.

Improving unfortunate shapes

It may well be that even after everything possible has been done the door openings are still badly proportioned, too square, too wide or too high. If a panelled door is used the shaping of the panels can be made to improve the situation. In figure *21a* the opening is square shaped and the panels are only fielded down the sides; (*b*) is a very wide door which could either have two doors or the panel could be divided into two with a muntin; (*d*) illustrates a well-proportioned door with its panels fielded on all sides.

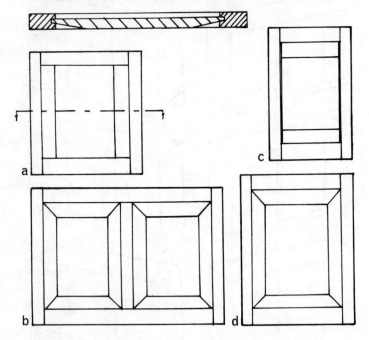

21 *a* Square door panel fielded on sides only
b Wide door divided by muntin into two panels
c Narrow door fielded top and bottom only with gap at sides to allow for movement
d Well proportioned door and panel

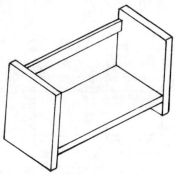

Designing a book rack

22 a-w Designing a book rack

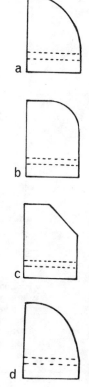

A bookrack makes a very suitable subject for an early exercise in design. It is reasonably small and its function is straightforward and easily understood. Only a limited quantity of wood is required enabling a mock-up to be easily and cheaply made and the completed article itself will not be very expensive. Finally, the hours involved are short and the results, pleasing or otherwise, are soon obtained. At the same time there are plenty of problems to be solved if the finished bookrack is to be worthwhile.

In this section an attempt will be made to follow the design through the usual stages to the point where it tends to get stuck, and take it further until the problem is approached in the abstract. At first the mind is clogged up with the very mediocre bookracks which usually serve the purpose and gradually, if enough time is spent, these can be forgotten and a new approach made.

The first pictorial view shows the usual bookrack in the 'square'. To be quite fair it is extremely functional and will hold books very adequately. The embryo designer is now faced with the problem of how to shape the ends since it is apparent that it would be unsatisfactory to leave it like that. If he is wise he will draw a number of rectangles to scale representing the end and see what he can make of it. If he fancies a curve, he will think in terms of a simple compass curve and figure *22* (*a*) or (*b*) is the result or, if straight lines, then (*c*). With any luck he will not like his efforts and will realise that a compass curve is rarely pleasing because it is monotonous and continuing will come up with (*d*) or (*e*) where an attempt is made to link up the back, top and front edges and make a more unified design. Cutting out a portion of the end could make for an interesting effect as shown in (*g*) and (*h*).

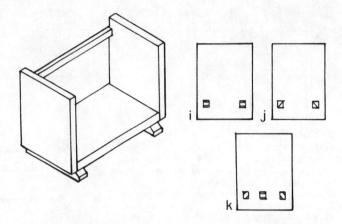

The joints can themselves be used as decoration if they are taken through and wedged. (*i*), (*j*) and (*k*) show three possibilities with the wedges inserted in different directions. The tenons could also be made to stand out proud for $\frac{1}{4}$ in. and be chamfered around the edges.

The second pictorial sketch shows another variation. Here the shelf or base is joined with lap dovetails to the ends. This method allows the introduction of feet which can be set in from the ends, as in the diagram, or made flush. These feet can be either parallel strips or they can be tapered from back to front. In the latter case it will incline the whole bookrack slightly backwards.

Looking at the front elevation of the bookrack there are several arrangements for the back rail. It could be single and narrow, single and wide, double or even panelled. At this point it becomes clear that the rail could just consist of one narrow rail placed low down. If this is done then the shaping could continue much further round and the 'squareness' of the back edge relieved. Explore these possibilities in figure *22 l–q*.

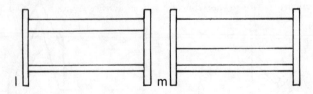

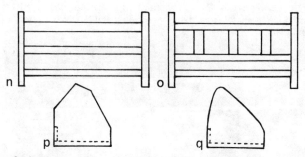

So far the books have been held upright or nearly so, but is this the only way? Would it not display the books to better advantage if they were leaning further back? This arrangement will be less formal and the titles will be more easily read. At first this new positioning is considered within the already accepted construction and (r) shows this new arrangement within a blank end, (s) and (t) show the new freedom this allows.

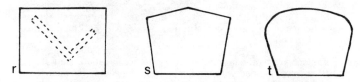

But why must the conventional construction be used? Draw the outline of the book in its new attitude and decide what is needed to hold the book in that position. There must be a support for the back and front of the book and something to stop them sliding off the end. A possibility is shown in (u). This looks as if it might be easily tipped forward and in (v) it is allowed to lean back further. (w) is a further extension along these lines with only rails supporting the books and here the old image of a book rack has completely vanished.

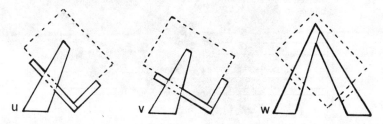

23 A book rack in English walnut. The shape has changed from the original sketch to achieve a stronger joint between the two end pieces.

24 A book rack in black bean with sycamore end pieces

Designing an easy chair

This project is taken right through from the time when it was decided that this was the next job to be undertaken until the completed chair. This chapter tries to show how the design came into being and the various factors which influenced it and the problems which had to be overcome.

25 Easy chair with English oak frame, laminated removable back and re-movable side panels

The brief was concise and controlled the design from the start. It consisted of the following eight points.

1 It must be comfortable.
2 It must be easily upholstered and when the time came re-upholstered.
3 To have wooden arms bare of upholstery because these seem to wear quicker than anywhere.
4 The back to have 'wings' to keep off the draughts.
5 The back to be high to support the head in comfort.
6 To be light enough to be easily moved.
7 To be less bulky than the average easy chair.
8 To be stable.

This was a formidable list to include in one design.

A long time was spent on preliminary sketches to try and get an idea of what a chair which answered all these criteria would look like. At the same time it was realised that there are certain essential dimensions which decide whether a chair will be comfortable or not. These will remain the same whatever design is eventually decided upon.

26   a–b

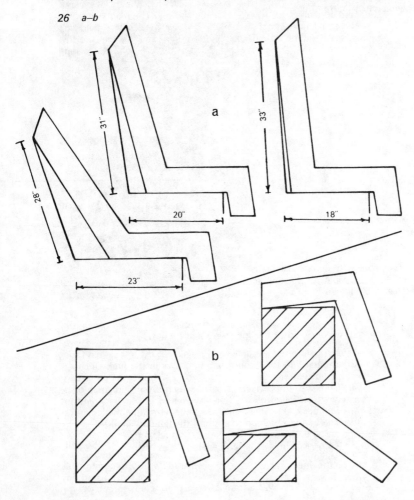

The chair must be wide enough across the front to admit any reasonably sized person. There are then three essential measurements; from the ground to the seat, from the front of the seat to the back, and from the back of the seat to the top of the back. A study of various chairs showed that the second two were complementary. (See *26a*.) Make the depth of the seat greater then the height of the back could be reduced and vice versa. There appeared to be quite a tolerance here. The height from the floor could not exceed a certain figure or the victim would find his legs dangling in space or on the other hand if it was too low his legs would be uncomfortable and tend to stick out a long way. (See *26b*.) These sizes settled themselves easily.

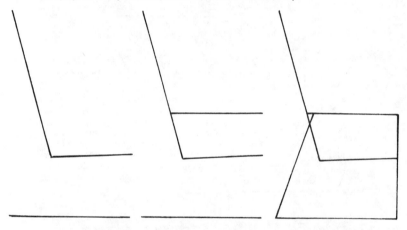

26 c

A lot of scale drawings were now made to get these sizes on to paper and see what they looked like. In the first sketch (*26c*) just the seat and the back were shown in single line. Once the seat height was established this fixed the height of the arms. Legs were added to make a stable chair which would not rock or be liable to tip backwards when anyone sat in it. The back and the arms had now to be considered as a shape to do a particular job; at this stage the constructional problems were ignored.

It was considered essential now to put together a 'mock-up' to test the design as far as it had gone. A chair which looked very fine on the drawing board could turn out to be most uncomfortable when it was made up. A frame was nailed together using any available wood and the various measurements altered until the most comfortable solution was found which fitted into the general plan. There was little to quarrel with at this stage.

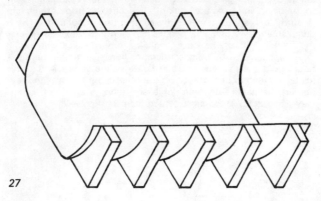

27

There were still many technical problems to be solved before the chair could be constructed. The original idea was to mould a back in fibreglass and this was in fact done. A mould was made of plywood on shaped battens (*27, 28*) and the fibreglass back formed inside. To make the back a sheet of polythene was draped over the mould and a layer of resin applied. On this was

28 The mould used to make the back of the chair

laid a sheet of glass mat and a further layer of resin added. Two more thicknesses of glass mat and resin produced the desired thickness. When this was dry it was removed from the mould, the polythene ensuring that it came away easily without sticking. The result was a very strong though springy back with the disadvantage of looking inadequate. This proved to be fairly expensive but it did produce a back of the desired shape. This was very useful used in conjunction with the mock-up and enabled the final shape to be decided upon and the best angle for the back was then found by trial and error.

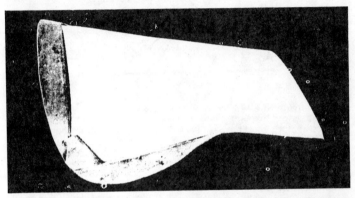

29

The sketching was continued in an attempt to fix on a construction which would unite the back and the legs. Finally the idea came of making the arms and the back rail as a unit and then tenoning this into the frame (*30a*). The only way thought to make the back rail strong enough was to laminate and join the arms with dovetails. This would have the advantage of keeping the joint between the back rail and the arms clear of the top of the back legs. The sketches were now taken to the drawing board and a working drawing made of the frame. This incorporated all the information gained from the 'mock-up'.

It became obvious, at this stage, that the dominant feature in the design would be the shape of the arms and sketch after sketch was rejected until the final shape was arrived at. The widening out inside seemed to suggest both comfort and a welcome while the more sever shaping on the outside matched the rather austere frame (*30b*).

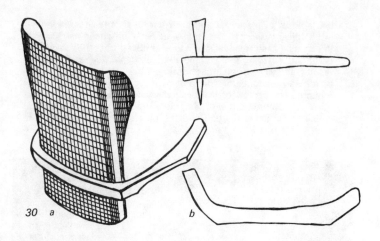

30   a   b

The frame was now made, although not all the details were yet solved. Enough was decided to enable a start to be made. Once this was done the fibreglass back was propped into position and different angles were tried out until the most comfortable one was discovered. People were asked to sit in the chair and their reactions were studied. They were deliberately chosen so that some were short and others tall in an attempt to discover proportions which would satisfy most people. Once the position of the back was finally established the length of the arms could be ascertained and the arm and back rail unit made up. The back rail was laminated from $\frac{1}{8}$ in. strips around a former and then dovetailed into the arms.

It was realised at this stage that it would not be very easy to upholster the back because of the impossibility of driving tacks into the fibreglass. At the same time a glance at the mould showed that plywood would take up the shape since it had already been used in its construction. Two sheets of plywood were roughly shaped, glued and cramped into the mould and allowed to set. When they were released they retained their shape and the first plywood back had been produced. It was only 8 mm thick and inclined to be a little 'whippy' as well as looking rather thin and light, although perfectly strong enough for the job. To stiffen the edges and give some thickening, strips of 4 mm Gaboon were glued around the top edge and down the sides to bring them up to about 1 in. in thickness. This was then shaped and tapered from the top edge to the point where the back would meet the back rail (29).

The chair sides were made in a similar way. Curved panels were made by gluing two sheets of plywood together. These were to be held in place by fitting into a groove in the front leg and a rebate on the back (*31*). They were to be fastened with a screwed batten thus allowing for their easy removal.

31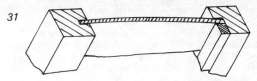

The arm unit was secured to the legs with stopped tenons wedged securely from the underside. The back was held in place with four screws into the bottom rail and it was rested on the back rail, there being no tendency for it to come forward. The chair was now put into use for a week. It must be appreciated that a chair that is comfortable for a few minutes may well give the occupant back ache after a few hours! This was the last opportunity to make any minor changes.

32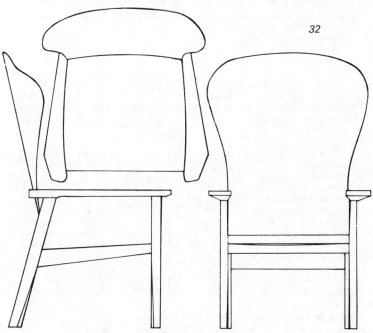

The chair, having now passed the test, was ready for upholstering. A 1 in. layer of foam was glued onto the inside of the back. It was not felt that any thicker was necessary because it had been quite comfortable during the test period without anything there at all. The inside was now covered with material which was tacked into the strips which had been glued on to thicken the back. The cover for the back was sewed in place making a seam around the edge. The two side panels were slipped into carefully made 'envelopes' and the two retaining strips secured. With the coil springs clipped into the seat and the foam seat placed on top the chair was complete. Figure *32* shows three views of the completed chair.

3 Joints

Tee joints

33   Half lap. This is a very easy joint to make but is not very strong. Usually reinforced with screws. Used in soft wood frames.

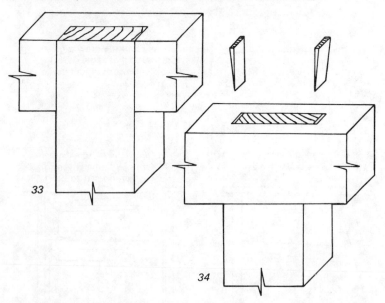

34   Through wedged mortise and tenon. This is an extremely strong joint. It can also be drawn pinned. See 'Bridle joint' *36*

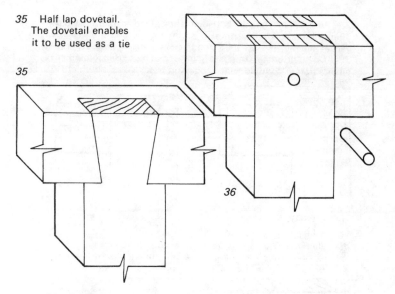

35 Half lap dovetail.
   The dovetail enables
   it to be used as a tie

36 Bridle joint. It can be used with or without the draw pin. To fit the pin, holes are drilled slightly out of line so that as the dowel is knocked in it pulls the joint up tight. Commonly used without pin to join centre leg to a plinth

Frame joints

37 Simple butt mitre. This is much used by the picture framer and strengthened with a nail across the corner. With the advent of modern glues this is a much stronger joint than it used to be.

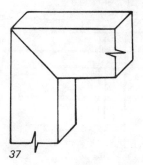

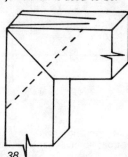

43

38 Veneer key. Here the butt joint is first glued and allowed to dry. Then the corners are sawn at a dovetail angle and the pieces of veneer glued in. If these are a good fit a very strong bond will result
39 Dovetail bridle. This is a joint sometimes used on a heavy picture frame. It would need modifying to take a rebate

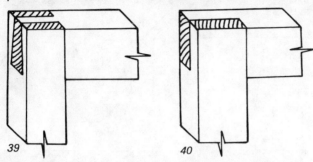

40 Half lap. This is suitable for a light frame like a kitchen cabinet door which is going to be strengthened with hardboard
41 Bridle or open mortise and tenon. Not a very attractive joint to use on furniture; it shows too much end grain. Any shrinkage of the rail is also very obvious

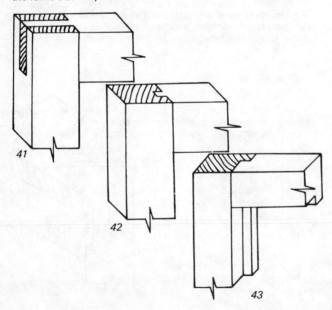

42 Stopped mortise and tenon. A very useful joint which can have a sloping haunch if it is visible and a square one if it is unsighted. It can be combined with a groove in which case it will require a square haunch to fill the gap left by the groove

43 Long and short shouldered mortise and tenon. If the frame is rebated, to hold glass for example, then this construction is indicated

Carcase joints

44 Pinned and glued. This is only suitable for small jobs where the joint is not expected to take a lot of strain

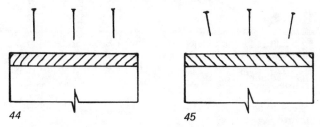

45 Dovetail pinned. The angle of the nails makes a stronger joint

46 Lapped and pinned. This is stronger than those mentioned above, it is also neater because it hides more of the end grain

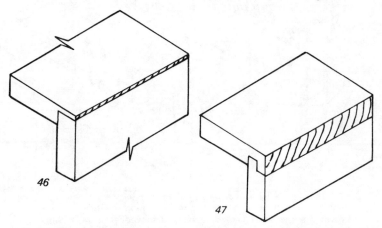

47 Tongue and groove. Used a lot commercially for chess boxes and similar articles

48 Dovetail tongue. This makes a strong practical joint

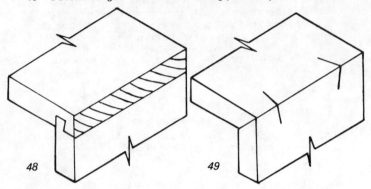

48 49

49 Butt mitre with veneer keys. The keys are added after the butt is glued and set making a very strong and easy construction
50 Through dovetail. A very strong and attractive joint which can be mitred at both or one edge

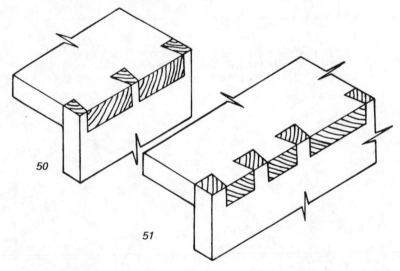

50

51

51 Through dovetail variations. The edge tails are smaller to achieve more holding power where it is most needed. It also provides added interest and this could be repeated on a wide board, i.e. two narrow tails followed by two wide ones. There are other variations which could be adopted

52 Lap dovetail. This is a suitable joint to use for a carcase bottom where only one part of the joint is visible

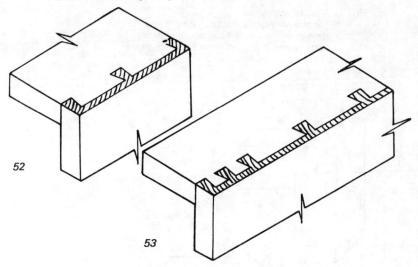

52

53

53 Lap dovetail. To achieve greater strength at the edges the two outer tails on each side of the joint are smaller to increase the gluing area

54 Secret lap dovetail. This avoids almost all the end grain and the lap can be moulded so that even that little bit is not noticeable

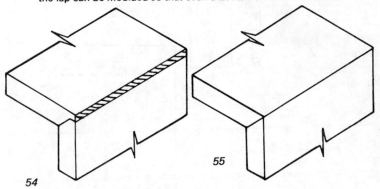

55

54

55 Secret mitre dovetail. No joint is visible and it is left to the grain of the wood to provide interest. This is used in high class cabinet work.

Stool joints

56   *a* Mortise and tenons
     b Tenons mitred to meet rails at right angles
     c Rails over 3 in. wide have double tenons
     d Extra strong thick rails have twin tenons
57   Open mortise and tenon or bridle joint
58   Lap dovetail

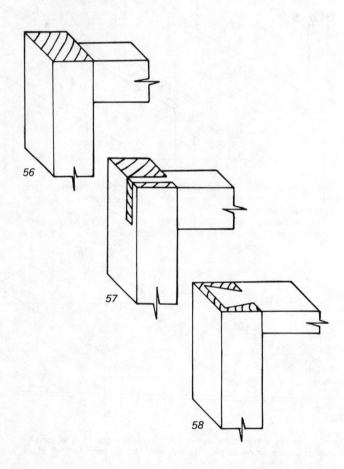

4 Joint construction Mortise and tenons

Marking out a corner mortise and tenon

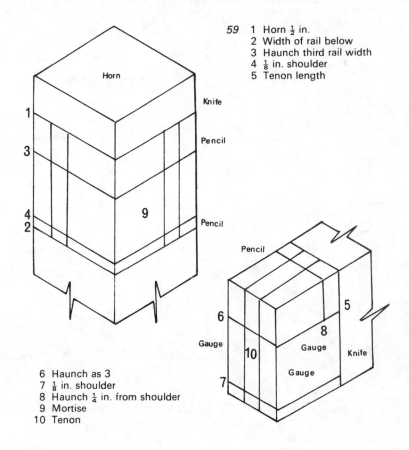

59 1 Horn $\frac{1}{2}$ in.
2 Width of rail below
3 Haunch third rail width
4 $\frac{1}{8}$ in. shoulder
5 Tenon length

6 Haunch as 3
7 $\frac{1}{8}$ in. shoulder
8 Haunch $\frac{1}{4}$ in. from shoulder
9 Mortise
10 Tenon

Chopping the mortise

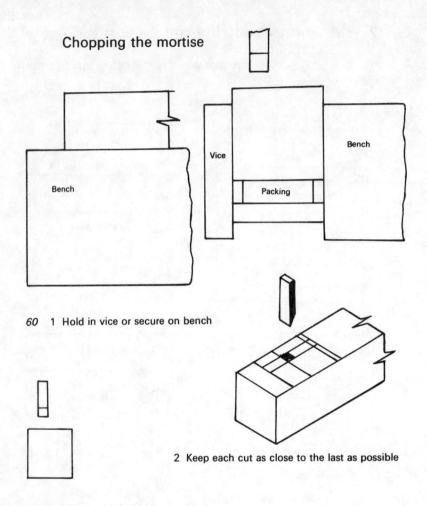

60   1 Hold in vice or secure on bench

2 Keep each cut as close to the last as possible

3 Keep chisel vertical and avoid any sideways leaning

4 Mark depth of mortise on chisel with pencil or plaster

50

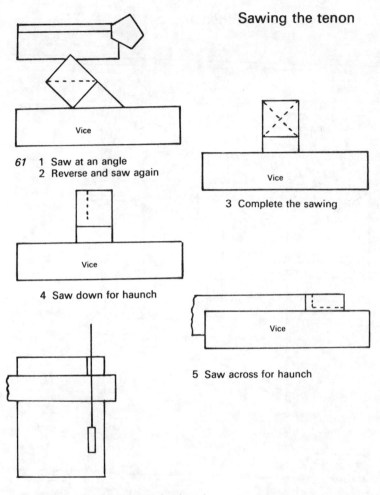

Sawing the tenon

61   1 Saw at an angle
       2 Reverse and saw again

3 Complete the sawing

4 Saw down for haunch

5 Saw across for haunch

6 Saw shoulders on sawing board

7 Reverse and repeat
8 True shoulders with shoulder plane
    if necessary
9 Chisel haunch to make it slope
10 Fit carefully

Corner mortise and tenon

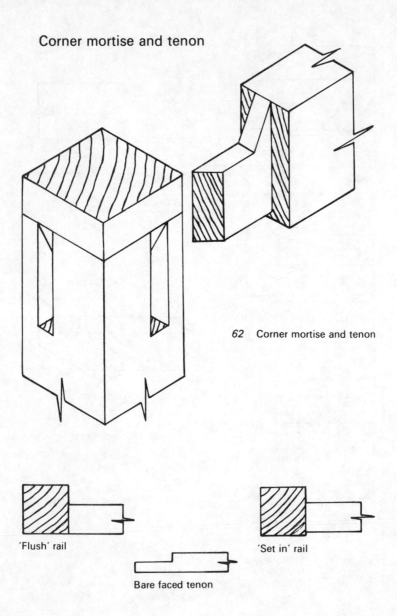

62   Corner mortise and tenon

'Flush' rail

'Set in' rail

Bare faced tenon

Grooved mortise and tenon

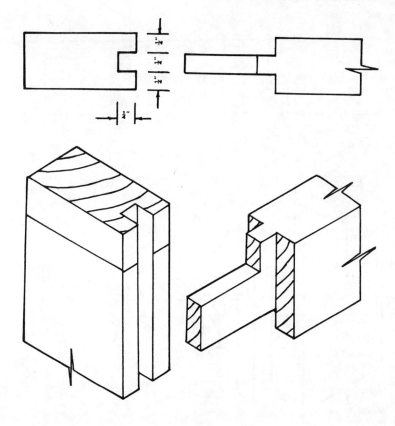

63 1 Mark out as for ordinary mortise and tenon but allow $\frac{1}{4}$ in.
   shoulder at lower edge for groove
 2 Square haunch to fill groove
 3 Chop mortise
 4 Saw down tenon but do not remove cheeks
 5 Work groove on both rails and stiles
 6 Remove cheeks of tenon
 7 Fit carefully

Long and short shouldered mortise and tenon

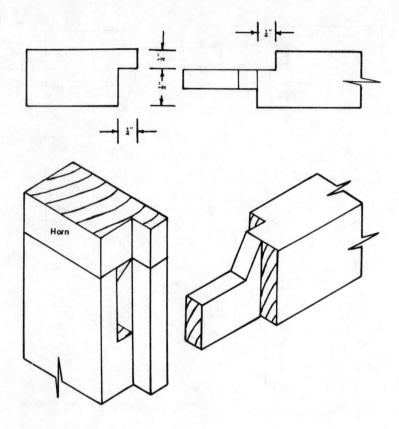

64 1 Mortise hole marked out as for ordinary mortise and tenon
2 Tenon marked out with one long and one short shoulder
3 Chop mortise disregarding rebate
4 Saw down tenons but do not remove cheeks
5 Work rebates on both stiles and rails
6 Remove cheeks from tenons
7 Fit carefully

Faults in tenons

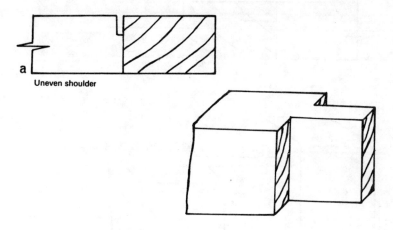

a Uneven shoulder

65a One shoulder is sawn too much in the waste or on the wrong side of the line

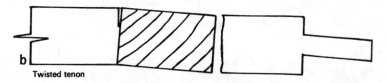

b Twisted tenon

65b and *c* The tenon is sawn at an angle in one direction or the other or it could be in both directions

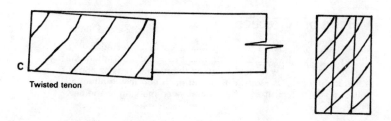

c Twisted tenon

65d A too tight tenon forced in is causing end splits

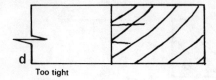

Too tight

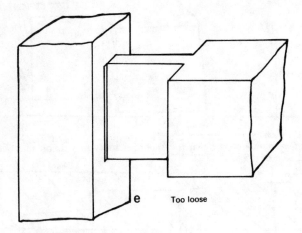

e   Too loose

65e Too thin a tenon

Method of correction

66a If one shoulder is too long this is easily corrected with a shoulder plane. If one shoulder has been undercut then the shoulder line must be re-marked when the procedure is as above. If this occurs on a rail with a tenon at each end it will affect all rails of a similar length and they will all need marking to the new length

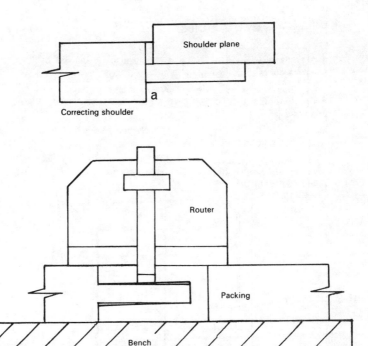

Shoulder plane

Correcting shoulder

a

Router

Packing

Bench

b

66b A tenon which is oversize or twisted can be corrected by cramping it on a bench top with a packing piece of the same thickness close by. Use a router across the gap and this will ensure that the tenon sides become parallel to the rail face

This may make the tenon too loose in which case it will be necessary to make up this thickness by gluing pieces of veneer on the tenon sides. Do not attempt to force the saw when sawing tenons since this will make it tend to leave the line and follow the grain.

Faults in mortise holes

The faults illustrated in *65b* and *c* may also be caused by in-accurate chopping of the mortise hole.

While chopping is in progress leave the chisel in the hole every now and then and check with a trysquare that the chisel is going in square (*67*).

Work within the lines and make each successive cut as near to the last one as possible.

Any untrueness must be corrected by paring and this will lead to an oversize mortise hole. Reasonable care in chopping should avoid this problem.

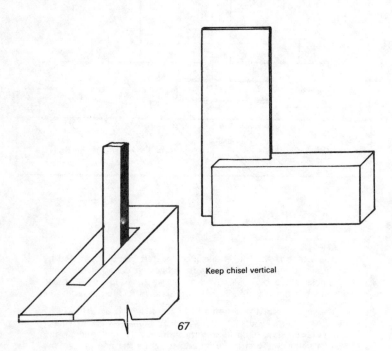

Keep chisel vertical

67

Fitting mortise and tenons

Careful fitting will save some mistakes from taking place.

1   Start by 'offering up' the corners of the tenon to the mortise
(*68a*); this will indicate if it is the tenon thickness which is
preventing the joint from going home.

68a

2   The second check is to try the tenon for length. If the tenon
passes this test as well as the first then, provided it isn't wedge
shaped it should fit (*68b*).

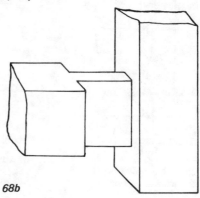

68b

Joint Construction   Dovetails

Slope

The slope of a dovetail is important. The usually accepted angle is 1 in 7, i.e. $\frac{1}{4}$ in. in $1\frac{3}{4}$ in. This can be set on a sliding bevel by marking the angle on a bench top. Square a line across the top and measure 7 in. along it. Measure 1 in. from this line along the edge of the bench and join these two points, see figure *69a*. This is the dovetail slope.

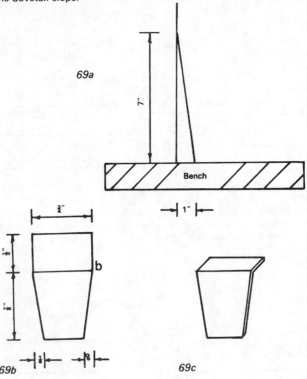

69 b, c A simple template can be made with a piece of mild steel or brass. Cut and file it to size and then bend the top half-inch to a right angle.

Common dovetail

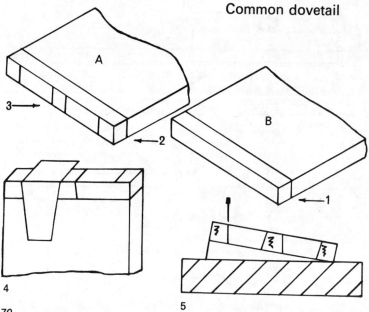

70

1 and 2 Cutting gauge set to thickness of wood on A and B
3 Mark out dovetails on end of A with pencil and square
4 Use dovetail template and pencil, also mark waste
5 Place at an angle in vice and saw alternate tails with tenon saw
6 Reverse and saw others
7 Saw corner pins with tenon saw
8 Remove centre pins with coping saw

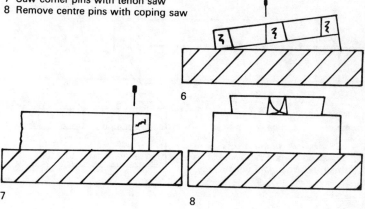

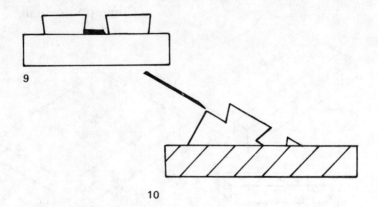

9   Clean out with bevel edged chisel
10 Clean out corners
11 Mark B from A using scriber
12 Square down sides in pencil, mark waste

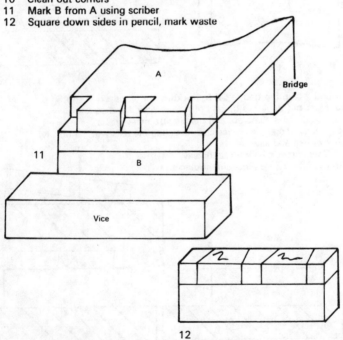

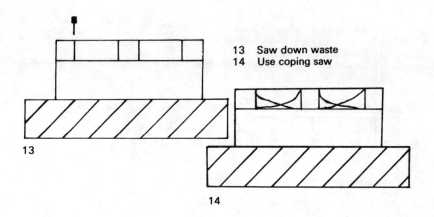

13 Saw down waste
14 Use coping saw

13

14

Lap dovetail

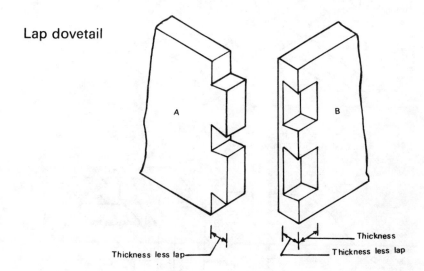

A   B

Thickness less lap

Thickness

Thickness less lap

71
1 and 2 Cutting gauge set to thickness less $\frac{3}{16}$ in. for lap
3 Cutting gauge set to thickness
4 Mark out tails and proceed as for Common Dovetail up to 11

12 Square down inside of B with pencil, mark waste
13 Hold in vice and saw down with tenon saw
14 Remove part waste with coping saw
15 Secure on bench, remove waste with chisel and mallet
16 Fit carefully

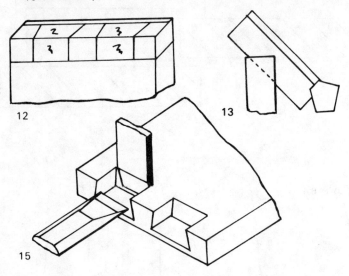

Clean out by paring on to chiselling board on bench (*a*) or on to chiselling board in vice (*b*)

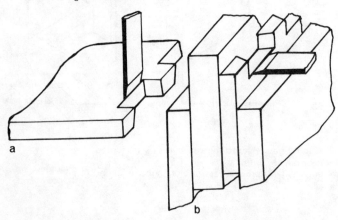

Dovetail hints

The recommended way to make through and lap dovetails is to tackle the tails first and to use them as a template. It is essential, therefore, that they should be accurately made.

Checking dovetails

72a   Look at the ends of the tails and check that they are square. A small engineer's square is invaluable for this. If any are inaccurate, place the wood in the vice (*b*) and pare carefully down while maintaining the dovetail slope

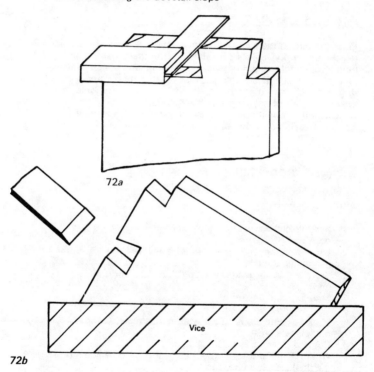

72a

72b

Vice

72c   The most common fault is to undercut the shoulders as illustrated. A line must be squared round the lowest point and the waste removed. The waste is shown blacked in. This fault should be avoided because the correction will nearly always alter vital measurements

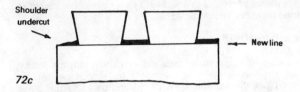

Shoulder
undercut

New line

72c

Fitting dovetails

Place the pins in the vice and 'offer up' the tails carefully. Do not remove any wood unless sure that it is the part that is causing trouble. Do not force it into place. A light tap with a tack hammer on each tail will indicate any tails that are sticking by producing a different note from the rather hollow tone of the free joint. Pare down the sides of any pins which require attention and fit again. Repeat until the joint can be pushed together. A too tight joint will cause splitting so do not use too much force.

Secret lap dovetail

Square both ends

1 Set the cutting gauge to $\frac{3}{16}$ in. and gauge lines 1 and 2 on A and B (*73a*).
2 Set the cutting gauge to wood thickness less $\frac{3}{16}$ in. and gauge line 3 on A.
3 Set the cutting gauge to wood thickness and gauge line 4 on B.
4 Mark out the pins on A.
5 Gauge mitres on A and B with marking gauge.
6 Mark out mitre on A and B with mitre square.
7 Mark waste on A.
8 Cut and clean up pins.
9 Work rebate on B leaving $\frac{1}{64}$ in. on the lip to be taken off at the final cleaning up stage.
10 Transfer markings from A to B. Place B flat on bench and cramp A on top with a sash cramp while this is being done (*73b*).

11 Mark the waste and make the tails.
12 Cut mitres and leave a small margin for final fitting.
13 Fit carefully. The lips of B's rebate can be finished off with a shoulder plane.

Note It is essential to make the pins first.

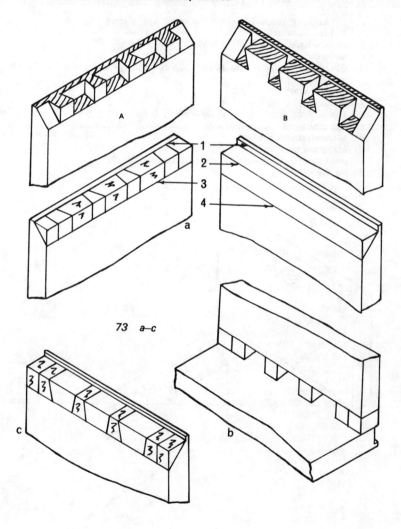

73 a–c

Secret mitre dovetail

Square both ends

1   Set cutting gauge to $\frac{3}{16}$ in. and gauge 1 and 2 on A and B (*74a*).
2   Set cutting gauge to wood thickness and gauge 3 on A and B.
3   Work rebates on A and B (*74b*).
4   Mark out tails on A.
5   Gauge mitres on A and B with marking gauge and mitre square (*74b*).
6   Mark in waste on A (*74c*).
7   Make pins.
8   Transfer the markings to B by placing B flat on the bench and cramping A onto it (*74d*).
9   Mark waste on B (*74e*).
10 Make the tails.
11 Work the mitres at corners and on rebates carefully.
12 Fit the joint.

Note   It is essential to make the pins first.

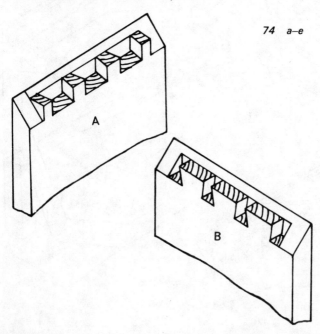

74   a–e

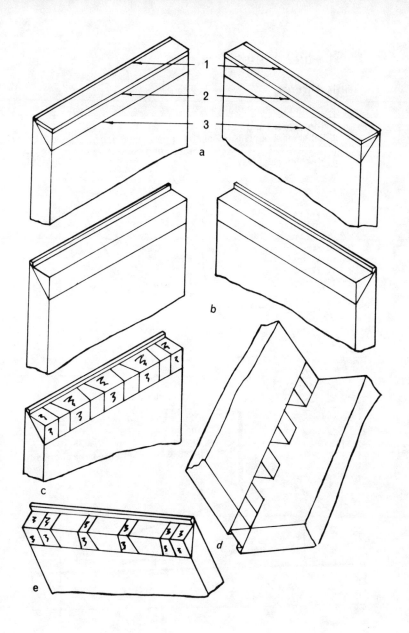

5 Special constructions

Angled joints

75 *a*
1 Through or lap dovetail
2 Either mark out tails from end before sloping at usual slope or afterwards with specially set sliding bevel
3 Make in usual way

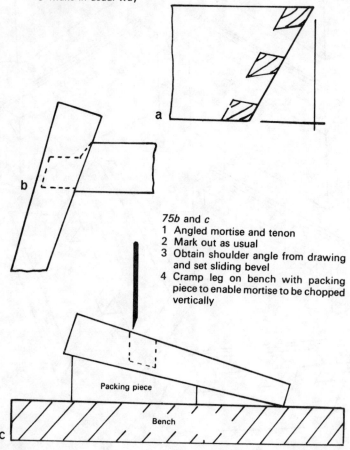

75b and *c*
1 Angled mortise and tenon
2 Mark out as usual
3 Obtain shoulder angle from drawing and set sliding bevel
4 Cramp leg on bench with packing piece to enable mortise to be chopped vertically

Packing piece

Bench

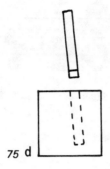

75 d

1 Front leg of dining chair with angled mortise and tenon
2 Cramp on bench and use chisel at angle
3 Set sliding bevel to an angle and use to check as work proceeds

Backs

76a Here the plywood or hardboard back is held in a rebate using either screws or panel pins.

76b Plywood or hardboard can also be held in a groove but in this case it cannot be removed once the carcase is assembled. It also makes gluing up a little more involved.

76c In this example a panelled frame is made up, a tongue worked along the top and two outside edges and the whole thing slid in place and secured with screws. The panel can be simple or fielded. It will be necessary on a wide back to have one or more muntins to reduce the widths of individual panels.

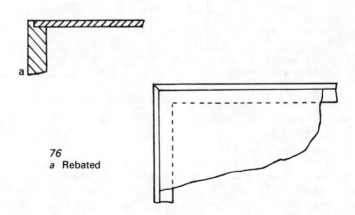

76
a Rebated

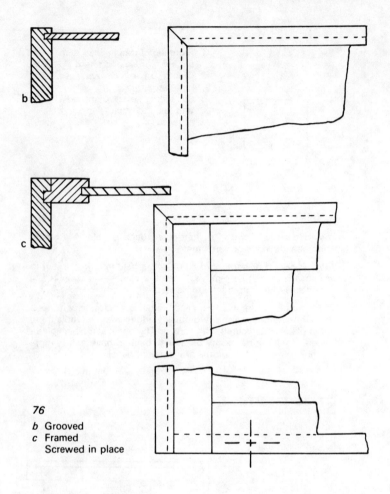

76
b Grooved
c Framed
Screwed in place

Bureaux

1   77*a* shows the traditional method for hanging a bureau fall.
The fall is hinged with strap hinges and a stop prevents it from
going in too far.

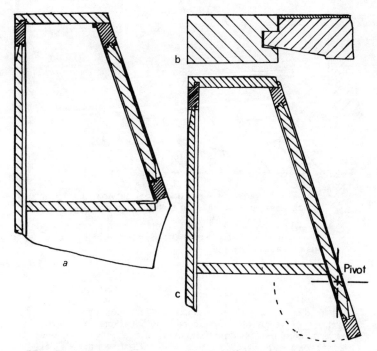

77b The panel is made to come nearly flush with the inside, allowing for the thickness of the skiver. An $\frac{1}{8}$ in. of cardboard under the skiver gives a pleasant surface to write on

2 Another method of hanging a fall is illustrated in *77c* and *d*. The fall is pivoted on a metal pin covered with a hardwood plug. This is most suitable for a small hanging bureau, if it was used with a drawer underneath there would be a lot of unusable space because the fall below the pivot moves in an arc as the fall is opened to support it.

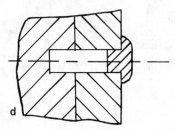

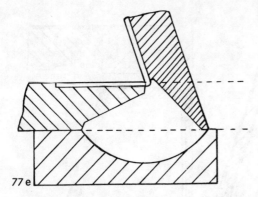

77e

3 *77e* illustrates the more traditional method of achieving (*c*) which does not involve more than an inch of waste space.

4 The stationery is usually contained in a separate fitment having the necessary pigeon holes which slides in place after the bureau is glued up.

Chairs

The method of constructing chairs has changed considerably over recent years. Although these new ideas are very much easier to carry out it is doubtful whether the resulting chairs will last as long as their predecessors. Figure *78* shows three styles of chairs: (*a*) traditional, (*b*) simplified and (*c*) laminated. The following are some notes on the points which have to be considered in each of these types of construction.

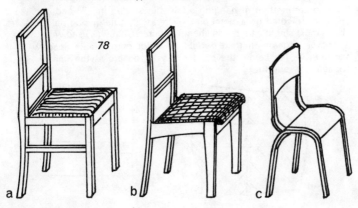

78

a   b   c

Traditional dining chairs

To give the maximum comfort the seat is slightly wider at the front than the back and slopes backwards while the back is wider at the top and gets narrower as it runs into the back legs. The points are illustrated in figure *79a* in which the plan is shown at seat level. All these factors cause complications which are explained.

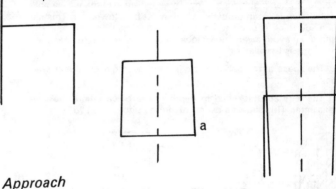

a

Approach

This follows the suggested plan in the design section.

1   Like the chair mentioned in that section a lot of experiment is necessary if the chair is going to be comfortable. Chairs of all sizes should be sat on to see how the body reacts; whether the seat is high enough or, most important, is the back at the right angle and height. Careful measurements should be made and notes taken. It is about these sizes that the chair will be built.

2   Make as many sketches around the basic dimensions, attempting to achieve many different designs, trying to think as freely as possible.

3   Pick out the sketch that looks most promising and draw this to scale. Repeat this scale drawing with a series of minor changes.

4   Amend the scale drawing as necessary and draw it out full size with the front and end elevations and plan superimposed on each other in order to keep the paper a reasonable size. If each view is given a different colour all confusion should be avoided.

79

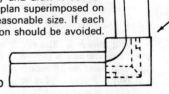

b

Constructional problems

Front legs   These are straightforward with a single rail joining them. Any stretcher rail must be out of reach of the feet of the sitter or it will be continually scuffed. (Stretcher rails are discussed later.) This joint is shown in *79b*.

Back legs   The main strength comes from a heavy rail at seat height. A chair is subject to a lot of stresses, most of them avoidable if the chair is sat in properly, which must be allowed for. This rail is made thick enough to have two tenons side by side, see *79c* and *d*. To avoid a very heavy look when viewed from the back the top edge is bevelled off.

The space at the back can be filled in according to the chosen design.

The legs are thickened in depth at the place where the side rails enter. This shows most clearly in the photograph (*81*).

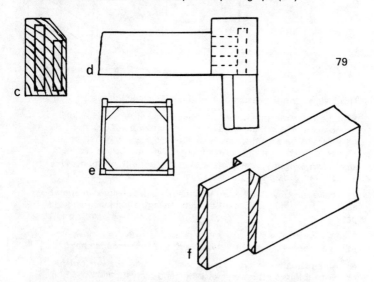

79

Seat   The tenons at the front of the side rail are left to run in line with the rails, making the shoulders angled across the width and thickness. The rail is not at right angles to the front leg in either the side elevation or the plan. The mortise holes in the front legs must be chopped at an angle to accommodate the tenons. Notice how the legs are set in a little so that they can be planed off at a later stage to finish flush and in line with the rails (*79b*).

At the back the tenons must run parallel to the axis of the chair otherwise it will be impossible to glue the chair up. At the same time the back legs slope inwards and the tenons must match this slope as well. This back tenon is angled in two directions and the shoulders are also off square. This is shown in *79d* and *30f*. These various angles are all taken off the full scale drawing.

The seat is greatly strengthened by the addition of carefully fitted corner blocks that are fastened with screws a little below the level of the seat rebate (*79e*). The actual seat is composed of a piece of 12 mm plywood upholstered with vinyl material over polyether foam. It is supported by a rebate which runs around the front and both side rails (*79g*). This rebate makes a modification necessary to the tenons which fit the front legs. The square haunch is reduced to a thickness of $\frac{1}{8}$ in. to keep it away from the side of the rebate. It is also stopped $\frac{1}{4}$ in. from the top so as not to show (*79h*).

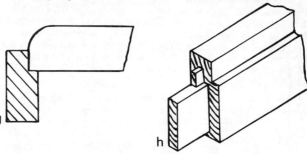

Marking out the back rails tenons

If a set of these chairs is required it is worth making two shaped blocks (one right hand and one left) which can be cramped to the rail so that a mortise gauge can be used. The slopes are taken off the full-scale drawing (*79i*).

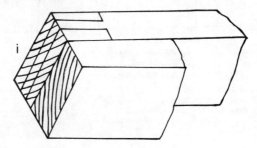

Stretchers These give considerable strength to the chair but care is needed in siting them. To give the most strength they should be as low as possible. In this position they will be scratched and damaged and unsightly. As usual a compromise has to be reached and the rails are kept fairly high with the front one possibly set back out of the way.

Gluing up

The back and front are glued up first and then the completed chair. If the back has a number of splats these may well be glued up separately making two gluings for the back.

Modified dining type chair

Most of the problems which occur in the traditional chair have been eliminated. The seat is still wider at the front than the back but the front and back legs are lined up with the rails. The sides of the chair are glued up first as two frames. The cross rails, which have angled shoulders, are through tenoned and wedged into the side rails. These rails support the seat which is built on a piece of 12 mm plywood and screwed on to them (*79j*). Corner blocks provide extra stiffness.

Here again there are many variations possible using this basic shape and construction.

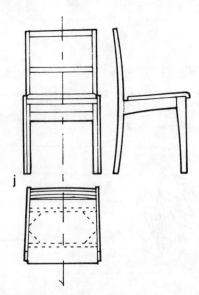

Laminated chairs

These are extremely easy to make. Once the design has been settled the formers are made (see section seven, which deals with laminations) and the various pieces are formed and cleaned up. The plywood back and seat can be glued on and the legs are screwed to the back rails. One advantage of a laminated construction like this is that it has a springiness built into it which adds to the comfort.

General

Needless to say there are many other solutions which will result in equally successful chairs and those illustrated are merely to show some of the possibilities. Try and tackle the design as just another problem, only in this case it has to support a body and not books or some other articles. Bear in mind that a person, because of his continuous movement and rather careless behaviour, exerts a great deal of stress and that this necessitates a very strong construction.

80

80 Dining chair in sapele illustrating the broadening out of the back and the heavy back rail with its bevel

81

81 Dining chair in sapele. Note the extra width of the back leg where the side tail comes in and the arrangement of the underframing with the front stretcher rail well out of the way

Constructions

Ellipse

1 Draw rectangle CDEF with major axis aa' and minor axis bb'. Divide Oa' and a'D into an equal number of parts (say 4) at 1, 2, 3 and 1', 2', 3' respectively. Draw b'3, b'2, b'1 to intersect b3', b2', b1'. These intersections are points on the ellipse. Trace a fair curve through the points and adopt a similar construction for the rest of the ellipse (*82a*).

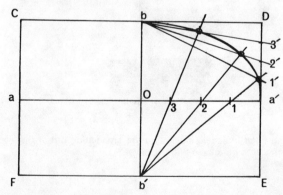

2 *Trammel Method* Draw the major and minor axes, aa' and bb'. On a strip of paper mark off three points E, G and H, making EG = Ob and EH = Oa. Keeping G on the major axis and H on the minor, move strip into various positions marking the position of E on the drawing. Trace a fair curve through the points.

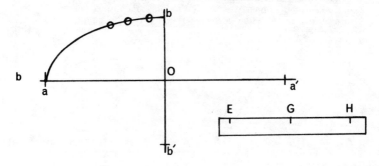

3 Figure *82b* Using cotton or string. Place three pins on f, b and f', having drawn the axes aa' and bb' (bf = bf' = Oa). Make a loop of cotton and place it over pin f', keeping the cotton taut, take it round pin b to pin f and wind it round the latter several times, taking care that the loose end is securely held. Withdraw pin b and replace with pencil point. Keeping the cotton taut and the loose end secure, trace the ellipse (*82c*).

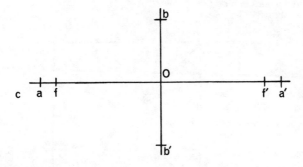

Hexagon

1   Given the length of one side AB, with the compass on A and radius AB describe an arc, repeat this on B intersecting the first arc at O. Using O as centre describe a circle using the same radius. With centre B step off the radius around the circumference. Join these points and the result will be a regular hexagon (*83a*).

2   Given the length of the diameter AB, take a compass with centre A and radius half AB, describe an arc, repeat on B. With centre O and same radius describe a circle. Join the points as shown in figure *83b*.

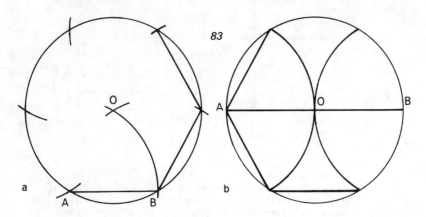

83

a

b

Octagon

Draw a square of a size to contain the octagon and draw its diagonals. With compass on each vertex and radius half the diagonals describe arcs cutting the perimeter. Join these points of intersection as shown in figure *84*.

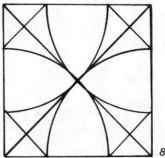

84

Doors

Figure *85a* shows a conventional door composed of stiles, rails, muntin and panels. Like all doors it is best made oversize and fitted to the actual opening when it is completed.

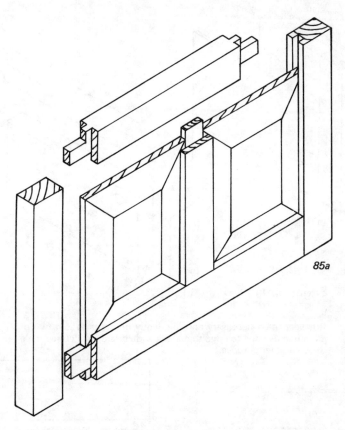

85a

85b is a quick construction suitable for a kitchen cabinet. It is made of soft wood with crosshalving joints at the corners which are glued and screwed and then both sides are covered with hardboard

85c can be used where a flush finish is required. Chipboard is used because it is a stable material and within limits any movement can be ignored. It is lipped to hide the unsightly edges which crumble easily and also to provide a firm anchor for the hinges. It will be veneered on both sides

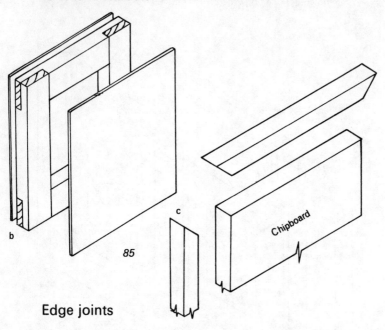

85

b

c

Chipboard

Edge joints

It is very often necessary and frequently desirable to join two or more boards edge to edge to make a wide board for a coffee table or some other purpose.

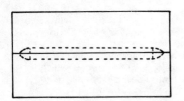

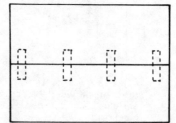

86a is a straightforward 'rubbed joint', that is two accurately planed edges glued together. Modern adhesives make this a very strong joint

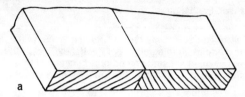

86b In this example a tongue and grooved joint has been used. This has the disadvantage that it shows at the ends

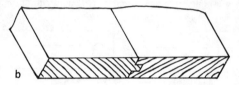

86c In this illustration a loose tongue is used. The drawing on the right shows how, if a circular saw is used, the groove can be stopped before the ends and the joint is then hidden

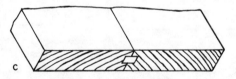

86d It is also possible to strengthen a rubbed joint with dowels but this is not recommended because of the difficulty of lining up the holes with sufficient accuracy

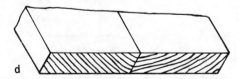

Handles

These are only a few suggested shapes to give an idea of possible scope of wooden handles.

In all the illustrations the tenons have been omitted. These would be turned at the same time as the handles or in the case of the others made as an integral part of the handle and used to hold it while the shaping is being carried out. Because of these tenons the handles must be made with the grain running into the tenon.

At least ¾ in. must stick out in order to be grasped.

87a and *b* These are two drawer handles shown in front and end elevations and plan. They have been left very simple and can both be improved upon

87c is a cupboard handle to match (*b*); again three views are shown

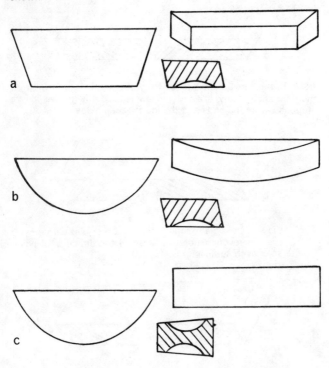

87d The lathe offers a whole range of possibilities. Those illustrated are all finished from the lathe except the second one which has the face chiselled to make a hexagon

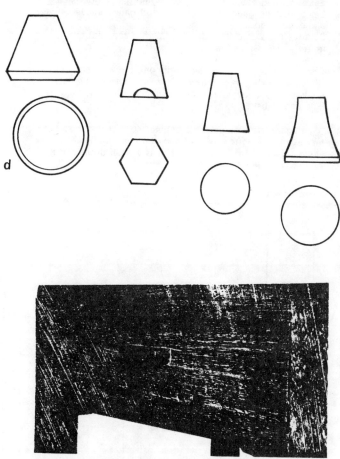

d

87e A wooden drawer handle on a small black bean table

1. Place door in position and mark length of hinge on door and carcase (*88a*), square inside carcase and round edge of door.
2. Set a marking gauge to thickness 't' and gauge door stile.
3. Set a marking gauge to width 'w' and gauge inside carcase and edge of door.
4. Remove the waste from the door with a saw and chisel and from the carcase with a chisel.
5. Screw the hinge on the door.
6. Screw the door in place using only one screw to each hinge. Check the swing of the door and if satisfactory complete the screwing. If not adjust one of the hinges using another screw hole until satisfied.

It is customary to fit hinges to a cabinet so that the top of the top hinge and the bottom of the lower one are in line with their respective edges of the door stiles. If it is a flush door then they will be their own length in *88b*.

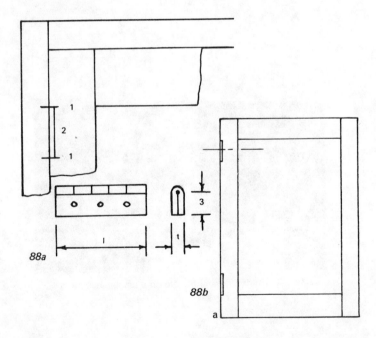

88a

88b

There are two usual methods of securing the hinges. *88c* is the best method with the hinge set in at an angle so that each leaf is partly set in either the door frame or the carcase. *88d* shows an alternative method with the hinge entirely cut into the door frame.

Box lids either have the hinge set out as in *88e* or let in flush as *88f*. In the latter case the hinging edges of the lid and bottom must be bevelled to allow the box to open.

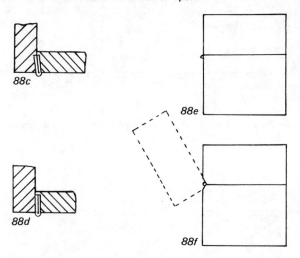

88c

88d

88e

88f

Lids, box

Figure *89a* shows the method of making a box and lid in one.

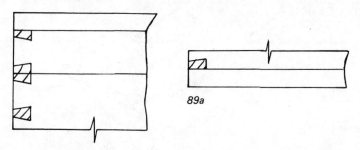

89a

This ensures a perfect fit when they are separated. The pin which coincides with the join between the lid and the bottom is made double size plus an allowance for a saw cut and cleaning up. The box is glued up with the top in place, the bottom is screwed in place and then the box is sawn into two. *89a* shows a tool chest where the top and bottom will be screwed on and *89b* the same construction applied to a jewel or cigarette box with top tongue and grooved and bottom rebated and screwed.

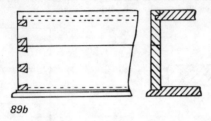

89b

89c This box has a sliding lid and two corners of the dovetails are mitred to accommodate the groove

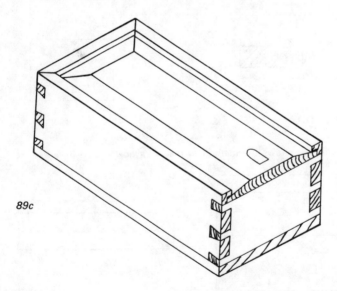

89c

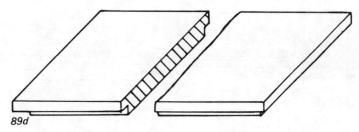

89d and *e* These are two types of drop in lid. *89d* is only suitable for a very small box, while *89e*, having battens to locate it, will be prevented from warping and could be a little bigger

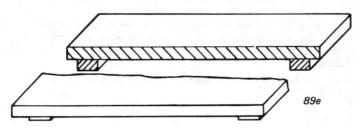

Panels

There are various forms that a panel can take and four of them are illustrated here.

90a shows the most common one with a rebate

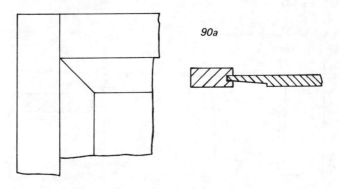

90a

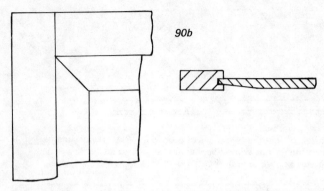

90b

90b   If the panel is too thin it can be made without a rebate but this is more difficult since the line has to be achieved by accurate planing. Care must be taken not to round this line when glass papering

90c is a flush panel usually reserved for somewhere out of sight

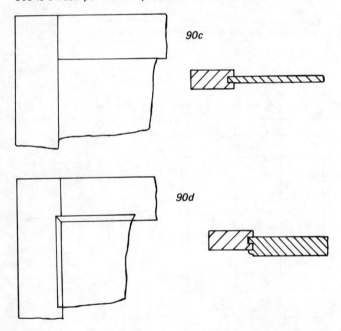

90c

90d

90d This is an overlaid panel and requires a thicker board. The moulding is worked with a shoulder plane after it has been defined with a cutting gauge

Plinths

As a general rule they should either fit right down to the ground or high enough to clean under. It is almost impossible to clean with less than 4 in. clearance.

The plinth is there to provide some means of protection from kicks accidentally given during normal use.

91a shows an outline sideboard with a framed plinth

1   This is of a simple mortise and tenon construction.
2   The rail is slightly reduced in width at the centre to improve the appearance.
3   The plinth is set in at the back to allow for the skirting board (see side elevation).
4   A large sideboard or other piece of furniture might require a centre leg to provide additional strength.

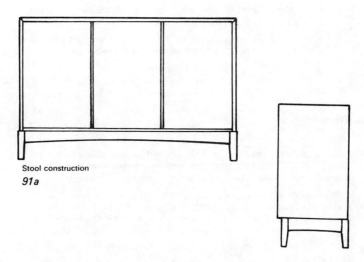

Stool construction
91a

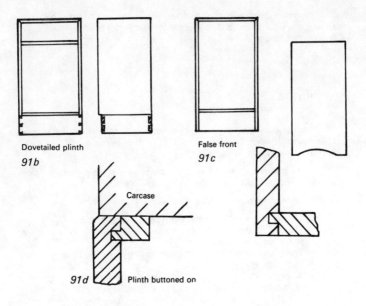

Dovetailed plinth
91b

False front
91c

Carcase

91d Plinth buttoned on

91b   Here a solid plinth with a dovetailed construction is used. This is usually reserved for small cabinets

91c   In this example the solid sides are continued right down and a false piece inserted to fill the space below the bottom shelf

91d   The plinths are normally buttoned on

Shelving

Shelves can either be fixed, in which case they add greatly to the strength of the construction or they can be adjustable and give a degree of flexibility to their possible arrangement.

Figure *92a* and *b* show fixed constructions. The mortise and tenon with housing should always be stopped at the front but the housing could be continued right through at the back. The tapered dovetail housing is a very strong joint which has the effect of tying the two sides together.

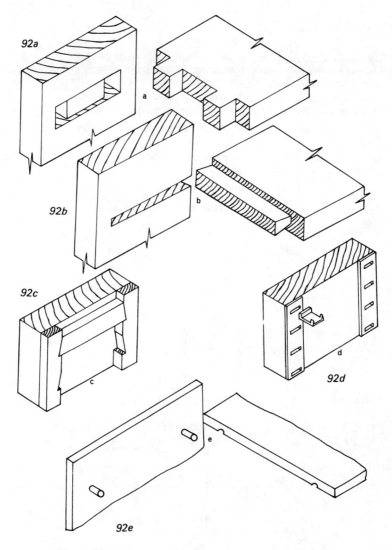

Figure *92c, d* and *e* are methods of allowing for adjustable shelves. The fittings for *92d* are easily obtained.

For a small job like a shaving cabinet it will be sufficient to screw two battens to the sides and let the shelf rest on top.

Securing tops

When table tops are held down due allowance must be made for subsequent movement. The method of holding must be such that it prevents warping while allowing expansion and contraction.

In figure *93a* a hole is drilled straight through the rail. This hole must be oversize or the top will be fixed too rigidly.

93b is similar but the screw is angled and sunk into the inside of the rail

93c A strip of 4 mm plywood is let into the rail with an oversize hole in the overhanging piece

93d This is the traditional method of the cabinet maker. The button is either held in a mortise hole or a groove ploughed all the way round

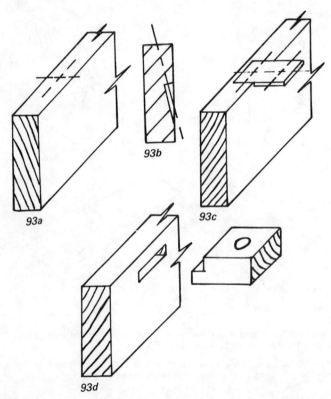

93a

93b

93c

93d

93e and *f* are two different types of metal fittings. It will depend on their position on the table which slot is used, remembering that timber moves about its width and remains constant about its length

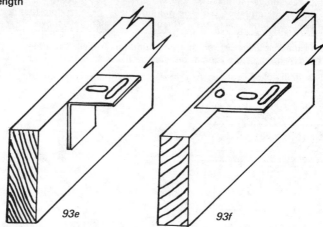

93g Where a cabinet is made with the 'false top' construction, that is rails lap dovetailed into the sides instead of the top being jointed, the top is secured by screwing through the rails. This should be done at a slight angle to allow a screwdriver to be used, especially if there is a shelf just underneath

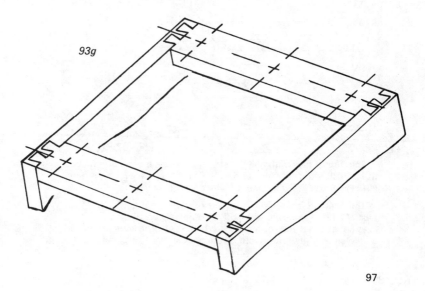

Warping—*Keeping boards flat*

Figure *94a* shows the usual way of keeping a drawing board flat. The boards are arranged with the grain deliberately at random to counteract the tendency to warp. The battens are then slot screwed onto the back. Each of the holes through the batten and the washers are slot screwed so that the round head screw can slide and allow for any expansion and contraction.

94b is the old-fashioned type of pastry board and is also used on the cheaper drawing boards. This is known as clamping

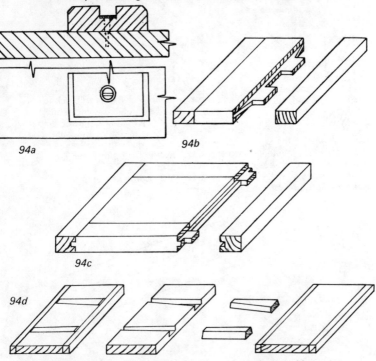

94a

94b

94c

94d

The next shows a framed construction where the panel is made to lie flush with the stiles and rails. There will have to be a gap left at the sides of the panel to allow for movement.

The method shown in *94d* is extremely neat and effective. First of all two strips are sawn off the edges. Then tapered dovetail keys are inserted and the strips glued on again. The keys are made a little shorter than the width of the middle piece of panel.

6 Drawers

Drawer construction

Drawers are not difficult to make if tackled in the right way. Such a method is laid out in note form. It will be seen that there are two different shaped drawer slips in the diagram. Which of these to use is decided by the use to which the drawer is to be put. If it is for stationery that requires to be kept flat then the top one is recommended, otherwise the rounded one is used. The rounded slip makes the tongues on the bottom in the same position both back and sides. The tongue is always at the top of the front edge to avoid any possibility of a gap showing inside the front of the drawer.

It is a good idea to leave the thickness of the drawer sides $\frac{1}{32}$ in. full instead of planing right down to the gauge line. This makes cramping up a lot easier because the tails at both back and front will stand proud and allow a cramping block to be laid straight across. When the drawer is glued up and ready for fitting the sides can be planed down. A heavy baulk of timber should be fastened to the bench with the end hanging clear. The drawer side can be supported on this while it is planed.

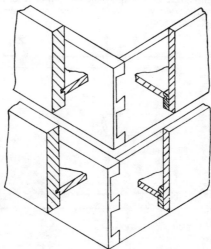

95 Diagram showing the tongue on a drawer bottom and the position of the groove in the drawer front and slips

Drawer construction

1 Leave drawer sides $\frac{1}{32}$ in. full in thickness.
2 Make drawer sides wide enough to include drawer slips.
3 Plough drawer slips while still attached.
4 Gauge and remove drawer slips.
5 Plane drawer sides to fit opening and letter 'Left' and 'Right'.
6 Plane front to fit opening end to end but leave width $\frac{1}{8}$ in. full.
7 Plane back to fit opening end to end and required width ($\frac{3}{16}$ in. less than width of sides).
8 Square ends of drawer sides.
9 Mark out lap dovetails and make and fit to front.
10 Mark out and make through dovetails at back.
11 Round off top edge of back. Take off top back corners of sides.
12 Chop mortise hole for handle in drawer front.
13 Clean up and polish inside omitting to polish where drawer slips are to be glued.
14 Glue up drawer.
15 Make bottom and work tongues (grain to run across drawer).
16 Hold slips onto ends of bottom and present to drawer frame.
17 If too wide, fit by planing off outside of drawer slips.
18 Glue slips onto drawer sides.
19 Fit bottom and, after polishing, glue into groove at front of drawer and leave dry in slips, slot screw into drawer back.
20 Fit drawer to opening.

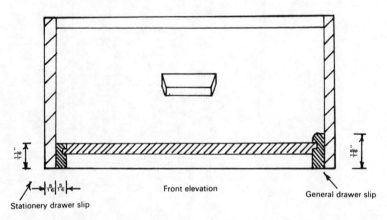

Stationery drawer slip

Front elevation

General drawer slip

96 a Draw construction front elevation

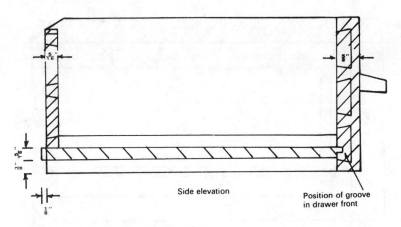

Side elevation

Position of groove
in drawer front

96 *b* Draw construction side elevation

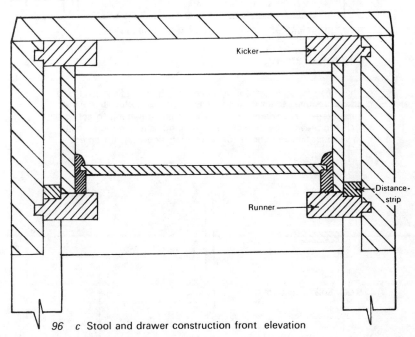

Kicker

Distance-
strip

Runner

96 *c* Stool and drawer construction front elevation

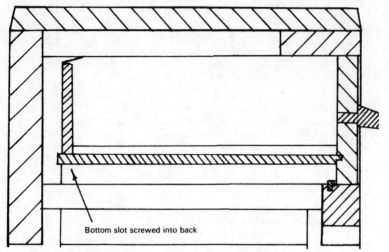

96d Stool and drawer construction side elevation

Bottom slot screwed into back

Drawer framing

The construction to support a drawer can be complicated since a drawer·requires three things if it is to run smoothly. It must be supported from underneath, there must be something to act as a kicker to prevent the drawer from dropping as it is withdrawn and there must be some means of preventing sideways movement.

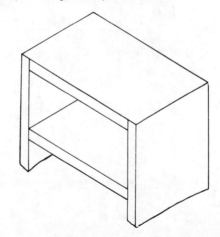

97a Solid construction

If the drawer is going into a solid construction then there is no problem. All the conditions are satisfied without any additions (*97a*).

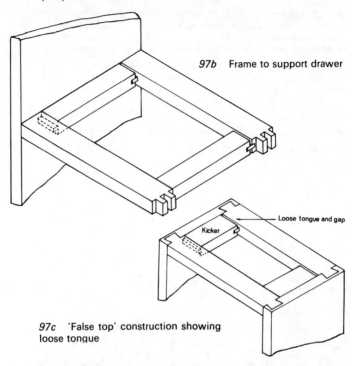

97b   Frame to support drawer

Loose tongue and gap

Kicker

97c   'False top' construction showing loose tongue

If, for reasons of economy, a frame is used to take the place of the solid shelf then allowance must be made for the expansion and contraction of the sides. The grain of the frame will be opposed to that of the sides. The front and back rails are tenoned into the sides and the side rails glued into the front. A gap is left at the back and a dry hardboard tongue inserted (*97b*). A similar method is used for the false top construction (*97c*).

It may be needed to fit a drawer into a stool construction and the method is shown in a series of diagrams where the drawer can be seen fitting into its position. This arrangement allows the rails and kickers to be glued in place at a second gluing after the main frame has set. The drawings show clearly the distance pieces that make up the difference in thickness between the legs and the side rails. The drawer stop is made with the grain running in the direction of the tenon.

Flush front drawer construction

Sometimes a design calls for all the drawer fronts to present a flush surface. The drawer fronts can then be matched up for grain or else veneered with matching veneers to give a very smooth appearance. Figure *98* shows three methods of doing this.

98a This can be made by making the drawer with the front $\frac{3}{16}$ in. thinner than usual and with through dovetails at the front instead of laps. The $\frac{3}{16}$ in. can now be glued on to form the rebate all round. It could also be made by using wood the normal thickness and making the rebate first and then making the joints

98b has the drawer sides secured with tapered dovetail housings

98c has a simple housing

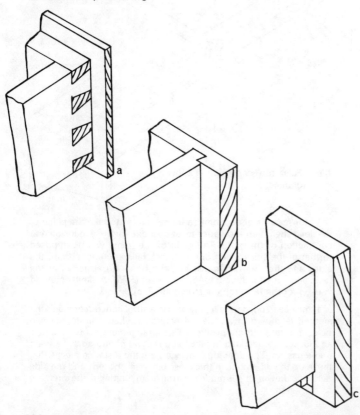

7 Laminating

Wood has natural limitation; it is strong about its length but weak about its width. This is common knowledge and who would make a see-saw with the grain running the wrong way? This weakness is clearly seen in a saw and the craftsman will be aware of the reason for the insertion of a length of dowel rod through the short grain in the handle. The shipwrights who years ago built wooden ships were aware of this and when they had need of a curved member they chose a tree with a natural curve which matched the one they were after.

The modern craftsman can follow the old method and select his wood so that the grain follows the desired curve but this is not easy and would require a large stock of timber being held. It is also inclined to be a very wasteful method, leaving a lot of odd shaped offcuts.

The modern solution is to laminate. If a timber is sawn into thin strips these will usually bend quite easily. The thickness is built up with a number of these strips and if they are cramped in the desired shape when the glue is dry they will retain their shape. The grain in all strips runs along their length and so maximum strength is achieved.

The major part of the work involved in laminating comes in the making of the formers. These must be very accurately made because the resulting lamination will repeat every bump, bulge or inaccuracy. If only a moderate curve is required then a solid block of wood will be adequate (*99a*), but heavier and more curved members will require a more elaborate former (*99b*). It is a good idea to always make the former at least $\frac{1}{4}$ in. wider and 2 in. longer at each end than is absolutely necessary. This will help to ensure that the edges and the ends are adequately glued. If a large surface is to be laminated, as for example the chair backs in Part 2, then a frame has to be made and surfaced. In this particular case plywood was used for this purpose.

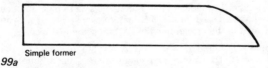

Simple former

99a

When the strips are held against the former for gluing some method must be adopted to transmit the pressure of the cramps evenly along the whole surface. One method is to make both a male and female former (see *99c*). An alternative and easier method

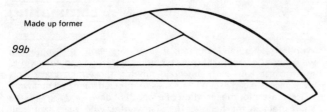

Made up former

99b

is to use a flexible steel blade which will take up any curve used. A length of old band saw blade 3 to 4 in. wide is excellent for this purpose. It is advisable to grind off the points of the teeth before using it to avoid a nasty accident

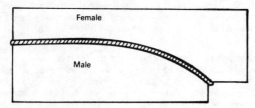

Female

Male

Two part former

99c

Having made the former it is cleaned, glasspapered, coated with two layers of shellac and glasspapered again. A layer of wax polish will help to ensure that the completed lamination will come away easily when the glue is set. As an additional pre-caution strips of waxed paper, such as that used to line cereal packets, are placed on either side of the laminations between both the former and the steel band

A two part resin glue is recommended for this work. It is extremely strong and allows sufficient time to get the whole thing cramped up before gelling starts. Spread some newspaper on the bench and lay out the laminations. Letter them as shown in *99d* with a large G to indicate that that is the side to glue. (Notice that the last piece has no letter G.) Now turn over and letter with an H as indicated in the figure, this time omitting the first piece

Tie some rag round a stick and apply the hardener to the strips lettered H. Turn them over when this has been done and apply the glue to the marked strips. To make sure that there is an even spread of glue use a photographer's roller. (This will last indefinitely if it is washed under the tap immediately it has been used.)

106

G	1	
G	2	H
G	3	H
G	4	H
	5	H

99d Strips marked for gluing

Put 2 on 1, 3 on 2, etc., until the pile is completed. Place a strip of waxed paper against the former, then lay the laminations in place, more waxed paper and then the band saw blade. Cramp up and leave until the glue is set, first removing any surplus glue with a damp rag.

Clean off and plane down to size as soon after uncramping as possible. The glue continues to harden for some days after it is safe to handle and the harder it becomes the more blunting is the effect on the tools.

Trial and error will show that there is a limit to the curve that can be achieved by this method and a trial gluing is essential if anything like a tight curve is contemplated.

Knife cut sheets of 4 mm wood are obtainable in limited variety or strips can be sawn with a circular saw. The first method is cheaper because it is more economical, the waste in sawing is considerable. There is no reason, especially if the edges are hidden, why an expensive wood should not be backed by a cheaper one.

100a Laminating a simple curved member, showing the former, waxed paper, laminations and steel backing

107

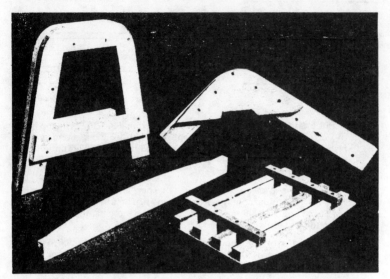

100b A selection of formers used for laminating purposes. The simple one, bottom left, was used to make the back rail of the easy chair (*25*) and the others to make a chair similar to the dining chair (*78c*)

8 Materials

Dowels

Dowels are obtainable in the following diameters in 3- and 4-foot lengths.

$\frac{3}{16}$; $\frac{1}{4}$; $\frac{5}{16}$; $\frac{3}{8}$; $\frac{7}{16}$; $\frac{1}{2}$; $\frac{9}{16}$; $\frac{5}{8}$; $\frac{3}{4}$; $\frac{7}{8}$ and 1 in.

When using dowels to make a joint make at least one groove down the length to allow the surplus glue to escape out of the hole. Also round the leading edge of the dowel to make for easy entrance.

Clear sheet glass

Clear sheet glass: 18 oz $= \frac{1}{12}$ in.; 24 oz $= \frac{1}{10}$; 26 oz $= \frac{1}{8}$ in.; 32 oz $= \frac{5}{32}$ in.

Polished sheet: $\frac{3}{16}$ in. and $\frac{1}{4}$ in. thick.

Handle grips can be ground in for sliding doors.

With grooves ploughed direct into carcase make the top groove twice the depth of the bottom groove to allow for removal of glass.

Glass plates

Glass plates to suspend mirrors or hanging cabinets.

Brass with round hole: 1 in. × 22 g; 1¼ in. × 19 g; 1½ in. × 16 g; 1¾ in. × 16 g; 2 in. × 16 g.

Brass with slotted holes: 1¼ in. × 19 g; 1½ in. × 19 g.

Particle board (chipboard and hardboard)

Chipboard Constructed of chips of wood which are glued and pressed to form a flat uniform board. It makes a very stable material while the movement is reduced to a minimum. It forms a very suitable base for veneers. It requires lipping for appearance sake as well as to protect the edges which are rather soft and liable to crumble. It can be obtained already veneered or covered with plastic laminate.

Standard sizes 8, 9, 10, 12, 16, 17 × 4 and 16, 17 × 5 (in feet) and 9, 12, 15, 18, 22 mm thick.

Veneered sheets 8 × 4 and 12 or 18 mm thick.

Hardboard Made from raw wood which has been processed.

Standard thickness ⅛ in. or 3/16 in.

Sheets 6, 8, 9, 10, 12 × 4; 8 × 5; 6 × 2; 6½ × 2½ (in feet).

Oiled Has greater density, strength and hardness.

Perforated with 3/16 in. holes at ½ in. or ¾ in. centres.

Sheets 6 or 9 × 4 ft, thickness ⅛ in.

Finishes Various, reeded, leather grained, etc., and covered with decorative laminate or stove enamelled.

Plywood

Plywood is made up of sheets of veneer glued with alternate veneers laid up at right angles to each other. This distributes the longitudinal strength of the wood in all directions. The small movement of the board is much less than that of solid timber and a greater stability is obtained (*101a*).

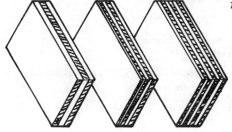

101a Three ply
Five ply
Multiply

It varies in the species of veneer used, its grade, thickness, type of adhesive, size of sheet and surface finish. A great variety of plywood is obtainable with many different woods. It is possible to have a decorative veneer on one side and a plain one on the other or to have both sides decorative or the plywood can be made of all the same timber, e.g. birch. Plywood is graded according to the quality of the veneers and adhesive which are used and these vary with the country of origin.

As an example the following details apply to *Finnish-Birch plywood:*

Grading

A Practically free from all defects.
B Some small pin knots, joints glued and matched, slight discoloration allowable.
S Good painting quality, knots, joints glued, discoloration allowed.
BB Knots plugged, joints and discoloration.
WG All defects allowed; only guaranteed well glued.

(Plugs exist where knots have been stamped out and filled and show as elliptical shapes.)

One side B and the other BB is quite a usual grading.

Glues Casein, Blood Albumen, Extended Resin and W.B.P. are used.

Sizes of sheet Thickness from 3 to 24 mm.

In inches
38 × 38; 42 × 42; 50/60 × 50/60/72/84/96/108/120/132/138/144; 72 × 50/60; 84 × 50.

Qualities A/BB; B/BB; B/WG; S/BB; S/WG; BB; BB/WG; WG.

Strips 1 in. wide are placed together with or without glue between outer veneers with the grain direction at right angles to the grain core (*101b*).

Finnish Birch blockboard

Core wood Pine, Spruce or Fir.

Thickness 16, 18, 19, 22 and 25 mm.

Glue Extended resin.

Sizes in in. 50 × 72/84/96/120/144; 60 × 72/84/96/120/144.

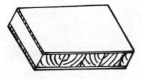

101b Blockboard
Core made up on strips
up to 1 in. wide with or
without glue between

Strips of wood which vary from 15 to 7 mm glued together face to face between outer veneers. This is more expensive and heavier (due to glue weight) than blockboard but more stable (*101c*).

Finnish Birch laminboard

Core wood   Pine or Birch.

Thickness   16, 18, 19, 22 and 25 mm.

Glue   Extended resin.

Sizes in in.   50 × 72/84/96/120/144; 60 × 72/84/96/120/144

Both blockboard and laminboard make a firm stable base on which to veneer but both require lipping.

101c Laminboard
Core made up of strips
between 1·5 and 7 mm
wide glued together

Protective covering (laminated plastic, vinyl and felt)

Thermoset plastic (or laminated plastic)

These can be obtained in a variety of colours and designs with either a high gloss or a semi-matt finish, in sheets $\frac{1}{16}$ in. thick. This is a very hard wearing material and will withstand normal heat and is reasonably scratch proof and entirely resistant to water. It is usually secured with an impact adhesive to its foundation. It can be purchased already bonded to hardboard or chipboard.

Standard sizes   10 × 4; 9 × 4; 8 × 4; 10 × 3; 8 × 3; 10 × 2½; 8 × 2½ (in feet).

Self adhesive vinyl

This makes a very useful material for shelf lining or tray bottom covering. It can be bought in a variety of colours and designs. The backing is removed and the sheet will adhere securely, requiring only a wipe with a damp cloth to keep it clean.

Standard sizes   Sold by the yard either 18 in. or 36 in. wide.

Self adhesive felt

Obtainable either red or green. This is excellent for putting on the underside of bowls or table lamps, etc.

Standard sizes   Sold by the yard either $16\frac{1}{2}$ or 33 in. wide.

Screws

Table of gauges available up to 10. Preferred sizes only

Length	Steel wood screws Countersunk heads	Brass wood screws Countersunk heads	Brass wood screws Round head
$\frac{1}{4}$ in.		1, 2	
$\frac{3}{8}$ in.	2–4	1–4	2–4
$\frac{1}{2}$ in.	2–8	2–6	2–6
$\frac{5}{8}$ in.	3–8	3–6	4–6
$\frac{3}{4}$ in.	4–10	4–8	4–8
$\frac{7}{8}$ in.	6–8		
1 in.	4–10	4–10	4–8, 10
$1\frac{1}{4}$ in.	6–10	6–10	6, 8, 10
$1\frac{1}{2}$ in.	6–10	6, 8–10	8, 10
$1\frac{3}{4}$ in.	8–10	10	
2 in.	6, 8–10	8, 10	
$2\frac{1}{4}$ in.	10		
3 in.	8, 10		

Mirror screw

Chromium plated brass countersunk head screws with chromium plated, polished brass dome tops.

$\frac{3}{4}$ in. by 8; 1 in. by 8, 10; $1\frac{1}{4}$ in. by 8, 10; $1\frac{1}{2}$ in. by 8, 10; 2 in by 8, 10.

Skiver

For bureau falls.

Smooth grained sheepskin, various colours.
Skins 6 to 10 square feet.

Dryad Handicrafts, Northgates, Leicester.

Upholstery materials and fittings

Foam   Various types of latex and plastic foam and practically any size is obtainable.

B & M (Latex) Sales Ltd, 35 Station Road, Addlestone, Surrey, will supply and advise.

Pass plates metal   These are $19\frac{1}{2}$ in. long with 9 spring holes and can be cut to a smaller size if required.

Springs, plastic covered tension   Obtainable in lengths 14 to 22 by inches. Add $1\frac{1}{2}$ in. for stretched length.

Webbing   Bonded fabric and rubber.
In widths of $\frac{3}{4}$ in.; $1\frac{1}{8}$ in.; $1\frac{1}{2}$ in.; 2 in.; $2\frac{1}{4}$ in.

Carpet fasteners   These consist of a screw to take a snap fastener and are useful to hold loose upholstery in position.

Vinyl   There are on the market a wide range of vinyl materials which are fist class for dining chair seats and other upholstery purposes. They are very hard wearing and can be easily cleaned. They are flexible, do not crack and can be obtained in different textures and a variety of colours. They will outlast most of the more conventional materials.

Commercial Plastics Ltd, Berkeley Square House, Berkeley Square, London W1.

9 Fittings

Bolts

102   Stamped brass barrel bolts. $\frac{7}{8}$ in. wide with $\frac{1}{4}$ in. shoot. 2 in. and 3 in. long

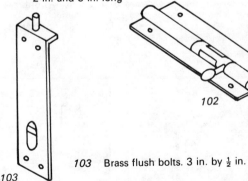

102

103   Brass flush bolts. 3 in. by $\frac{1}{2}$ in.

103

Castors

104 Heavy duty castors. Nylon socket requiring $\frac{1}{2}$ in. D hole
$1\frac{3}{4}$ in. deep. Wheels, black plastic, moulded nylon or off-
white rubber tyred $1\frac{5}{8}$ in. or 2 in. wheels

105 Plain trolley castors. Off-white rubber tyres. Steel socket
requiring $\frac{3}{8}$ in. D hole $1\frac{3}{4}$ in. deep

106 Ball type castor. Either plate mounting as illustrated or
socket type. Plate $1\frac{3}{4}$ in. square with 4 screw holes. Nylon
socket requiring $\frac{1}{2}$ in. D hole $1\frac{3}{4}$ in. deep

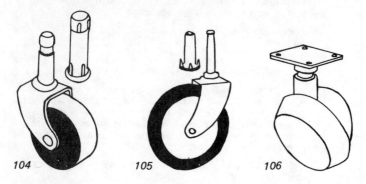

104   *105*   *106*

Catches

107 Ball catches—brass. Diameter of barrel $\frac{3}{16}$ in.; $\frac{1}{4}$ in.; $\frac{5}{16}$ in.;
$\frac{3}{8}$ in.; $\frac{1}{2}$ in.; $\frac{5}{8}$ in.
Roller catch—nylon. As above with nylon instead of brass
and nylon roller in place of steel ball. $\frac{3}{4}$ in. barrel

108 Brass catch as illustrated. Gripped by two steel balls
adjustable for pressure. $1\frac{5}{16}$ in. long

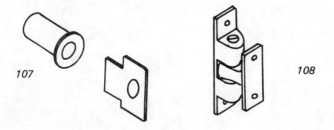

107   *108*

109 Nylon catches. Available in many slightly different forms
110, 111 Magnetic catches. Various patterns, some with the magnets enclosed in plastic, others in brass

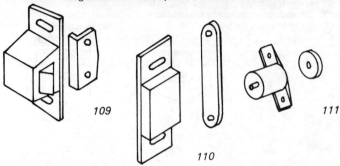

109

110

111

Hinges

112 Brass butt pressed steel pin. 1 in. $\times$ $\frac{1}{2}$ in.; 1$\frac{1}{4}$ in. $\times$ $\frac{5}{8}$ in.; 1$\frac{1}{2}$ in. $\times$ $\frac{3}{4}$ in.; 2 in. $\times$ 1 in.; 2$\frac{1}{2}$ in. $\times$ 1$\frac{1}{4}$ in.; 3 in. $\times$ 1$\frac{1}{2}$ in.

113 Brass butt broad suite solid machine iron or brass pin. 1$\frac{1}{2}$ in. $\times$ $\frac{7}{8}$ in.; 1$\frac{3}{4}$ in. $\times$ 1 in.; 2 in. $\times$ 1$\frac{1}{8}$ in.; 2$\frac{1}{2}$ in. $\times$ 1$\frac{3}{8}$ in.; 3 in. $\times$ 1$\frac{5}{8}$ in.

114 Brass butt narrow suite solid machine iron or brass pin. 1 in. $\times$ $\frac{5}{8}$ in.; 1$\frac{3}{4}$ in. $\times$ 1$\frac{11}{16}$ in.; 1$\frac{1}{2}$ in. $\times$ $\frac{3}{4}$ in.

115 Brass back flap solid machine steel pin. 1 in. $\times$ 1$\frac{5}{8}$ in.; 1$\frac{1}{4}$ in. $\times$ 1$\frac{7}{8}$ in.; 1$\frac{1}{2}$ in. $\times$ 2$\frac{3}{8}$ in.

116 Continuous hinge brass. Widths open 1 in.; 1$\frac{1}{4}$ in.; 1$\frac{1}{2}$ in. Available any length up to 6 ft with holes at 2 in. centre or without holes

117 Brass cranked kitchen cabinet hinge. Also supplied uncranked. 1$\frac{1}{2}$ in. for either $\frac{3}{8}$ in. or $\frac{1}{4}$ in. wood

118 Brass strap or desk hinge. First measurement length of strap, second width. 1 in. $\times$ $\frac{5}{16}$ in.; 1$\frac{1}{4}$ in. $\times$ $\frac{3}{8}$ in.; 1$\frac{1}{2}$ in. $\times$ $\frac{1}{2}$ in.; 2 in. $\times$ $\frac{1}{2}$ in.; 2$\frac{1}{4}$ in. $\times$ $\frac{5}{8}$ in.

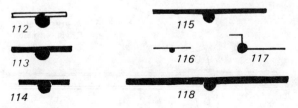

112   *115*

113   *116*   *117*

114   *118*

Lamp fittings

119 Threaded to fit lamp holder at top
 Coarse thread to grip in wood at bottom
120 Threaded at top to fit lamp holder
 Held in place by screws

  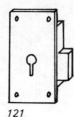

119 *120*

121

Locks

121 Straight brass double hand lock
 Brass cap 2 levers
 2 in. and 3 in.
122 Drawer locks
 Brass cap 2 levers
 2 in. and $2\frac{1}{2}$ in.
123 Chest locks
 Brass cap 2 levers
 2 in. and $2\frac{1}{2}$ in.

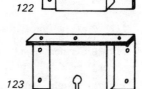

122

123

Stays

124 Bureau and desk stays
 Brass, left or right hand
 Sizes closed 3 in.; 4 in.; 5 in.; 6 in.

125 Wardrobe stays
 Brass with nylon slide
 Length overall $8\frac{1}{2}$ in.

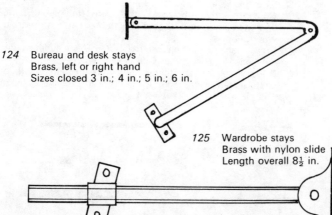

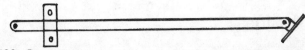

126 Brass
Length overall $7\frac{1}{2}$ in.; $10\frac{1}{2}$ in.

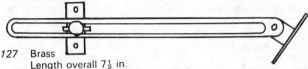

127 Brass
Length overall $7\frac{1}{2}$ in.
With phosphor bronze friction washer also $7\frac{1}{2}$ in.

Sliding doors

128 Fibre channel
Black plastic for $\frac{1}{4}$ in. plate glass
Single channel
      Bottom section $\frac{13}{32}$ × $\frac{3}{8}$ in., depth of groove $\frac{1}{4}$ in.
      Top section $\frac{13}{32}$ × $\frac{1}{2}$ in., depth of groove $\frac{3}{8}$ in.
Double channel
      Bottom section $\frac{25}{32}$ × $\frac{3}{8}$ in., depth of groove $\frac{1}{4}$ in.
      Top section $\frac{25}{32}$ × $\frac{1}{2}$ in., depth of groove $\frac{3}{8}$ in.
Both obtainable in 6 ft and 7 ft lengths
129 Fibre track
Inserted type   A $\frac{1}{2}$ in. high × $\frac{5}{32}$ in. wide
                 B $\frac{9}{16}$ in. high × $\frac{7}{32}$ in. wide
130 Surface type   C $\frac{7}{16}$ in. base × $\frac{1}{4}$ in.
                 D $\frac{1}{2}$ in. base × $\frac{5}{16}$ in.
Both obtainable in 6 ft to 6 ft 6 in. lengths
131 Fibre slides to run along track
                 E $\frac{13}{16}$ in. × $\frac{11}{32}$ in. × $\frac{3}{8}$ in. high
                 F $2\frac{3}{8}$ in. × $\frac{7}{16}$ in. × $\frac{1}{2}$ in. high

128

129

130

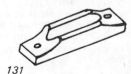

131

10 Glues

There are many different adhesives on the market and it is essential that the right choice is made. It is no good expecting a satisfactory joint to be made with the wrong glue. A glue which will give an excellent bond between wood and wood will not necessarily be effective for other materials.

The furniture maker is mainly concerned with wood to wood and so glues that are suitable for that purpose are most fully dealt with. These glues can be classified according to certain factors. The craftsman wants, ideally, a glue that allows him plenty of time to assemble and adjust his work; will then set quickly so that he can start cleaning up; will not stain; is durable; will last a long time on the shelf; a glue that while not exactly 'gap' filling will at least make up the normal space left in a joint. The various types of glue which are available are dealt with separately and then a table of these wood to wood glues is given to summarise their advantages and disadvantages.

The process of gluing takes place in three stages. The first stage is the period allowed for adjustment before everything must be in its final position with cramps tight and frames square. This is called the gelling time and it must be long enough to allow the essential adjustments to be made. The second is the time for which the cramps must be left on and before any more work can be done. The last period is that which must elapse before full strength has developed.

Glues have been evolved which are practically indestructible by micro-organisms, damp, wet, heat and physical stress. If two boards are carefully glued edge to edge, with one of these glues, and an attempt made to break the joint it will be found that the wood fractures not the glue.

With the modern adhesives it is essential that the manufacturer's instructions are faithfully followed. Most of these have a technical service and will be only too willing to help and advise.

Scotch glue

This has been largely superseded by more efficient glues, except for hand veneering. Its disadvantage is that it requires heating to prepare and must also be applied hot. When it has to be kept hot for a long time it tends to become too thick and should it boil its strength is dangerously reduced. In a cold workshop it is liable to chill too quickly and gell before the joint is properly together. It is not waterproof and requires longer in cramps than most modern adhesives.

It is useful for veneering because it has tack, that is it has a certain amount of immediate grip; it can also be softened by heating through the veneer with a hot iron over a damp cloth. (This overcomes the problem of gelling when veneering a large surface.)

There have been developed cold setting animal glues which are very useful for gluing in bands and strings. They have a much longer working time than ordinary hot glue. They remain liquid at normal temperatures experienced during the summer but in winter it may be necessary to stand the tin in warm water to make it fluid.

Resin glues

The group of glues which come under the heading of urea-formaldehyde provide a very strong bond which is almost indestructible. It is put out in two forms, two part and single application.

Two part application   Here the adhesive comes in two parts, a hardener which is a colourless liquid and a white powder. The hardener is ready for use but the powder requires dissolving in water. The powder should be added to the water. It is advisable to allow some hours between mixing and using so that all the air bubbles which develop during mixing have time to disperse. Once the solution, which should be of a syrupy consistency, has been made it will last for at least a month.

The glue and the hardener are applied separately. In the case of a mortise and tenon the easiest method is to apply the hardener to the tenon, using a stick to which has been tied a piece of rag. (Do not use a brush with any metal because this will cause staining.) The glue is put in the mortise hole with a stick. Keep the two containers well away from each other because it will only take a drop of hardener in the glue to set it and render it useless.

All the joints have the glue and hardener applied before any are put together. Since no reaction takes place until contact, the gelling time does not start until then. This allows a much longer time for a complicated assembly. (The hardener-coated surface must still be damp when the two halves of the joints are finally brought together.)

The work will require cramping until the glue is set. The cramps should not be so tight that they exclude all the glue. The gelling and setting time can be controlled by the temperature of the room and the hardener used. The manufacturers supply a table showing the effect of temperature on these times and the variety of hardener available.

The average working time is 15 minutes and it can be un-cramped in 3 hours, even though full strength has not yet been achieved. It is an advantage to remove any surplus glue while it is still fluid. The longer it is left the harder it becomes and the more blunting the effect will be on the tools.

To prevent any staining resulting from the glue, the iron of the cramp and the wood itself coming into contact, it is advisable to insert a piece of paper between the cramp and the glue where this could occur.

Single application This same type of glue can be purchased as a powder to be dissolved in water and applied as a single operation. The hardener, in dehydrated form, being already present in the glue powder. This will have a limited life and only sufficient for immediate application should be mixed. It will not allow for the same manoeuvering time as the separate application glue because 'gelling' will start once the glue is mixed with water.

While temperature does affect the setting time the glue is cold setting. A hot workshop will shorten the setting time and a cold one lengthen it.

P.V.A.

This stands for polyvinyl acetate and is a thermoplastic glue. This means that after it sets it can be softened by heating. Since furniture will not normally be subjected to temperature increases of this order this does not make it in any way an unsuitable furniture glue.

It is supplied ready for use, requiring no heating or mixing, as a white liquid. It is applied to one half of the joint only and is clean and easy to use. This makes it an extremely useful adhesive for a school or home workshop.

The joint will require cramping although some tack will be experienced. The setting time is down to about an hour depending upon local conditions. The glue itself is liable to stain some woods and for this reason must be used carefully.

Casein glue

This is a glue made from curds derived from filtering off the whey from skimmed milk and treating it with chemicals. This is another white powder which requires mixing with water. It is a single application glue and requires cramping. It will stain some woods with a high tannin content, e.g. oak. Only sufficient glue for immediate use should be mixed. It sets by chemical action and evaporation of water. After mixing allow 20 minutes for the powder to dissolve (add powder to water).

Epoxy resin

These glues do not produce volatile components and so can be used between non-porous surfaces, i.e. metal to metal. As with all glues it is essential that the two surfaces to be joined are perfectly clean. It is equally suitable for joining wood and metal. It is supplied in two tubes, one of glue and the other hardener. A sufficient quantity for immediate use is squeezed out and mixed in equal proportions from each tube.

Impact adhesive

This is a synthetic rubber and resin glue especially designed for gluing laminated plastic sheeting to wood. All surfaces should be clean and slightly roughened. The glue is applied to both surfaces and allowed to dry for 10 to 15 minutes. If they are then brought into contact with hand pressure they will immediately knit together. Although full strength is not developed for 48 hours the work can be handled immediately.

Great care must be taken to ensure that the laminate goes into its correct position because re-adjustment will not be possible. When surfacing a table top or other large area some means must be found of making a stop or ledge along the far edge so that the sheet can be lowered into position pressed against it. This can be done by cramping a lath along it or by drawing pins placed so that their edges stick above the level of the top.

Latex and resin

Particularly useful for upholstery work, being strong and clean to use. Comes ready for use as a white liquid. Braid, for example, which used to be fastened with gimp pins can now be held in place with glue.

The information in this section comes from manufacturer's technical sheets and the following booklets:

Forest Products Research, Bulletin No. 20, *Requirements and Properties of Adhesives for Wood*, H.M.S.O. Department of Scientific and Industrial Research.

Timber Research and Development Association, Construction Research, Bulletin No. 2, *Glues and Their Uses*.

Makes and types of glues

	Scotch	*Resin*
Bardens (Bury) Ltd, Hollins Vale Works, Bury, Lancs.	Calabar	—
Bostik Ltd, Leicester	—	—
CIBA(ARL), Duxford, Cambridge	—	Aerolite 306
Croid Ltd, Imperial House, Kingsway, London W.C.2	Aero	—
Evo-Stik, Evode Ltd, 450/2 Edgware Road, London W.2	—	—
Leicester, Lovell & Co. Ltd, North Baddesley, Southampton	—	Cascamite One Shot

P.V.A.	Casein	Impact	Latex	Epoxy
—	—	—	—	—
Bostik Bond P.V.A.	—	Bostik Contact 3	—	Bostik 7
—	—	—	—	Araldite
Polystik	—	—	Fabrex	—
Resin W	—	Evo-Stik Impact	—	—
Casco P.V.A.	Casco	—	—	—

This only shows certain manufacturers; there may well be others making glues equally efficient.

Comparative table of glues

	Useful life Unmixed	Mixed	Gelling Time
Casein	1 year	5 hours	
P.V.A.	1 year		15 mins
Resin Separate Hardener	2 years	2 months	15 mins
Resin Combined Hardener	1 year	1–3 hours	20 mins
Scotch Hot	Unlimited		5–10 mins
Scotch Cold	Unlimited		20 mins

Setting Time	Full Strength	Staining	Durability	Preparation
2–4 hours	12 hours	Slight	Interior	Mixed cold
1 hour	20 hours	Slight	Interior	Ready mixed
3 hours	48 hours	In contact with metal	Moisture resistant	Mixed cold
2–4 hours	48 hours	In contact with metal	Moisture resistant	Mixed cold
12 hours	48 hours	Nil	Interior	Mixed hot
2 hours	48 hours	Nil	Interior	Ready

All the times quoted above should be taken as only a rough guide because local conditions will be the deciding factor.

The Durability Grades are those assigned to the particular types of glue by the Forest Products Research.

Gluing up

The notes are intended as reminders because this is such a vital stage. A lot of good work is spoilt through a lack of attention to essential detail and a failure to allow sufficient time.

Using a simple frame as an example

1   Assemble the work 'dry', that is without glue. If the joints do not fit then the addition of glue will not correct this.

2(a)   Test for squareness by comparing the diagonals. This can be done with a lath sharpened to a flat point at one end. If both diagonals measure the same then the frame is square. If not, move the diagonals in the direction of the long diagonal until they are (*132a* and *b*).

(b)   Sight the frame carefully in the direction indicated by the arrow to see if it is 'out of wind' (*133c* shows a frame in wind). Raise the low corners by slacking the cramps and lifting them until the front and back rails are in line. When this happens they are out of wind. Should the frame be badly out and resist this correction it means that one or more mortise holes or tenons are out of true and these must be corrected.

3   Uncramp, clean up and polish the inside faces.

4   Glue up following the procedure outlined in 2(a) and (b).

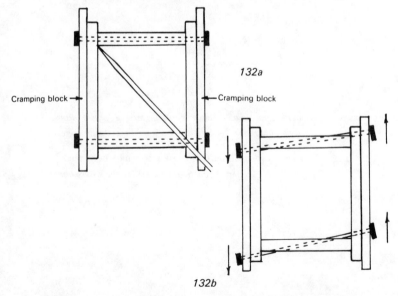

132a

Cramping block →   ←Cramping block

132b

Gluing up a stool

This is a more difficult proposition and must be glued in stages rather than all at once.

1   Each of the four frames must be cramped up dry as indicated in 2(a) and (b) for the simple frame.

2   Two opposite frames are cleaned up and glued. In *133a* that is either frames A and C or D and B.

3   When these are ready the complete stool can be cramped up for the first time. Using *133a*, assuming that frames A and C are already glued, the diagonals of D and B must now be checked.

4   The diagonals of the top and bottom must next be tested proceeding as shown in *133d*.

5   The final gluing can take place followed immediately by the tests which were made during the preliminary check.

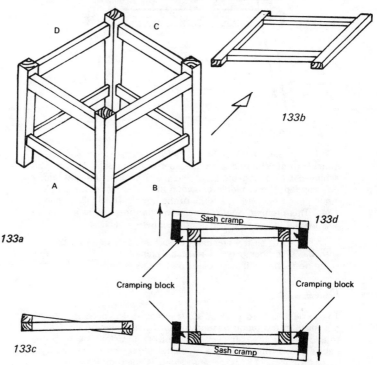

133a

133b

133c

133d

Sash cramp

Cramping block

Cramping block

Sash cramp

Cramping blocks

The work should always be protected from the face of the cramps. This is done by using a piece of soft wood. This has the added function of spreading the pressure of the cramp over a much wider area. In the case of the frame mentioned earlier they should stretch the full length of the frame. These are shown in *132a* and *b*.

It may sometimes be necessary to shape the blocks when gluing an assembly where the angles are not right angles. An example of this is a coffee table with splayed legs. When the legs and rails are glued, in order to cramp them up, shaped blocks are introduced (see *134a*). If the angle is at all great the blocks will slide as soon as pressure is applied. If this happens they should themselves be glued on to the legs before the actual gluing takes place. They can be easily removed when they are no longer required by sawing and planing.

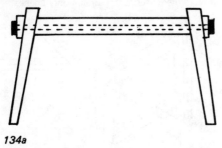

134a

When gluing a shelf into a wide carcase it is sometimes difficult to get the necessary pressure in the middle. This can be achieved by curving the cramping block so that the pressure is first applied in the middle and then at the edges as the block is straightened out with the force of the cramp. This is illustrated in *134b*. This problem does not occur at the top or bottom because 3 or even 4 cramps can be introduced here if necessary.

The faces of all the cramping blocks which come into contact with the piece being glued must be planed and smooth. If this is not done they will leave dents and marks behind.

Dovetails

The easiest way to glue up dovetails is to leave $\frac{1}{32}$ in. on the thickness of the wood bearing the tails when planing up. Gauge to thickness in the usual way but stop $\frac{1}{32}$ in. before reaching this gauge line. If this is done a cramping block can be put straight across the joint (*134c*), because the tails stand proud.

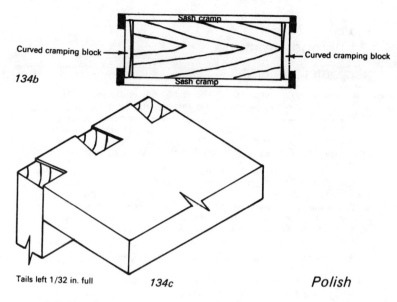

134b

Curved cramping block →

← Curved cramping block

Sash cramp

Sash cramp

Tails left 1/32 in. full

134c

Polish

It is best to exclude all polish from the joints but it is absolutely essential that any wax should be kept out. If this is not done there will be a failure of that joint.

135

11 Wood finishing

Preparing for polish

As much cleaning up as possible should be done with a smoothing plane which is sharp, has its mouth and cap iron set close and is finely set. This gives a very clean finish and is economical of time. A more difficult piece of wood with contrary grain may require a cabinet scraper but this should be used with caution to avoid making hollows which will show when the final polish is applied.

Follow this up with 'O' glasspaper and then 'Flour' grade, wrapped round a cork block. It must be realised that the success or otherwise of the finish is being laid down now. The polish will not disguise or hide any imperfections but only exaggerate and make them more obvious. The glasspaper must be used with the grain or the result, even with these fine grades, will be a series of scratches across the grain.

When woods are dampened there is a tendency for the grain to lift and this occurs with some polishes. This can be minimised by damping the surface, causing the grain to rise and then glass-papering again. This will ensure a smooth surface.

If the surface has been dented this can be corrected with a damp cloth and iron. Place a damp cloth over the mark and apply a hot iron. Provided that it is just a dent and no wood has been removed the steam will draw it up. Continue until the wood is slightly higher than the rest and then glasspaper it down.

Most of the dents which are discovered are due to a lack of thought during making. Each time a piece of wood is put down on the bench the surface of the bench should be cleared otherwise there will be small chips of wood trapped between the wood and the bench top and these will cause dents to form.

All polishing should be done in as near a dust free atmosphere as possible. This is particularly important with the harder finishes where the dust particles will form little blebs all over the surface.

Wax polish

There is no polish which leaves the wood as near its natural colour and which improves with the passage of time, like a good wax polish. Unfortunately it is not very durable and is spoilt with a drop of water or spirit (although this damage is repairable) and is inclined to show finger marks and has no resistance to abrasion.

All these defects would seem to rule it out as a finish but this would be wrong. It is admirable for such purposes as dining room chairs, the underframing of tables, bureaux and bookcases but unsuitable for table tops or uncovered dressing-table tops.

It has the great virtue that it is very easy to apply. First prepare the surface of the wood. Now brush on a coat of bleached shellac which has been diluted with 50 per cent methylated spirit. (It will be found to be too thick for this purpose undiluted.) This is done to fill the grain and prepare the wood for the wax. When the polish is dry, and this can be speeded up by rubbing it in with the ball of the hand, remove any polish left on the surface of the wood with flour paper. This should leave the surface perfectly smooth and shiny. A very absorbent wood may require two coats. The glasspaper is used without a block and as soon as it clogs a fresh part must be used or it will scratch the wood. The wax is now applied sparingly with a stiff cloth and left a little while for the solvent to evaporate and then polished. Several coats may be necessary and at the end the wood should gleam and show itself to full advantage.

The wax can be made by dissolving beeswax in turpentine but a proprietary brand of chilled wax gives a more lasting and harder polish. The beeswax will also give a yellow tinge, but the chilled wax can be obtained much lighter in colour and avoids this effect. As the finished article is regularly polished it will build up a most attractive shine.

Chilled wax

If a wax polished surface is damaged, by water for example, the old wax can be removed by rubbing with very fine wire wool and turpentine and then re-polished. If it is only a small mark a piece of flour paper charged with wax polish will usually suffice.

J. Nicholson & Sons, Longlands Works, Windermere

Polyurethane varnish

There are a number of these varnishes on the market which are available in small quantities. The first coat can be applied with a cloth or brush. Care should be taken to 'float the coat on, and any attempt to brush it out like a paint will spoil the finish. Watch the edges carefully so as to avoid tears.

When this coat is dry it should be flatted down with either flour paper or a very fine wire wool. This will remove any of the little blebs which may have formed and which would spoil the finished surface.

The second coat, which is best applied with a brush, should not be started until the first coat is hard, which will take about six hours depending on the temperature. A thin even coat should be put on, again watching the edges carefully.

Two coats are sufficient for most purposes but a third one can be added if desired. If the wood has a very open grain it may be necessary to use the first coat as a filler and rub it right down and then apply the normal two coats. The resulting finish is very hard wearing and is resistant to water, heat and spirit. It will keep its gloss and only require a wipe with a damp cloth to keep it clean.

Polyurethane varnish

Ronseal

Izal Ltd,
Thorncliffe,
Sheffield,
S30 4YP

Catalyst lacquer

To achieve the maximum protection of the wood it is necessary to use one of the catalyst lacquers or plastic coatings, or cold catalyst polishes. These names used by different manufacturers make for some confusion.

They consist of a mixture of three parts, a resin, a catalyst and an accelerator. The accelerator is to enable the reaction to take place at normal temperatures and without the catalyst nothing would happen at all. In most cases the accelerator has already been added to the resin and it only requires the addition of the catalyst to make it ready for use. The resulting mix varies with different makes but most will remain in a usable condition overnight.

The first coat should be diluted with thinners to act as a grain filler. The second one, full strength, can be brushed on as soon as this is dry. When this also has had time to dry rub over the surface lightly with a fine grade of wet and dry paper (used wet) to denib (that is remove any blebs that have appeared). The final coat can now be put on. Leave this overnight to harden.

The degree of gloss depends upon the amount of work that is done at this last stage. First of all rub down with fine wet and dry paper, again used wet, and follow this up with a burnishing cream. As the work proceeds the gloss will appear and as soon as it is satisfactory it can stop. The polish is practically indestructible under normal conditions and has a high resistance to abrasion.

Plastic coating (Complete with thinners and burnishing cream)

Rustins

Rustins Ltd,
Waterloo Road,
London, N.W.2

With an article like a coffee table it is useful to use this finish for the top and to polish the underframing with wax.

Read the manufacturer's instructions carefully before starting.

Bourne seal

This is a most efficient wood seal and is mentioned by name because there does not seem to be another equivalent product on the market. It is recommended for table tops and similar surfaces which are liable to experience hard wear and have water and other liquids spilt on them. It is also reasonably heat proof.

The first coat is floated on with a rag and allowed to dry overnight. The surface should be lightly rubbed down with flour paper to remove any blebs. Carefully dust the surface and apply the second coat with a brush with light easy strokes, only brushing enough to ensure an even flow.

Teak oil

For those who require an oiled finish teak oil is the answer and it is very easy to apply with a cloth and does not darken the wood unduly. Apply one coat and after a few minutes remove any surplus oil. When this coat is dry in about six hours, put on another coat in the same way.

Bourne seal

Floor Treatments Ltd,

Lloyds Bank Chambers, High Street, High Wycombe, Bucks.

Other items

Fillers, plastic wood and stains are best avoided. The former will show through natural finishes, the second is used only to fill holes which should not be there and is immediately obvious and if you select the right wood then stain is unnecessary.

Abrasive materials

Glass paper Preferably of the dark glass variety which is recommended for uniformity of cut. Grades 00, 0, 1, $1\frac{1}{2}$, F2, M2, S2, $2\frac{1}{2}$, 3.
Garnet paper Close or open coat, the latter being better for soft or resinous wood. Grades 5/0, 4/0, 3/0, 2/0, 1/0, $\frac{1}{2}$, 1, $1\frac{1}{2}$, 2. (These are arranged to correspond with the glass paper grades, i.e., 5/0 is equivalent to 00, etc.)
Waterproof carborundum (Wet and Dry paper) Used with water and having a back proof against water, petrol, oil and alcohol. Grades 400, 320, 280, 240, 220, 180, 150. (The finest grade comes first.)
Lubrisil Non-clogging. Grades 400, 320, etc., as for Waterproof carborundum.

12 Useful sizes

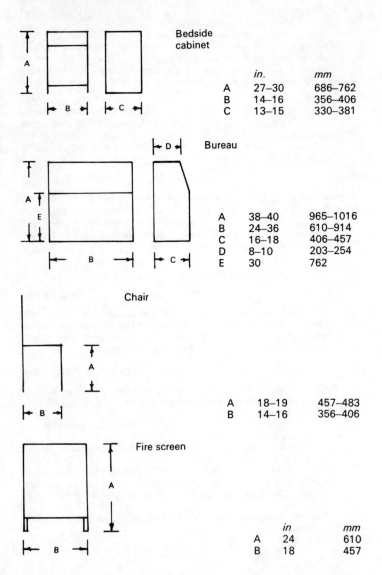

Bedside cabinet

	in.	mm
A	27–30	686–762
B	14–16	356–406
C	13–15	330–381

Bureau

A	38–40	965–1016
B	24–36	610–914
C	16–18	406–457
D	8–10	203–254
E	30	762

Chair

A	18–19	457–483
B	14–16	356–406

Fire screen

	in	mm
A	24	610
B	18	457

Piano stool

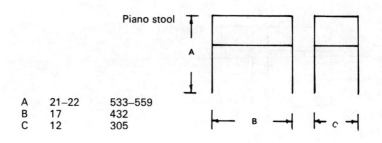

A	21–22	533–559
B	17	432
C	12	305

Stool

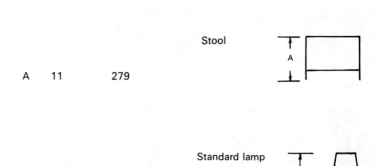

A	11	279

Standard lamp

A	60	1524

Table lamp

A	8–11	203–279

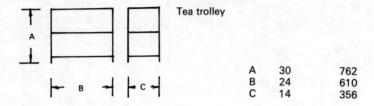

Tea trolley

A	30	762
B	24	610
C	14	356

Conversion table from inches to millimetres

1 in. = 25·4 mm

Decimals of an inch	in.	mm	in.	mm	ft	mm
0·0312	$\frac{1}{32}$	0·79	1	25	1	305
0·0625	$\frac{1}{16}$	1·59	2	51	2	610
0·125	$\frac{1}{8}$	3·18	3	76	3	914
0·1875	$\frac{3}{16}$	4·76	4	102	4	1219
0·25	$\frac{1}{4}$	6·35	5	127	5	1524
0·3125	$\frac{5}{16}$	7·94	6	152	6	1829
0·375	$\frac{3}{8}$	9·53	7	178		
0·4375	$\frac{7}{16}$	11·11	8	203		
0·5	$\frac{1}{2}$	12·70	9	229		
0·5625	$\frac{9}{16}$	14·29	10	254		
0·625	$\frac{5}{8}$	15·88	11	279		
0·6875	$\frac{11}{16}$	17·46	12	305		
0·75	$\frac{3}{4}$	19·05				
0·8125	$\frac{13}{16}$	20·64				
0·875	$\frac{7}{8}$	22·23				
0·9375	$\frac{15}{16}$	23·81				
	1	25·4				

All metric measurements are quoted in millimetres although no firm decision on the unit to be eventually used has yet been made.

Suitable sizes for common articles

		in.	*mm*
Books	Large	15 × 12	381 × 305
	Medium	8½ × 5½	216 × 140
	Small	7 × 4½	178 × 114
Crockery	Dinner plate	11	279
	Tea plate	7	178
	Saucer	6	152
	Cup	3	76
Cutlery	Large knife	9½	241
	Small knife	8	203
	Large spoon	8	203
	Small spoon	6½	165
	Teaspoon	5	127
	Carving knife	13	330
Letters	Large	9 × 4	229 × 102
	Regular	6 × 3¾	152 × 95
Magazines		13½ × 11	343 × 279
Milk bottle		9 × 3	229 × 76
Music		13 × 10	330 × 254
Paper	Foolscap	13 × 8	330 × 203
	Quarto	10½ × 8	267 × 203
Pencil		7	178
Records	L.P.	12½ × 12½	318 × 318
	E.P.	6½ × 7½	165 × 191

Index

WOODWORKING AND FURNITURE MAKING

By G. W. Endacott

DRAKE PUBLISHERS INC.

NEW YORK LONDON

Published in 1976 by
Drake Publishers Inc.
801 Second Avenue
New York, N.Y. 10017

ISBN: 0-8473-1161-9

Printed in The United States of America

Contents

Chapter 1

Basic Essentials

THE WORKSHOP

There are many difficulties in using the same building as both workshop and garage, or workshop and garden shed. A separate workshop is preferable, though often one has little choice. It is a consoling fact that many fine pieces of work have been constructed under conditions far short of ideal.

The workshop should be large enough to store tools and materials easily in an uncluttered way. It should be possible to use the bench without constantly having to rearrange things. The ceiling should be high enough so that an assembled article can be placed on the bench without hindrance, and there should be sufficient floor space to contain racks for all hand tools. Tools are best stored under the bench or upon the wall so that the floor space is kept to a maximum. Orderly tool racks provide safety and accessibility.

Careful planning is required to make sure the workshop can contain all the items required. If more than one person is to use the room at a time then machinery must be placed well away from the benches. It is important to leave a clear space for the unhindered passage of timber through a machine. The workshop must have places allocated to store tools and timber, to glue-up, to sharpen tools; or alternative arrangements must be made for these activities. If the bench is to serve for sharpening and glueing-up this must be planned into the scheme from an early stage.

The roof and walls of the building should be insulated if they are of light construction, so that the room is reasonably warm in winter yet remains cool in summer. A safe form of heating must be considered for the winter months. The building must be dry inside in order that tools do not rust and timber does not change its shape unduly. A large door is important. Remember that large sheets of plywood and planks of timber will on occasion need to be brought in. For this reason double opening doors are advantageous.

Large windows will provide good, natural lighting on the workspace. Artificial lighting required during the evening and on dull winter days should be provided by an ordinary electric light bulb. Fluorescent lighting should be avoided as it makes the colours false and flattens the appearance of the work because it shows no shadows. It is a good idea to consider siting the workshop in such a position that electricity for lighting and power can be connected without difficulty. Hot and cold running water are also useful.

A wooden floor is better than concrete. Sharp edge tools dropped on such a floor are unlikely to chip or blunt, and steel planes are less likely to break. A wooden floor is also more pleasant to stand on and is warmer in winter. However, the floor must be firm and give good support to the bench so that heavy work such as chopping out large mortises can be carried out effectively on the bench top.

THE BENCH

The woodwork bench is an essential part of the equipment. Figure 1 shows the typical arrangement of a traditional bench.

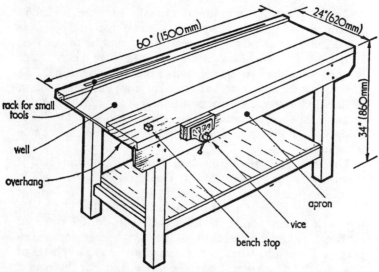

Fig 1 The woodwork bench

The Lervad bench, of Scandinavian design, is shown in plate 1. Either type of bench would be suitable for the work described in this book.

The sketch shows the principal dimensions for a bench. The most important size shown is the height. If the bench is not at the correct height then it will be found uncomfortable to work at for a lengthy period. A tall person will require a bench that is a little higher than the one shown and a short person will require a bench that is lower. As a general rule it is best to have the height of the working surface the length of a chisel below the level of the elbow. This allows the person to work as comfortably on the top of the bench as at the vice.

The parts of the bench which are indicated in figure 1 have various functions that may not be apparent at first sight. The well is the place to put tools that are needed to hand in the immediate future. The proper place for tools when they are not being used is in a rack, but they may be laid down temporarily in the well, where there is little fear of them rolling off onto the floor.

The apron is a wide board running the length of the front. This is notched around the legs and secured in place by screws. It makes the construction rigid and prevents a see-saw motion of the bench when planing a piece of wood.

The bench stop prevents the work from sliding off during planing. It is a block of wood that projects above the bench top. Figure 2 shows how the bench stop is adjusted by use of a wing nut.

The bench must have an overhang at the end for cramping wood when sawing or chiselling. The top is 1¾in (45mm) thick and is usually made of a solid piece of beechwood to give good support to the work. This way the energy produced by blows of the mallet upon a chisel is not lost in the spring of the bench. Look after the top of the bench because if it is worn hollow by tool marks then it cannot be expected to support the work when planing flat. It must be remembered that the bench is a tool and should be treated with the respect given to other tools.

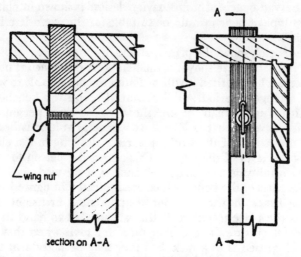

wing nut

section on A-A

Fig 2 How the bench stop is adjusted. The bench stop slides through a hole in the bench top and is held in position by a wing nut and bolt

THE VICE

The vice is the most important part of the whole equipment needed in a workshop. A jaw width of 7in (180mm) and opening of 8in (200mm) will be found adequate for most work. To open the vice to maximum aperture one has to turn the handle many times. An improved vice, fitted with a quick release lever, saves time. With this lever pressed the vice can be opened by pulling the jaw straight out. However, this vice is more expensive and for the kind of work envisaged in this book the quick release mechanism is in no way essential.

The jaws of the vice should be lined with wooden packing to prevent bruising the work. Countersink bolts can be bought to fit the two threaded holes provided in each jaw and may be used to hold the wooden packing in place.

The portable vice is a handy temporary measure. It can be easily fitted to a table by tightening the screw underneath, and when work is finished for the day the vice can be removed with equal ease to be stored elsewhere. This tool could be useful to those people who have very limited space to establish a workshop, but for the sort of work envisaged in this book the plain screw woodworkers' vice will be found more serviceable.

THE BENCH TOOLS

The nine bench tools that are most commonly used are best located near to hand in a rack fitted to the bench or fastened to the wall directly above it.

☐ STEEL RULE

The steel rule should be about 12in (300mm) long. The rule has two uses in the workshop: first, and most obvious, measuring, and second, checking the work for flatness. To check for flatness place the edge of the rule on the work and arrange the light behind the work. Gaps that show between the rule and the surface of the work are hollows. It will be seen that the markings on the steel rule start from the very end. There is no extra piece as on most wooden rulers. This enables one to measure accurately into a corner, for instance when measuring the inside depth of a drawer. The end of a steel rule is not liable to wear so the rule remains true. Its edges will also remain straight and accurate for a very long time. Figure 3 shows how to check a rule for straightness.

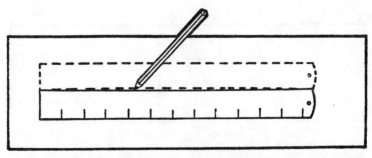

Fig 3 Testing the steel rule for straightness. Mark against the edge with a sharp pencil and then turn the rule over and repeat, a trick that 'doubles' any discrepancy

☐ TRY SQUARE

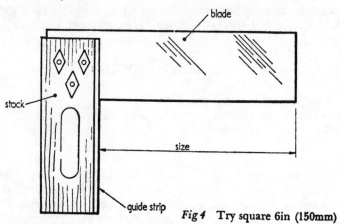

Fig 4 Try square 6in (150mm)

The try square consists of two main parts: the steel blade and the stock, which is made from rosewood. These two parts are fastened together by three steel rivets. The ends of each rivet are fitted with a diamond-shaped brass washer to prevent the rivet from splitting the stock. A brass guide strip on the inside edge of the stock prevents the rosewood from wearing. This tool must be handled with care and never dropped if it is to retain its accuracy.

The try square is used to check if one surface of the work is at right angles to another. It may also be used as a guide when

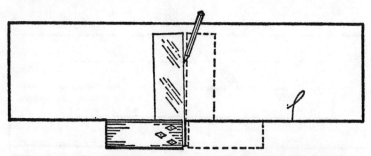

Fig 5 Checking a try square for squareness. Place the square against a straight edge and mark with a sharp pencil. Reverse the square and repeat. The marks will coincide only if the square is accurate

marking lines across the wood at right angles to an edge. Figure 5 shows how to check a try square for squareness. Any inaccuracy can be corrected by judicious use of the file. A handy size for the try square is 6in (150mm).

☐ MARKING KNIFE

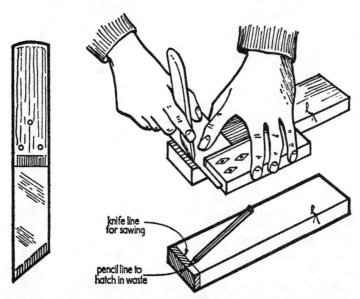

knife line
for sawing

pencil line to
hatch in waste

Fig 6 Marking knife and how it is used. Grip the knife like a pencil and hold it upright. Pull the knife towards the person to make a clean line

The marking knife has a steel blade and a handle made of either beechwood or rosewood. The two parts are held together by three rivets. The knife is used to mark all lines that are to be sawn, whereas the pencil is used for hatching waste, numbering joints, and marking shaping on the wood. The advantage of the marking knife over the pencil is that it produces a more accurate mark on the wood and also severs the fibres of the grain in advance of the saw. The knife is used in an upright position and pulled firmly against the try square. The knife is held by the blade rather than the handle. It should be kept sharp so as to produce a clean cut. A small penknife will always serve as a marking knife. Remember to use a marking knife for lines that are to be sawn.

☐   TENON SAW

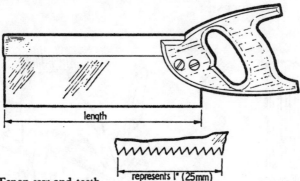

Fig 7   Tenon saw and teeth   represents 1" (25mm)

The tenon saw is used for sawing accurately to length and for general bench work. As its name implies it is used also for sawing the tenon of the mortise and tenon joint. This saw is about 10in (250mm) long. The handle is made from beechwood and the thin blade is cold rolled steel stiffened by a back of brass or steel. For this reason the tenon saw belongs to a family of saws called *backed saws*. The handle is fastened to the blade by two saw bolts.

The sketch shows that there are fourteen points per inch on the tenon saw. Obviously the more teeth there are the smaller they are. The teeth can be made so small they become difficult to sharpen. The number of points per inch mentioned here is considered adequate for general bench work.

The bench hook is used to support the wood when cutting across the grain with a tenon saw. It should be made from hard wood—beech or oak—for a long life. The two blocks are fastened to the base by wooden dowels instead of screws so that the teeth of the saw may not be damaged. It will be noticed that the block of the bench hook is short on the right-hand side. This is to provide protection for the bench top and prevent the saw making any marks on the bench. Because of this

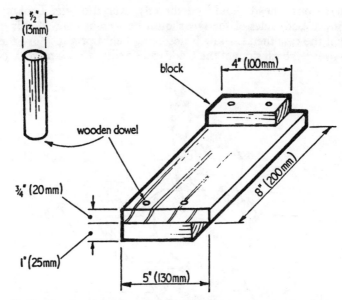

Fig 8 Construction of a bench hook. Made from beechwood and fastened with dowels, the bench hook should have a long and serviceable life

the bench hook shown in figure 8 is only suitable for a right-handed person. A left-handed person should remove part of the left-hand end of the block.

In use the bench hook can be made firm by clamping the lower block in the vice. The wood is then placed across the bench hook and gripped tightly against the front block by the palm and fingers of the left hand. Grip the tenon saw firmly, with the forefinger outside the handle and pointing forward. This will ensure positive control over the saw. Start the cut on the far corner of the wood. Guide the saw by the thumb of the left hand and draw the saw backwards three times to make a groove on the corner of the work. Then commence sawing and lower the handle of the saw with each stroke until the saw is horizontal. Normally one is following a line on the wood and as the saw is brought into the horizontal position the line is watched carefully to give an accurately positioned cut. At this stage one's head should be directly over the line. Looking down, both sides of the saw should be seen at once. If this is not the case then the saw is not being held upright. Move the saw until both sides of the blade can be seen. Check most care-

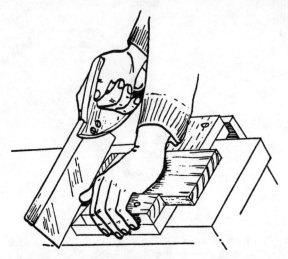

Fig 9 Starting a cut with the tenon saw. The thumb positions the blade as the saw is drawn backwards three times on the corner of the wood

fully that the saw is held upright. When all is correct continue sawing. Use all the teeth of the saw by making long steady strokes. This way the saw will stay sharp for a long time. Take the last three strokes more slowly until the cut is completed. The end of the work should be sawn sufficiently square that the piece can be stood upright on the cut surface.

☐ FIRMER CHISEL (fig 31)

The firmer chisel is used for general bench work. The handle is shaped into a comfortable grip for pushing the chisel into the work. The blade is fastened to the handle by the tang. The shoulder prevents the tang from pushing too far into the handle. The ferrule is a seamless ring of brass or steel and it prevents the tang from splitting the handle. A handy size of chisel for bench work has a blade that is $\frac{5}{8}$in (16mm) wide.

Three safety rules apply when using a chisel. Firstly, always keep the cutting edge sharp. Sharp tools are less dangerous than blunt ones. A blunt chisel has to be forced to make it cut and when forcing the tool into the work it is easy to be taken off balance if the wood splits, or when the chisel reaches the end of the cut. Secondly, always cut away from the body. Keep all fingers behind the cutting edge. Hold the handle of the chisel in the right hand and the blade between the thumb and forefinger of the left hand. This way there is good control over the chisel and there is no risk of cutting oneself should a slip occur. Thirdly, always carry a chisel by the blade and near the cutting edge. Should someone nearby not realise there is a chisel in your hand and step back quickly, they are thus protected from the cutting edge.

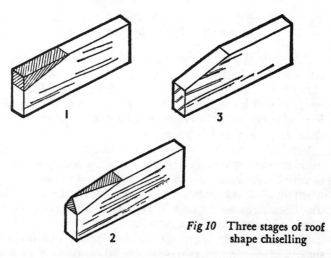

Fig 10   Three stages of roof
shape chiselling

The firmer chisel is used frequently for shaping wood held in the vice, and for vertical paring on the bench. All the marking out should be done first with pencil. Then place the piece of wood in the vice at such an angle that the line representing the finished surface is horizontal. Select a large chisel and hold it with the axis horizontal and the cutting edge tilted to 45°. Start by removing a small shaving from the top of the work as shown in figure 11. Note that one should stand half way along the side and work towards the left end of the bench. One only works in the opposite direction if left-handed.

Fig 11   Starting the cut. The work is held firmly in the vice, allowing both hands to grasp the chisel, as shown

Continue to chisel working down to the finished line until only the line itself is left. Then tilt the cutting edge of the chisel to 45° the other way and tackle the second side of the work. It will be apparent why this is called *roof shape chiselling*. It only remains to remove the ridge of the roof with the chisel and the shape is completed.

Vertical paring is used when rounding the corners of the wood or making a small 45° cut across the corner as shown in figure 12. Use a coin or tin lid of suitable curve as a template when drawing the shape on the wood. Lines are squared across the edges of the work to mark the exact limit of the curve. The waste is hatched in with a pencil.

The work is laid flat on a chiselling board. This is simply a smooth piece of wood laid on the bench to protect the surface of the bench from chisel marks. The handle of the chisel is held in the right hand with the thumb on top. The thumb and forefinger of the left hand guide the blade of the chisel. The left hand is placed on the work to hold it in position.

Start work on the corner of the wood by pushing down on the chisel. Take a modest cut and there should be no reason to hit the chisel with a mallet. This cut will create two corners which can be removed in turn. The work continues and the line is approached gradually. The many facets made by the chisel will form the curve.

With the straight 45° cut work starts on the corner of the wood and the chisel is moved back to the line in stages. The

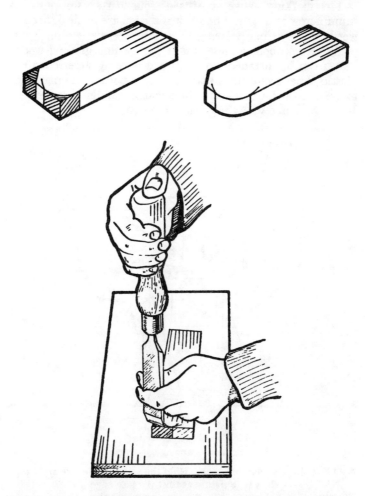

Fig 12 Vertical paring. All marking for shaping is done with a pencil. Support the work on a chiselling board and hold the chisel as shown. Keep fingers behind the cutting edge and take modest cuts

shavings taken are forever increasing in width. The last cut is made on the line.

The marking gauge consists of four parts: stock. stem, thumbscrew and spur. The stock and stem are made of beechwood, which is hardwearing. The thumbscrew is sometimes made of boxwood because this is such a fine grained wood that it can be threaded, but boxwood is being superseded by plastic. The steel spur is sharpened to a point. The marking gauge is used for marking a line that is parallel to an edge. It is always used with the grain of the wood.

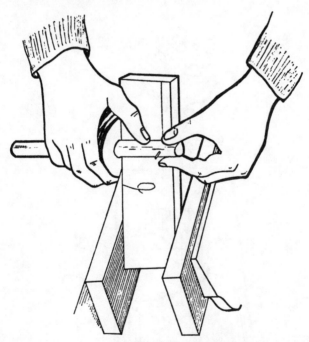

Fig 13   Using the marking gauge. Hold the wood in the vice and keep the gauge tightly against the face edge

□ JACK PLANE

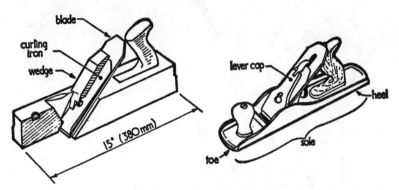

Fig 14   Wooden and metal jack planes. The wooden jack plane *(left)*
is shown in part section

The jack plane is used chiefly to remove a lot of waste as
quickly as possible. It receives its name from the expression
jack of all trades. There are two types of jack plane. One is
made of metal, the other of beechwood. Both planes are 15in
(380mm) long. The wooden plane is lighter and therefore
easier to use over a long period. It also slides over the surface
of the work better than a metal plane and therefore requires
less effort. Another advantage of the wooden plane is that it is
less likely to break if dropped. Despite these three advantages,
the metal plane is still the more popular because it is easy to
adjust.

Figure 14 shows the chief parts of the plane. The blade cuts
the shavings from the work and the curling iron curls the
shavings, thereby preventing tears (pronounced 'tares') on the
surface of the wood. The blade and curling iron are fastened
together by a large screw, and the pair of irons are retained in
the body of the planes by either a wooden wedge, as in the case
of the wooden plane, or a lever cap in the case of the metal
plane.

When using the plane the wood should be placed against
the bench stop, although the vice may be used when planing
the narrow edge of a piece of timber that will not stand properly on top of the bench. Take an easy but firm position

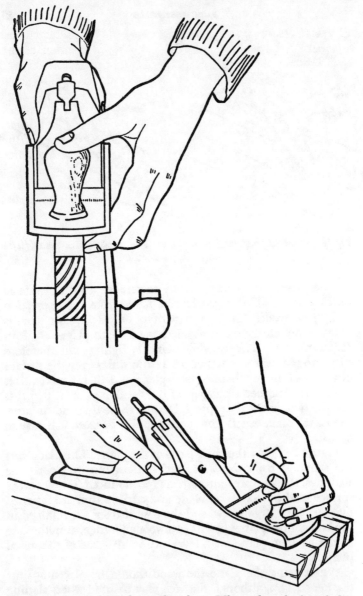

Fig 15 Position of hands on the plane. When edge planing timber, the fingers can act as a guide

directly behind the work. Stand at the side of the bench and work towards the end. Figure 15 shows the position of the hands on the plane. The chief function of the right hand is to push the plane forward. It is the left hand that presses down and holds the plane on the wood. When planing a narrow edge let the fingers of the left hand act as a fence under the sole of the plane, guiding the work to the centre position of the cutter. Start each cut by pressing down firmly at the toe of the plane with the left hand. Push the plane along the wood with the right hand but release the pressure applied to the front of the plane towards the end of the stroke. If the wood tears it is because the plane is being used against the grain. In this case turn the wood around and plane from the other end of the work.

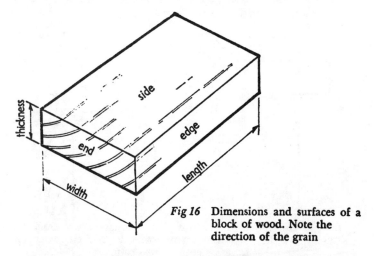

Fig 16   Dimensions and surfaces of a
block of wood. Note the
direction of the grain

The beginner will often round over the end of the work. To avoid this a pencil mark can be made about 1in (25mm) in from each end of the wood. Place the plane on the work so that the cutter avoids the first mark, and remove one shaving up to the second mark. Continue planing in this matter until the plane stops cutting. The work has now been planed slightly hollow but the plane will not make a deeper hollow because it rests on the high parts at each end. Finally, remove one shaving from the length of the work. This will remove most of the high parts at the ends.

The side of the wood that has just been planed is called the *face side* and should be marked in pencil with the symbol shown (fig 17). This symbol is called the *face side mark* and it points to the best edge called the *face edge*. The object of planing the face edge is to produce a flat smooth surface at right angles to the face side. Check for flatness with the steel rule then check for squareness with the try square. Place the stock of the square against the face side of the work and hold it up to the light. Again, any gaps that show are hollows. Look for the high parts and mark these with a pencil. The cutter of the jack plane is slightly rounded. Move the plane over so that the thickest part of the shaving will be taken from the highest part of the edge. When the face edge is correct mark it with a face edge mark pointing to the face side.

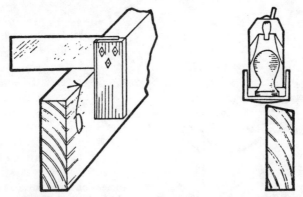

Fig 17   Checking for squareness and planing square. Check from the face side. Move the plane over to correct as the thickest shaving is cut from the centre of the cutter

The piece of wood has now been planed on two surfaces. In order that the work finishes parallel a line must be marked on the wood parallel to the face edge. Set the marking gauge to the width of wood required. Measure the size from the stock of the gauge to the point of the spur (fig 18). Hold the gauge by the stock and tap the stem on the bench to make fine adjustments if necessary.

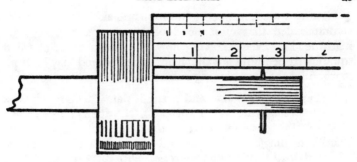

Fig 18 Setting a marking gauge. Measure from the stock to the point of the spur

Place the wood in the vice face edge towards the centre of the bench, and slope the wood to 45° before tightening the vice jaw. Put the stock of the gauge against the face edge and hold the gauge with both hands. Press the gauge tightly against the face edge and tilt so that the spur trails behind as the tool is pushed slowly along. People often forget that the object of using a gauge is to produce a line that is parallel to an edge, so hold the gauge tightly against the work.

Turn the wood end for end in the vice and mark the line all the way around. Always take care to use the gauge from the face edge so that the gauge line is nearest the rough edge of the wood.

Look at the wood before planing down to the line. If there is greater waste at one end than the other then shavings will have to be planed off the high point first. Otherwise there is a tendency to plane past the line at one end of the work (fig 19). Check for flatness with a steel rule and squareness with a try square.

Finally, gauge to thickness from the face side. Plane to thickness and test for flatness.

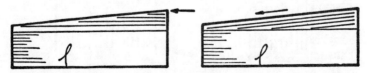

Fig 19 Planing to width correctly *(left)* and incorrectly *(right)*

Planing a piece of wood takes time and skill. It is therefore recommended that most wood be bought ready planed by machine. However, knowing how to plane a piece of wood square will be found advantageous. The method may be summarised by the four planing rules as follows:

1 Choose the *face side* and plane it flat. Check for flatness with a steel rule. When correct mark with a *face side mark* pointing to the face edge (ie the best edge).
2 Plane the *face edge* flat and square. Check for flatness with a steel rule and squareness with a try square. When correct mark with a *face edge mark* pointing to the face side.
3 Gauge to *width* from the face edge. Plane to width. Check for flatness and squareness.
4 Gauge to *thickness* from the face side. Plane to thickness. Check for flatness.

Planing end grain is not as easy as side grain. If the plane is taken straight across, then splitting will occur at the end of the cut (fig 20). One way to avoid this is to cramp a piece of waste wood tightly to the end of the work; then splitting occurs only

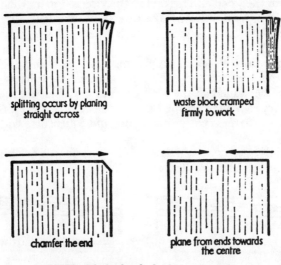

splitting occurs by planing
straight across

waste block cramped
firmly to work

chamfer the end

plane from ends towards
the centre

Fig 20   Methods of planing end grain

in the waste piece. Another method is to remove the far corner of the wood at an angle of 45°. This prevents splitting, but can be done only if the cut corner of the wood will not show because later shaping of the work will remove the cut. The usual method to adopt for planing the end grain of a wide board is to plane half-way from each end.

To plane the end grain of a small piece of wood requires the use of a simple appliance called a shooting board. This device helps one plane a straight square surface. The letters in figure 21 show the purpose of the parts more clearly.

A This block is put in the vice to hold the shooting board securely.
B Is the surface which the plane moves along.
C Is the stock which helps to hold the work square to the plane. The stock has to be at right angles to B.
D Is a piece of wood which rests in the well of the bench and helps to hold the shooting board in place.
E Is where the work is rested and held in place against the stock.

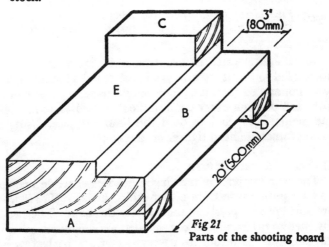

Fig 21
Parts of the shooting board

☐ MALLET

The mallet is made from beechwood, which is hardwearing and does not split easily. It is used chiefly for hitting chisels when working on top of the bench. The usual size for a mallet

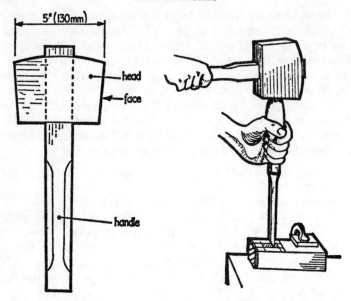

Fig 22 Parts of the mallet *(left)* and using the mallet *(right)*. The
face of the mallet is angled so that it hits the chisel squarely

is 5in (130mm) which is measured as in figure 22. The faces
are angled so that they always hit the chisel squarely. If they
were not angled then the elbow would have to be lifted to an
awkward position every time the tool is used. The handle of
the mallet is tapered to hold the head in place. Using the
mallet forces the head tighter on the shaft.

☐ WARRINGTON HAMMER
   The warrington hammer has a head of crucible cast steel
and a handle made from either ash or hickory. These woods
are springy and pass few shocks into the hand. The head is
fastened to the handle by one wooden wedge of hornbeam (fig
23) and two malleable iron wedges that are barbed to hold
them in place. Should the head become loose on the handle
then the metal wedges can be tapped further into the eye of
the hammer. The pein of the hammer can be used for tapping
small nails which are held upright between the fingers.

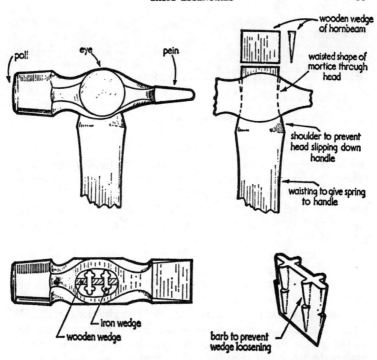

Fig 23 Parts of the warrington hammer. One wooden wedge of hornbeam and two iron wedges are used to fix the hammer head to the shaft

Chapter 2

Saws, Chisels and Planes

HANDSAWS

Wood consists of a mass of closely packed fibres all running in the same direction. These patterns made by the fibres are called the grain of the wood. The handsaw cuts by making a channel either through the grain or across the grain and the wood that is removed from the channel becomes sawdust. The rip saw is designed to cut with the grain. The crosscut saw is designed to cut across the grain.

These saws have three major differences as shown in figure 24. Firstly, the rip saw is longer. It is therefore the faster cutting saw, as longer strokes can be used. Secondly, the teeth of the rip saw are sharpened like chisels, whereas the teeth of the crosscut saw are sharpened like knives. The rip saw can chisel a path through the fibres of the wood. The crosscut saw has to cut across the fibres; it makes two parallel cuts close together so that the wood between these cuts crumbles away. The third difference is that the rip saw has bigger teeth. The size of the teeth is measured as the number of points per inch (per 25mm) or ppi. Alternatively the number of teeth per inch, tpi, can be measured. It will be realised that there is one more point per inch than there are teeth per inch as both outside points are counted. An easy way to recognise the rip saw from the crosscut is to remember that the rip saw has bigger teeth.

Figure 24 also shows that the teeth on both saws are bent outwards alternately. This is called the set of the saw and provides clearance for the blade to pass through the saw cut. Without set the path cut by the saw would be the same width as the thickness of steel in the blade. The saw would then bind in the cut and be difficult to use. A well set saw makes it possible to slide a sewing needle between the teeth of the upturned saw from heel to toe. Best quality saws are taper ground. That is to say the steel blade is thinner at the back than along the roots of the teeth. This way clearance can be provided for the

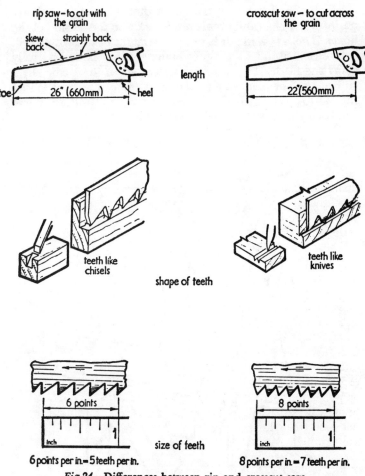

Fig 24   Differences between rip and crosscut saw

saw with less set. The saw cut is therefore narrower and less work has to be done by the craftsman to achieve the same results.

Of the tools listed in Appendix A a crosscut saw is recommended since it is the only type of saw that can cut both with and across the grain. However, cutting with the grain is slower by crosscut saw than rip saw.

When choosing a new saw check that the teeth are sharp, uniform in shape, and evenly set. Check also the tension of the blade. The saw blade does not stay straight of its own accord. It is tensioned like a spring, by hammer blows placed skilfully along the blade. This work is carried out in the factory by a craftsman. The blade of a good quality saw can be bent so that the toe touches the heel. It should bend in a uniform curve and spring back straight when released.

Fig 25 Crosscutting a plank. The thumb of the left hand guides the blade as the saw is drawn backwards three times

The sawing stool, sometimes called a trestle or horse, is used to support a plank when sawing with a handsaw. Lines to be followed are marked on the work with a pencil giving a generous allowance to the sizes to allow for planing at a later stage. Use two stools to support long work, then the board is held in a horizontal position. The stools must be of sufficient height to prevent the toe of the handsaw striking the floor. A height of about 22in (550mm) is adequate.

Figure 25 shows how a shorter piece of wood may be placed on the sawing stool for sawing. Notice also how the saw is held. Three fingers pass through the handle and the forefinger points alongside in the direction of the cut. This grip is more positive than passing all the fingers through the handle. The work is held firm by placing the left knee on the wood. To commence sawing draw the saw backwards for three strokes guiding the saw by the thumb of the left hand. These three strokes will make a groove on the corner of the wood. This groove acts as a guide for the saw and a forward stroke can be made as soon as the groove is of a reasonable size. Take care with the first few strokes as it is these that determine the accuracy of the cut in regard to the line. Remember that the teeth of the saw are sharpened from toe to heel. Use all the teeth of the saw by making long strokes. Using only the teeth in the middle of the blade will cause them to blunt rapidly. Complete the saw cut by holding the overhanging part and sawing more slowly. Letting the wood fall to the ground can cause a split to run into the work.

BACKED SAWS

Backed saws are so called because the thin blade of the saw is weighted and stiffened by a back of brass or steel. It has been mentioned that the blade of the handsaw is stiffened by skilfully placed hammer blows. The back saw has a thinner and narrower blade and cannot be tensioned in the same way.

The back of the saw is a strip of brass or steel folded tightly over the blade. To tension the blade the back is tapped lightly with one blow of the hammer at point A and again at point B. The natural tendency is for the back to straighten, pulling at the blade at the same time. This pulling action tensions the blade. Best quality backed saws are usually backed with brass, which grips more firmly than steel.

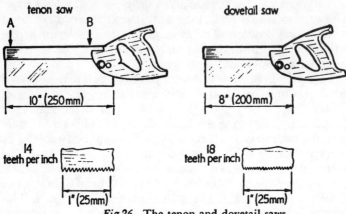

Fig 26   The tenon and dovetail saws

There are two types of backed saws (fig 26). These are the tenon saw and dovetail saw. The main difference is in the length of blade and size of teeth. It has been mentioned that the tenon saw is 10in (250mm) long and has 14 teeth per inch. It is used for accurate bench work. The dovetail saw is only 8in (200mm) long and has 18 teeth per inch. It is used for very fine work, in particular for cutting the dovetail joint. The tenon saw is the most used. Its teeth are relatively large and easy to sharpen. The dovetail saw is reserved for the finer work as its teeth are small and tedious to sharpen.

FRAME SAWS

The majority of work can be undertaken using the saws already mentioned. All straight cuts can be performed by the handsaw or backed saw. However, not all sawing is limited to straight cuts. There are two saws used to cut most curves: the bow saw and coping saw (fig 27). These are sometimes referred to as frame saws because a frame of wood or steel keeps the thin blades taut.

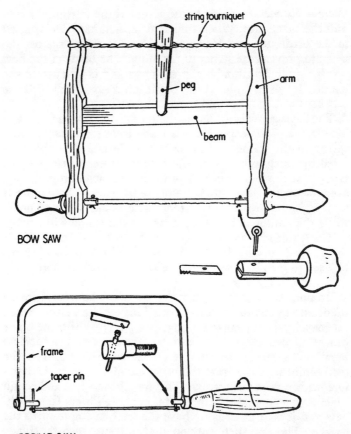

Fig 27 Frame saws. The bow saw has a blade length of 10in or 12in (250mm or 300mm) and is used for cutting curves in thick wood. The blade of the coping saw is 6½in (165mm) long. The coping saw is used on thinner wood

The frame of the bow saw is made of beechwood. It consists of two arms loosely jointed to a beam. At one side of the beam there is a loop of string, in the centre of which is a peg. When the peg is turned the string is twisted and thereby shortened. It acts as a tourniquet, the arms being pulled closer together. At the other side of the beam the arms are forced apart. The blade is fastened that side so the action of the tourniquet is to pull the blade taut. When sufficient tension has been applied to the blade, the peg of the tourniquet is rested against the beam to prevent the string unravelling. The blade of the bow saw is supplied with a hole at each end and is fastened to the handles by a small pin. If the pin is lost a small nail with the end bent over can be used.

The coping saw is similar to the bow saw in only a few ways. The frame of the coping saw is made from steel and it is the spring in the frame that keeps the blade taut. The blade is fitted by partly unscrewing the handle, thereby bringing the taper pins closer together. A pin fitted at each end is slipped over the taper pin to hold the blade in place. The handle is then tightened to its full extent. The blade will not break while the handle is being tightened as the frame will spring.

The frame saw cuts a curved path because the narrow blade can be made to turn in the saw cut. Because both hands must be used to grip the handle of the saw, the work is most easily supported in the vice.

On both types of frame saw the blade can be turned inside the frame to cut in any direction. This can be helpful when sawing a long cut near to the edge of a plank. Whilst the blade can be turned every care must be taken not to twist it or a break will occur. Generally the craftsman prefers to have the teeth pointing away from the main handle. The cut is therefore made on the push stroke. This way the sawdust and rough edges do not conceal the line that is being followed. In schools, however, it is quite usual to have the teeth facing towards the handle. The saw then cuts on the pull stroke so the blade is less likely to buckle and be broken. The teeth of frame saws are never sharpened. The blades are cheap and easily replaced.

Frame saws can be used to make an enclosed cut. This is done by drilling a hole in the waste part of the wood and threading the blade through the hole. The blade is fixed to the frame and the shape is sawn. This is only possible when the frame is in reach of the cut.

SPECIAL SAWS

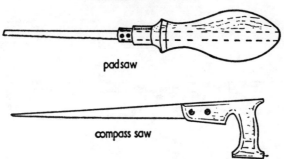

pad saw

compass saw

Fig 28   Special saws. The pad saw *(top)* has a blade length of 8-10in (200-250mm). The compass saw *(bottom)*

These saws are particularly useful when cutting a hole in the middle of a large panel. In this instance work can begin from a drilled hole. The padsaw is slow and it is difficult to keep the blade straight. It is therefore convenient to have only sufficient blade showing. The rest of the blade slides inside the hollow handle. The blade of the padsaw is replaceable and not worth sharpening when blunt. The compass saw would be used for curves of larger radius than the padsaw.

CHISELS

One type of chisel has been mentioned already—the firmer chisel. Sketch (a) represents the $\frac{5}{8}$in (16mm) firmer chisel, and sketch (b) represents the 1in (25mm) firmer chisel. Both sizes are recommended in the tool list given in Appendix A. Notice that the handles are the same size. This is because despite the size of blade the handle must fit the hand. Sketch (c) shows a 1in (25mm) bevelled edge chisel. It looks as though it is sharpened on three edges but there is in fact only one cutting edge. The long edges are not sharp. The bevelled edge chisel is very similar to the firmer chisel. If one imagines the blade of the firmer chisel divided into three equal parts then the bevelled edge chisel is formed by grinding away the outside thirds to form a slope leaving only the centre section flat. Figure 30

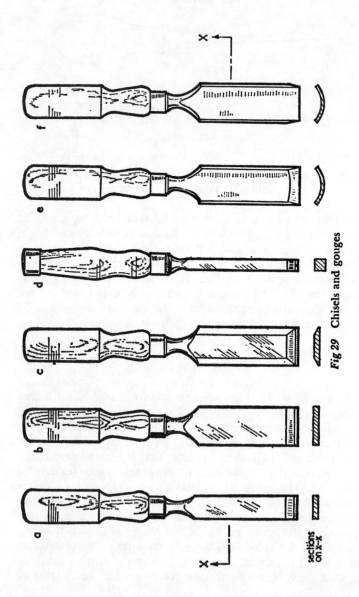

Fig 29 Chisels and gouges

sections on x-x

shows the bevelled edge chisel being used to cut away the centre section between two dovetails. The bevels on the chisel allow the tool to work into the undercut corners. This would be an impossible job for the firmer chisel.

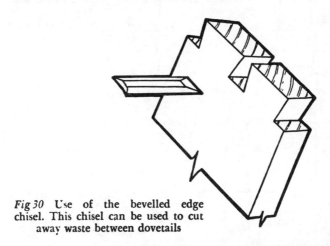

Fig 30 Use of the bevelled edge chisel. This chisel can be used to cut away waste between dovetails

Sketch (d) shows a mortise chisel. It will be noticed that the blade is nearly square in section, and therefore very strong. Sketches (e) and (f) show a tool called a gouge. If one imagines the blade of a firmer chisel heated to red heat and then bent one can see how the gouge is formed. Thinking of a firmer chisel, it is possible to curve the blade in two different ways. Sketch (e) shows the gouge with the sharpening bevel on the inside. This is called the scribing or in-cannel gouge. Sketch (f) shows the gouge with the sharpening bevel on the outside, and this is called the firmer or out-cannel gouge. The firmer gouge is used for hollowing out to make dishes and bowls, whereas the scribing gouge is used for the vertical paring of internal curves.

Figure 31 shows the main parts of the firmer chisel. The blade is fastened to the handle by means of a tang. The tang and the blade are all one piece of tool steel. The tang is a spike forced into the chisel handle. The shoulder prevents the tang from driving up inside the handle when the chisel is struck with a mallet. The ferrule is a seamless brass ring pushed on

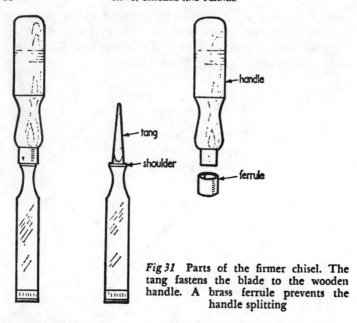

Fig 31 Parts of the firmer chisel. The tang fastens the blade to the wooden handle. A brass ferrule prevents the handle splitting

the handle and held in place by a punch mark. The ferrule prevents the handle from being split by the tang, especially when a new handle is fitted. The bevelled edge chisel is similar to the firmer chisel but it is not as strong and should not be hit heavily with a mallet.

The mortise chisel is rather different. It has a leather washer fitted between the shoulder and the handle to absorb some of the shock to the hand, as this chisel is always used in conjunction with a mallet. Some patterns have a ferrule at the top of the handle to prevent splitting after repeated blows of the mallet. It will be seen that it is not the ferrule that is hit with the mallet but the wood inside the ferrule. The beechwood mallet is never used against metal. Modern chisels have plastic handles. These are very strong and may be hit with a mallet. The advantage of the wooden handle is that it will absorb perspiration.

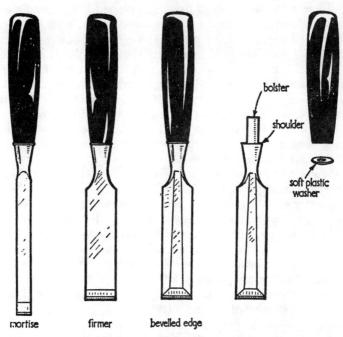

Fig 32 Stanley range of chisels. The mortise, firmer and bevelled edge chisels have handles made of tough plastic. A bolster type construction is used to fasten the handle to the blade

BENCH PLANES

Two planes that have been mentioned previously are the wooden and metal jack planes. All planes have three things in common. Firstly, they each have a cutter. Secondly, they each have a device for holding the cutter in position. In the case of the wooden jack plane it is a wedge; the metal jack plane has a lever cap. The third feature of all planes is the stock or body. This is simply a device used to present the chisel-like blade in a controlled manner to the surface of the wood. Beechwood is used for the stock of the wooden plane because it is a stable and hard wearing timber. The body of the metal plane is made from cast iron.

To remove the cutter of the metal plane lift the lever; this loosens the cap and allows it to be removed, enabling the cutter to be lifted out of the plane. Above the toe of the wooden plane is a small piece of boxwood. This is partly let into the body and is called the button, presumably because of its similarity in shape to the wooden buttons worn on coats years ago. To release the wedge of the wooden plane the stock is held in the hand while the button is tapped two or three times with the hammer. The vibration of the stock causes the wedge to shake out of place. Once the wedge has been removed the cutter can be taken out.

It will be seen that the cutter consists of two parts, the blade and the curling iron (fig 33). The two are held together by a large screw. A large cabinet screwdriver is required to undo this screw but special care must be taken. It is dangerous to hold the blades in the hand while applying pressure with the screwdriver. A slip could cause a bad cut. Instead, place the blades on the bench. Release the screw one turn. It is not necessary to remove the screw entirely as the cutting iron may be slid back from the cutting edge until the screw head can pass through the hole in the blade.

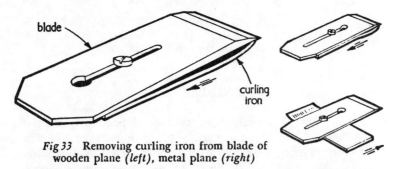

Fig 33   Removing curling iron from blade of wooden plane *(left)*, metal plane *(right)*

When removing a cutter from a metal plane greater care is required, as the release hole in the blade is near to the cutting edge. In this instance slacken the screw one turn with the screwdriver. Do not use the lever cap although it seems an ideal fit; the metal is not specially hardened and tempered to act as a screwdriver. Slide the curling iron back from the cutting edge, then swivel the curling iron through 90°. It may now be removed from the blade by sliding forward without the risk of damaging the cutting edge.

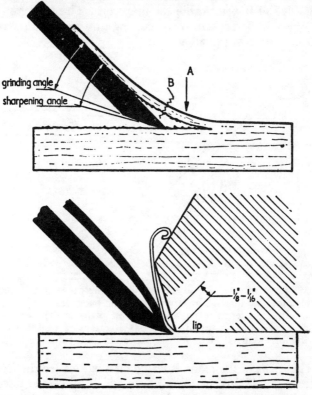

grinding angle

sharpening angle

Fig 34 Tearing occurs with single iron

A blade on its own may be tapped into a block of wood with a hammer but splitting occurs ahead of the cutting edge (fig 34) because the blade is acting like a wedge and prising the wood away. This results in a rough surface. Three things can be done to prevent splitting. Firstly, the surface of the wood must be pressed down immediately in front of the cutter to prevent the shaving lifting (*A* fig 34). Pressure is applied by the lip of the plane. Secondly, if the shaving were broken at *B* then it would be prevented from rising up the blade forcing the wood to tear up in front of the cutting edge. This is done by the addition of the curling iron placed about ⅛in (3mm) from the cutting edge for coarse work and as close to the cutting edge as is practicable for fine work. Thirdly, only fine shavings can be broken by the curling iron so the cutter is set to protrude only a small amount.

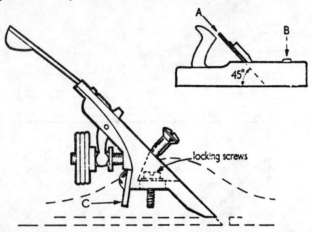

Fig 35 Frogs of wooden and metal planes. The cutter of the wooden plane is adjusted forward by tapping at A and backward by tapping the button B. The depth of cut of the metal plane is adjusted with a knurled knob and lateral adjustment is by means of a lever. Further, the frog of the metal plane may be moved to adjust the size of mouth

The blade of the plane is seated on a part called the frog at an angle of 45° to the sole. This angle is called the pitch of the plane. In the case of the wooden plane the cutter and curling iron are placed on the frog, the wedge pushed in place and the blade is set by tapping at *A* (fig 35) for a coarser shaving or at *B* for a finer shaving. Set also for evenness of cut by tapping the blade sideways. Finally secure the blade by tapping the wedge. Figure 36 shows how to check for cutter projection by holding the plane sole upwards with the light coming from behind the plane. One can then sight along the sole.

The frog of the metal plane is cast as a separate piece from the stock. It is fastened to the stock by two locking screws (fig

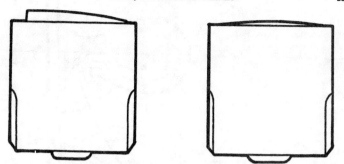

Fig 36 Sighting wooden plane for cutter projection: *(left)* too coarse
and uneven; *(right)* correct

35). It will be noticed that the locking screws pass through
slots in the frog, and that a lug (*C* fig 35) locates on an adjusting screw on the stock. The principle is that the two locking
screws are released one turn and the frog adjusting screw
revolved to move the frog forward or back, thereby opening or
closing the mouth of the plane. Close the mouth for timbers
that are inclined to tear; open the mouth to take coarse shavings and for general purpose work. Should shavings choke in
the mouth of the plane do not try to push them through with
a steel rule. Remove the lever cap and blade to release the
shaving. Choking can indicate that the opening of the mouth
is too small or that too coarse a cut is being attempted. Occasionally the edge of the curling iron may be seated incorrectly.
This can be remedied by careful use of a file on the curling
iron. To alter the amount of cut on the metal plane the
knurled adjusting screw must be turned. To set for an even
cut the lateral adjustment lever is moved towards one side.

Figure 38 shows the three common metal planes. Each, because of its length, does a particular job best. The smoothing
plane, being short, is light, handy and comfortable to work.
As its name implies, it is used for finishing off where smooth-
ness is more essential than flatness. It is the plane that is used
before the polishing stage of the work. The jack plane is the
jack-of-all-trades. It is a general purpose plane. It is used for
planing wood to size, trueing edges, and planing ends square
on the shooting board. It is long enough to be accurate but
light enough to be in use for a long time. The trying plane is

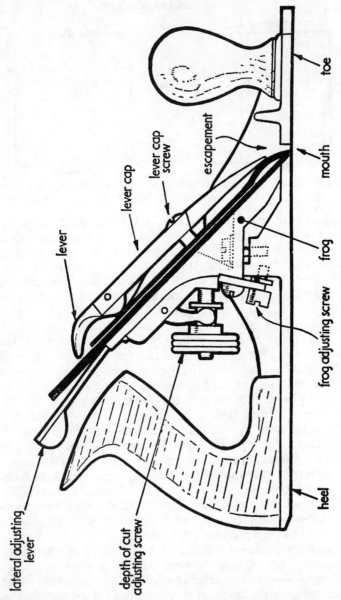

Fig 37 Elevation of metal smoothing plane, with one side removed

toe

mouth

frog

frog adjusting screw

heel

escapement

lever cap screw

lever cap

lever

lateral adjusting lever

depth of cut adjusting screw

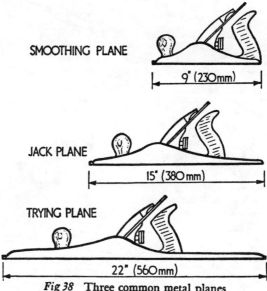

SMOOTHING PLANE

9" (230mm)

JACK PLANE

15" (380 mm)

TRYING PLANE

22" (560mm)

Fig 38 Three common metal planes

about 22in (560mm) long. It is used for trueing long surfaces, and particularly for edge jointing. Its length allows it to ride over minor undulations and take the crests off bumps, thereby achieving a flat surface. This plane should be set to take off only a very fine shaving.

All the metal planes have wooden counterparts. The relative advantages of the wooden and metal planes may be summed up as follows:

Wood	*Metal*
1 Runs more easily over the wood	The sole is machined true
2 The body is robust and more likely to withstand rough treatment	It is less liable to wear
3 Lighter and less tiring to use	The cutting iron is more easily adjusted
4 It is cheaper	The size of the mouth may be adjusted by moving the frog

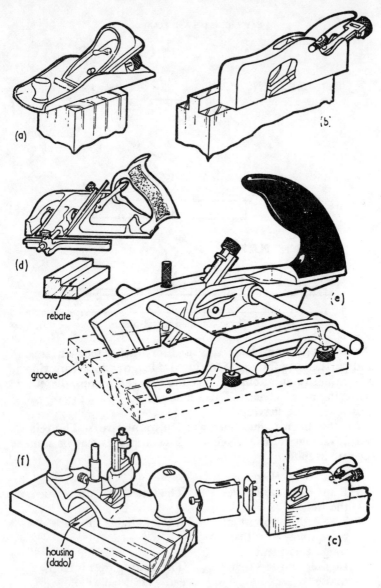

(a)

(b)

(d)

rebate

(e)

groove

(f)

housing
(dado)

(c)

Fig 39 Special planes: (*a*) block plane, (*b*) shoulder plane,
(*c*) shoulder/bullnose/chisel plane, (*d*) rebate (rabbet) plane.
(*e*) plough plane and (*f*) router

It is recommended in the tool list given in Appendix A that chiefly metal planes are acquired because easy adjustment is a considerable advantage to the beginner. Using the wooden jack plane to plane wood down to size is now largely an anachronism as timber can be easily acquired planed to size by machine. The metal plane is however required to remove the ripple marks left on the wood by machine planing. Many of today's timbers have difficult grains requiring the use of a finely set plane.

All planes work much better if the sole is wiped with a pad moistened with light machine oil. A little linseed oil well rubbed into the stock of the wooden plane serves to preserve the wood.

SPECIAL PLANES

There are several planes that have not yet been mentioned because they have special purposes. The small block plane (fig 39a) may be worked single-handed. It is used chiefly for small work and for trimming end grain. The original function of this plane was to trim the surfaces of butchers blocks, which were made of hardwood with the end grain upwards. This tool has a single blade set into the body of the plane at a shallow angle, bevel uppermost. Owing to its handy size and its efficiency for planing end grain the block plane has been adopted not only by the cabinet maker, but by the model maker as well. It has also been found an exceedingly handy tool for trimming plastic laminates, though in this case the tool works better if it has a low angle of pitch.

The shoulder plane (fig 39b) is used chiefly for trimming shoulders, tenons and rebates. The blade cuts the full width of the body so that this tool can trim right into the angle of the corner. This plane is obtainable with a detachable front section for use as a bullnose plane (fig 39c). As such it may be used to trim right into corners.

The rebate, or rabbet plane (fig 39d), is used to cut a rebate on the corner of a piece of wood. This plane has two fences. One is a stop for cutting the correct depth and the other is a guide for cutting the correct width. These are easily adjusted to suit the size of rebate required. There are two blade positions. The centre position is used for all normal open-ended rebating. The forward position is used for bullnose work when cutting stopped rebates. The blade cuts bevel downwards and adjustment is made with the lever behind the blade. As there is no curling iron work must begin in progressive stages to minimise tearing of the grain. Start from the front end by making a short cut and work backwards until the entire rebate is made.

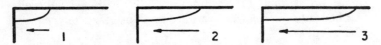

Fig 40   Working a rebate in progressive stages

The plough plane (fig 39e) is used to make a groove inside the boundaries of the wood but it can also work a rebate. This plane is supplied with a set of cutters of different widths. A cutter is chosen to match the width of the groove required. The plane is then set for depth of the work. As with the rebate plane, start work at the far end and move backwards gradually. Clear shavings from the mouth of the plane frequently as it quickly becomes choked. The most common fault when working with this plane is not holding the fence tightly to the work. Remember to press inwards with the left hand when cutting. This requires a little practice but is easily mastered. A spot of oil on the fence and sole of the plane eases the effort required.

Figure 41 shows the plough plane being used. Grooving the edge of a wide board is easy as the wood may be held in the vice. Often, however, the groove is required in the side of the work. The wood is then best placed in a sash cramp and the cramp held in the vice. Always allow the wood to overhang the vice as part of the plough plane is likely to work below the wood. The most common trouble is caused by the plane rubbing on the vice.

The router (fig 39f) is used for making grooves of uniform depth across the grain. A groove cut across the grain is called a housing or dado (pronounced *day'doe*). The sides of the

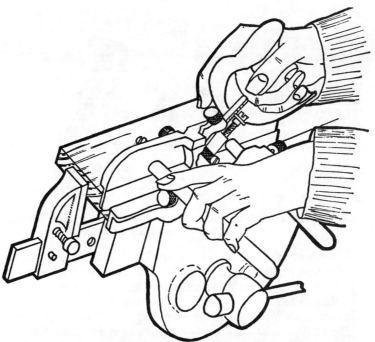

Fig 41 Using a plough plane. The work can be supported in a sash cramp and the sash cramp held in the vice

housing are cut first with the tenon saw and most of the waste is removed with a chisel before the router is used. The router is worked from the edge of the wood towards the centre to avoid splitting. The depth is gradually increased if necessary until the required depth is reached.

The replaceable blade plane (fig 42) is the latest development in plane design. The replaceable blades are made of tungsten steel and are sharpened in the factory ready for use. Three shapes of blade are available. The curved blade is for general planing, the straight blade for rebate work and edge and end grain planing, and a special blade is available for planing hard laminated plastics and manufactured boards such as Formica and chipboard.

A blunt or chipped blade may be easily replaced by slackening the blade clamping screw and allowing the old blade to

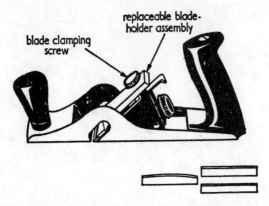

Fig 42   Replaceable blade plane. No sharpening is required because the worn out blades are simply discarded

drop out of the assembly. The plane is then held sole upwards and a new blade slipped in place. Care must be taken to position the blade bevel upwards and to seat the blade squarely in the blade holder assembly. While the plane is still in the inverted position, the blade clamping screw is retightened. The blade can be adjusted for depth of cut and lateral alignment in the usual way. A fence is available and can be used in conjunction with a straight blade to convert the ordinary plane into a rebate plane.

The advantages of the replaceable blade plane are lightness and ease of use. The plane is 10in (250mm) long and has a 2in (51mm) cut. No sharpening is required as the worn out blades are simply discarded.

Chapter 3

Other Hand Tools

MARKING TOOLS

☐ MORTISE GAUGE

The mortise gauge is similar in appearance to the marking gauge, the chief difference being that the mortise gauge has two spurs. This tool is used to mark two lines on the wood parallel to an edge and with the grain. Its use is marking guide lines to be followed with the saw and chisel when cutting the mortise and tenon joint; hence its name.

The distance between the spurs may be varied by adjusting

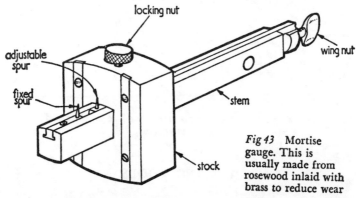

Fig 43 Mortise gauge. This is usually made from rosewood inlaid with brass to reduce wear

a wing nut on the end of the stem. The position of the lines from the edge of the work may be adjusted by moving the stock. The stock can be locked by turning the nut provided. It is usual to set the spurs of the mortise gauge to suit the chisel to be used when cutting the mortise, rather than to a set measurement. When the gauge is set correctly the mortise chisel just rests between the points of the spurs.

☐ CUTTING GAUGE

The cutting gauge is used to mark a line on the wood *across* the grain. This tool is similar to the marking gauge but the spur is replaced by a small knife held in place by a brass wedge. The end of the wood must be square and true before this gauge can be used with accuracy.

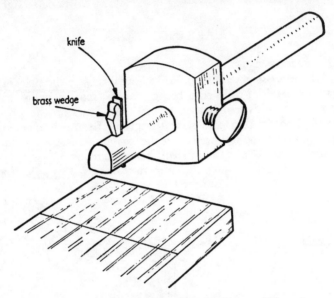

knife

brass wedge

Fig 44 Cutting gauge. This marks one line on the wood across the grain

TESTING TOOLS

☐ MITRE SQUARE

The mitre square is similar to a try square, the difference being that the blade is inclined at an angle of 45° to the stock. It is used therefore for marking out and checking angles of 45° and 135°.

☐ SLIDING BEVEL

The sliding bevel is used for transferring angles other than 45° or 90°. The angle of the blade is adjustable and is locked in place either by a wing nut or a set screw.

It is usual for the angle required to be given not in the

numbers of degrees but as a ratio, in a method similar to that used for informing motorists about the gradient of a hill. Suppose the sliding bevel is to be set to a slope of 1 in 14. It is first necessary to choose a setting out board with one straight

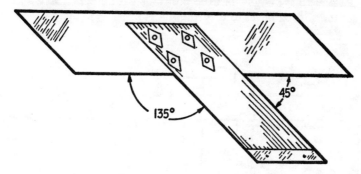

135°   45°

Fig 45 Mitre square. Used for checking the mitre angle of work such as picture frames

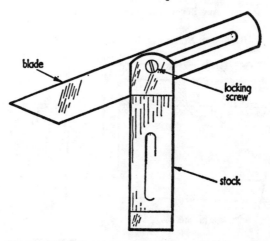

blade

locking screw

stock

Fig 46 Sliding bevel. Used for transferring angles to the work of other than 90° or 45°

edge; the top of the bench may be used provided it is in good order. Mark a line at right angles to the edge of the board with a pencil and try square. Now it will probably be impracticable to measure along this line a distance of 14in; it will be more convenient if the numbers in the ratio are divided by 2. This will not change the amount of slope. Measure 7in (140mm) along the line from the edge and $\frac{1}{2}$in (10mm) from that point parallel to the edge. Join the positions with a pencil line and set the sliding bevel to this line (fig 47).

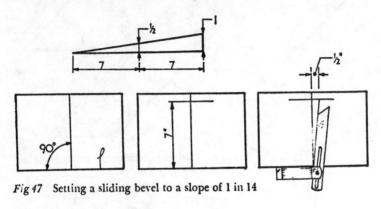

Fig 47　Setting a sliding bevel to a slope of 1 in 14

□　DOVETAIL TEMPLATE

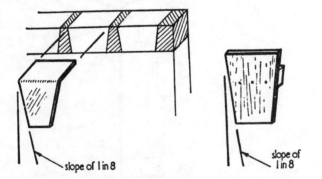

Fig 48　Dovetail templates: *(left)* made of metal;
(right) made from wood

The dovetail template is used as a pattern when marking the slope of a dovetail. This device can be made from a piece of steel bent and filed to shape, or a piece of shaped plywood.

☐ WINDING STRIPS

Winding strips are two parallel strips of well seasoned wood placed at opposite ends of the work; by sighting across the tops of the strips any wind (twist in the wood) can be easily detected. The best way to correct a twisted piece of wood is to place the work against the bench stop and plane diagonally to remove the high spots.

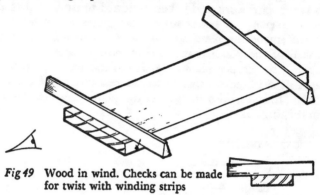

Fig 49 Wood in wind. Checks can be made for twist with winding strips

CUTTING TOOLS

☐ CABINET SCRAPER

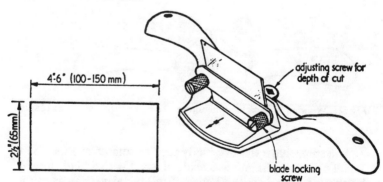

Fig 50 Cabinet scraper and scraper plane. The cabinet scraper has to be sprung in the hands and pushed away from the operator. The scraper plane springs the blade with an adjusting screw and makes the work easier

Some timbers will tear slightly no matter how well the smoothing plane is sharpened and set, and the cabinet scraper may be used to remove these blemishes after the surface has been planed.

The cabinet scraper is used sprung in the hands so make sure the blade is relatively easy to bend. The centre of the convex edge is pushed forward to remove a ribbon of shaving. It is fairly hard work and is best confined to timbers that are difficult to plane. A better surface can generally be achieved with the smoothing plane so it is more worthwhile mastering the skill of the plane than making too frequent use of the scraper. The scraper plane is easier to use than the cabinet scraper as the blade is sprung by a screw instead of pressure from the thumbs. Also the sole of the plane prevents the tool from digging in.

☐   SPOKESHAVE

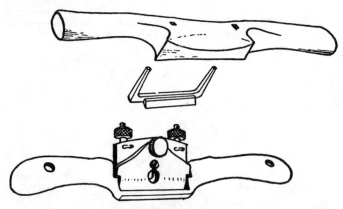

Fig 51 Wooden and metal spokeshave. The metal pattern is available with a flat or curved sole

The spokeshave was originally used to smooth the spokes of wooden cart wheels and was made of wood with a blade forged by the local blacksmith. Today an all-metal version is available. The wooden spokeshave is made in only one form but there are two types of metal spokeshave: the flat sole spokeshave is used for convex shapes, gentle hollows, and flat cutting; the round sole spokeshave can be used only to make concave shapes.

As well as shaping a curve the spokeshave may be used for smoothing a curve that has been cut to shape with a frame saw. It is possible with this tool to produce a surface which requires no further cleaning up. Care must be taken to always work with the grain.

BORING TOOLS

☐ BRADAWL

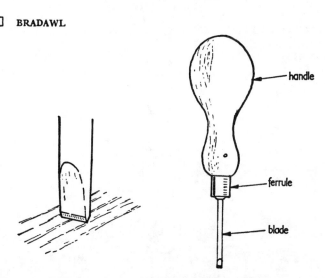

Fig 52 Bradawl. Used for making small holes. Set the blade across the grain and twist and push on the handle

The bradawl is a small chisel-pointed tool used for making holes to start screws. It is used with a semi-rotary action starting with the blade at right-angles to the grain of the wood. The sharp edge of the bradawl cuts the fibres of the wood and the blade pushes the fibres to the sides. A pin through the handle and blade secures the latter and prevents it pulling out from the handle when the bradawl is withdrawn from the work.

☐ HAND DRILL

By far the most satisfactory method of boring small holes in wood is by means of the hand drill. The drill shown in figure 53 has a double pinion drive which is stronger than the less expensive drills with single pinions. The hand drill has a three-jaw chuck which will only accept round-shanked drills. This limits its use to the twist drill and round-shanked countersink. It will grip drills up to at least $\frac{1}{4}$in (6mm) in size.

The point of a drill is rather blunt, and so it is good practice

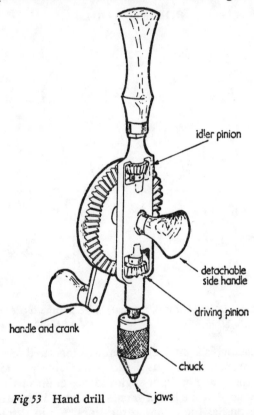

idler pinion

detachable
side handle

driving pinion

handle and crank

chuck

Fig 53 Hand drill   jaws

to locate the required centre of the hole by means of a centre punch. This prevents the tendency of the blunt point to wander from the correct position at the start of drilling.

Hold the drill straight. Do not wobble while turning as it makes the hole oversize and is likely to break the drill. Turn the crank at a constant speed and not too fast. The same rules apply when withdrawing the drill, when there is even greater danger of the drill breaking. Always keep the drill turning in a clockwise direction or the waste will be left in the hole.

☐ TWIST DRILLS

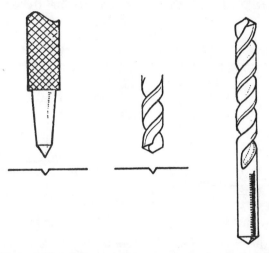

Fig 54 Twist drill and the use of the centre punch to locate the drill

The twist drill is used for making small holes into which screws are fitted. These drills can be bought in sizes from ₁₆in (1.5mm) to ¼in (6mm) for use in the hand drill. Larger sizes are obtainable but these require more powerful drilling machines to turn them. Twist drills may be made of carbon tool steel or high-speed steel. The high-speed steel, though more expensive, is the better type as it is stronger and can be used with greater reliability in the electric drill.

When drilling deep holes the twist drill is liable to clog with waste. To prevent this the drill should be withdrawn frequently from the hole and the flutes cleared. The twist drill is sometimes called the Morse drill after the name of the American inventor.

☐   BRACE

The bits used for boring large holes require considerable leverage to turn them. The power of the brace is dependent upon the sweep. This tool can be bought with different amounts of sweep. A brace with a large sweep will exert more power on the bit. A useful size is an 8in (200mm) sweep. The head of the brace is fitted with ball bearings so that it may be held steady as the brace is turned. A more expensive brace has a ratchet fitted above the chuck. This enables the brace to be

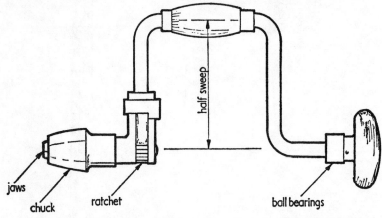

Fig 55   Brace. Used to bore holes greater than ¼in (6mm) in diameter

used in awkward places, against a wall for instance, where the brace cannot be swung through a complete circle. The chuck of the brace has two jaws that will in general only grip square shank bits. It will not accept the twist drill which should of course be used in a hand drill.

☐   BITS

Figure 56 shows the most common types of bits made to fit the brace. The centre bit is used for cutting a clean hole in thin timber. In operation the brad point is placed onto the centre mark on the work. Turning the brace causes the point to penetrate. The scriber then cuts a circular path through the grain of the wood. Finally the cutter lifts the waste. The bit operates successfully when drilling holes in thin wood but is inclined to wander with the grain when drilling to a good depth.

The Jennings pattern twist bit may be used successfully when deep boring. The spiral twist not only removes the waste from the bottom of the hole, but also the edges of the spiral press against the side of the hole making the bit follow a straight and accurate path. This is the bit most frequently used by the cabinet maker.

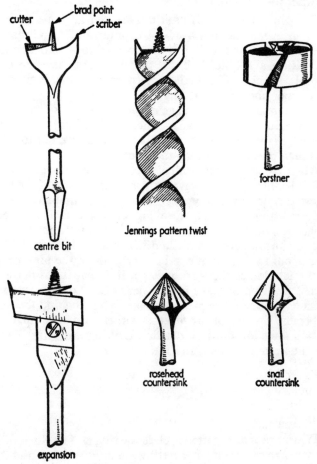

Fig 56 Common types of bit

The Forstner bit is used for drilling holes when an almost flat bottom is required. This bit is rather more specialised than the previous two but sometimes it is invaluable.

All the bits mentioned can be bought in a range of sizes from $\frac{1}{4}$in (6mm) to at least 1in (25mm). It is useful to have a selection of these so that holes in the more common size range can be readily produced. The expansion bit, however, can be adjusted to make holes from $\frac{7}{8}$in (22mm) to 3in (76mm) in diameter.

The countersink bit is used to bore conical holes in hardwood in order that the heads of countersink screws may be fitted flush with the surface of the work. Two types of countersink bit are available. The rose pattern may be used on brass as well as wood. The snail pattern countersink is used for wood alone and provides a slightly better finish.

A useful addition to a range of bits is the turnscrew bit. As its name implies it can adapt the brace for use as a screwdriver. It is so efficient that one has to take care not to apply too much pressure and snap the screw.

When using any bit to drill a hole right through a piece of wood splitting will always occur on the far side of the work unless certain precautions are taken. The simplest way to avoid splitting is to drill through the wood until the point penetrates, then reverse the wood and drill in from the other side. Unfortunately this method will not work when drilling thin wood. In this instance when the point of the bit emerges on the far side of the work it is possible that it has not even started to shape the hole on the near side. To overcome this difficulty place a waste piece of wood directly behind the work and cramp the two firmly together either with a cramp, or by placing them low down in the vice. Drilling through the work into the waste will result in a clean cut hole.

MISCELLANEOUS TOOLS

☐   SCREWDRIVER

There are many patterns of screwdriver. The duties of a cabinet screwdriver involve setting the mortise gauge and sliding bevel, undoing the blade and curling iron of the plane, as well as turning screws. Some people say this tool is misnamed. It is argued that the hammer is used to drive nails and the screwdriver is used to turn screws. Perhaps this tool should therefore be called a turnscrew.

The handle of the screwdriver is made of beechwood and is shaped for pushing and turning. The part of the blade that enters the handle is rectangular to prevent the handle from turning on the blade. The large handle over a small blade produces great turning power. Several screwdrivers should be bought to fit screws of different sizes.

☐ NAIL PUNCH

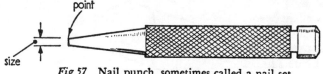

Fig 57 Nail punch, sometimes called a nail set

The nail punch is used to sink the heads of nails below the surface of the work. Place the punch on the nail and tap the head of the punch with a hammer. The resulting hole may be hidden with filler, such as hard beeswax pressed in with a bradawl on work that is to be polished, or putty on work that is to be painted. Two punches are needed, small and large, and the hollow point pattern are better, being less liable to jump from the head of the nail.

☐ PINCERS

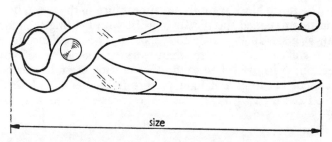

Fig 58 Pincers. Protect the surface of the work by levering on to a pad of waste wood

Several types of pincers are available and the tower pattern illustrated is the most popular. These may be bought in a range of sizes, the 8in (200mm) size being the most useful. When using the pincers to withdraw a nail it is advisable to place a piece of waste wood between the jaw and the surface of the work. This prevents the jaw from damaging the surface. The claw may be used to withdraw nails from awkward places.

AIDS AND APPLIANCES

☐   MITRE BLOCK

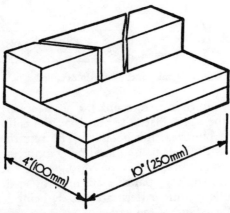

Fig 59   Mitre block. Used in conjunction with a tenon saw '. r cutting the ends of small beading to an angle of 45?

The mitre block is similar in appearance to the bench hook, but it is designed specifically to assist with holding the tenon saw at a steady 45° angle to the work. This appliance is seldom sufficiently accurate when working mouldings of large section, so its use is best confined to cutting the mitre corners of small beadings and light picture frames. Made of beechwood and used with care this tool can have a reasonably long life.

☐   MITRE BOX
The mitre box is used to guide the saw at a controlled angle

of 45° to the work. This tool is better than the mitre block as the saw is guided on both sides of the work. This device can be used on mouldings of large section. Accurate mitre joints can be cut straight from the saw if a fine tooth tenon saw is used and the moulding is cut so that the ragged edge is produced on the back of the work.

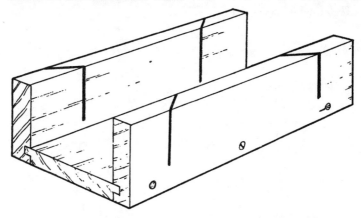

Fig 60 Mitre box. This has similar uses to a mitre block, but is much sturdier and may therefore be used on larger pieces of work. Insert a piece of waste wood inside the box to prevent the saw cutting into the base

☐ MITRE SHOOTING BOARD

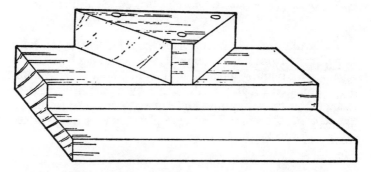

Fig 61 Mitre shooting board. Used for trimming the ends of moulding previously sawn to 45°

This device may be used for trimming the ends of mouldings cut to shape previously in the mitre box. It is similar in use and appearance to the shooting board. The work may be placed in either of two positions because mouldings can seldom be reversed to trim the mitre.

☐   GUILLOTINE

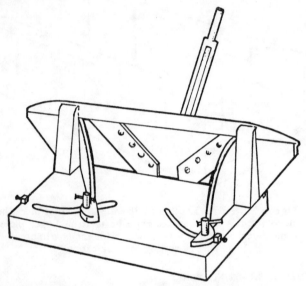

Fig 62   Guillotine. A powerful machine that can be used to trim the ends of wood to any angle between 45° and 90°

The guillotine is a sturdy hand powered cutter used for trimming end grain. With large blades and a long handle it is capable of trimming mouldings of large section. The moulding is prepared roughly to the angle by saw then accurately trimmed on the guillotine. Only fine shavings should be removed from the work. The angle plates have a range of adjustment from 45° to 90°.

CRAMPS

☐ G CRAMP

The G cramp is so called because it is in the shape of a
letter G. It can be used for holding two pieces of wood together while the glue sets between them, or it can be used to

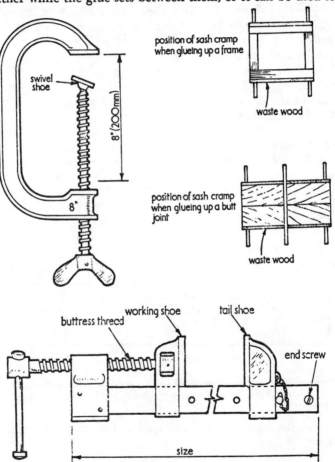

Figs 63 & 64 G cramp *(top left)*. Sash cramp *(right and below)*, showing how to position the cramps when glueing up a frame and a butt
joint between boards

hold the work steady on the bench leaving both hands free to work with the tools. A useful size of G cramp is 8in (200mm). One G cramp is essential amongst a kit of tools and a good workshop will have many of different sizes.

☐ SASH CRAMP

The sash cramp is mainly used for holding work together while the glue sets. It has a short thread on the working shoe and main adjustments are made by sliding the tail shoe along the bar. A useful size of sash cramp is 36in (910mm). It is best to buy a pair of cramps because usually two are needed on the work. Always use a piece of waste wood between the shoe of the cramp and the work as this helps to spread the pressure and prevent the shoe from marking the work.

☐ T-BAR CRAMP

The T-bar cramp is similar in appearance to the sash cramp but the section through the bar is in the shape of a letter T. This gives the cramp greater strength and rigidity. It is intended for use on large and heavy work. There are disadvantages in using a cramp that is too big for the job. It can

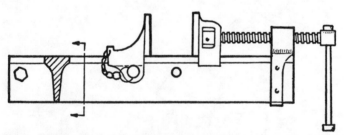

Fig 65   T-Bar cramp. The T-bar section produces a very strong cramp but these cramps are usually too heavy for furniture making

distort the work and one cannot feel how much pressure is being applied.

☐ HANDSCREW

The handscrew is a useful cramp sometimes made entirely of wood but more commonly made with beech chops and metal screws. To open or close the handscrew grasp the handles firmly one in each hand and spin the wooden chops head over heels. In operation arrange the jaws parallel and the same distance apart as the thickness of the work. Fasten to the work by tightening screw A and then turn screw B so that the chops pinch firmly in place.

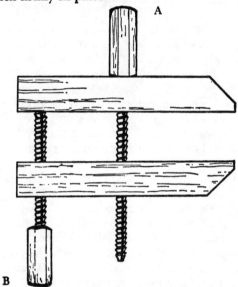

Fig 66 Handscrew. A very useful cramp

Chapter 4

Maintenance of Hand Tools

CARE OF TOOLS

Good tools are expensive and they should be carefully maintained. This will not only avoid the unnecessary expense of premature replacement, it will also mean that the tools are always ready for use. Nothing can be more irksome than having to sharpen or mend tools before work can commence. Probably the most satisfactory method of organising these chores is to perform them as one works, and above all to make sure that the workshop and its equipment are left in good order at the end of the day ready for a prompt start on the next occasion.

Rather like the motor car, servicing of tools depends on the amount of work they are given. A well-used jack plane will require frequent sharpening. Remember, though, that tools left idle for long periods will also require maintenance. The biggest problem is the deterioration of steel tools through rust. A rust-pitted chisel will not sharpen; the face must be reground to a smooth, flat surface and this is very time consuming. There are several ways of preventing the formation of rust. Primarily, the finer the surface finish given to the steel then the greater resistance there will be to rust. Well polished tools as supplied by the manufacturer will help maintain themselves in a good state, but some protection should be given to tools that are to be stored for a period of time or are used only occasionally. Water and air must be excluded from the surface of the metal, and even in the best ventilated workshop moisture can be transferred to the metal by contact with sweaty hands. Petroleum jelly should be applied liberally and thoroughly to form a protective barrier. By wrapping the object in newspaper one can prevent the transfer of petroleum jelly to other things. Grease is a good substitute for petroleum jelly; in fact some people find it more efficient. A vapour barrier paper such as *Banrust* is frequently used by manufacturers to save the time and trouble of greasing their tools in transit. It is of course more convenient for the customer if the tool is not covered with grease. The tool must be placed in an enclosed container with the white side of the paper, which is the treated side, facing the steel parts of the tool. This will ward off rust for lengthy periods of time. One of the latest products for treating steel is *Lubysil 717*. This is sold in 8oz (227g) aerosol cans. The liquid consists of a non soap based grease and mineral oil base containing silicone resins. This has excellent dielectric, corrosion resisting and lubricating properties. Furthermore this liquid is not inflammable. Sprayed on to metal, Lubysil forms a smooth transparent layer with an imperceptible skin, which resists condensation, water, and salt- and sulphur-laden air. Equipment treated this way is ready for use without time spent unpacking and cleaning.

In the same way that steel tools require periodic maintenance, so wooden tools require some preservative treatment. All wooden parts of tools deserve wiping with a rag soaked in linseed oil once a year. This drying oil, made from the exudation of the crushed seeds of the linen (flax) plant, helps preserve the wood and eases the work by reducing friction. Sometimes a little turpentine is added to the oil to make a kind of teak oil. This will impart a little shine to the wood.

Maintenance can be looked at in two ways. There is the more general maintenance of all tools to preserve them and to ensure they work at optimum efficiency, and there is the normal sharpening procedure required for all cutting tools, except of course the replaceable blade plane.

Spare parts are available for all the tools supplied by reputable manufacturers. Make sure that the tool supplier is given the exact serial number of the tool, and full details of the part required.

The following is a list of common hand tools. More specific advice is given here on the maintenance and sharpening of these tools though it is suggested that all tools be looked at in this light at least once a year, and preferably twice a year, say spring and autumn.

☐ BENCH

It should be remembered that the bench is as important to

the craftsman as the saw and the plane. The working surface should be protected from saw cuts by a bench hook, and a chiselling board should be used when doing vertical paring or chopping a through mortise.

An occasional inspection for nails and panel pins driven into the bench top will save nasty snags to sharp cutting edges. Any nail that can be withdrawn must be taken out with pincers even at the expense of making a hole in the top of the bench. Use a screwdriver and mallet to cut the wood from around the nail. Pliers can sometimes reach where pincers fail. The most stubborn of nails should be punched well below the surface of the bench.

Despite all one's efforts to protect the top and keep it flat and true, the timber will move in time and gradual wear will take place particularly in the region of the vice. The movement of wood and tools on the surface of the bench will gradually wear a hollow. Placing wood on a hollow bench top for the purposes of planing is obviously not possible. The top must be retrued. For this task there is no better tool than the trying plane. Make sure the plane is sharp and finely set, as beech is hard to work. A little oil on the sole of the plane will ease the work. Plane first across the grain, then diagonally, and finish with the grain. A long steel rule or straight edge will help to check the trueness of the work. Remove the sharp edge around the top of the bench with a few strokes of the plane.

☐ BENCH HOOK

The bench hook will last only a few years. Its purpose, apart from helping to hold the wood when sawing, is to protect the surface of the bench from the teeth of the tenon saw. A new bench hook can be quickly made in the workshop from a hardwood such as beech. Rather than drill and dowel first, it is easier to glue the blocks in place and drill for the dowels after the glue has set. As mentioned in Chapter I it is not good practice to secure the blocks with screws as these can easily damage the teeth of the saw. Try to avoid dropping the bench hook as it will break just like other tools.

☐   BRACE AND BITS

The wooden handles of the brace require only occasional attention. Wiping them over with a rag previously dipped in linseed oil will help preserve the wood. Braces fitted with plastic handles require little maintenance to the plastic other than wiping clean with a damp cloth. The metal frames that are unplated can be polished with wire wool or fine emery cloth dipped in mineral oil. This treatment is not suitable for braces plated with chromium or nickel as it would remove the plating. Plated braces are cleaned and maintained by wiping the frame with an oil soaked rag. Remember to use mineral oil for metal work and linseed oil for wooden parts. The latter, being a vegetable oil, is a drying oil and not suitable for the oiling of metal parts.

The brace will usually benefit from a few drops of oil placed on the ball race under the head. A brace fitted with a plastic head can have the mouldings separated with a pen-knife, but it is advisable to read the manufacturer's instructions first. A spot of lubricating oil can be placed on the bearing inside the head and the plastic mouldings will snap together with firm pressure. Remember that woodworking tools are kept in a dusty atmosphere and this quickly dries the oil. Consequently it is advisable to oil all moving parts little and often.

Grease applied to the thread of the chuck and a little spread on the inside cone of the chuck will aid smooth operation of the brace. A grease recommended for the workshop is *Lubysil GPI* grease. This is a soft silicone grease and works well in enclosed gearboxes and bearings. Never use a high pressure oil on hand tools as this promotes very rapid wear of the tool. Always try to prevent over oiling or over greasing, which can at the least make things very messy.

Bits for the brace are sharpened with a needle file (fig 67) and occasionally an oilstone is employed to provide that extra keen edge. Various sectional shapes of needle file are obtainable, but chiefly square, triangular, flat, round and half-round files are suitable for our purposes. It is worth obtaining a set of needle files as they have other uses such as sharpening saws (see later in this chapter).

The sharpening of bits consists chiefly of following the

angles already established by the manufacturer. Never touch the outside of the bit with a file or the bit will bore an undersize hole and probably, worse, it will get stuck in the hole being drilled.

A centre bit is sharpened by pushing the point into a spare

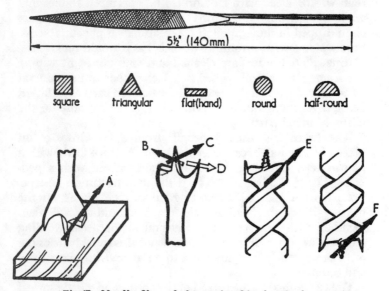

Fig 67   Needle file and sharpening bits for the brace: *(top)* sections through some of the needle files available; *(bottom)* try to follow the bevels already established on the bits and never sharpen on the outside of the bit

piece of wood. The bevel can then be filed until the cutting edge is sharp (fig 67a). The inside of the scriber may be touched with a file (fig 67d), and with the bit upturned the brad point can be sharpened (fig 67 b c). Remember to follow the angles existing on the bit and use the safe edge (non-milled surface) of the file where necessary to prevent damaging an adjoining surface. The sharpening of the twist bit is also detailed in figure 67.

☐   BRADAWL

The bradawl is easy to sharpen if one considers how it

works. The cutting edge should be sharp in order to sever the fibres of the grain, and the gently sloping faces are used to force the fibres outwards. A small metalworking vice is handy for holding small tools, such as the bradawl, while working on them with a file. Such a vice can be conveniently mounted on a wooden block and the block held in the woodworking vice.

□ CHISELS

It is not easy to say how often a chisel will need to be sharpened as this very much depends on the type of wood being cut. Certain timbers will require that the chisel be sharpened after every six cuts. Other timbers may necessitate sharpening the chisel only every half-hour of use. The beginner is not always sure when a chisel is blunt and may find the following guidance helpful There are four signs used by the craftsman:

1 Inspect the work for the quality of cut
2 Think about the ease with which the chisel performs the desired operation
3 Look to see if the cutting edge is polished with use as this will be seen as a reflection of light from the rounded edge
4 Check the quality of the cutting edge by drawing the tip of the thumbnail across it

An oilstone is used to sharpen the chisel. The oilstone, as its name implies, is oil on stone. The stone may be quarried, in which case it is likely to have come from *Washita* or *Arkansas*, USA, and will be called after its place of origin. Quarried stones are known as natural stones and are expensive, but cheaper artificial stones such as *Carborundum* and *India* make good alternatives. The artificial stones generally belong to one of two types, silicon carbide or aluminium oxide. Both types make excellent stones. Having been produced in an electric furnace these artificial stones have a great consistency in their quality.

Oilstones are generally 8in x 2in x 1in (200mm x 50mm x 25mm). This size is convenient for sharpening plane irons as well as chisels. As the stone is delicate is is usually stored and used in a shallow tray (fig 68 i). At either end of the stone a

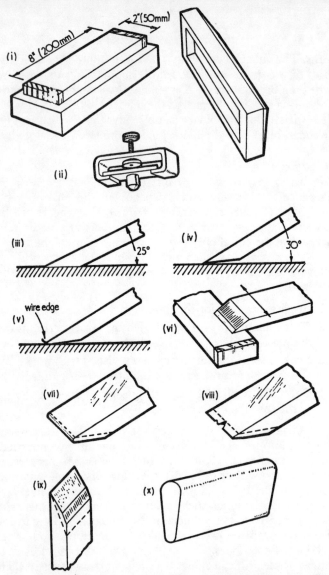

Fig 68 *Sharpening a chisel*: (*i*) oilstone in case with lid to keep dust off, (*ii*) honing guide to help maintain the correct sharpening angle of 30°, (*iii*) chisel stood on oilstone at 25°, (*iv*) chisel raised to 30°, (*v*) wire edge (burr) turned up by sharpening, (*vi*) place chisel flat on stone to remove wire edge, (*vii*) rounding of edge caused by careless sharpening, (*viii*) gashed edge, (*ix*) chisel with large sharpening bevel is slow to sharpen so requires grinding first, (*x*) oilstone slip used to sharpen gouge

piece of hardwood is fitted end grain uppermost and level with the surface of the stone. This provides a run-off for the tools. It ensures even wear of the stone, allowing the whole surface to be used when sharpening. Only a flat oilstone will sharpen correctly. A hollow stone can be flattened by rubbing on the surface of a sheet of glass using carborundum paste as an abrasive. This is a tedious task and should be avoided. A lid should be provided to keep the stone free from dust.

The surface of the stone is lubricated with neatsfoot oil or thin lubricating oil such as that used for bicycles. Neatsfoot oil is used for softening saddles and leather goods and is usually obtainable from stores specialising in this equipment. A drying oil such as linseed oil would gum up the stone. Such a stone has to be cleaned by soaking in a bath of paraffin. Therefore a non-drying oil must be used: (1) It cleans the stone by washing away the particles of metal. (2) It reduces friction. (3) It cools the edge of the blade. (4) It helps to polish the metal and produce a finer edge.

A new chisel has a grinding bevel of 25°. Chisels are ground to this angle in the factory but, to avoid danger during transit, are not sharpened. From the variety of chisels in the tool kit, it is recommended that the beginner choose a large firmer chisel to practice sharpening.

To sharpen a chisel on the oilstone, first stand the blade on the grinding bevel (fig 68 iii), then lift the blade through 5° to the sharpening angle of 30° (fig 68 iv). Various guides are available to help maintain this angle and can be a great help to the beginner (fig 68 ii). In time one learns to do without these devices, finding the 30° angle as a matter of habit. Push the blade from one end of the stone to the other keeping the angle constant. Avoid rocking the chisel as this will cause the sharpening bevel to be rounded and result in a dulled edge. Sharpen at the 30° angle until a burr, or wire edge, appears on the back of the blade (fig 68 v). This can be felt by sliding the finger down the blade and across the edge. The burr is removed by rubbing the back of the chisel FLAT on the oilstone (fig 68 vi). To remove the burr hold only the blade of the chisel. Bunch the fingers over the cutting edge to provide pressure and polish only the first inch of the blade on the stone, making every effort to keep the blade flat. After a short time the blade will acquire a mirror-like finish. Some crafts-men like to spend time honing the back of every new chisel to this mirror finish. An extra edge can be produced by strop-ping the cutting edge on oiled leather dressed with jewellers' rouge, but this practice is usually restricted to the tools of the woodcarver.

From time to time all chisels, and for that matter plane irons, have to be reground to restore them to the single bevel angle of 25° as supplied by the tool manufacturer. Firstly, careless sharpening may have produced a cutting edge that, while sharp, will not work satisfactorily because it is rounded and rollerskates from the work (fig 68 vii). This may be due to using a hollow stone, or lifting the blade as it is sharpened on the flat side. Secondly, careless use can result in a chipped blade (fig 68 viii). This will leave score marks on the surface of the work. The third reason for grinding results from normal and proper use. A blade that has been sharpened many times acquires a large sharpening bevel (fig 68 ix). This becomes a lengthy task to sharpen on the oilstone. In these three cases the cutters require grinding back to the areas indicated by broken lines. Grindstones are used because they are quick-cutting stones. However, they leave a rough edge on the blade which is unsuitable for cutting wood. The slower-cutting oil-stone is therefore used to achieve the final cutting edge.

Three types of grindstone are in general use. The high-speed dry grinding wheel to be found in most metal working establishments, and often offered as an accessory for the elec-tric drill, is unsuitable for our purpose. It is fast-running and quickly overheats the metal despite frequent quenching in water. All steel tools are specially heat treated. Reheating the steel will remove many of these qualities. A tool damaged in this way will fail to sharpen as it will not retain a cutting edge, and furthermore it is likely to break in use. Such damage can be caused unwittingly in a few seconds by using the high-speed wheel. Breakage can be recognised on the blade as a striated band of colour but when this appears it is too late. Though one can remove the colours from the surface of the metal the damage has been done.

The traditional type of grindstone made from natural grit sandstone is slow-running and powered by an electric motor.

The cutting edge is cooled and the surface of the stone cleaned by water dripped from a tank above the stone. This method of grinding requires a fair amount of skill but it gives a good edge to the tools. The stone should not be left standing in water as it will soften one portion and wear out of shape. These stones can be maintained true and square by occasionally applying the end of an iron pipe across the working surface. All sludge and water from the stone must be drained from the tank after use and tipped on waste ground.

The modern horizontal grindstone is successfully replacing the traditional sandstone. In appearance it is not unlike a large record player. The wheel is artificial and has an extremely long life. Oil is used as a coolant and lubricant, and for washing away the metal swarf. A filter inside the machine traps all the metal particles before the oil is returned in another cycle. An excellent toolrest holds the blade at the chosen angle to the stone and helps one achieve great accuracy.

One of the benefits of attending evening school is that grinding facilities will be available. When working alone one seldom has these facilities. Enquiries then have to be made at the tool shop. Remember, however, that though tools require frequent sharpening they should be infrequently ground as grinding rapidly shortens the life of a tool.

Figure 68 (x) shows an oilstone slip. This is used for sharpening gouges. It is used with oil on the inside of the scribing gouge to sharpen it, the burr being removed on a flat oilstone. The firmer gouge is sharpened in a figure of eight movement on the flat oilstone and the burr removed from the inside of the gouge with the oilstone slip.

☐ CRAMPS

Cramps are often used but seldom maintained. Left in a neglected state the cramps are a curse. Moisture left when glueing up causes the bar to rust, glue itself sticks to the bar and the shoes will not slide easily. Cramps not fitted with the Deacon Patent tail slide (a Woden product) can be missing the peg where the chain has snapped.

The bar of the cramp should be regularly cleaned to remove all traces of rust and glue. Polish the bar if necessary with emery cloth and oil. This will help the tail shoe to slide easily with gentle hand pressure. Oil the screw thread. Check the condition of the chain that secures the peg. Replace the chain if necessary. Fit a nut and bolt to the end of the bar to prevent the loose shoe from falling onto the floor and becoming lost in the shavings. New cramps are supplied with a bolt at the end of the bar; if these are removed to extend the cramp, remember to replace them.

☐ GAUGES

The three gauges—mortise, marking and cutting—should have the wooden parts wiped with a rag dipped in linseed oil. The metal screw of the mortise gauge will benefit from a few drops of light machine oil. The spurs of the mortise and marking gauges become blunt after a period of use and require sharpening with a file. The cutter of the cutting gauge can be sharpened on a fine oilstone. Some people like a rounded shape whereas others prefer a pointed one. If the shape of the cutter as supplied by the manufacturer suits you, then follow this as closely as possible when sharpening.

☐ HAMMER

Everyone knows of the hammer that bends nails. This usually happens when the hammer has a dirty face. Carelessness can result in paint or varnish adhering or glue still covering the face of the hammer after the assembly of a job. Polish the metal parts of the hammer with emery cloth and oil. The pein of the hammer should be made to shine as well as the poll (face end). The handle of the hammer can be rubbed with a linseed-oiled rag and inspected carefully for splits. Test the head for any play and if necessary tap the metal wedge further into the eye.

☐ MALLET

The mallet requires very little maintenance. The wood will benefit from a wipe with a linseed oil rag.

☐ MARKING KNIFE

The marking knife requires fairly frequent sharpening. It must be able to cut the fibres of the wood cleanly. Some people prefer the knife sharpened on one side like a chisel, but the most popular method is to sharpen the knife with bevels on either side. Penknives are usually sharpened in this fashion and indeed penknives can make excellent marking knives. Push the blade of the knife forward on the oilstone at a low angle. Turn the knife over and pull it back. This way the problems that can be caused by a burr are eliminated. Polish the wooden handle with a linseed oil rag and check the rivets for tightness.

☐ PLANES

Planes, like chisels, require frequent sharpening. The pitch angle of most planes is 45°. If the blade was sharpened at 45° friction would be great because the bevel would rub the surface of the wood (fig 69a). If the blade was sharpened at a low angle (fig 69b) either the edge would snap off or the blade would be bent against the frog until it gained sufficient energy to spring forward. This springing movement, heard as chattering, would result in a poor finish. Practice has shown that a 5° clearance angle is sufficient for a plane (fig 69c). The blade is given plenty of support from the frog and friction is reduced to a minimum. However, sharpening is still a lengthy procedure as a lot of metal has to be removed on the oilstone to gain a new edge. Most of the metal is therefore removed first on the grindstone, and the final edge is given to the cutter on the oilstone. The grinding angle is about 25° and the sharpening angle about 30°. This gives a clearance angle of about 5°, but as many people sharpen at an angle a little greater than the 30° angle normally recommended, then the clearance angle usually lies somewhere between 5° and 15°. In the case of the bench plane never sharpen the iron at an angle greater than the pitch angle of the plane.

The method of sharpening planes and chisels can be considered identical except for one important factor: the profile shape of the plane blade has to vary with the function of the plane. The blades of the rebate and plough planes are sharpened straight and square (fig 69d). It is not easy for the beginner to achieve this shape. It requires care and practice. The cutters of the plough plane are usually ground by the manufacturers to an angle of 35° and the manufacturers recommend that these cutters are sharpened on their grinding bevel.

The block, smoothing and trying planes are sharpened similar to the rebate plane but the corners of the cutting edges are rounded off on the oilstone to prevent the cutter digging in and scoring the work (fig 69e). The jack plane has a cutting

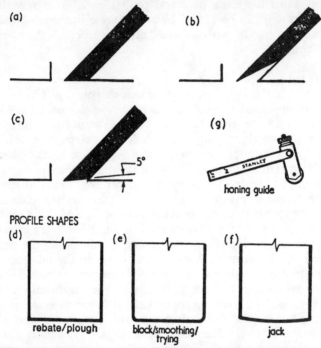

Fig 69 Sharpening plane irons: (*a*) bevel rubs, (*b*) sharpening angle too acute causing chattering, (*c*) 5° clearance angle is sufficient, (*d*) (*e*) (*f*) profile shape of cutters and (*g*) honing guide

edge that is rounded in profile so it may be used to remove coarse shavings (fig 69f). When planing wood from the rough state this is most useful, but if most of the wood arrives machine planed it is better to sharpen the plane as at figure 69 (e) and use it like a small trying plane.

The sharpening of plane irons is never an easy task for the beginner but the job can be simplified by using a honing guide (fig 69g). This device locks onto the blade and helps achieve a constant sharpening angle.

Much of the advice already given applies equally well to the special planes. Take care to assemble the block and shoulder planes with the blade bevel upwards. Sharpening the golf club shape cutters of the router is not easy. They should be sharpened on the bevelled side only, merely wiping off the wire edge on the flat side. Place the oilstone on the edge of the bench so that the stem of the cutter can hang down. Occasional regrinding will be necessary and this can be done on the side of the grinding wheel.

☐ SAWS

If treated properly a good quality saw will last a lifetime. It requires sharpening at least once a year, but it is probably the one tool that most amateurs neglect to sharpen, probably because they fail to understand how the saw works. Much has been written concerning this point in Chapter 2, but a few additional points may be helpful here.

The bluntness of the teeth may not be readily apparent, but each time the saw is used the teeth become a little more worn, losing their keen edge (fig 70a). This will be recognised as a dull glint of light on the points of the teeth, the light being reflected by the dulled edges. Any truly sharp edge, be it a chisel, plane blade or saw tooth, cannot be seen. A saw with dulled teeth will require needless effort and eventually the blade will jamb in the cut as the teeth lose their set.

Misuse of a saw will result in broken teeth, or if the saw has been badly sharpened in the past then the teeth may be uneven (fig 70b). A saw consists of a gang of teeth and each tooth must do its fair share of the work. The first stage in sharpening the teeth of a saw must therefore be to level them out with a long flat file. Even a saw in good condition should have the teeth 'topped' in this way before sharpening. The blade can be held in a special saw vice which grips the saw near the roots of the teeth (fig 70k). It is usually advantageous to remove the saw handle from the blade before the latter is clamped in the vice. Top the teeth of the saw by running the file lengthwise down them. Discontinue filing when the smallest of the teeth have been touched (fig 70c).

If the teeth have been badly mishapen by previous efforts at sharpening, then they will need reshaping with a triangular

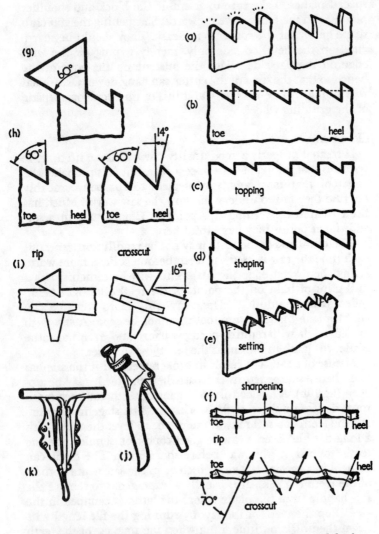

Fig 70 Sharpening saws: (*a*) dulled teeth, (*b*) irregular and broken teeth, (*c*) topping with a flat file, (*d*) shaping with a triangular file, (*e*) spring setting, (*f*) sharpening rip and crosscut, (*g*) choice of file size, (*h*) shape of rip and crosscut teeth, (*i*) sloping the saw when sharpening crosscut saw, (*j*) plier type saw set and (*k*) saw sharpening vice

file. Choose a file sufficiently large that, having been used once and turned to present a new face to the work, part of the old blunt surface is not in contact with a tooth (fig 70g). The file manufacturers recommend that a worn file be used to sharpen the teeth of a new saw. Treat the file with respect as a slip may not only damage the saw, but it may also damage the teeth of the file. Keep the file clean with a wire brush. A new file can be rubbed with chalk to prevent metal clogging (pinning) the teeth. Never stack the files against each other, and store them in a dry place to prevent rust.

It must be remembered that the teeth of the rip saw have to be shaped differently from the teeth of the crosscut saw. Figure 70 (h) shows that the gullet angle of all hand saw teeth is 60°. This is the reason for using a triangular file. However, the leading edge of the tooth of a rip saw is vertical, whereas the leading edge of the tooth of a crosscut saw leans back through an angle of 14°. The correct shape tooth for the rip saw is achieved relatively easily, but the crosscut saw is most difficult. It is useful therefore to be able to slope the saw and saw vice through 16° when sharpening the crosscut saw. This puts the back of the file in the horizontal plane (fig 70i). File the teeth straight across at this stage until they are all even and the small flat on the top of each tooth has just been removed.

The third stage of the work is setting the teeth. Hand saws are spring set. That is to say the teeth are bent outwards alternately (fig 70e). The best setting is generally considered to be done with a hammer, and indeed some modern saw factories set their best quality saws in this fashion. The saw is placed on a chamfered metal block and every other tooth tapped over. The saw blade is then turned over so that the other teeth may be bent to a similar extent. In this process only the top half of the tooth is bent; otherwise cracking is liable to occur at the base of each tooth. The alternative method of setting a saw is by using the plier type saw set (fig 70j). This is a self-contained tool that is adjustable to suit handsaws from 4 to 12 points. It is built like a pair of pliers. When the handles are squeezed together, the tool first grips the saw and then sets the top half of each tooth to the required angle.

The fourth stage of the work is the sharpening of the saw. This is performed with the file that was used for sharpening the teeth. The file is always held in the horizontal plane. With the rip saw it is taken straight across; with the crosscut saw the file is held at an angle of 70° to the blade (fig 70f).

Often all that is required is a light topping, followed by sharpening. The tenon saw can be sharpened as a crosscut saw, but the dovetail saw with tiny teeth is more easily sharpened straight across. Occasionally the backed saws will require re-tensioning. This can be done with gentle blows of the hammer as explained in Chapter 2.

□ CABINET SCRAPER AND PLANE

The cutting action of the cabinet scraper depends on the quality of the burr put on the edge of the blade. The edge must be trued with a long second cut file (fig 71). Hold the blade in the vice and, keeping the file lengthwise on, file a few strokes making the edge flat and square. This edge may be further trued on an oilstone. Rub both the edge and sides of the blade in turn to produce an accurate 90° corner. This corner has to be bent outwards to form the burr. Replace the blade in the vice and, using either a special tool of hardened steel called a burnisher or the back of a gouge, pass this firmly down the edge at 90° to the surface of the blade. Tilt the burnisher through 10° and make another pass pressing firmly to polish the edge. One more pass at 15° to the horizontal will cause sufficient burr to be pushed out for the scraper to cut cleanly.

Instructions for sharpening the scraper plane are usually supplied with the tool. The cutter is ground at 45° but it must

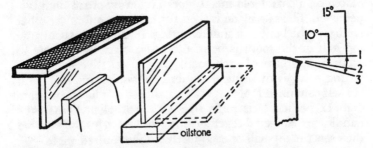

Fig 71 Sharpening the cabinet scraper: file the edge flat then oilstone the surfaces and burnish the edge over to create a burr

be sharpened before it can be used by polishing the ground surface with a fine or medium oilstone. This should throw up a burr on the flat side but this burr must be removed by rubbing the blade flat on the oilstone. A much stronger burr can be created by using a burnisher. Burnish first the flat side, holding the burnisher flat to the surface of the blade. This will consolidate the metal. Then place the blade in the vice and start burnishing on the 45° bevel. Work steadily and press quite hard, raising the burnisher through 30° until it is 15° below the horizontal (fig 72).

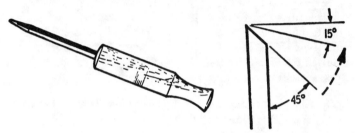

Fig 72   Sharpening the scraper plane: *(left)* hardened steel burnisher; *(right)* burnishing the blade

☐   SCREWDRIVER

Several screwdrivers should be bought and ground or filed to fit screws of differing sizes. The blade should be the same width as the bottom of the slot in the screw head (fig 73). This will prevent the screwdriver from scoring the work. The blade should be just sufficiently thin to fit to the bottom of the slot. When filing or grinding a screwdriver do so across the blade; it will hold the screw more securely. Always keep the thickness of the blade even at the tip. Do not file to an extreme taper shape or it will cause the screwdriver to jump from the slot when pressure is applied.

☐   SPOKESHAVE

The blade of the spokeshave is sharpened like the cutter of a smoothing plane. The problem is that of size. A block of wood with a saw cut at one end (fig 74) can act as a useful holder, helping one maintain a firm grip when sharpening the blade on the oilstone. The blade of the wooden spokeshave

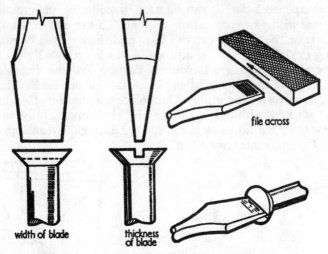

Fig 73   Filing a screwdriver to size. By filing carefully across the blade, the screwdriver can be made to grip the screw firmly

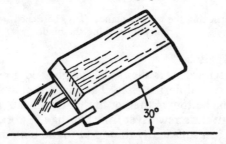

Fig 74   Shapening the blade of a spokeshave. This is sharpened as a plane iron or chisel. A wooden holder helps one to grip the blade

is another problem. The usual method is to hold the blade steady in the vice and move the oilstone over the cutting edge.

☐   TWIST DRILLS

Twist drills for use in the hand or electric drill are sharpened on the high-speed grinding wheel. This difficult technique can only be mastered with practice. Figure 75 should help to explain it. Choose a fairly large drill as the smaller sizes make it difficult to see what is happening.

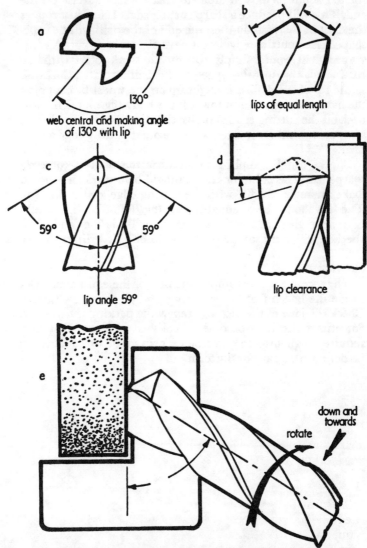

a

130°

web central and making angle
of 130° with lip

b

lips of equal length

c

59°   59°

lip angle 59°

d

lip clearance

e

rotate

down and
towards

Fig 75 Sharpening a twist drill. This is performed on the
high speed grinding wheel

The drill is applied to the side of the wheel and has to be rotated about its axis in order to create a new surface on the end. This will produce a sharp cutting edge. If one just rotates the drill in this fashion then the end of the drill will be cone-shaped. Any cutting edge must have clearance to cut. A cone-shaped drill would simply rub on the work. Start with the cutting edge against the wheel; as the drill is rotated clockwise so the tip of the drill is brought up on the wheel by dropping the hands downward and towards the body (fig 75e). This will back off the cutting edge and give the clearance required. The same movement is repeated with the other cutting edge on the drill.

Checks can be applied to see that the drill is correctly sharpened. The point, or chisel, should be central and should make an angle of 130° with the cutting edge, or lip (fig 75a). The lips should be of equal length (fig 75b). The lips should be at an angle of 59° to the axis of the drill (fig 75c), and when checked with a try square there should be a little lip clearance

□ VICE

The vice is the most important part of the equipment. Get inside the bench from time to time and oil the screw thread. Check the jaws of the vice and renew the packing if necessary. Sometimes the jaws become so polished with use that they require roughening to give a better grip to the work. This can be done with a rasp or Surform.

Chapter 5

Timber

GROWTH OF A TREE

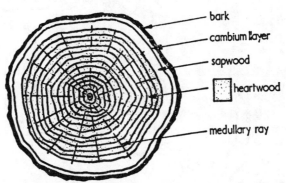

bark
cambium layer
sapwood
heartwood
medullary ray

Fig 76 Cross-section through a tree to show names of principal parts

A cross-section of a tree (fig 76) reveals many features result-ing from its growth. The new wood cells form a band just under the bark which is always present but not clearly dis-tinguishable in every species. The band, usually paler in colour than the rest of the tree, is called the sapwood.

The sapwood of a tree is of little use, being soft and prone to attack by fungi and beetles. The useful part of the tree, the heartwood, is composed of older cells that are no longer grow-ing.

Probably the most noticeable features on the end of a log are the concentric circles called annual rings. Each ring gener-ally indicates one year's growth, so by counting the rings from the bark to the centre of the tree one can calculate the tree's age. The annual rings are formed by the difference between the spring growth and the summer growth. Spring growth, being the most rapid, is the lighter, greater part of each ring. It is usually softer and more porous than the thinner and darker band of summer growth.

At right angles to the annual rings are the medullary rays.

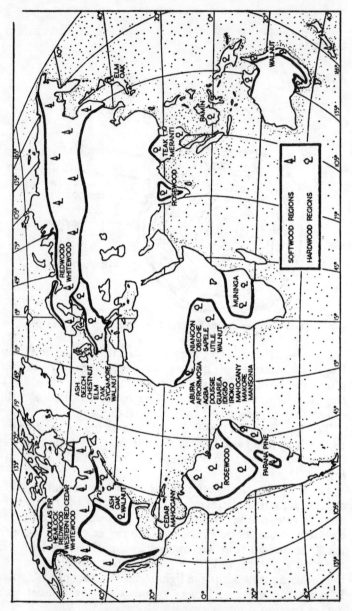

Fig 77 A general guide showing the chief sources of hardwoods and softwoods

These are more discernible in some woods than others. In oak, for instance, they are particularly attractive.

HARDWOOD AND SOFTWOOD

Commercially, timber can be divided into two groups, hardwood and softwood. This description is, however, misleading. For instance a hardwood like balsa can be softer than some softwoods, while a softwood such as yew can be quite hard.

Softwood is the generic term for timber produced from coniferous trees. With certain unimportant exceptions these are the evergreens and are easily distinguishable by scale or needle type leaves. There are two types of softwood. The first, commonly known as European redwood, but also called Scots pine, or red or yellow deal, is the most important structural and general purpose timber in Europe. Most of the timber in our houses, the rafters, flooring, and second fittings, is European redwood. The second type of softwood is called European whitewood, or Norway or European spruce. It is familiar to everyone as the Christmas tree. Besides having the same uses as redwood, whitewood is also the principal raw material for the manufacture of wood pulp for newsprint.

Hardwood is the generic term for deciduous trees. These timbers are used for fine cabinet making. Such timbers are grown in warmer climates than the softwood trees. The variety of hardwood timbers compared with softwoods is enormous, but despite the wide range the trade in softwoods is nine times larger than the trade in hardwoods. Softwood is both strong and cheap and has extensive uses from window frames in the building industry to packing cases for exports.

CONVERSION

The conversion of timber means cutting the log into useful thicknesses of board to obtain the greatest quantity of good quality timber possible.

Plain or through and through sawing is the quickest and least expensive method of conversion as there is little wastage

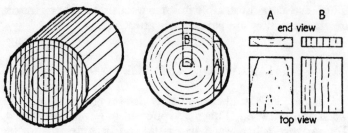

Fig 78 Slash sawing, also known as plain or through and
through conversion

(fig 78). This is therefore the most common method of converting a log into planks. Many of the boards cut this way are
tangentially sawn. That is to say they are cut tangential to the
annual rings. Some of the middle boards however are cut at
right angles to the annual rings, and these are said to be
radially or quarter sawn (fig 78).

Some woods possess particularly attractive features and are
sawn in a deliberate fashion to reveal their most decorative
surface, sometimes called the silver grain or figure of the wood.
It is revealed by cutting planks along the line of the medullary rays (quarter sawing).

The method of quarter sawing shown in figure 79 (left) is
expensive and leads to a great amount of wastage. It is therefore more usual for a log to be quarter sawn as shown in figure
79 (right). Although such timber is not truly quarter sawn
this method will produce many decorative boards. As well as
producing a good figure, quarter sawn timber is very stable.

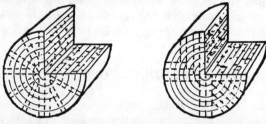

Fig 79 Quarter sawn oak: *(left)* is the only method of conversion that
will produce solely quarter sawn boards; *(right)* shows economical
methods of quarter sawing. This shows two less wasteful methods of
obtaining boards that are all nearly quarter sawn

This factor can at times be more important than the figure on the surface of the timber.

To reveal the full flame figure in a softwood such as Douglas fir (Columbian pine) the log must be tangentially sawn. However, boards cut in this manner have the disadvantage of cupping. They do not keep their shape as well as quarter sawn boards.

Figs 80 & 81 Method of tangentially sawing a log, and disadvantage of tangential sawing. This produces a flame figure that is most attractive in Douglas Fir. Unfortunately tangentially sawn boards are liable to cup

SEASONING

The timber is seasoned (dried) at a controlled rate to remove the sap. Seasoned timber has many advantages, the chief one being that it is less likely to shrink or warp. It is also easier to work on, and will polish, paint, or varnish better. Because such timber is also lighter in weight it is easier to handle. It is also less likely to be attacked by fungi.

☐ AIR OR NATURAL SEASONING

In this traditional method of seasoning the planks of wood are stacked neatly, leaving a space between each plank with a sticker to allow the air to circulate and carry away the excess moisture. The weight of the stack also keeps the planks flat. When one has to store timber for a period of time this is the way it should be done. The stickers must be placed accurately in line one above the other to prevent distortion of the lower boards. The planks at the bottom are built up off the ground away from frost and dew.

A good roof will shed the rain and prevent the heat of the sun drying the timber too rapidly. Fast drying of the timber can cause surface cracks to appear. It is usual for boards in the seasoning process to be end coated to prevent rapid drying from the ends. The coating can be thick paint or paraffin wax applied hot.

The type of seasoning shed described will ensure that the timber is open to the wind but not the sun or rain. Under such conditions an inch (25mm) thick plank takes one year to season. Every additional inch (25mm) increase in thickness of board requires another year of seasoning.

☐   KILN OR ARTIFICIAL SEASONING

A quicker method of seasoning is kiln or artificial seasoning. This is an industrial process and requires a kiln in which warm air and steam can be circulated by means of fans. The rate of drying and the final moisture content of the timber in the kiln is controlled by adjusting the temperature and humidity of the circulating air.

Depending upon the timber, kiln seasoning can take from three days to three weeks. It is a skilled job the success of which is reflected in the way the timber can be utilised after seasoning. Bad drying can result in loose knots, twisted timber, and fuzzy grain that is awkward to plane.

MOISTURE CONTENT

Wood will absorb or give up moisture until the moisture content of the wood is in equilibrium with the surrounding air. It is possible by kiln seasoning to extract all the moisture from the wood. This, however, is seldom required as bone dry timber will only take on moisture to suit the conditions in the workshop, and will later change that moisture content to suit the conditions existing in its final surroundings. This happens despite the thicknesses of polish, paint or hard varnish. Everyone knows that on a wet day wooden windows and doors can stick, whereas on a hot summer day they may rattle in their frames. The expansion and contraction of timber is due to the taking on or giving up of moisture.

It is important to the timber merchant, particularly when kiln seasoning, that the moisture content of the timber in stock is accurately assessed from a fair sample. This is done by excluding the wood from the first 9in (230mm) of a plank. The sample piece is first weighed, then dried in an oven until bone dry. As it cannot be seen at a glance when the sample is bone dry, it is usual to weigh when it is thought to be dry, then place back in the oven for a further twenty minutes before reweighing. If the second reading is the same as the first then it is safe to assume that the figure represents the oven dry weight. The moisture content of the sample can then be calculated as follows:

$$\frac{\text{weight of wet timber} - \text{weight of oven dry timber}}{\text{weight of oven dry timber}} \times 100 = \text{moisture content}$$

ie,
$$\frac{\text{wt of moisture}}{\text{wt of oven dry timber}} \times 100 = \text{moisture content}$$

It is possible with very wet stock to have moisture content readings of well over 100% as there can be a greater weight of moisture in the sample than the timber. Air seasoned timber will generally reach a level of about 20%. Further drying necessitates the use of a kiln. It is usual for the craftsman to bring the wood indoors for a short period before it is used; this can reduce the moisture content to about 14% which is suitable for most applications. Placing the stock in a situation with a high degree of central heating can however reduce the moisture content even further to about 10%.

TIMBER DEFECTS

A defect in timber is any flaw that can affect the strength or the appearance of the finished article. Figure 82 shows the major faults found in unselected stock. The most common defects are known as shakes (splits); the name of the shake often refers to the pattern these splits have formed.

A heartshake is caused by decay at the centre of the tree

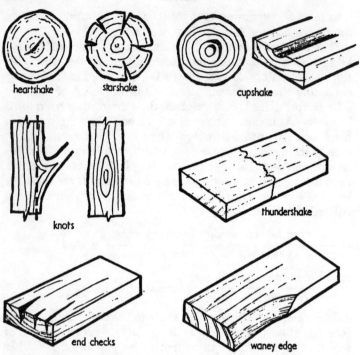

Fig 82 Timber defects. Any of these can spoil the work. Look out for
them when selecting timber

spreading along the lines of the medullary rays. It can largely
be prevented if the tree is not allowed to lie too long in log
form.

A star shake is caused by the drying and shrinkage of the
log more rapidly on the outside than at the heart. The splits
occur along the line of the medullary rays.

Cup shakes occur between the annual rings in the spring
wood, due to the inner part of the wood shrinking from the
outer layer. This often happens with pine and fir trees but is
usually small and not a serious defect.

Knots are the cross sections of branches. Live knots are firm
in place whereas dead knots are loose or have fallen out.
Knots weaken the timber but can be placed to look attractive.

A thunder shake is a crack across the grain which is probably caused by bad felling. African mahoganies are prone to this defect.

Checks are small splits, usually not more than 2-4in (50-100mm) long, which occur at the ends of long lengths of wood which have dried too rapidly during seasoning. This can largely be prevented by end coating as noted earlier.

Wane is the natural edge of the tree that remains on the plank after conversion. It may have the bark left on. It is best to work well inside the waney edge of a board in order to avoid the sapwood, the latter, as has been mentioned, being prone to attack by insects.

SHRINKAGE

As the timber dries out the loss of water will result in shrinkage and warping. Figure 83 shows the end view of a log with various boards indicated. Tangential shrinkage is nearly twice that of radial shrinkage. The tangentially sawn board will also tend to cup, as though the annual rings try to straighten when they shrink. The board cups away from the heart side. To overcome this stack the timber carefully during the seasoning process. The weight of the stack will hold such boards flat between the stickers. When glueing several boards together, it is usual to arrange the pattern of the end grain as shown in figure 83 to keep warping to a minimum. Occasionally a wide board will warp but this can be partially corrected by damping the cupped (hollow) side of the board to swell the pores. The board is then left over-night with weights on top to hold it flat.

The quarter sawn plank shown in figure 83 is very stable. The round stock, however, will shrink to an oval section and square stock cut in the fashion indicated tends to a diamond shape. Because of diamonding the stocks of the best wooden jack planes are selected so that the annual rings cross them from side to side. Such wood will not distort from the square section.

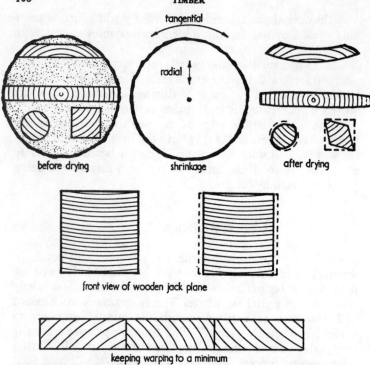

Fig 83 Shrinkage and change of shape during seasoning. Select timber carefully as it can change shape even after drying. Quarter sawn boards are always the best, but are not freely available. Stack wide boards between stickers prior to use and this will keep them flat. Note the care taken in the selection of wood for the stock of a wooden plane. When edge jointing boards, avoid placing the grain the same way in each piece

STORAGE OF TIMBER

The quality of timber can be easily reduced by bad storage. It can decay, warp, and split if handled incorrectly. Timber bought as seasoned stock is unlikely to be sufficiently dry to withstand the rigours of a centrally heated house or workshop. Such stock should be stored in a cool dry place. If the material feels dry then it may be worked on immediately. Otherwise it should be stored for a period of time.

The only acceptable alternative to stacking timber is to stand the boards upright. This will prevent bowing of the planks along their length but cannot prevent cupping. On no account should one leave the timber in an untidy heap, or leave a plank leaning against a wall as the wood will take on a permanent sag.

SOME TIMBERS AVAILABLE

The following is a list of some of the woods suitable for use by the home craftsman. When selecting boards from the timber yard do not be put off by the grimy surface of some of the stock. This surface dirt is in no way a defect but rather an indication that the stock is well seasoned. The grimy exterior will soon be removed by one or two shavings of the plane.

☐ HARDWOODS

Abura (West Africa) A pale, reddish to light-brown wood with an even texture. Very stable when seasoned. Resistant to acids. Works well and cleanly by hand and machine. It takes a good finish but it lacks character in its appearance.

Afrormosia (West Africa) A brownish-yellow timber with darker streaks often thought of as a substitute for teak. It is, however, a fine wood in its own right, and a good show-wood. It is extremely durable and has good resistance to decay. It is the worst timber for the problem of colour change, no finish being available to prevent this.

Agba (West Africa) Light yellow in colour, straight grained with a fairly close, even texture. It has good durability and is very resistant to decay. It works well and is largely used as an alternative to oak.

Ash (Europe and America) Pale yellow in colour and usually straight grained. This is a tough and flexible timber and is used chiefly for sports goods and tool handles. It has good bending properties and is invaluable for bent wood furniture.

Beech (Europe) Pinkish-red to yellow-brown in colour and usually straight grained with a fine texture. It is exceptionally strong, and machines and works well. It is a good wood for chairs, tool handles, planes, benches, and is widely used in the furniture industry. It holds tacks well, and is therefore used for the frames of upholstered furniture.

Cedar (British Honduras) Pinkish-brown in colour, it resembles true mahogany, but is lighter in weight. It is easily recognised by its characteristic scent which is so familiar because of its use in cigar boxes. It is fully resistant to decay and therefore used in boatbuilding, but is also used for the linings of wardrobes and chests, and for the bottoms of drawers on account of its moth-resistant qualities and pleasing aroma.

Chestnut, Sweet (Europe) Yellow-brown in colour and sometimes used as a substitute for oak. It works and finishes well but is rather soft.

Doussie, Afzelia (West Africa) Strong, durable and light brown in colour. It is a high grade wood producing a good finish and has a wide variety of uses similar to Iroko and Teak. It has a low shrinkage factor.

Elm (Great Britain, Holland, Japan) A light brown wood with distinctive grain pattern. It is strong and durable and does not cleave easily. It is resistant to decay under water. It is used for furniture, wheelmaking, coffins, and boat building. Generally a rather handsome timber. Japanese Elm is milder and more straight grained than English Elm.

Guarea (West Africa) Pinkish brown in colour, with a fine texture and cedar-like scent. It is fairly mild and easy to work. It is probably closer in appearance and properties to Cuban and American (Honduras) mahogany than any other timber. Its lack of dimensional movement makes it popular for drawer sides. It has good finishing properties. Its chief disadvantage is that dust from this timber is very irritating.

Idigbo (West Africa) A large tree providing timber that is pale yellow to light brown in colour with little distinction between heartwood and sapwood. Resistant to decay. It is soft to medium hard and can be easily worked by hand or machine. Not a widely known timber.

Iroko (West Africa) This wood is yellow in colour when freshly cut, but on exposure to light quickly becomes a rich golden brown. It is well figured and extremely handsome. Its strength compares with that of home-grown oak and it is very resistant to fungus and insect attack. Owing to its resistance to wear and to acids and its durability under damp conditions, it is particularly suitable for bench tops and workshops.

Mahogany (West Africa) This timber is mid-red in colour and is probably the most widely used of the mahoganies at present. Many of the logs are 6ft (up to 2m) across and can produce very wide boards. It is coarser in texture than Honduras mahogany and sometimes has an interlocked grain which produces an attractive figure but is difficult to plane by hand. It has small dimensional movement and is often used for drawer sides.

Mahogany, Honduras (British Honduras) This is one of the finest woods, being stable and extremely strong. It works well with all types of tools, and glues and finishes well. It is durable and has many uses, but is rather expensive.

Makore (West Africa) This wood is similar to a close grained mahogany but with a much finer texture. Makore is also denser, harder and heavier than mahogany. It is often used for high-class work.

Mansonia (West Africa) The heartwood is a purple-brown. It is a fairly hard timber, usually with a straight grain, and has a smooth and fine texture. It is a durable timber and makes a substitute for walnut. It is used for much high-class work. Its chief disadvantage is that dust from this wood can be particularly irritating.

Meranti, Light Red (SE Asia) As its name suggests this wood is red in colour. It works well and is suitable for general interior work. Pinhole-borer attack can cause wastage if the timber is not carefully selected.

Muninga (East Africa) This timber has a warm brown colour and a pleasing grain pattern. It is mild, stable, and works well by hand and machine. It has good finishing properties and is an excellent show-wood. Its only disadvantage, compared to species such as teak and afrormosia, is that logs sometimes contain some white spotting which can look unsightly, but this can to a great extent be overcome in the finishing process.

Niangon (West Africa) This is a reddish wood similar to African mahogany in all respects except that it has a rather more open grain and, when quarter sawn, shows dark flecks on the rays. It is quite popular in the furniture trade.

Oak (European) A creamy yellow wood with a distinctive grain. If cut on the quarter the medullary rays are revealed as an attractive feature. This wood is immensely strong and durable; however it splits easily and the grain is open. This wood is at present out of fashion in modern domestic furniture but this should not deter the hand craftsman.

Oak, American (N America) American oaks are divided into two classes, white oak and red oak. White oak approximates to European oak, with a pinkish tinge. Red oak, as its name implies, is pinky-red in colour, harder and coarser, and not durable. The white oak can be used instead of European oak.

Oak, Japanese (Japan) This oak is different in character from oaks native to Europe and the Americas. It is mild and more easily worked, lighter in weight, and reliable. It is not suitable for exterior work but can be used for all classes of furniture. The appearance of the European species is, however, often preferred.

Oak, Slavonian (Yugoslavia) European oaks vary considerably according to conditions of growth. Slavonian oak, which grows in very suitable conditions, is of slow even growth, of uniform colour and straight grain. It is mild and easy to work and has a handsome figure when quarter sawn. It is used for church work and wherever the highest class work in oak is required.

Obeche (West Africa) This timber is creamy-white to pale yellow in colour and light in weight. It is fairly soft, but firm and fine in texture. Obeche is one of the largest of the forest trees of West Africa and from its cylindrical trunk, clean timber of exceptional lengths is obtainable. This timber is popular because of its reliability in quality and dimensional stability.

It is used mainly in the field of lower-priced domestic cabinet work and in kitchen furniture.

Ramin (Sarawak) This timber is of uniform pale straw colour, moderately hard and heavy. It is very clean and straight grained and for this reason used extensively for picture frames and small mouldings. Ramin is valued for its strength and similarity to beech as a general utility wood. It paints, varnishes and machines well. It is generally unsuitable for use in large sections because of its tendency to checking.

Rosewood, Rio (Brazil) A rich reddish-brown wood with contrasting dark grain markings. A very decorative wood suitable for high-glass interior work and makes most impressive furniture. Its chief disadvantage is that a purple dust from the wood will stain the hands and clothes.

Rosewood, Bombay (India) This wood is slightly plainer in appearance than the Brazilian timber. It is suitable for high-class cabinet work but requires careful polishing.

Sapele (West Africa) Of typical mahogany colour, Sapele is characterised by a marked and regular stripe, particularly prominent on quarter sawn surfaces. Harder and heavier than African mahogany it is, nevertheless, very similar in appearance. It is a tough, hard timber, resistant to decay. It works well by hand and machine tools, but can be difficult to hand plane due to its interlocking grain.

Sycamore (Europe) Milky white weathering to a golden yellow colour, this is an easy timber to work. Being tasteless it is often used when wood has to come in contact with food. It is used in furniture mainly as a contrast to other woods, in the form of decorative inlay or beading. It is sometimes used for the sides and bottoms of drawers.

Teak (Burma) This timber varies in grain and colour from a clear golden shade to a chocolate brown. It is one of the most valuable and expensive of all woods, being extremely durable, strong, stable, resistant to moisture, termites, fire, acids and non-corrosive. It has a wide range of uses including furniture, garden furniture, laboratory bench tops, and ships' decking. Afrormosia is a good substitute for teak since it is not so expensive. However, as teak presents less of a problem with colour-change, this can be a false economy. It is a popular timber for furniture, being a good show-wood.

Utile (West Africa) Utile is a mahogany coloured wood, very even in colour and texture. Although similar to Sapele, it is more stable and is one of the most popular hardwoods. It is very resistant to decay and works well. It has been found a very satisfactory timber for drawer sides.

Walnut, African (West Africa) This is not a true walnut, but a very handsome wood, golden brown in colour with occasional thin black streaks and a lustrous surface. It is sometimes referred to as Nigerian Golden Walnut and often used for high-class work.

Walnut, American Black (USA) This is a handsome wood of a rich dark brown colour, which works easily and takes a fine finish. It is of medium-heavy weight. It is a true walnut, related to the European species, and used in high-quality work.

Walnut (European) This wood has an unusually wide range of colour that may vary from a cold grey to a warm brown. The grain can vary from a straight pattern to a flowery contrast. It is the favourite of all woods, being excellent to work and taking a good finish. It is used only for high-quality work, but increasing difficulty is found in obtaining good quality solid timber, especially of English walnut. French and Italian walnut are fairly satisfactory substitutes.

Walnut, Australian (Queensland, Australia) This is neither a true walnut nor is it related to African walnut. The quarter sawn boards can show an attractive figure.

☐ SOFTWOODS
Douglas Fir, Columbian Pine (British Columbia, and some British) The heartwood is reddish to brownish in background colour, with a darker, very prominent growth ring figure, often quite attractive in appearance. The grain is usually straight but may be slightly wavy, while the texture is moderately coarse. The yellow background is soft whereas the darker growth rings are quite hard. This timber has excellent

strength qualities, is very knot-free, and is used extensively for ladder construction. It is highly water resistant.

Hemlock, Western (Canada and NW USA) This wood is pale yellowish-brown in colour, sometimes with a faint red tinge. It is straight-grained and has a moderately fine texture. This is a general utility wood often classed as a whitewood.

Parana Pine (South America) This timber is variable in colour from light to dark brown, and often marked with distinctive bright red streaks. The grain is normally straight and the texture moderately fine and even. It takes varnish and paint well, and is usually available in knot-free lengths.

Redwood, Scots Pine, Red Deal, Yellow Deal (Russia, Baltic countries, Scandinavia, Canada, and some British) The colour is light reddish-brown or yellowish-brown. It is moderately resinous but usually straight grained. It has fairly good strength properties and works, nails and finishes well. Redwood is more frequently used where painting over is not necessary, being usually left bare on the interior of built-in cupboards, or given a clear finish.

Whitewood, European Spruce ie Christmas Tree (Russia, Baltic countries, Scandinavia, Canada, and some British) This is very light yellowish-brown in colour, almost white. It has a mildly lustrous surface when planed and is very slightly resinous. The grain is straight and the texture moderately even. Its use is usually confined to cupboard framing.

Yew (Europe) The heartwood is reddish when freshly cut, but soon darkens to a deep orange-brown that often shows an attractive growth ring figure. It is finely and uniformly textured, and straight grained. For a softwood species it is very heavy. It was used in the early days for archers' bows. The leaves of this tree are poisonous to animals and so its growth is generally confined to churchyards, and it is not in plentiful supply. It is occasionally used for high-class furniture.

VENEER

A veneer is a thin slice of wood usually taken from a species showing attractive grain or figure. It can be an economical way of making an attractive item of furniture, as a veneer of expensive show-wood can be used to cover a groundwork of cheaper timber. Using veneers can also conserve rare and exotic woods, making a little go a long way. In some instances there may be insufficient timber available in a certain colour, grain pattern, or figure to be able to make an item of reasonable size from the solid wood. Modern adhesives help to form veneers into new and exciting shapes. Sometimes a fundamental part of the design is impossible to construct in the solid wood. Techniques of lamination and veneering on particle board have produced new fashions in furniture design. However, those master craftsmen as far back as Chippendale, Sheraton and Hepplewhite used mahogany veneers in their work, as did the Egyptians 3,000 years ago.

Veneers are cut from the bole of the tree, above the roots up to the first limb. Veneer can be made using a saw or a knife. Saw cutting is very wasteful and is now reserved for extremely hard woods, difficult woods such as curls, small diameter logs, and when a thick veneer is required.

Prior to knife cutting a veneer, the log has to be softened by steaming in a vat, from a few hours to several weeks according to the hardness of the wood and the thickness of the cut to be taken. Machinery is employed that moves either the knife or the log. Veneer is cut from the log to a determined thickness which can be as thin as a few thousandths of an inch and as thick as 5/16in (0.1mm-8mm).

There are two traditional methods of laying veneer, the hammer and caul methods. The hammer method involves the use of a veneering hammer. This tool is a handled wooden block, one edge of which is fitted with a strip of brass. The hammer is used to press on the veneer and push out surplus glue from underneath the veneer.

Prior to laying veneer the groundwork should be keyed to permit maximum adhesion. This is done with a toothing plane, a wooden plane with a serrated edge cutter set at a high pitch angle.

Brush a thin even coat of scotch glue (see chapter 6) on the groundwork and allow to tack. Lay the veneer in position and press down. Lightly sponge the veneer with hot water then work an electric iron over it with the control at silk. The iron should be hot but not hot enough to cause water to spit on the sole. The heat from the iron will melt the glue and draw it up into the pores of the veneer. An iron that is too hot will allow the glue to penetrate the surface of the veneer and this will cause discolouration. With the veneer hammer work squeegee fashion to exclude air from under the veneer and to force out surplus glue. The sequence of damping, ironing and working with the veneer hammer can be repeated many times until the job is finished.

Simple joins can be made with the grain of the veneer by laying the first veneer, overlapping the second by an inch (25mm), then cutting through both veneers using a sharp knife and straight edge. Remove the surplus from the top veneer then lift the veneer slightly to peel away the strip from underneath. Iron the veneer back home and place gummed tape across the join to prevent a gap forming by contraction of the veneer. Always trim the veneers to size after the glue has set.

The method of caul veneering is suggested for the veneered box (chapter 9). It is simpler since it requires less equipment. Again the veneer is cut oversize. The groundwork is prepared flat and true and a caul is made from $\frac{3}{4}$in (19mm) blockboard or similar. The caul should be just larger than the work in hand.

A synthetic resin glue should be used. Spread the glue evenly on the groundwork taking special care to glue the edges. Place the veneer in position and a clean sheet of paper (not newsprint) on top of the veneer in case glue should penetrate to the surface. The caul is then placed on top and pressure is applied with G cramps. On large work thick crossbearers are used to spread the pressure of the cramps.

Most of the timbers listed in the section dealing with hardwoods are available as veneers. Certain more important additions are as follows.

Olive Ash (UK) Attractive contrasting light and olive colour

Figured African Cherry (W Africa) An exceptionally highly figured block mottle veneer. The plain veneer is referred to as makore.

Eucalyptus (Australian) Rather an unusual colour, pink to beige, and can be beautifully mottled. It is available in long lengths.

Lacewood (UK) A pink, highly figured veneer with attractive lace rays.

Figured Indian Laurel (India) Dark rich colour and attractively figured. It can be used successfully in association with other lighter timbers.

Bird's Eye Maple (N America) A cream colour veneer which has unique figure, with masses of tiny eyes or knot formations.

West Indian Satinwood (W India and Ceylon) A golden colour, stripy, with beeswing mottled figure. Once very much used for cabinet work. When well figured it has a depth of light not seen in other woods. It takes and holds a polish well. The colour remains fast.

Tola (W Africa) A reddish, straight grained, striped veneer widely used by veneered chipboard manufacturers.

Figured Willow (UK) A creamy golden colour. This veneer is exceptionally attractive and usually well figured.

Zebrano (Africa) As the name implies, a contrasting light and dark stripy wood. It is straw colour with brown stripes, generally used in small decorative pieces.

MANUFACTURED BOARDS

☐ PLYWOOD

Plywood is made from three or more odd number of wood veneers glued face to face with a suitable adhesive and with the grain of each veneer running at right-angles to its neighbour. Plywood is many times stronger in bending strength than its equivalent thickness of solid wood, and is available in very large panels. By varying the species, thickness of veneer,

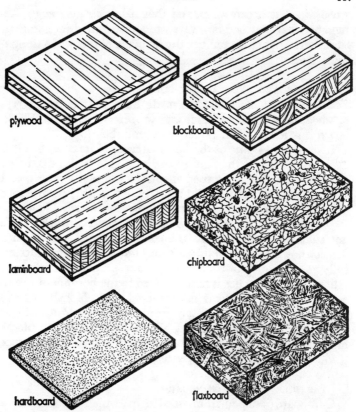

Fig 84 Manufactured boards. All these boards are available in very large sheets. Their rate of expansion and contraction in changing humidity is negligible, and apart from plywood, they will not warp

and type of glue it is possible to manufacture plywood for a great variety of purposes. One instance of this is the waterproof plywood used for building marine craft which will withstand exposure to weather, immersion in water, and is unaffected by micro organisms.

Plywood is commonly used when making furniture but it is generally restricted to the cheaper and more every day items such as the backing of framed kitchen cuboards and cabinets, and shelves and drawer-bottoms. The disadvantages of plywood are that it can warp, and that it has an ugly edge. Remember that plywood is always stronger in one direction than the other. Advantage can usually be made of this when designing an item.

☐ BLOCKBOARD AND LAMINBOARD

These board materials are made from long narrow strips of wood, edge-glued together and veneered both sides. Blockboard is made of wider pieces than laminboard.

Laminboard is one of the best materials of its type, but it is expensive. Most of the laminboard available is manufactured to high standards. It is used in places where a strong board material is required for solid construction, chiefly for the tops of tables where the design dictates long, unsupported lengths.

Blockboard is not a suitable base for veneered work as it is not sufficiently even across the surface. Its use results in a defect known as telegraphing. It may however be used successfully as a groundwork for lino, leather, or plastic laminates. Other than this its use is best confined to the bottoms of cabinets. The main problems encountered with blockboard are a result of an inferior standard of manufacture. Much of this material supplied has missing blocks, gaps where the blocks have not been pushed tightly together, and a poor surface through using badly peeled veneer.

☐ PARTICLE BOARD—CHIPBOARD

Chipboard is made from wood chips which are dried to a constant moisture content, and bonded together with synthetic resin under heat and pressure. It is available in different densities, the most dense being the best grade. Chipboard is obtainable with a plain or veneered surface. It is an excellent base for veneer but is rather heavy.

It is used chiefly as a material for solid construction and as such lends itself more readily to mass-production than to craftsmen-made items. It is a fairly stable material and good supplies of consistent quality are available. It is rather expensive and in many instances the home craftsman is better off buying solid timber. Although chipboard can be worked by hand it is difficult to groove and rebate as the wood is of a fairly stable nature. Dowel joints are the most practicable method of construction. Screws must not be overtightened or they will lose their holding power. A special screw with coarse thread is available for chipboard. When designing for this material remember that it is not a good structural material. A chipboard shelf, for instance, will require plenty of support as it can gradually sag under its own weight.

☐ PARTICLE BOARD—FLAXBOARD

Flaxboard is made from chemically treated flax shives, the residue of the flax plant after being divested of its linen fibres, mixed with synthetic resins and hot-pressed. The flax plant, which grows as a crop like oats or corn, is dried in the open after cutting and then transported to the factories for scutching. This is a beating process producing large numbers of small fine shives, which are hard in section, and from which all soft fibres are separated. The shives are graded so that the long ones may be further processed to make linen, whereas the shorter, less suitable fibres are used in the manufacture of cigarette paper. The remaining small shives are selected and the most suitable made into panels.

This is a board of increasing importance. It is lower in price than chipboard, and it has the advantage of lightness. It may be used, for instance, in the construction of wardrobe doors, which if too heavy can cause a light-weighted frame construction to overbalance.

☐ HARDBOARD

Hardboard is manufactured from pine logs, chipped, defibrated and felted by mechanical process into highly compressed rigid sheets. Its homogeneous construction makes it free from warping and other drawbacks common to laminated materials.

Hardboard has many uses, chiefly cladding or backing framed kitchen cabinets. It has an advantage over plywood where painting is required since it does not need sanding. Other uses include exhibition stands of peg board, toys, flush doors, picture frame and mirror backs. The thickness most commonly used is about $\frac{1}{8}$in (3mm) but $\frac{1}{4}$in (6mm) is also available.

Chapter 6

Materials

This chapter deals with the principal materials in their order of use. It is normal practice to clean up the inside and other inaccessible surfaces of the work with a smoothing plane, cabinet scraper, or glasspaper, then polish the inside surfaces before glueing the construction together. The outside can then be polished and the back can be screwed or nailed in place and all other fittings applied. Hence the order abrasives, finishes, glues, nails, screws and fittings.

ABRASIVES

Abrasives are part of the final finishing process. Once they have been used on the wood, cutting tools must not be reverted to as particles of abrasive embedded in the grain will quickly dull a sharp edged tool. To prepare a surface to a good finish clean it up first with a sharp, finely set smoothing plane. Make every effort to remove all tears with the plane, which will produce a better surface than that achieved by the heavy use of abrasive. If the wood is difficult cross-grain then use a scraper plane before succumbing to an abrasive. A cut surface will be sheer but an abraded surface will not possess the same sparkle because the fibres have been scrubbed back and forth. This is important when a transparent finish is to be applied.

☐ GLASSPAPER

The most common type of abrasive in use in the workshop is glasspaper. This is made by coating a stout paper with glue, and then, while the glue is still wet, sifting on finely powdered glass. This work is usually carried out in an electrostatic field so that the grains of glass are set on end. Various grades of fineness are obtainable, the first being called flour, then 0 (nought), 1, 1½, fine 2 (F2), middle 2 (M2), strong 2 (S2), and

$2\frac{1}{2}$. The smaller the number the finer the particles of glass used. For general use grades $1\frac{1}{2}$ and fine 2 are adequate.

The sheets are usually supplied 11in x 9in (280mm x 230mm) in size. Each sheet can be torn against a steel rule into 4 pieces. Glasspaper should be used wrapped around a cork block. This secures the paper and lengthens its life; it also increases the pressure that can be applied, and makes for a flatter surface. Always glasspaper with the grain when work is to be polished. For good results damp the wood to raise the grain then glasspaper flat.

☐ OTHER ABRASIVES

Other types of abrasives are Garnet, Aluminium oxide, and Silicon carbide. Any of these can be used for hand sanding but they are more commonly used when machine sanding. Garnet, which is a mineral, is crushed to form sharp individual grits. It is glued on to a paper backing in a similar fashion to glasspaper. Aluminium oxide (Al_2O_3) is a tough artificial abrasive. The grit is silver-grey in colour and is very hard. Silicon carbide (SiC), another artificial abrasive, is also very hard but brittle. All abrasive papers (except glasspaper) can be bought with the abrasive grains spread wide apart. This is called an open-coated paper and is recommended by the manufacturers for use on soft wood and when sanding gummy materials. For all other sanding, the close-coat type of paper is more satisfactory.

A paper recently introduced by the English Abrasives Corporation Ltd is called Lubrisil. This is a Silicon carbide paper which is stearate lubricated. This paper is non-clogging and will last at least twice as long as glasspaper. Type A lubrisil paper is preferred for hand sanding. Type C is for machine sanding. The grades recommended for hand sanding are 150 and 180. Store all abrasive papers away from any source of dampness or excessive heat and keep them in their original package until required.

A useful abrasive is fine wire wool grade 0000. This may be used for flattening down french polish or polyurethane varnish. If the surface is to be left semi-matt then wire wool will work into every hollow resulting in an even finish.

FINISHES

Finishes are applied to the wood to preserve the timber and to make the work look more attractive. If the pores of the wood are filled then the surface is easier to dust and keep clean.

☐ FRENCH POLISH

Polishing has always been a trade of its own, with special techniques and skills, but one of the interests of making one's own furniture is seeing the job through from beginning to end, and it is quite possible to produce a surface that is french polished to an adequate standard.

French polish is a traditional finish which still possesses considerable merit. It is easier to apply than the modern plastic type finishes, particularly when making individual items of furniture. It is neither heat resistant nor waterproof, but these two qualities are not required on the underframe of a coffee table or on the ends of a bed. A french polished table top has to be treated with care, but a plastic finished surface cannot be given unlimited rough treatment without showing signs of wear, and of the two finishes a french polished surface is much easier to repair. French polish must not be despised because we have modern alternatives; it has its own merits and disadvantages as have the modern finishes, and each must be taken into consideration before the craftsman makes a suitable choice.

Only two ingredients are used in the manufacture of french polish, shellac and industrial methylated spirit. Shellac is formed in the digestion process of the Laccifer Lacca insect which flourishes in certain provinces of India. It lives in colonies and feeds on tree sap. As the insect feeds a secretion is formed which eventually covers the whole swarm. This secretion hardens on contact with the air and it is collected for processing. The shellac is usually heated and then passed through a cloth screen which separates twigs and other impurities. Sometimes it is dissolved in industrial alcohol, which removes the trace of wax otherwise present in shellac. Transparent polish is made from bleached dewaxed lac, and is colourless as its name implies; alternatively white polish may be used, also made from bleached lac, but this is milky white in appearance. Button polish, another grade, has a deep yellowish tone. It is slightly cloudy and opaque, and is made from shellac which has not been dewaxed.

Transparent polish is recommended, being clear and harder than the other forms of polish. It can be obtained in liquid form, having been dissolved in industrial methylated spirit. Usually a little of this spirit will have to be used to thin the polish and make it a more watery consistency. Methylated spirit bought over the counter contains a blue dye. This can sully the colour of the polish but a little will do no harm.

After the surface of the work has been carefully prepared with the plane and perhaps a little glasspaper, brush on one thin coat of polish, working quickly, with a camel hair mop. Do not worry about bubbles in the polish as these soon disappear. Wait three minutes for the polish to dry, then lightly go over the work using flour grade glasspaper on the fingers. Do not use a cork block as the glasspaper must be worked into all the hollows. Brush on another *thin* coat, again working quickly. This will take a little longer to dry. Then gently flour paper the surface for the second time.

Some people complete the polishing at this stage with beeswax (see later in this chapter). If one requires more than a semi-matt finish then the work can be polished to a good shine as follows, though it is worth noting that the more shiny the surface the more easily all marks and blemishes can be seen.

Prepare a polishing pad from a small piece of non-fluffy cloth such as cotton or linen, containing a ball of cotton-wool about the size of a golf ball. Soak the cotton-wool in french polish, place this in the centre of the cloth and squeeze out as much as possible of the polish through the cloth. Now the polishing pad is ready charged and must be pulled over the surface of the work without scrubbing. Work very speedily in straight rows following the direction of the grain. The pad is working correctly if the surface dries almost instantly. Repeat this process several times, occasionally working the pad in tight circles across the work to spread the polish evenly. Gradually a really good shine will appear giving a very handsome finish. Should the pad stick during this process put a smear of linseed oil on the finger and apply this to the sole of

the pad. Remember that one is not oiling the work but just
lubricating the pad, so use only a trace of oil.

☐ WAX POLISH

Wax polish is probably the oldest method of applying a surface finish to an article. It is prepared from beeswax and
turpentine. Pure beeswax is yellow in colour, but a white
beeswax (bleached) can be obtained. The wax must be shredded and this can be easily done using a *Surform* tool. Cover
the wax with best quality pure turpentine (not white spirit)
and let the wax dissolve. This process can be speeded up by
placing the container with the wax in hot water. Do not heat
with a naked flame as turpentine is highly inflammable. The
wax should be used in the form of a thin paste that is about
the consistency of butter in the summer.

Beeswax should be applied with a soft cloth and rubbed
well into the pores of the wood. This will produce a dull lustre
suitable for the treatment of furniture and most indoor work.
Beeswax is fairly soft and the finish can finger-mark. The
polish can be hardened by the addition of carnauba wax (prepared from a Brazilian palm) in the proportion of about 1 part
carnauba wax to three parts beeswax. Lighter fuel petrol is
sometimes added to wax polish to speed up evaporation.

A proprietary brand of wax polish called *Briwax* can be
used with excellent results. *Ronuk,* a non-sticky wax, is also
useful for drawers and sliding parts.

☐ LINSEED OIL (AMER. FLAXSEED)

Linseed oil is prepared from the seed of the flax plant which
is crushed to extract the oil. This oil dries slowly by absorbing oxygen from the air and forms an elastic film. When
heated to about 200°C for several hours the linseed oil can
absorb oxygen more rapidly. It is then known as boiled oil.

Linseed oil is applied to the wood as a preservative. It en-
riches the colour of the wood and for this reason is frequently
used on oak and chestnut. Several applications are usually
made with a rag, allowing drying intervals of a day between
each coat.

Linseed oil can be mixed with an equal quantity of turpentine to form a kind of teak oil. Teak, being a greasy timber, takes a good oil finish.

☐ PAINT

A covering of paint protects the wood and gives a colourful appearance to the work. When carefully applied it can have a superior finish.

Glasspaper the work thoroughly to begin with. Work across the grain diagonally and finish with the grain. Brush on one coat of priming to seal the pores.

The next operation is to fill the pores with a thin paste called a filler; this will make the surface of the work level. The filler can be a plaster of paris type mixture such as *Alabastine* or *Polyfilla*. Work the filler across the panel with a painter's broad-knife. Allow 1 day for the filler to dry, glasspaper with a fine paper and cork block, then repeat the filling operation using the broad-knife with the grain. Allow another day for this to harden; then glasspaper the panel. The work should now be smooth and the grain completely filled. Inspect the work carefully and if the surface is not satisfactory repeat the filling operation a third time.

The work can now receive two applications of undercoat. The undercoat is the colour and bodying coat for the work. It is a flat finish (no gloss). Dust off the work using a rag slightly moistened with linseed oil. This tacky rag will pick up the dust but not apply linseed oil to the work. Using a worn but cared for brush, apply an even coat and feather off by letting the brush lightly touch the work. Travel across the panel, then diagonally, and finish lengthwise. Allow at least one day for this to dry thoroughly; then glasspaper, dust, and apply the second undercoat.

The top coat is the enamel or gloss coat and should be applied with the same care as the undercoat. If possible keep the work flat to prevent runs.

Maintain all brushes with thoroughness and care. Wash them out with white spirit and clean them with warm soapy water. Wrap brushes in paper to store them. Keep the paint in good condition by pouring sufficient quantity for the work in hand into a paint kettle and use it from there. Keep the tin sealed to avoid evaporation of the solvents.

□ POLYURETHANE VARNISH

Polyurethane varnish is a hard plastic coating. It provides a transparent finish that can both enhance and protect the wood. This varnish is available in two different forms. Firstly the twin pack type which is generally recognised to be a tougher finish, but requires mixing immediately before use. Secondly the one pack type which is more straight forward to apply as it consists only of opening the tin and brushing the varnish straight onto the work. With this second type no mixing or stirring is required. Once the tin is re-sealed the contents will stay fresh for a long period.

Polyurethane varnish can be applied similarly to paint; that is to say for best results on hardwood a grain filler should be used which is compatible with the varnish and of the same colour as the wood. Apply the filler and leave to set overnight before rubbing down with fine glasspaper (flour). Remove all dust with a tacky rag and then flow one coat of varnish onto the work with a brush. Some people prefer to thin this first coat with the thinners recommended by the manufacturer in order to gain maximum penetration. There is usually a time limit with this type of varnish at which stage the surface must be rubbed down and the next coat applied. Working beyond this time limit can have disastrous results.

The final coat must be allowed to harden for several days and then it can be flatted with fine glasspaper or grade 0000 wirewool. Alternatively good results can be obtained by using an electric finishing sander (not a rotary disc sander) with fine aluminium oxide paper. The surface should not be cut through to the bare wood, but it can be flatted to a smooth, even finish. This will provide a matt surface akin to ground glass. It may be left like this or it can be polished using either liquid metal polish such as *Brasso,* or a special polyurethane polishing cream. This will result in a high gloss and excellent finish.

As with all products, read the manufacturer's instructions carefully before starting the work.

□ TANALISED TIMBER

Tanalith C, a preservative, is suitable for the treatment of outdoor woodwork. It is forced into timber by a vacuum/pressure impregnating plant at a pressure of 180lb per sq in. Chemicals which are naturally present in the wood react with Tanalith C to make it water insoluble. The water content of the preservative dries out in the air and the preservative salts remain fixed in the timber.

This treatment imparts a soft greenish colour to the wood and looks attractive as it blends well with natural surroundings. Tanalised timber can be painted if so desired and may be glued in the normal way. Tanalised timber is exceedingly durable. Treated pine fencing has a life of well over thirty years.

☐ FORMICA

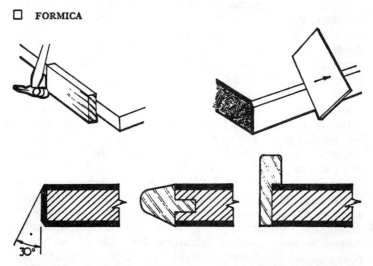

Fig 85 Methods of edge lipping plastic laminate. The edge of plastic laminate is unattractive and requires concealing. Self edging can be performed as shown. Trim to 30° with a cabinet scraper or block plane.
Edging strips made of hardwood can make attractive alternatives

Formica is basically a plastic laminate. It consists of three layers of paper impregnated with resin and bonded together under great pressure and high temperature. The first layer is the base paper. Over this is placed a white or coloured sheet on which the pattern has been printed. The top layer is a cellulose paper which becomes transparent during the curing process in manufacture, and forms a protective skin. This skin will resist heat, impact, abrasion and staining. All laminates emerge with a glossy surface, but where a matt surface is required sheets are dull rubbed with a fine abrasive at the factory. The laminate is 1/16in (1.6mm) thick. It is easier to apply than veneer and does not require polishing. It is widely used as wall panelling and working surfaces, and has very special advantages in kitchen areas.

The technique of cutting, trimming and applying Formica is not difficult to master. It can be cut by circular saw. A high peripheral speed is required, so use the biggest saw blade the saw bench can accommodate. A fine tooth saw is essential since it reduces the amount of finishing required. Cut the sheet with the decorative face upwards, making sure that it is held firmly down to the table. Portable electric saws may be used. The rotation of these saws demands that the sheet should be cut from the back to avoid broken edges. Travelling saws are the most convenient way to cut, since the sheet is held firmly while the saw moves across the work. It is most likely that the local supplier will have this type of saw. Add $\frac{1}{4}$in (6mm), for overhang, to the sizes required, and let the supplier do the work of cutting; this way one can usually buy 'off-cuts' at a cheaper price.

Laminates can be cut by hand. Use a fine toothed tenon saw at a low angle. Mark lines on the surface of the sheet with a soft pencil, these being easily removed later with soap and water. Take care to support the sheet to prevent splitting. Alternatively a Stanley trimming knife fitted with the purpose-made blade can be used for cutting the laminate. Lay the sheet on a firm base, decorative face upwards, score the surface about five times using the Stanley knife against a thin straight edge, then keeping pressure on the straight edge, lift the off-cut side gently. The sheet will start to break along the scribed cut.

When using Formica the core material (groundwork) should be chipboard, blockboard or plywood. Solid timber is not suitable due to its movement. As with normal veneered work, the panels should be counter-veneered. This is achieved by balancing the work by another sheet of laminate of the same thickness bonded to the back of the core. For this purpose the manufacturers produce backing boards which are considerably cheaper than the standard laminate. Counterveneering is essential for free-standing panels such as doors, but is not necessary if the work is to be secured to a solid carcase or wall cladding.

Synthetic resin adhesives (Cascamite, Aerolite, etc) are the most successful bonding agents, having good heat and water resistance, but they do need sustained pressure whilst setting takes place. For this reason synthetic rubber-based adhesives (Bostik, Evostik, etc) are often more suitable. These adhesives, though generally more expensive, are able to stick on touch without sustained pressure, but in certain conditions of heat and humidity they too can be unsuitable. Therefore, if in doubt it is better to use a synthetic resin glue.

When working with the synthetic rubber adhesive, spread a thin film of the adhesive onto both contacting surfaces and wait twenty minutes. By this time the adhesive will appear touch dry. It is important to place the laminate on the core material accurately as once touched down it has no opportunity to slide. Location can be done by locating pins at 3 corners, or by sandwiching a sheet of brown paper between the work. The paper will not stick but it allows one to locate the work accurately, then the paper may be withdrawn, allowing the surfaces to meet. Take care to avoid trapping air.

Careful consideration should be given to the finish of edges, not only for reasons of appearance, but also because it is vital if resistance to wear and abrasion is to be maintained. One of the most successful methods is self-edging with laminate. The laminate can be applied slightly over-size and then trimmed down to the surface finish. Trimming can be done quickly with a power router, or with a low angle block plane. The bevel angle should be about 30° to the perpendicular as this gives less emphasis to the dark core line. A final finish can be given using a cabinet scraper.

When using contact adhesives the core edges should be given two coats, the second coat being applied after the first has dried. After applying the edging make sure it is firmly fixed by tapping with a block of wood and hammer.

Various extruded metal mouldings with plastic inserts are

available. These are particularly suitable for kitchen furniture.

Laminated plastic provides a colourful and hardwearing surface, though it does have limitations; it can be cut by sharp knives and worn out by abrasion. The surface should be cleaned with a damp rag; never use furniture polish as this will in time form a grimy layer and spoil the appearance. Do not iron directly onto the laminate but protect the surface with a thick blanket of cloth. Similarly do not place hot dishes straight from the oven onto a Formica surface. When using a hand mincing machine always place a pad between the screw and the table edge. Alcohol, soft drinks, tea or coffee will not affect Formica, but take care with strong chemicals such as caustic soda, hydrogen peroxide, lavatory cleaner and washing bleach, as these can affect the surface.

GLUES

☐ ANIMAL GLUE—SCOTCH GLUE

Scotch glue, which is the traditional glue of the cabinet maker, is still derived from abattoir waste. The dry glue is usually sold in pearl form and is prepared in the workshop using a double container. The glue placed in the inner container is heated by water held in the outer container. The water does not exceed 100°C so the glue will not burn. Thermostatically controlled electric pots are obtainable.

Fill the inner pot one-third with pearl glue and top up with cold water. Stir once every two minutes for at least ten minutes. The pearls will swell and stirring prevents them forming a lump which would be slow to dissolve.

It takes about half an hour to prepare the glue. When ready it should flow in a continuous, thin, unbroken stream from the brush; it should make a spattering noise when it falls onto the glue in the pot; it should feel sticky between the fingers as it begins to gel.

When using Scotch glue always make sure the room is warm, close all windows and keep the glue pot in the water jacket to maintain the glue at the correct temperature. Work quickly.

Always cramp up before glueing. This will set the cramps to size and ensure there are no hidden snags. Take the work apart, glue up and cramp up for the second time. Glued work should be left cramped until the next day. This allows the glue to harden.

Scotch glue is not waterproof, it takes time to prepare and some form of heating—either gas ring or electric glue pot—is essential; it is not the glue for an ambitious assembly job requiring time in the glueing up stage, as it chills easily.

However, although rather out of favour at the present time, this is a good glue, being very strong, seldom staining the wood, and surplus glue can be easily removed from the corners of the work with hot water. Scotch glue forms a bond between two porous materials by soaking into the pores and setting like little dowels. This explains why the glue may be used successfully only on materials such as wood, leather or hessian. It will not stick glass, plastic or metal.

☐ ANIMAL GLUE—CASEIN GLUE (eg casco)

Casein glue is manufactured from skimmed milk, which has a 3% casein content. It is usually supplied in dry powder form and is mixed with water following the instructions on the tin.

Casein glue must be stored dry and sealed against contact with carbon dioxide in the air. There is a tendency for this glue to stain so its use is generally confined to the building industry. It must also be realised that this glue is not sticky, so cramps must be used until the glue sets hard.

However, it is easy to prepare, is used cold, and has good resistance to moisture. It will bond wood to linoleum, Formica, cardboard, paper, cloth, leather and cork.

☐ SYNTHETIC RESIN GLUES

Mineral Glues—Polyvinyl Acetate (eg Casco PVA, Extra Bond, Resin W) One of the more recent glues is called polyvinyl acetate emulsion glue, or PVA for short. This glue has the components of coke and lime. PVA glue is obtained in liquid form, as an emulsion, that is minute particles of PVA are dispersed in water. It is a very swift gripping glue on porous materials. As the water is quickly absorbed this has the effect of forcing the particles of resin together until they unite and form a firm bond.

The disadvantages of PVA are that it must not be allowed to freeze in storage or it will coagulate and cannot be reconstituted. Similarly, it must be worked at normal room temperature for the best results.

The advantages of PVA are that it requires no mixing, it is fairly waterproof, colourless, and has a certain amount of natural flexibility. The last is a good point, as many modern glues dry hard to the extent of being brittle. In all respects PVA makes a very good substitute for Scotch glue and is probably the best type of wood adhesive for the home craftsman. It will glue everything except rubber, PVC and polythene.

Urea Formaldehyde (eg Cascamite, Aerolite 300) This glue is produced by the reaction of Ammonia with Carbon Dioxide and Formaldehyde. If the process were continued until saturation it would produce a solid but brittle glass-like substance. For the manufacture of glue the process is only partly completed, and by the addition of a hardener which is a catalyst the reaction is completed in the joint. A joint glued in this way is very strong and highly resistant to water, heat and bacteria. This is the most suitable type of glue for boat building and all outdoor work and can be used for Formica work.

Urea formaldehyde adhesives are available in two forms, separate resin and hardener or powder form with hardener added.

☐ CONTACT ADHESIVES (eg Evostik, Bostik, Superstik)
This is a synthetic rubber adhesive and is formed as a by-product of the petroleum industry.

A thin, even film of adhesive should be applied to both surfaces and allowed to touch dry (about 20mins). Then the two surfaces are pressed together over the whole bond area, hand pressure usually being sufficient. This glue is suitable only for butt jointing operations and cannot be used where joints have to be slid into place, eg mortise and tenon joints, dovetails, etc. Impact adhesives will glue most materials, but are not suitable for expanded polystyrene.

NAILS

Nails are used as a quick method of fastening pieces of wood together, but they are not as strong as screws, nor as easy to remove.

Special types of nail are available according to the job in hand. The round wire nail is the most common; it has a large head which is easy to hit and may be put in flush with the surface of the work. If the nail is outsize the ends can be clenched round underneath to make a firmer job. Staggering the nails can prevent splitting. The oval nail has only a small head and can be punched below the surface of the work, the resulting holes being filled with putty and painted over, or filled with solid beeswax, glasspapered over and polished in the normal way. Oval nails may be placed with the grain and this reduces the chance of splitting the wood. Panel pins are very thin and may be used on small work such as boxes and picture frames. They may be punched below the surface and are easy to conceal. The clout nail is used for fixing roofing felt; it has a large head which secures the felt firmly and reduces the risk of tearing. The tack is the upholsterer's method of fixing fabric and webbing. It is available in sizes from $\frac{3}{8}$in (10mm) to $\frac{3}{4}$in (20mm) and can be ordered as either ordinary or improved. The improved type has the larger head and under the head are two small lugs which secure the webbing or fabric when the tack is hit firmly home. A good tack is sharp and stands up with little pressure. A sprig is a small nail used for holding pictures in a frame. It is usually inserted with the side of a large chisel acting as a hammer.

SCREWS

There are three head shapes in common use. The countersink screw is used when the head of the screw must finish flush with the surface of the work, the raised countersink may be used for a more pleasing appearance, and the roundhead is generally used for fastening metal to wood with the exception of hinges which are always fitted with countersink screws.

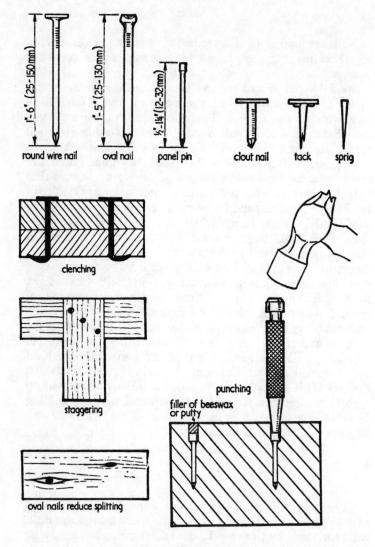

round wire nail 1"–6" (25–150mm)

oval nail 1"–5" (25–130mm)

panel pin ½"–1¼" (12–32mm)

clout nail

tack

sprig

clenching

staggering

oval nails reduce splitting

punching

filler of beeswax or putty

Fig 86 **Types of nails**

These three types of screw may be turned by either a slot or a pozidriv recess.

The pozidriv, a recent improvement in the form of recess, has four major advantages over the slotted type head. The primary advantage is that the screwdriver cannot slip. This reduces accidental damage and brings about increased effici-

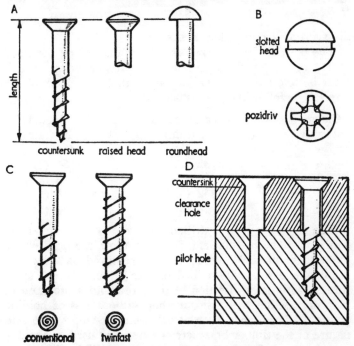

Fig 87 Types of screws: (*a*) types of screw head (*b*) method of driving (*c*) types of thread and (*d*) fitting a countersink screw

ency. The second advantage is that the same screwdriver will fit both large and small screws. This reduces the handling time and means fewer tools are required for the job. The third benefit is that the screw is always aligned with the screwdriver. Finally, the pozidriv screw tends to look more decorative than the slotted head, though this is a matter of personal opinion.

There are two principal types of thread. The pozidriv twin-fast woodscrew is designed for use in low density chipboard, blockboard, fibreboard and softwoods. This screw has a two-start thread which offers increasing holding power, and because it buries two thread pitches each turn this screw can be inserted almost twice as quickly as the conventional screw. The twinfast screw is also threaded nearly to the head. The relieved shank eliminates wedge action and minimises splitting.

☐ FITTING A COUNTERSINK SCREW

The position for the screw should be marked on the wood with a centre punch to prevent the drill wandering. A drill must be selected which is just bigger than the shank of the screw. The following table is helpful:

Gauge of screw	Clearance hole in (mm)	Pilot hole in (mm)
4	$\frac{1}{8}$ (3)	5/64 (2)
6	5/32 (4)	5/64 (2)
8	3/16 (5)	3/32 (2.5)
10	7/32 (5.5)	$\frac{1}{8}$ (3)
12	$\frac{1}{4}$ (6)	$\frac{1}{8}$ (3)

The clearance hole is drilled followed by the countersink which must be of sufficient depth to allow the head of the screw to fit flush. No countersink is required on softwoods. A pilot hole is usually drilled to take the core of the screw thread. This eases insertion of the screw and a lubricant of soap or vaseline will assist further without loss of holding power. In hardwoods, such as oak, where owing to the acid nature of the timber brass screws are always used, preferably a steel screw is first inserted to cut a thread. This will help to prevent the softer brass screw breaking.

Screws are available in a variety of metals and finishes. The commonest metal is steel, which is strong and suitable for most ordinary applications. Brass screws are less strong but offer medium corrosion resistance and look well on furniture. Stainless steel is used for good resistance to corrosion. Silicon bronze screws are used for marine applications and aluminium alloy screws are used with aluminium fittings. In general it is good practice to use screws of the same material as the metal fittings they are to accompany.

Certain finishes can be applied to screws either to make them more decorative or to protect them from weathering. These finishes are listed with descriptions and suggested uses.

Steel *plus*—

Bright zinc plate	Bright attractive protective coating	All dry interior uses and with a paint finish outdoors
Sheradised (zinc)	Dull grey protective coat; may turn brown	Most exterior uses on buildings; good surface for painting
Nickel plate	Bright reflective finish; may tarnish	Dry interior fasteners, eg shelves
Chromium plate	Attractive bright reflective finish	Fairly dry interior work in kitchens and bathroom
Brass plate (electro-brass)	Reflective bright yellow finish	Furniture for matching against brass; dry interior work only
Bronze metal antique	Dark brown finish	Interior use with oxidised copper fittings
Dark florentine bronze	Near black finish	Interior use with oxidised copper fittings
Antique copper bronze	Uniform bronze colour	Interior use with copper, bronze and matching timber finishes
Black japanned	Overall black enamel	General interior use; must be re-painted outdoors for protection
Berlin blacked	Overall dull black enamel	General interior use; must be re-painted outdoors for protection

When ordering wood screws the following information is required:

1 Quantity: screws are usually sold singly, by the dozen, or by the gross
2 Length
3 Diameter by screw gauge: a number 8 screw is a general size. For thinner use number 6, or for stouter number 10
4 Material or finish
5 Type of head: eg 10 1½in (38mm) No 8 pozidriv countersink head screws

HINGES

☐ TYPES OF HINGES

Figure 88 shows a best quality butt hinge made from extruded brass. The knuckle is solid and therefore very strong. Such a hinge will always have an uneven number of knuckles, generally five. The plate with three knuckles is fastened to the cabinet side and the plate with two knuckles to the door. This is the strongest method of fitting this type of hinge. Brass hinges will always be fitted with brass countersink screws. The pin in the hinge may be either brass or steel. Such a hinge is expensive but good quality work deserves good quality fittings.

Common sizes are
1½in x ⅞in	38mm x 22mm
2 in x 1⅛in	51mm x 29mm
2½in x 1⅜in	63mm x 35mm
3 in x 1⅝in	76mm x 41mm
4 in x 2⅜in	101mm x 60mm

A poorer quality hinge is made from folded brass. This is cheaper but less strong and can usually be distinguished by an even number of knuckles.

Common sizes are
1 in x ½in	25mm x 12mm
1¼in x ⅝in	32mm x 16mm
1½in x ¾in	38mm x 19mm
2 in x 1 in	51mm x 25mm
2½in x 1¼in	63mm x 32mm
3 in x 1½in	76mm x 38mm
4 in x 2 in	101mm x 51mm

Such hinges may also be obtained in chromium plate.

The backflap hinge (fig 88c) is used for work such as the drop leaf on a table.

The piano hinge (fig 88D) is used for piano lids and work of a similar nature requiring an extra long hinge. A usual size is 36in x 1in (915mm x 25mm).

The strap hinge (fig 88E) is obtainable in natural brass with a steel pin. Open sizes: $\frac{3}{8}$in x $1\frac{7}{8}$in (10mm x 47), 7/16in x 2$\frac{3}{8}$in (11mm x 60mm).

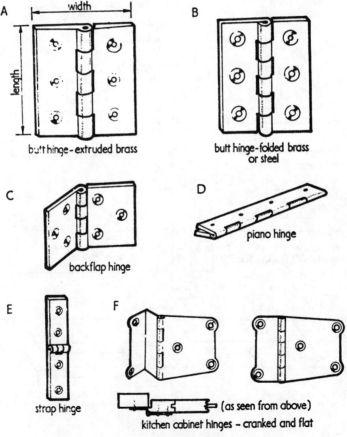

A — width — length
butt hinge - extruded brass

B
butt hinge - folded brass or steel

C
backflap hinge

D
piano hinge

E
strap hinge

F
(as seen from above)
kitchen cabinet hinges - cranked and flat

Fig 88 Types of hinges

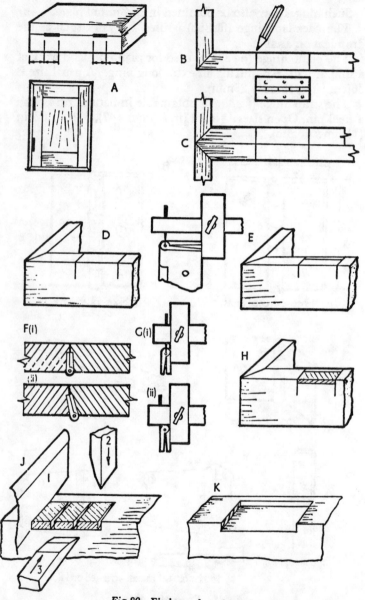

Fig 89 Fitting a butt hinge

Kitchen cabinet hinges are extremely useful. These are surface fitting and the cranked type may be used on a framed and rebated door (fig 88F).

☐ FITTING A BUTT HINGE

A On a box allow the length of the hinge in from the ends. For a door it is usual to allow a little more space under the bottom hinge.

B Mark the exact length of the hinge on the work in pencil.

C Transfer these marks to the lid and square across with a try square and pencil.

D Partly square these pencil marks onto the adjoining surface, where the butt of the hinge has to be let in.

E Set a marking gauge to half the width of the hinge, as shown, and gauge the hinge positions from the outside of the box.

F There are two methods of fitting a hinge:
   i The hinge is let equally into both parts of the job. This is the method shown for the box in figure 89A.
   ii The knuckle of the hinge is let entirely into the moving part. This method is shown on the cabinet in figure 89A. It can result in a better final appearance as the line of the carcase is not broken visually.

G Depending on the method of hinging used, set a marking gauge to either one-half the thickness of the hinge knuckle, or to the full thickness.

H Gauge for the thickness of the hinge, then knife in the pencil lines where required.

J Saw across the fibres for as much of the way as is possible, and remove the waste with a chisel.

K The completed recess will have a sloping base to suit the flap of the hinge. Fit the hinge with the centre screw only. Adjust this as necessary by pelleting the hole (levering the fibres across with a bradawl). When correct insert the other screws.

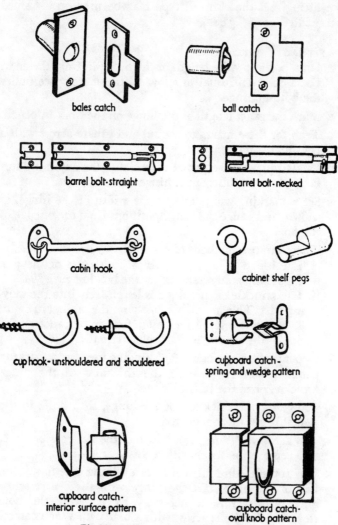

bales catch

ball catch

barrel bolt-straight

barrel bolt-necked

cabin hook

cabinet shelf pegs

cup hook-unshouldered and shouldered

cupboard catch-
spring and wedge pattern

cupboard catch-
interior surface pattern

cupboard catch-
oval knob pattern

Fig 90 **Metal and plastic fittings**

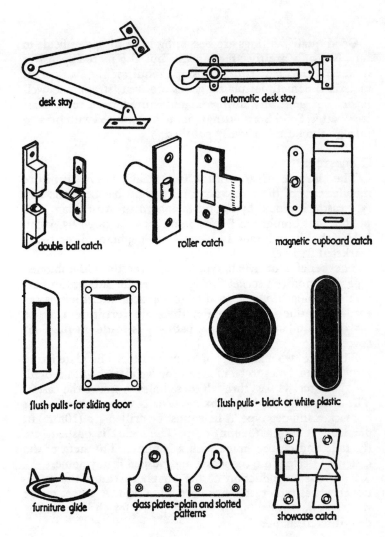

desk stay

automatic desk stay

double ball catch

roller catch

magnetic cupboard catch

flush pulls – for sliding door

flush pulls – black or white plastic

furniture glide

glass plates – plain and slotted patterns

showcase catch

FITTINGS

Good quality fittings are becoming increasingly difficult to buy. Not only are they more scarce but also more expensive; however, the best workmanship requires the very best materials. Sometimes plastic goods are neat, strong and well made, but generally fittings manufactured from solid brass look better. Solid brass fittings, not to be confused with brassed fittings, should be carefully polished.

☐ CASTORS

The purpose of any castor is to make heavy furniture mobile. One of the most successful designs has been the ball type castor invented by George Shepherd, an Australian. The product was brought to England and manufactured by Archibald Kenrick and Sons Ltd, the first Shepherd castor being marketed in 1950.

The benefits of a ball type castor over the old-fashioned type are improved socket fitting, no need for lubrication, exceptional long life, and good castoring action. Criticisms are that the castor is too mobile; therefore furniture may be moved around so often that a pathway is made on the floor covering.

There are two main ways of fixing a castor. The plate fixing requires four holes to be made in the woodwork with a bradawl. Four screws pass through these holes to secure the castor. The alternative method of fixing, usually more convenient, is the socket and peg type. A hole must be drilled $\frac{3}{8}$in (10mm) in diameter and $1\frac{1}{4}$in (32mm) deep. The socket is pushed into the hole and tapped home with a hammer. The stem of the castor is inserted into the socket and pushed firmly home.

Since the introduction of the Shepherd castor the traditional wheel type castor has been improved. A wheel castor was chosen, because of its elegant looks, for the tea trolley described in chapter 9.

MASONRY WALL FIXING

Wall fixings can be made by putting a screw into a plastic

or fibre plug inserted into a pre-drilled hole. The screw expands the plug against the sides of the hole, making a firm fixing.

Care must be taken to drill a hole the correct size for the plug and the screw. Generally a number 8 screw is fitted into a number 8 plug and the hole is drilled with a number 8 masonry drill. Wall plugs of the plastic type will usually fit screws of three different gauges but may require a larger size drill.

A masonry drill, though similar in appearance to a morse drill, has a hard metal insert of tungsten carbide to form the cutting edge. The bit must be turned at slow speed, using either a hand drill or slow running electric drill. Drills turning faster than 1000 revolutions per minute can cause the masonry bit to overheat, resulting in the hard steel edge coming adrift.

The plain shank of the screw must not enter the plug, as it can cause the screw to seize and break at the thread to shank junction. A depth stop can be provided for the drill by wrapping sticky tape around the drill. This way the plug may be made to sink $\frac{1}{8}$in (3mm) below the surface of the wall.

Long battens can be fitted by securing the ends firmly to the wall. Further plugs and screws can be inserted by drilling directly through the batten into the wall behind with the one masonry bit. The spiral twist of the masonry bit will withdraw all dust from the hole. A plug of the fibre type can then be inserted and pushed to the bottom of the hole with the screw. This avoids all difficulties of locating the hole in the batten with the hole in the wall. Remember too that a little lubricant of vaseline or soap will help the screw to enter easily.

A fairly recent innovation is the masonry nail. This is made from hardened steel and has a specially shaped point. Take care to choose the correct size of nail for the job in hand by reading the manufacturer's instructions. These nails are hard but brittle and can 'fly'. Wear protective goggles to shield the eyes when working.

Chapter 7

Woodworking Machinery

THE PURPOSE OF MACHINERY

Not so long ago the machine was thought to be of no benefit to the craftsman working in wood. It was believed that craft items should be made entirely by hand. It was argued that machines were expensive, that the same work could always be done by simple hand tools, and that the use of machinery dictated a poor design, being planned around the machine to the detriment of the final product.

Nowadays most people will accept the machine as part of the workshop situation, having realised it can save time and effort. Machines will help with laborious chores such as sawing the length of a plank or cutting out several rails from one wide board. Work can be tackled in minutes by a circular saw which would take hours by hand.

SAFETY

All tools are safer when they are sharp. Learn how to maintain every machine tool in your workshop, thereby keeping them in prime condition. Many people buy a circular saw without knowing how to sharpen the blade; pushing against a blunt circular saw causes the majority of machine accidents.

When setting up a machine it is often necessary to place the hands near the moving parts, so isolate the machine before making adjustments. Apart from the push button switch on the machine there should be an isolator switch on the wall. This may be a fuse box type switch which can be turned to OFF, or it may be a plug and socket, in which case switch off the socket and REMOVE THE PLUG. One can then adjust the machine in complete safety.

Certain other precautions can also be taken. Belt drives must be guarded as must all revolving parts. It should be made quite difficult, if not impossible, to get fingers near to anything that turns at speed. Furthermore, the machine should be securely fixed either to the floor or to a solid bench; there should be no possibility of it toppling over in use. When a machine has been set up check the revolving parts, see that they can turn freely and make sure all nuts are tight before switching on.

Loose clothing should not be worn; ties are a particular hazard and should be either removed or tucked securely into the shirt. A good workshop smock without loose cuffs or dangling strings will protect clothes. If the machine creates swarf in the direction of the operator wear an eye shield as protection (appendix B).

All machinery can be divided into two basic types, fixed and portable. Both types should be made safe electrically and must be earthed (grounded). However, portable machinery is the more dangerous from this point of view as it can be carried into new and potentially dangerous situations. This particularly applies to the electric drill. This tool is only as safe as its insulation and as the earthing (grounding) of the socket. One assumes that every socket is earthed efficiently but this is not necessarily the case. A fault can occur, such as metal swarf entering the rubber lead and causing a drill to become live. In this event only a good earth connection will prevent electricity flowing through the body to the ground. There are three main ways of preventing an electrical accident.

1. Make sure the drill is efficiently earthed and when working stand on a wooden floor or in rubber boots. On no account hold onto a metal water pipe or gas pipe.

2. The safest method is to reduce the voltage (as in the USA) to no greater than 115 volts, using a step down transformer. This should employ a centre tapped earthed connection, then either lead will supply about 55 volts to the drill. The transformer should be wired with a short flex to the mains supply and a long working flex to supply current at low voltage to the drill (plate 4).

3. The cheapest method of ensuring electrical safety is to use only a double insulated tool. This is signified by the symbol of one square inside another stamped on the tool, as on the Stanley Bridges XK 360. This is a glass filled nylon

bodied drill. Even the metal chuck is insulated from the armature of the drill. This form of insulation will not protect the operator should the lead be cut but in all other respects it has a high degree of safety.

CIRCULAR SAW

The circular saw is obtainable either as a bench or a portable machine. It is known by the largest diameter of saw blade it will take.

☐ THE BENCH MACHINE

All circular saws should be provided with sufficient power for the blade to perform its normal quota of work without protest. The rule of thumb is to allow one horsepower for every inch (25mm) depth of cut. It must be realised that circular saws require a lot of power to work effectively.

The power is usually transmitted to the saw spindle by means of a v belt. This is similar to the fan belt of a car. On larger machines two or even three belts are fitted in order to transmit adequate power from the motor to the blade. These belts need no attention. On no account should they be fitted spring tight.

The motor is seldom connected directly to the blade. Only on smaller saws, usually fitted as attachments to an electric drill, is the saw blade fitted directly to an extension of the motor. The reason for this is that circular saws have to revolve at a certain speed for optimum efficiency and seldom does this speed comply with the speed of the motor.

Tensioning is required with circular saw blades as with handsaws. Without tension the rim of the blade becomes slack at speed. The blades are usually tensioned to suit a peripheral speed of 10,000ft per minute (50 metres per second). The table below gives the approximate spindle speed of the machine against the diameter of the saw blade.

Speeds of Circular Saws

Diameter of saw		Approximate spindle speed (peripheral speed 10,000ft per minute)
in	mm	rev/min
6	150	6,370
8	200	4,770
10	250	3,820
12	300	3,185

Saws not designed for these normal applications have to be specially tensioned to suit the speed of rotation.

When ordering a circular saw blade the following information is usually required:

1 The type of saw—this is normally a plate saw but other saws, eg hollow ground, swage, are obtainable for special purposes.
2 Diameter of saw.
3 Size of centre hole to suit machine spindle.
4 Type of tooth—rip saw, crosscut saw or combination shape. This is dictated by the timber that is to be cut.
5 The spindle speed.

All bench circular saws have some means of adjusting the amount of blade that shows above the table. On cheaper machines it is usual to have a rise-and-fall table. More expensive machines have a rise-and-fall saw arbour which is better as it means the operator is always working at a constant table height, usually about 34in (860mm). The reason for adjusting the depth of cut is not only to make it possible to saw grooves and rebates but also to enable the saw to be set so that the upper surface of the timber is just penetrated by the blade. It will be found that the circular saw will cut more smoothly in this set-up as more teeth are engaged (fig 91). Frequently

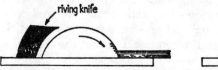

riving knife

Fig 91 Use of rise-and-fall arbour. When the saw is set low in the table, more teeth are in engagement with the work. This results in smoother cutting

the saw blade can be adjusted on the machine to operate at any angle from 90° to 45° with respect to the table. This allows bevel cuts to be performed. The more expensive machines have a tilting arbour (saw spindle), whilst cheaper machines are fitted with tilting tables.

It is desirable to have some means of crosscutting accurately. Often a longitudinal slot is provided in the table to take a simple mitring and crosscutting fence. This is satisfactory for small work but for anything large it is usual to prepare a suitable wooden jig.·

The ripping fence should be adjustable not only across the table but also to and from the blade. When used for ripping and deep sawing the fence should guide the work only to the blade. The leading edge of the fence should project about half the gullet depth of the saw and should be shaped to the approximate curve of the blade. This prevents the wood binding between the fence and the saw blade. The latter would cause loss of power and could result in the work being thrown back at the operator. When crosscutting it is more convenient to have the fence extended to the full depth of the table. For those saws fitted with a long and non-adjustable fence a false timber plate can normally be attached with machine screws.

Certain timbers, notably elm, will pinch on the saw blade once the cut has been started. To prevent this happening and to keep the cut open a riving knife is fitted directly behind the blade. The riving knife should be of a thickness equal to the kerf of the saw.

The circular saw is the most dangerous woodworking machine; hence the need for certain safety precautions. Firstly, the blade should be well protected. It should be guarded underneath the table by the cabinet and above the table there should be a special (crown) blade guard. This can be a metal shield attached to the riving knife. Alternatively a spring guard is fitted which encloses the teeth of the saw and only opens as wood is fed through. Always use a push stick (a stick of wood notched at one end) when working near the teeth of a saw; it matters little if the push stick gets sawn in half. Oil the machine little and often and make sure it works as efficiently as possible. The fence should work easily and so should the rise-and-fall mechanism.

☐ THE PORTABLE MACHINE

There are times when it is easier to take the saw to the work than the work to the saw, for example when sawing large panels. It is easier to place the panel on trestles and cut with the portable saw rather than man-handle the timber to a bench machine which will require at least double the amount of operating space.

The portable saw may be regarded as a powered handsaw, its chief uses being ripping and crosscutting. It is essential that the work is held securely. A satisfactory method is to set the depth of cut to just greater than the thickness of the material being sawn. A waste batten may then be placed under the work and the saw arranged to cut through the work and into the batten. This prevents the sawn off piece of timber from dropping down at the completion of the cut.

☐ SHARPENING A CIRCULAR SAW

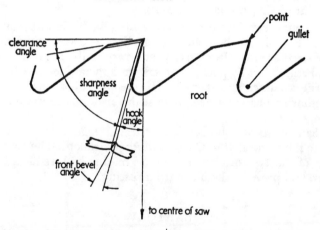

Fig 92 Combination circular saw blade. This is the typical type of blade that is supplied as an electric drill attachment. Clearance angle 10°, sharpness angle 65°, hook angle 15°, top bevel 5°, front bevel 10° and set 0.015 in

An ordinary circular saw blade (not tungsten tipped) requires sharpening about every four hours of use.

1 Before removing it from the machine lower the blade so

that the teeth are level with the table. Whilst the saw is running, place an oilstone on the table to just touch the points of the teeth. This will cause sparks but will level all the teeth and produce a guide to sharpening.

2 Remove the blade from the machine and secure it in the vice between two circular pieces of wood a little smaller than the blade. A bolt through the middle will hold everything together.

3 With a millsaw file sharpen every tooth which is set *away* (alternate teeth) by (a) filing across the top with the handle about 5° below the horizontal, until the topping mark has just disappeared; (b) three strokes of the file in the gullet of the saw, working on the leading edge of the tooth at an angle of about 10° from the square position. Such a blade will then rip and crosscut and is called a combination blade. Should the blade only be required for ripping then sharpen the leading edge of each tooth at 0° (ie parallel to the axis).

About every sixth time of sharpening the blade will require setting. This can be done with a pliers-type saw set suitable for circular saw. Alternatively, and very easily, the teeth may be hammer set by placing the saw on a metal block with one corner chamfered to about 5°. Hit the top half of the alternate teeth with a hammer, then reverse the blade and repeat for the other side.

Saw blades are obtainable coated with *teflon*. This is fused onto the blade at 400° C and is quite permanent. The advantage of this type of blade is that the coating both reduces friction and prevents the blade from rusting.

BANDSAW

The bandsaw has a blade that is an endless ribbon of steel with teeth shaped on the leading edge. The blade can be ⅛in (3mm) to 7in (180mm) in width, depending upon the size of the machine. Generally in the home workshop the blade is no more than ⅜in (10mm) wide. The narrower the blade the tighter the curve the bandsaw is capable of cutting. The blade revolves around two large pulleys. The top pulley is freewheeling whereas the bottom pulley is powered by an electric motor. A bandsaw suitable for a large woodworking machine shop can have pulley wheels up to 60in (1.5m) in diameter. Some smaller machines have wheels that are only 10in (250mm) in diameter. The maximum distance for a cut into a board (the throat size) can never be greater than the diameter of the wheel on a two-wheel machine. It is common for small machines to have three wheels, which increases the throat capacity without increasing the wheel size.

The wheels of the bandsaw are usually fitted with rubber tyres. These are crowned so that the speed of rotation causes the blade to climb to the highest point of the camber. The top wheel is normally adjustable for tensioning the blade and for tracking. Narrow blades, having less mass, require less tension than the wider blades. At the end of the day's work it is a good practice to reduce the tension on the blade. The tracking screw is a means of adjusting the tilt of the top pulley so that the blade follows the correct path as it moves.

The bandsaw has an adjustable saw guide which gives support to the back of the blade by a bronze thrust wheel and gives lateral support by the means of fibre pads. This saw guide is always adjusted so that it just clears the surface of the work, thereby giving maximum support to the blade.

This is generally considered to be a very safe machine to use. The rule is to tension the blade before starting the machine to check the tracking. Set the guide to just over the thickness of the work and keep the hands away from the right-hand side of the blade because if the blade should break it will generally fly out on that side. Keep the blade sharp and set.

MACHINE PLANER

These machines consist of a steel cylinder fitted with either two or three knife-like blades. The machine size is known by the length of the cutting cylinder and can be from about 4in (100mm) to 20in (510mm). Obviously the larger the machine the more power it consumes and the more expensive it is to run. The cutting cylinder normally revolves at about 6,000 revolutions per minute.

Mounted on either side of the cutting cylinder are two sturdy steel tables. These are adjustable in height and can be operated independently of each other. The method of adjustment is effected by moving each table along a ramp by means of adjusting screws. In this fashion it is possible to work to very fine limits. The machine tables are normally graduated in 1/16in (1.5mm) but there is every possibility of working to 1/64in (0.5mm).

In operation the back table is always set level with the tips of the cutters. This can be checked by switching the machine on and running a piece of previously planed wood from the back table onto the cutters. A snicking noise should be heard as the cutters just touch the wood.

The depth of cut is arranged by lowering the front table the desired amount below the back table. Most machine planers can deal with a thickness of cut up to $\frac{1}{2}$in (12mm) at one pass. It is wrong to attempt to cut less than 1/16in (1.5mm) as the cutters will only be rubbing and will quickly dull. Similarly it is wrong to attempt to machine plane timber of less than 8in (200mm) in length as the gap between the two tables where the cutting cylinder revolves is about 1$\frac{3}{8}$in (35mm) wide and it is easy for the fingers to be caught.

To help prevent accidents it is normal to have a bridge guard fitted to the machine. This must always be set so that the wood can just pass between the guard and the cutters, the hands having to pass over the top of the guard.

When working at this machine always place the wood hollow side down on the infeed table. Check the direction of the grain on the timber as the work can be reversed to keep tearing to a minimum. A machine planer always cuts a ripple finish. The best finish is obtained from the planer by slow feeding; the ripples are then closest together and less conspicuous. On first class work, however, even this fine finish can be improved by hand planing. Remember that a high gloss finish will always expose marks on the wood rather than conceal them.

If the machine planer works unsatisfactorily it may be that the back table is incorrectly set, or that the cutters are blunt. It is easier to sharpen this machine if the cutters are left in place. Turn the block so that one cutter is $\frac{1}{4}$in (6mm) forward of the top position and lock the block in place with a wedge. Wrap two-thirds of a fine oilstone (8in x 2in x 1in size) with paper and rest the covered part of the stone on the back table, with the exposed stone over the cutting blade. Lower the back table until by sliding the stone along it touches the blade. Sharpen the cutting edge. A little oil will help. Turn the block around and sharpen the other cutters in the same manner. The stone, having been run along the blade, will not raise a burr. Most cutters are made from high speed steel and require sharpening about every two days of continuous use. Eventually the cutters will require re-grinding, and for this they are sent away to specialists, who will also balance them to reduce vibration and increase safety.

The purpose of the machine planer is

1 To prepare sawn timber to a smooth finish.
2 To make the surfaces flat and out of wind, and square to each other.
3 To prepare the timber to an even thickness.

There are three types of planing machine. The simplest, the overhand or surfacer, is the one that has been described. This will make the surface smooth and flat and can prepare surfaces square to each other, but it will not thickness the material. This has to be done on a special machine called a thicknesser. These two machines can be bought combined in one, and they are then known as an over and under. Wood is surfaced over the top of the machine and thicknessed by passing back under the cutting block of the machine. The third type of machine, the four-cutter, will perform the whole planing procedure in one operation.

PORTABLE ELECTRIC ROUTER

The electric router is capable of performing many more tasks than the simple hand router. It is in effect an inverted spindle moulder and can be used to produce all manner of mouldings.

The electric router consists of a powerful motor (about 1 horsepower)· which runs at a very fast speed (20,000-30,000 rpm). The motor fits into a housing which is fitted with two handles to help guide the tool. The whole tool weighs less than 10lb, is fairly quiet and easy to handle.

Cutting bits are fitted directly to the spindle of the motor by means of a collet type chuck. The motor is adjustable inside the housing so that the bit can be extended to a predetermined depth below the sole of the machine and the depth can be set to an accuracy of about 0.004in. In operation the fast spinning cutter of the machine cuts very cleanly. It will make easy work of a groove. The router is always fed from left to right. A fence is provided to follow the edge of the work. Alternatively a batten can be cramped down to the work and the edge of the machine allowed to follow the batten.

Many different shaped cutters are available in either high speed steel or tungsten carbide. The latter is very expensive but stays sharp for a long time. The cutters can groove and rebate, flute, round over edges, cove, chamfer and dovetail. Furthermore, the tool can make joints such as housings, dovetail housings, tongue and groove. The electric router will also trim Formica.

ELECTRIC DRILL

The electric drill consists of a fast revolving armature which is geared down to produce a chuck speed of about 3,000 revolutions per minute. Slower running drills of about 1,000 revolutions per minute are available for masonry drilling. Two-speed drills are also available and these offer considerable versatility. The size of the drill is known by the maximum diameter circular bar that the chuck can hold. This varies between $\frac{1}{4}$in (6mm) and $\frac{1}{2}$in (13mm).

The early electric drills were fitted with plain three jaw chucks, as fitted to the hand drill, but these have now been superseded by Jacobs geared chucks. A chuck key is used to tighten the grip of the chuck on the bit. Having closed the chuck jaws on the shank of the bit, the chuck key should be placed in one of the three spigot holes in the chuck body and normal pressure applied to the key. Check if further tightening is required, however slight, by applying the chuck key to the other spigot holes in turn.

Maintenance of the electric drill should be performed occasionally, according to instructions supplied with the tool. This will usually concern the carbon brushes which should not be less than 5/16in (8mm) in length and should always be replaced in pairs. The front gearbox will also require replenishing with grease. To do this the front section of the drill is removed by releasing two or three screws. Clean out the old grease with a stick. It is seldom advisable to wash out the gearbox with paraffin as this can thin the grease contained in the front bearing. Replenish with the correct grade of grease and do not exceed the original amount. When warm, grease expands and can cause loss of power and excessive overheating.

The electric drill can be given a long life by taking certain precautions. Do not clamp the drill in the vice as this will distort the frame. Coil the cables when not in use and keep them free of oil and grease. Do not lift the drill by the lead. Always keep the drill bits correctly sharpened and avoid switching the drill on under load. Switch on and run for a few seconds before drilling. This allows the drill to reach maximum speed. Do not apply excessive pressure as slowing the motor will cause overheating. If the machine becomes very hot allow to cool by running with no load for a few minutes before switching off.

Various attachments are available for most electric drills, chiefly sawing, sanding and grinding. Sawing is hard work for a drill so keep saw blades sharp. The electric drill is usually capable of sawing to a depth of 1½in (38mm). When bench sawing the drill is supported in a bench stand. Bolt the stand securely to your bench. The chuck of the drill will have to be removed by holding the spindle of the drill steady with the spanner provided whilst turning the chuck in the *same direction as it normally revolves,* using the chuck key as a lever. Some types of drill have no position for a spanner, in which case put the chuck key into one of the chuck spigot holes and tap the key with the handle of the hammer. The inertia of the gearing will oppose the force you apply.

A saw mandrel is screwed onto the drill in place of the chuck. The saw blade is then bolted to the mandrel with a metal washer either side of the blade for support. On some machines a spring saw guard is also bolted onto the mandrel with the blade. It is possible for the saw blade to be fitted backwards. A correctly fitted blade will have the points of the teeth of the saw coming over the top and towards the operator. Fit the table in position then check that the blade is free to revolve by rotating it by hand. Plug in the machine and start it up. Allow a short pause before cutting for the machine to reach maximum speed. Do not force wood through the saw or damage will occur to the motor. The machine cuts at its best when it is revolving at its fastest speed.

A useful sawing attachment is the jig saw. A short blade is moved rapidly up and down. This machine tool can be used for straight or contour sawing. Hold it so that the sole plate rests firmly on the work and feed along the line without forcing.

The disc sander as a bench machine is a handy accessory. A circular steel plate is attached to the spindle of the drill and to this steel disc is glued a circle of garnet paper. Usually the glue (disc cement) is in stick form and is applied to the disc as it rotates. Friction melts the glue. Stop the machine and press the sanding disc firmly in position. The finish obtained is quite good. Feed the work steadily without applying too much pressure as this would burn the wood. If a good thickness of material has to be removed feed the work through several times until the cut is completed. Generally a little hand sanding afterwards in the direction of the grain will further improve the finish.

The portable disc sander is a more difficult tool to operate successfully. A rubber backing pad is attached to the chuck of the drill and the sanding discs, supplied with a central hole, are bolted onto the pad with a recessed nut. The disc should not be placed flat on the work but held at an angle with only the trailing edge working. Allow the speed of the disc to do the work. Do not press as this will slow the motor and cause rings to appear on the work.

The finishing sander cuts slowly and gives a very smooth finish for painting or sanding. Rectangular sanding sheets are clipped across a rubber sole which either oscillates or moves in very small orbits. Do not press on the machine but pass it over the work as if ironing a sheet. This machine is not suitable for finishing a rough sawn surface but it will remove the ripple marks left on the surface by a machine planer.

Chapter 8

Basic Procedures

DESIGN

The process of design is composed of four steps.

1   Consider the function of the article. This will at the very least suggest the overall sizes and can give ideas on the layout and form. For an item to be truly successful it must work well.

2   Think about the construction. Consider how it is to be made, whether it can be put together easily and the size and strength of the various members.

3   Consider the proportion of the pieces. Perhaps a wider rail may make the article look more balanced, more aesthetically pleasing. A little shaping can alter the appearance and indeed make the item more functional.

4   Some carefully applied decoration can add appeal to the article. This could be achieved by the colourful effect of different timbers. Texture, too, can be thought about in the quality of finish that is to be used. Decoration can also be added by the use of chamfers, carving, or inlay.

The current fashion is for simply decorated designs, the main effect of the item being its shape and form. Whatever you think of this you must design things so that they are relevant to your needs. Use the opportunity to create things the way you wish, avoid using direct copy, and you will achieve greater satisfaction.

PREPARING A DRAWING

A sketch should be made at the beginning of any job. It can be invaluable both as an aid to memory and to prevent constructional mistakes. For those people who find drawing difficult it can take the form of a thumbnail sketch showing principally the overall dimensions.

Most designers begin by making many simple sketches, developing their ideas as they work. A small scale drawing always looks most realistic if it is drawn to a scale of $\frac{1}{8}$ or 1/10, as the view shown on paper in front of you looks approximately the same as the finished object standing at the normal viewing distance.

These scale drawings can be turned into models using either balsa wood or the wood that is to be used in the final construction. Balsa cement or PVA glue will hold the parts of the model together. A full-size model can always be made using cheap softwood (or cardboard) with parts roughly nailed together. People often say they can work well without making sketches or models by designing the job as they go. In point of fact they are trying to take a short cut and this can lead to mistakes that are impossible or expensive to rectify.

The final drawings can show greater detail if important parts are drawn full size. Many examples of such working drawings are included in chapter 9. Due to difficulties in reproduction these drawings may not show parts exactly full size.

MAKING A CUTTING LIST

Having prepared the drawings, the next stage is to make a cutting list. The timber merchant will not want to see the drawings but he will expect to be given a detailed analysis showing exactly the materials required.

The first essential is the type of timber required. Sometimes two or three timbers are used in the construction of an article and the parts needed should be separated under their respective headings, viz African mahogany, chipboard, plywood, etc.

The next requirement is the quantities of similar items, viz 4 legs, 2 side rails, 2 end rails.

Demensioning of the items requires care. The first dimension is always the length. This is taken in the direction of the grain and it may not be the greatest dimension of a piece of wood. In fact it is quite common for a piece of wood to be wider than it is long. Included in the length should be an extra $\frac{1}{2}$in (12mm). This will allow $\frac{1}{4}$in (6mm) at each end for sawing the ends square. The second dimension given is the width, and to this should be added $\frac{1}{4}$in (6mm) to allow for planing. This is then called the nominal size, though a better system is to ask for the finished size (f). This means planed and finished to this size, so 3in (nom)$=2\frac{3}{4}$in (f). The third dimension given is the thickness. To this can be added $\frac{1}{8}$ (3mm) for planing, although most times the finished size is the most convenient to use.

An example of a cutting list for four legs of a stool which must finish 16in (410mm) high, $1\frac{3}{8}$in (35mm) wide and $1\frac{1}{4}$in (32mm) thick, is:

4 legs teak $16\frac{1}{2}$in (422mm) f x $1\frac{3}{8}$in (35mm) f x $1\frac{1}{4}$in (32mm) f

ORDERING TIMBER

There are usually a variety of places in every town where one can buy timber, but it is not always appreciated that each firm specialises in certain woods and manufactured boards. The do-it-yourself (handyman) shop is always helpful but it specialises in softwood and manufactured board. Only a few of these shops stock hardwood. The advantage of a do-it-yourself shop is that it will usually cut to any size, and this can save time and money.

Many joinery and shopfitting firms can be very obliging, and they are well equipped with machinery and can supply your exact requirements. It should be realised that these people are manufacturers rather than suppliers so be prepared to wait two or three weeks for your order to be processed.

The large firms usually specialise in either hardwood or softwood. The softwood section of the timber trade is an entirely distinct division from the hardwood section; even the units of measurement are different. Hardwoods are bought by the cubic foot, whereas softwoods are bought by the standard. A standard of softwood is 165 cubic feet. This is now changing in the UK where the standard is being replaced by the cubic metre. Some large firms will not serve the customer with a small order, but others can be quite helpful. It is a question of finding the right firm.

Always try to order the timber planed on four surfaces as this will save you much time and effort. Make it clear to the timber merchant that the sizes given are the finished measurements of the timber after machine planing, indicating this by the letter (f).

ORDER OF CONSTRUCTION

With all jobs there is an order of construction that can be followed. This will speed up work and make mistakes less likely. The procedure is as follows.

1 Set out the parts and number adjacent joints. Pencil the number on the *outside* surface. The reference marks will then remain on the work until after the job has been glued together. Mark the face sides and face edges if this will help.

2 Mark the pieces of wood to length. Knife lines should be used as these are guide lines for the saw. Do not saw the wood to length too early. If the first joint is not successful it may be that sufficient wood remains to cut another without reducing the dimensions of the article.

3 Mark out the joints.

4 Make sure all the necessary marking out is done before commencing to cut; then choose the most important joint and cut this first. Follow the advice of checking twice and cutting once! Do not remove the wrong part for waste. A sound idea is to hatch in the waste areas with a pencil before cutting.

5 Fit the joints using either a hammer and block of wood or a sash cramp to close the joint. Do not glue up yet.

6 When all the joints have been fitted take the pieces apart and clean up the inside surfaces with a smoothing plane. Remove just two shavings and keep the use of glasspaper to a minimum.

7 Polish the inside surfaces, as these will be inaccesible after glueing up. Wax the inside surfaces to prevent glue from sticking, but take care not to put wax on the joints, as this will reduce their strength.

8 Cramp up without glue and use waste wood to prevent the shoes of the cramps from marking the work. This will set the cramps to length. Check that the joints fit really well; check too for squareness and twist before proceeding.

GLUEING UP

Before glueing up check that the room is warm. Scotch glue gels too quickly in a cold room, and formaldehyde glues are slow to set. Mark where each joint goes as this will speed up work. Do not be over ambitious. It is better to glue up some of the work the next day rather than find the glue setting before you are finished.

Always glue both surfaces of the joint. Work quickly and wipe off excess glue with a damp rag before it hardens. Do not overtighten the cramps as this will distort the work.

Make careful tests before leaving the work to set.

1   Check the diagonals for equal length. This will ensure squareness. If incorrect try moving the cramps slightly in the direction of the long diagonal.

2   Sight for twist. This can be corrected by moving the cramps. or packing the end of one cramp off the bench with a piece of wood.

3   Check that the joints are closed and fit up tight.

Next day the cramps can be removed and the outside surfaces of the work cleaned up with a smoothing plane. Plane protruding parts of the joints flush and remove all pencil and knife lines. Round over any sharp corners on the work and this will add a professional touch making the item much nicer to handle. Polish the outside of the work to match the treatment given to the inside surfaces.

LAP BUTT JOINT (fig 93)

☐   MARKING OUT THE JOINT

Assuming that the wood has been planed to size and sawn to length. square up the ends on the shooting board.

A Arrange the parts and if necessary number them in pairs.
B Set a cutting gauge to just over the thickness of the wood.
c Use this setting to gauge the shoulder line across the inside surface and one-third way across the edge.
D Set a marking gauge to one-third thickness of the wood. Hold the wood in the vice and gauge across the end and

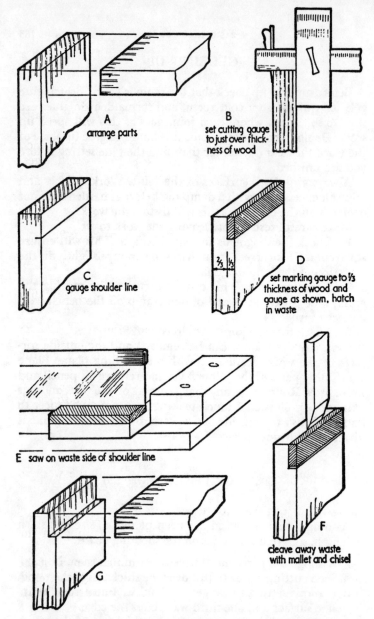

A
arrange parts

B
set cutting gauge
to just over thick-
ness of wood

C
gauge shoulder line

D
set marking gauge to ⅓
thickness of wood and
gauge as shown, hatch
in waste

⅔ | ⅓

E saw on waste side of shoulder line

F
cleave away waste
with mallet and chisel

G

Fig 93 Lap butt joint. Marking out and cutting this joint

down to the shoulder line. Hatch in the waste with a pencil.

☐ CUTTING THE JOINT

E Place the work on a bench hook and saw along the waste side of the shoulder line with a tenon saw.

F Stand the wood upright in the vice and with an inch (25mm) chisel and mallet, cleave away the waste in stages. Alternatively the waste may be removed with a tenon saw as when sawing a tenon (see later in this chapter).

THROUGH DOVETAIL JOINT (figs 94 & 95)

☐ MARKING OUT THE TAILS

A Number the joints on the outside surfaces, then mark the shoulder lines the thickness of the wood plus 1/16in (1.5mm) in from the ends using a marking knife and try square. If the ends are square a cutting gauge may be used as an alternative.

B Mark out the position of the tails in pencil on the shoulder line of one of the pieces.

C Use a dovetail template to complete the marking out. A slope of 1 in 6 is used for softwoods and 1 in 8 for hardwoods. Hatch in the waste.

☐ CUTTING THE TAILS

D & E Place the wood for the tails low in the vice to prevent undue vibration when sawing. Slope the work so that the lines are vertical and with a dovetail saw cut down *on the lines* to the shoulder line.

F The waste on the outsides may be removed by placing the wood horizontally in the vice and cutting on the waste side of the line with a dovetail saw.

G & H The coping saw may be used to remove most of the waste between the tails. The remainder can be chiselled back to the shoulder line with a bevelled edge chisel. It is a good policy to work on a chiselling board using a straight piece of wood cramped along the shoulder line as a guide.

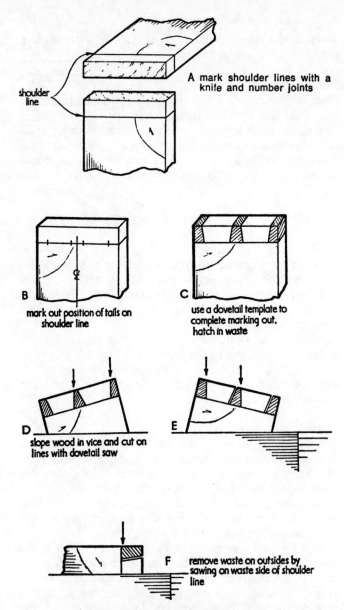

shoulder line

A mark shoulder lines with a knife and number joints

B mark out position of tails on shoulder line

C use a dovetail template to complete marking out, hatch in waste

D slope wood in vice and cut on lines with dovetail saw

E

F remove waste on outsides by sawing on waste side of shoulder line

Figs 94 & 95 Through dovetail joint

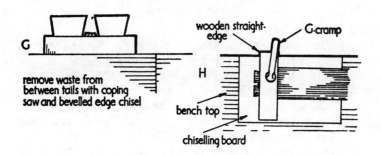

G

remove waste from between tails with coping saw and bevelled edge chisel

wooden straight-edge

G-cramp

H

bench top

chiselling board

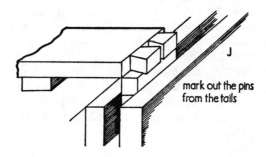

J

mark out the pins from the tails

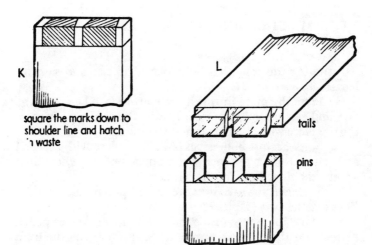

K

square the marks down to shoulder line and hatch in waste

L

tails

pins

☐ MARKING OUT THE PINS

J Place number 1 piece for the pins in the vice and arrange the tails for number 1 across it. Check for squareness with a try square and ensure that the tails are positioned correctly over the wood for the pins. Mark around the tails with a scriber. This can be a piece of broken hacksaw blade sharpened to a point or the blade of a small penknife. Sometimes it is difficult to see the scriber marks, in which case the end grain of the pins can be rubbed with chalk before marking.

K Square the marks down the sides of the wood to the shoulder line with a pencil. Hatch in the waste.

☐ CUTTING THE PINS

When cutting the pins there is no need to slope the wood in the vice. Cut down on the *waste side of the lines* with the dovetail saw and remove most of the waste with a coping saw. The waste that remains may be carefully pared away with the bevelled edge chisel in a similar manner to that used when cutting the tails. It is easiest to work from each side into the centre of the wood.

STUB MORTISE AND TENON JOINT (figs 96 & 97)

☐ MARKING OUT THE JOINT

Assuming the wood has been planed to size and sawn to length

B Place the piece in which the mortise is to be cut in the vice and rest the other piece across it. Check the position of the top piece with a steel rule and try square.

C Mark against both edges of the top piece with a pencil and square these marks across the upper surface. These lines are the shoulder lines for the joint.

D If several similar joints are to be cut mark all shoulder lines together with a pencil.

E Mark ⅛in (3mm) *inside* the shoulder lines with a pencil and square these marks across. These are the mortise-limit lines and will allow a cover on the tenon to conceal the mortise.

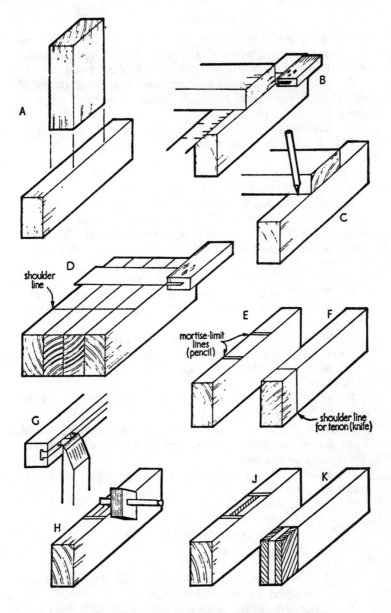

Fig 96 Stub mortise and tenon joint. Marking out the joint

F   Mark the shoulder line for the tenon with a marking knife and square the line all the way round. The length of a stub tenon is usually two-thirds the width of the wood.

G   Set a mortise chisel nearest one-third the thickness of the wood, then check the marks made from both edges to make the joint central.

H   Gauge the mortise and the tenon from the face side.

J & K   Hatch in the waste with a pencil.

☐   CUTTING THE MORTISE

L   G cramp the wood to the end of the bench.

M   With the flat part of the chisel facing towards oneself make two cuts and remove the wood from the notch.

N   Using a mallet, work away from the notch. Mark the depth of the mortise on the chisel with chalk or coloured tape to prevent cutting too deep. Several passes will have to be made to enable the chisel to reach full depth.

O   To remove the waste put the wood in the vice and carefully lever out the chips. Do not use a mallet and take care not to round the corners.

P   Hold the wood upright in the vice. Place the tenon saw just outside the gauge line and saw a shallow groove.

Q   Slope the wood in the vice to 45° and saw down to the diagonals.

R   Hold the wood upright in the vice and cut straight down to the shoulder line.

S   Place the work on a bench hook and, keeping on the waste side of the shoulder line, remove the cheeks taking care not to cut into the tenon.

T   Finally mark $\frac{1}{8}$in (3mm) and remove waste at ends of tenon for covers.

DOWEL JOINTS (fig 99)

☐   METHODS OF LOCATING THE DOWEL

A   A manufactured jig (fig 98). This will require a centre line to be marked for the joint in pencil.

B   A home-made jig. This will only work on a flat frame with all pieces the same thickness.

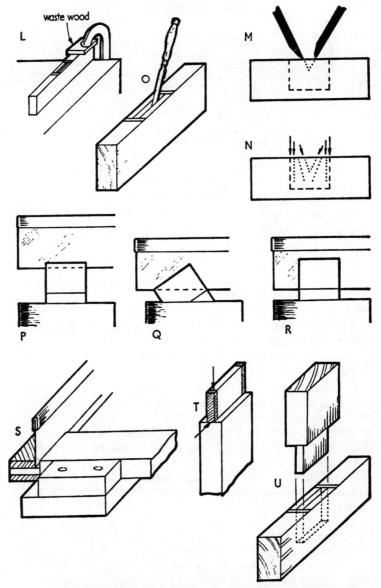

Fig 97 Stub mortise and tenon joint. Cutting the joint

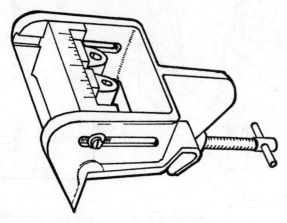

Fig 98   Dowelling jig

C   Panel pins. The panel pins should be driven part way in one piece and the heads cut off just above the surface of the wood. Align the two pieces and tap both together. This transfers the dowel positions onto the other piece. Remove pins with pincers before drilling.

☐ MAKING DOWEL

D   Square straight-grained stuff should be prepared which is cleft, ie cut with a chisel or axe. Point one end and hammer the piece through a dowel plate. This is a steel plate drilled with a series of holes, $\frac{5}{8}$in, $\frac{1}{2}$in, $\frac{3}{8}$in, (16mm, 13mm, 10mm). Place the dowel plate over a hole in the bench, eg remove the bench stop.

Dowel may be bought in lengths up to about 7ft (2m). Thickness of dowel varies from $\frac{1}{8}$in (3mm) to about 1in (25mm).

☐ FITTING DOWEL

Cut dowel to lengths just shorter than that required to fill the holes. This will prevent the dowels resting on the bottom of both holes thereby preventing the joint from closing.

A tight dowel should be eased before glueing to prevent glue from bursting open the wood.

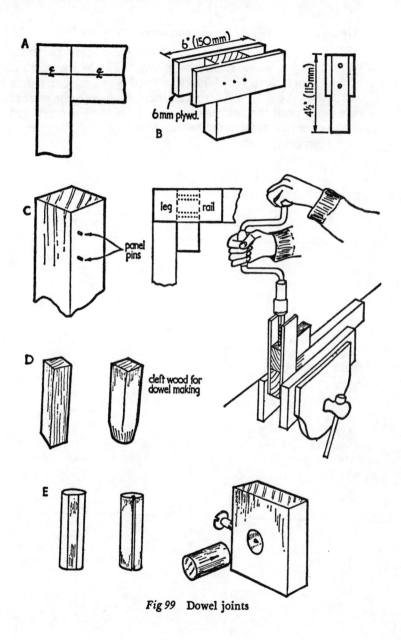

Fig 99 Dowel joints

E   To provide for glue escape the dowel may be either planed with a flat or it may be grooved. The groove method can be simply achieved. A block of wood is drilled with a drill the size of the dowel. A screw is inserted through the edge of the block until the point emerges in the hole. The dowel rod may be tapped through the hole and the dowel will be grooved as it emerges.

Chapter 9

Designs in Wood

WOODWORK BENCH

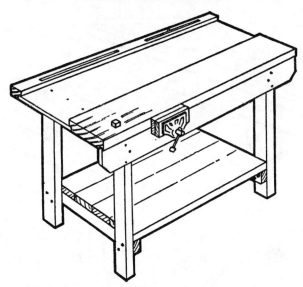

Fig 100 Woodwork bench. Pictorial view

This bench has been designed for the person who has a workshop or spare room large enough to contain a bench but with limited tools to hand. It can be built without the aid of another bench; the frame of the bench may be used to aid the work while the rest is being completed. The bench can easily be taken apart and put together again when moving house.

Despite its ease of construction this bench is most substantial. It has a solid hardwearing top of 1¾in (45mm) thick beech which is suitable for supporting work even when heavy morticing is being done by hand. Large section legs provide plenty of support for the top which has a 4in (100mm) overhang at each end to facilitate the use of G cramps. A wide apron at the front and a diagonal brace at the back of the bench top so it is not transmitted to other parts of the build-saw movement when planing. Rubber feet let into the legs help to isolate the noise made by machinery being used on the bench make the whole construction rigid and prevent a see-ing by the floorboards.

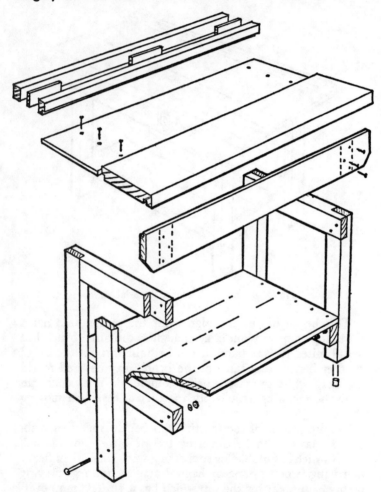

Fig 101   Woodwork bench. Exploded view with brace omitted

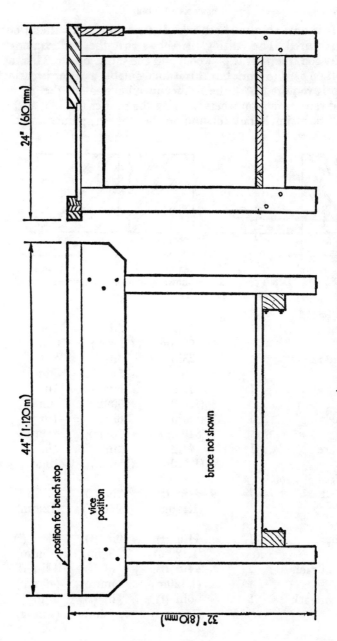

24" (610 mm)

44" (1·120 m)

32' (810 mm)

position for bench stop

vice position

brace not shown

Fig 102 Woodwork bench. Working drawing

It is advisable to check overall sizes and make alterations if required. The cutting list shows that the underframe is softwood, the well is plywood, and the top is beech. This top will be hard to work but this is unavoidable as a hardwearing top is required. Ask the timber merchant to cut the groove and rebates for you when ordering the timber (fig 103) as this will be a simple task for him on the machine planer and circular saw.

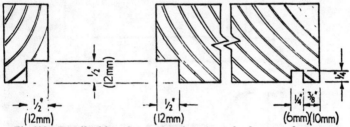

Fig 103   Detail of bench top showing sizes of rebates and grooves

☐ CUTTING LIST

Softwood

Legs	4	31in (790mm)	3in (75mm)	2in (50mm)
End rails	4	23in (580mm)	3in (75mm)	2in (50mm)
Apron	1	45in (1.140m)	6in (150mm)	1in (25mm)
Shelving	4	33in (840mm)	6in (150mm)	1in (25mm)
Brace	1	44in (1.120m)	3in (75mm)	1in (25mm)

Birch Plywood

Well	1	44in (f) (1.120m)	12in (f) (305mm)	12in (12mm)

Beech

Top	1	44in (f) (1.120m)	10in (f) (250mm)	1¾in (f) (45mm)
Tool rack	2	44in (f) (1.120m)	1in (f) (25mm)	1¾in (f) (45mm)
Tool rack	3	6in (f) (150mm)	¾in (f) (20mm)	1¾in (f) (45mm)

Hardware	8	4in x ¼in (100mm x 6mm) coach bolts with nut and washer
	4	rubber door stops for feet, about 1in (25mm) diameter

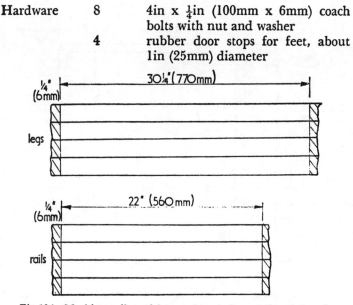

Fig 104   Marking rails and legs to length for woodwork bench

Mark out the legs and rails to length as shown in figure 104. Mark the pieces together as a set using a marking knife, try square, and steel rule, then separate the pieces and square the lines around each. Saw accurately to length with a tenon saw.

Mark out the position of the joints (fig 105) in pencil. W refers to the exact width of the timber and will of course be in the region of 2¾in (70mm).

Set a marking guage to half the thickness of the wood and gauge the corner halving. Mark the shoulder line with a marking knife working against a try square. Cut the corner halving joint either as you would a lap butt joint or a one-sided (barefaced) tenon. Screw and glue the corner halvings together.

Place the bottom rail in position and cramp firmly to the leg. Drill through the leg and rail. Bolt the rail in position with two coach bolts at each point.

Notch the apron around the legs by carefully marking the position then sawing across the grain and removing the waste with either a chisel or router to ¼in (6mm) depth.

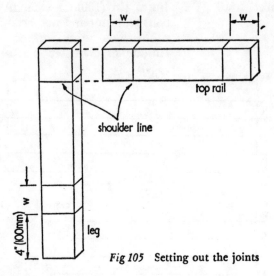

Fig 105 Setting out the joints

Prepare a tongue on the apron to fit the groove in the bench top. Use a rebate plane for this. Make sure that the correct part of the apron is removed—check twice and cut once! The tongue and groove may be glued together.

Make the rack for small tools by glueing the pieces together. Cramp until the glue has set.

Screw the apron front to the end frames. Leave this as a dry joint (do not glue); then the bench can be dismantled. The top can be fastened to the rails by metal brackets. Screw the plywood well to the rails and attach the tool rack with metal angle brackets. The shelf boards may be screwed to the lower end rails. Drill into the bottoms of the legs to take the rubber feet.

Figure 106 shows how the vice is fixed to the bench. A hole has to be cut in the apron front to allow part of the vice to pass through. Four ⅜in (9mm) coach screws hold the vice securely in place under the bench top. Coach screws are merely wood screws that have a square head, these being turned with a box spanner. A clearance and pilot hole must be drilled to enable the screw to be tightened with reasonable ease. In most instances a packing piece has to be inserted between the vice

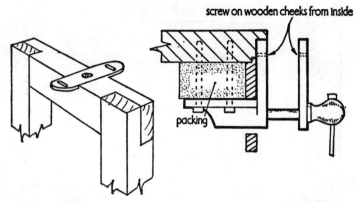

Fig 106 Fixing of bench top to rails with metal plates. The elongated screw holes allow the top to expand and contract across the width

and underside of the top so that the top of the jaws may be ½in (12mm) below the surface of the bench. This is necessary to keep the teeth of the tenon saw away from the steel jaws of the vice. In this way accidential damage to the saw is prevented. A small rebate will have to be worked in the edge of the top with a chisel.

Two pieces of wood 10in (250mm) x 3½in (90mm) x ⅝in (15mm) must be fitted to the jaws of the vice. These will prevent bruising of the work. Two threaded holes are provided in each vice jaw to take 5/16in Whitworth set screws. These will hold the wooden cheeks in place.

PAINTED CABINET

☐ CUTTING LIST

Softwood

Top	1	23¾in	x	5¾in (f)	x	⅞in (f)
		(600mm)		(145mm)		(22mm)
Bottom	1	23¾in	x	5¾in (f)	x	⅝in (f)
		(600mm)		(145mm)		(15mm)
Sides	2	12¾in	x	5¾in (f)	x	⅝in (f)
		(325mm)		(145mm)		(15mm)

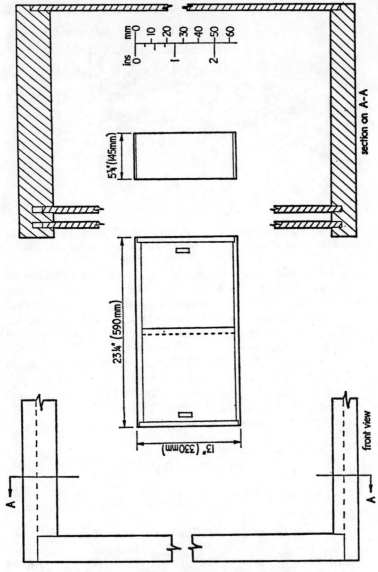

Fig 107 Painted cabinet. Working drawing

Shelf	1	22½in	x	4in (f)	x	⅜in (f)
		(570mm)		(145mm)		(10mm)
Hardboard						
Back & Doors	2	24in	x	13in	x	⅛in
		(610mm)		(330mm)		(3mm)

Choose the face side and face edge of each piece and mark with a pencil. These will be the outside surfaces.

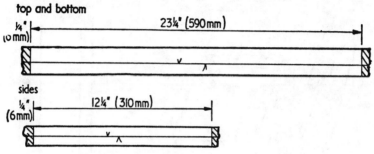

Fig 108 Painted cabinet. Marking to length

Mark out to length.

Mark out and cut a lap butt joint on top and bottom pieces to leave a ⅜in (9mm) tongue.

Plough grooves ⅛in (3mm) wide in top and bottom to contain the hardboard doors. Note that the groove in the top has to be twice the depth of the groove in the bottom. This is to enable the doors to be fitted after glueing up.

Rebate the bottom and sides ¼in (6mm) x ⅛in (3mm) for the hardboard back, and the top ½in (12mm) x ⅛in (3mm).

Clean up the inside surfaces. Pin and glue the joints together. Fit the back with number 16 gauge panel pins before cleaning up the outside and painting. Complete by fitting the doors with a 1¼in (30mm) overlap at the centre.

TRINKET BOX

The box is made as a hollow block, then a saw cut is made all the way round to remove part for a lid. In this way the lid always fits the bottom of the box.

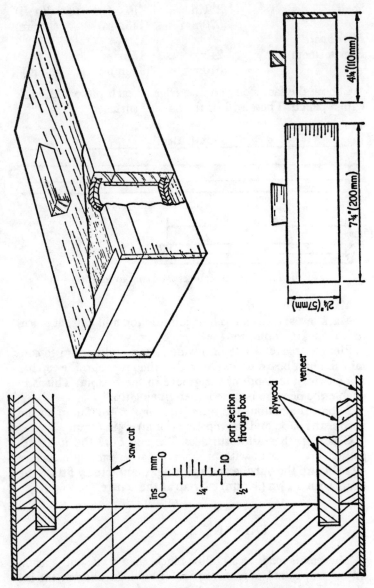

4¼" (110mm)

7¾" (200mm)

2¼" (57mm)

saw cut

part section
through box

mm 0
ins 0   ¼   ½   10

veneer

plywood

Fig 109   Trinket box. Working drawing

☐ CUTTING LIST

It is advisable to cut the sides and ends together so that the grooves may be made more easily.

Top & bottom	4	12¼in (310mm)	x	2⅜in (f) (60mm)	x	7/16in (f) (11mm)
Sides & ends	2	7¾in (200mm)	x	3¼in (f) (110mm)	x	3mm ply
Veneer	2	8in (210mm)	x	4½in (120mm)		
Lining	2	12in (310mm)	x	1½in (f) (40mm)	x	¼in (f) (6mm)
Handle	1	2½in (65mm)	x	¾in (f) (19mm)	x	⅜in (f) (11mm)

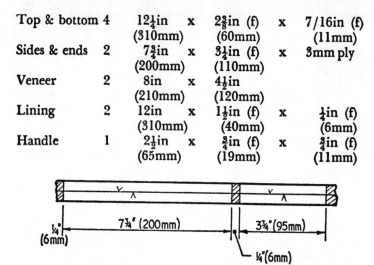

7¾" (200mm)   3¾" (95mm)

¼" (6mm)   ¼" (6mm)

Fig 110   Trinket box. Marking to length

Mark out to length but do not cut until after the grooves have been worked. Support the wood in a sash cramp and hold the sash cramp in a vice when ploughing the grooves.

Cut the lap butt joint in the side pieces in the normal way. Clean up and polish the inside surfaces. Fit the box together and measure for the plywood top and bottom. Plane the plywood to size, then clean up with glasspaper and polish the inside surface.

Check that the box will go together, then glue up the main joints including the plywood top and bottom in the assembly.

When the glue has set fill in the well in the top and bottom with the other pieces of plywood. Glue these in place.

Now sand off the top and bottom surfaces *flat* on a disc sander. Alternatively a smoothing plane can be used to level these surfaces.

There are several methods of veneering but caul veneering is favoured in this instance. Spread an even layer of PVA glue

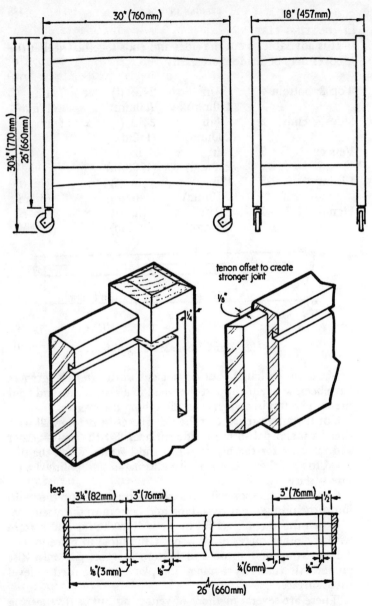

30" (760 mm)

18" (457 mm)

30¼" (770 mm)

26" (660 mm)

tenon offset to create stronger joint

⅛"

¼"

legs

3¼" (82 mm)

3" (76 mm)

3" (76 mm)

½"

⅛" (3 mm)

⅛"

¼" (6 mm)

⅛"

26" (660 mm)

Fig 119   Tea trolley

to the top and bottom of the box taking particular care to glue up to the edges. Lay the veneer on the glued surface, then a blanket of paper, followed by a stout piece of plywood or blockboard. The latter is the caul and must be pressed down on the veneer with G cramps.

Carefully trim the overhanging veneer with a sharp knife. Glasspaper up the whole.

Mark a pencil line on the box for the lid position and separate either with a fine-toothed back saw or on a circular saw with the blade set low. Clean up the raw edge on the disc sander or by hand.

Polish the outside of the box and fit the lining by cutting a mitre on the corners.

A knob for the lid may be shaped with a plane, polished, and secured by two screws from the underside of the lid.

RECORD HOLDER

☐ CUTTING LIST

Hardwood	4	$14\frac{3}{4}$in	x	$3\frac{1}{2}$in (f)	x	$\frac{1}{2}$in (f)
		(370mm)		(90mm)		(12mm)
Birch						
Plywood	2	$14\frac{1}{2}$in	x	$14\frac{1}{2}$in	x	4mm
		(370mm)		(370mm)		

Place the wood face edge upwards in the vice and mark to length (fig 111). Hatch in the waste with a pencil then mark in the shoulder line for the joint with a knife. Remove the wood from the vice and square the lines around each piece.

Saw off the waste and number the neighbouring joints on the outside surface (fig 112). Try to arrange the pieces with the grain matching on the corners.

Mark out the dovetails and cut in the normal way for a thorough dovetail joint. Fit the joints carefully. Tap them together with a hammer and block of wood. When correct, clean up and polish the inside surfaces.

Cramp up dry, then glue up. Check the diagonals for equal length. When the glue has set clean up the edges with a smoothing plane.

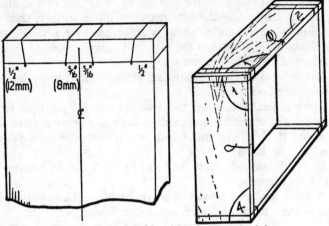

Fig 112   Record holder. Marking out the joints

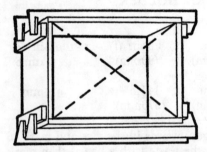

Fig 113   Record holder. Cramping up the frame and checking the diagonals for equal length

Fit the plywood to front and back. Secure in place with ¾in (19mm) No 4 chromium plated raised head screws. Avoid putting screws where they will interfere with sawing off the lid.

Mark a line for the lid position and cut through the box with a fine toothed back saw. Plane ⅛in (3mm) from the plywood back to create a gap at the hinge position. Glue a 2in (50mm) wide strip of linen on either side of the plywood with contact adhesive. This forms a cloth hinge which is simple and unobtrusive, yet very strong. Cover the outside of the plywood with sticky-back plastic and allow some to wrap around the edges onto the inside. Cover the inside surface of the plywood

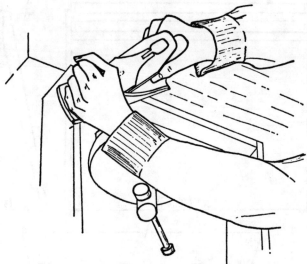

Fig 114   Record holder. Place the frame in the vice and clean
up the edges with a smoothing plane

with another piece of plastic and screw back onto the box. Fit
the handle with round-head screws and the catches with bi-
furcated rivets.

FLOWER TROUGH

☐ CUTTING LIST

Trough	1	36in (915mm)	x	5in (130mm)	x	$\frac{5}{8}$in (f) (16mm)
	2	7in (180mm)	x	8in (200mm)	x	$\frac{5}{8}$in (f) (16mm)
	2	36in (915mm)	x	1in (f) x (25mm)		$\frac{3}{8}$in (f) (10mm)
	2	36in (915mm)	x	$1\frac{3}{16}$in (f) x (30mm)		$\frac{3}{8}$in (f) (10mm)
	2	36in (915mm)	x	$1\frac{3}{4}$in (f) x (35mm)		$\frac{3}{8}$in (f) (10mm)
Legs	4	32in (810mm)	x	2in (50mm)	x	1in (25mm)

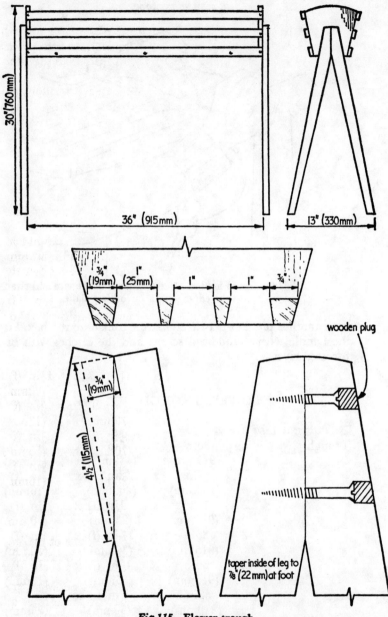

30" (760mm)

36" (915mm)

13" (330mm)

¾" (19mm)

1" (25mm)

1"

1"

¾"

¾" 1" (19mm)

4½" (115mm)

wooden plug

taper inside of leg to ⅞ (22 mm) at foot

Fig 115 **Flower trough**

The main strength of the flower trough is given by the two sets of through dovetail joints. When the legs are fitted these joints are concealed. The legs may be either screwed together, as illustrated, or dowel jointed.

This trough fits well in the alcove of a french window. Alternatively the legs can be replaced by feet and the trough stood on the window-sill. A plastic tray will catch drips from the flower pots.

COFFEE TABLE

This is a coffee table of traditional design. The original was made entirely from solid mahogany.

To overcome the problem of continual expansion and contraction, the top is fastened to the frame with wooden buttons. The construction of buttons is explained later. Notice how the underside of the top has been chamfered to give a thinner, more delicate appearance to the edge of the table top. The legs are not square in section. The wider surface is placed on the side frame to balance the proportions.

☐ CUTTING LIST

Legs	4	18in (460mm)	x	$1\frac{3}{8}$in (f) (35mm)	x	$1\frac{1}{4}$in (f) (32mm)
Rails	2	30in (760mm)	x	$2\frac{3}{4}$in (f) (70mm)	x	$\frac{3}{4}$in (f) (19mm)
	2	14in (360mm)	x	$2\frac{3}{4}$in (f) (70mm)	x	$\frac{3}{4}$in (f) (19mm)
Top	1	33in (840mm)	x	$16\frac{1}{2}$in (f) (420mm)	x	$\frac{5}{8}$in (f) (16mm)

The top may have to be several pieces which are edge jointed together.

Make a face side mark on the best $1\frac{3}{8}$in surface of the leg, then make a face edge mark on the best edge. These reference sides will be on the outside of the finished job.

Mark the legs to length and hatch in the waste. Mark the mortise limit lines with a pencil. Square the knife lines all the way round each leg but square the pencil lines only onto

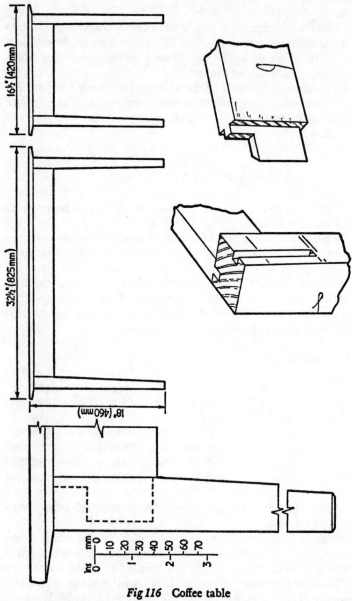

Fig 116   Coffee table

the other inside surface. Mark the rails to length and mark in the shoulder lines. Saw the rails to length.

Set the spurs of a mortise gauge to $\frac{1}{4}$in (6mm) mortise chisel. Set the stock of the gauge $\frac{1}{4}$in from the adjustable spur in order to mark in the centre on the edge of the rail. Gauge the mortises and tenons the normal way working from the face side in each case.

Cut the mortise proper. That is to say leave the haunch alone. The mortises will meet inside the leg. Saw the tenon in the normal way. The tenon has now to be cut down to size. Mark $\frac{1}{8}$in (3mm) cover at the bottom in pencil. The tenon will occupy two-thirds the width of the rail. The haunch is like a shorter tenon, being $\frac{1}{4}$in (6mm) long. Mark the haunch in pencil and remove the waste with a tenon saw. Saw down the sides of the mortise to $\frac{1}{4}$in deep and chisel out the waste to form the haunch in the leg. Mitre the ends of the tenons to prevent fouling in the mortise.

When the joints fit correctly, number them and clean up and polish the inside surfaces. Cramp up the two big frames dry. Check each framework carefully and when correct glue the two large frames separately. *On no account attempt to glue the whole table together in one stage.* When the glue has set cramp the whole up dry. Check carefully and when correct glue up.

Clean up all the outside surfaces. Do not leave sharp corners (arrises). Round corners to about $\frac{1}{8}$in radius circle using a smoothing plane or glasspaper. Polish when ready.

The top can be prepared as for a normal piece of timber. Should it be made up from several pieces, place pairs of boards together in the vice and plane the adjacent edges flat and square. Glue the edges and cramp the boards together (see sash cramp). The edges of the top should be carefully rounded. Glasspaper the end grain to make it smooth. When well pleased with the surface, it can be polished.

Table tops can be secured to the rails with metal angle plates but the traditional method of holding the top in place is with wooden buttons (fig 117). For this a mortise is chopped $1\frac{1}{4}$in (32mm) long with a $\frac{1}{4}$in (6mm) mortise chisel. The mortise is positioned $\frac{1}{2}$in (12mm) from the top edge of the rail.

The buttons for one table can be constructed together. For

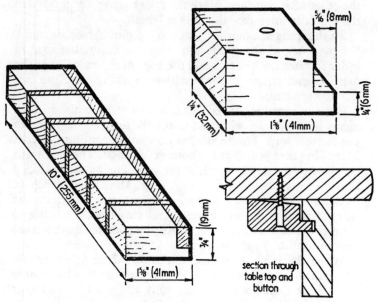

Fig 117 Buttons

six buttons select a sound piece of hardwood finished to 1⅝in
(41mm) x 10in (260mm) x ¾in (19mm). Note the direction of
the grain.

Mark each individual button 1¼in (32mm) wide and leave
¼in (6mm) space for waste between each. Now draw the diagonals on each button. This will give the position for the screw.
Rebate the edge to leave a 𝟷/₁₆in x ¼in tongue (fig 117) and drill
𝟷/₁₆in for the screws. Countersink for a No 8 screw and plane
the strip to finish as shown in the sectional diagram. Finally
saw the buttons from the strip and polish them.

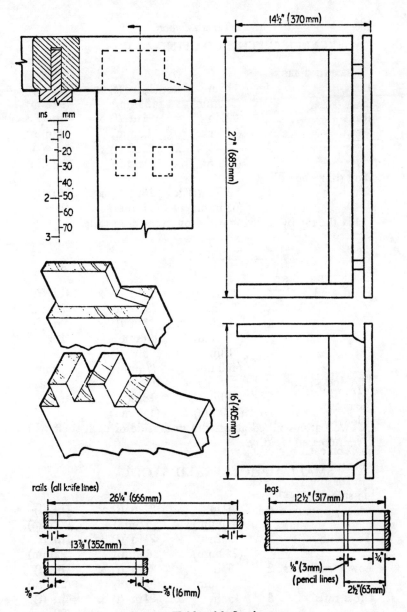

ins mm

Fig 118 Table with floating top

TABLE WITH FLOATING TOP

☐ CUTTING LIST

Legs	4	13in (330mm)	x	$1\frac{3}{8}$in (f) (35mm)	x	$7\frac{1}{4}$in (f) (32mm)
Rails	2	27in (700mm)	x	$2\frac{1}{2}$in (f) (63mm)	x	$\frac{7}{8}$in (f) (22mm)
	2	16in (400mm)	x	$3\frac{3}{4}$in (f) (95mm)	x	$\frac{7}{8}$in (f) (22mm)
Top (blockboard)	1	27in (f) (685mm)	x	16in (f) (410mm)	x	$\frac{3}{4}$in (f) (19mm)

Fix the top by screwing up through the cross rails.

TEA TROLLEY

☐ CUTTING LIST

Hardwood	4	$26\frac{1}{2}$in (680mm)	x	$1\frac{1}{4}$in (f) (32mm)	x	$1\frac{1}{4}$in (f) (32mm)
	4	30in (760mm)	x	3in (f) (76mm)	x	$\frac{3}{4}$in (f) (19mm)
	4	18in (460mm)	x	3in (f) (76mm)	x	$\frac{3}{4}$in (f) (19mm)
Plywood shelves	2	30in (760mm)	x	18in (460mm)	x	4mm

Two battens glued across the underside of each shelf will give increased rigidity.

SMALL UPHOLSTERED STOOL

☐ CUTTING LIST

Legs	4	$16\frac{1}{2}$in (420mm)	x	$2\frac{1}{4}$in (f) (57mm)	x	$\frac{7}{8}$in (f) (22mm)
Top end rails	2	$9\frac{1}{2}$in (240mm)	x	$2\frac{1}{4}$in (f) (63mm)	x	$\frac{7}{8}$in (f) (22mm)
Lower end rails	2	$9\frac{1}{2}$in (240mm)	x	$2\frac{1}{2}$in (f) (57mm)	x	$\frac{7}{8}$in (f) (22mm)
Cross rails	3	$15\frac{1}{2}$in (400mm)	x	$2\frac{1}{4}$in (f) (57mm)	x	$\frac{3}{8}$in (f) (22mm)

Materials for the seat are also required.

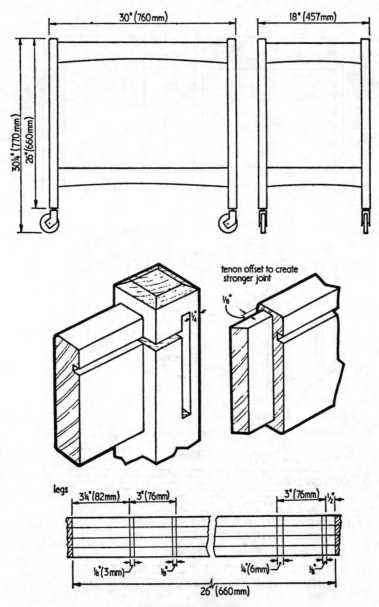

30" (760mm)

18" (457mm)

30¼" (770mm)

26" (660mm)

tenon offset to create stronger joint

⅛"

¼"

legs

3¼" (82mm)

3" (76mm)

3" (76mm)

½"

⅛" (3mm)

⅛"

¼" (6mm)

½"

26" (660mm)

Fig 119 **Tea trolley**

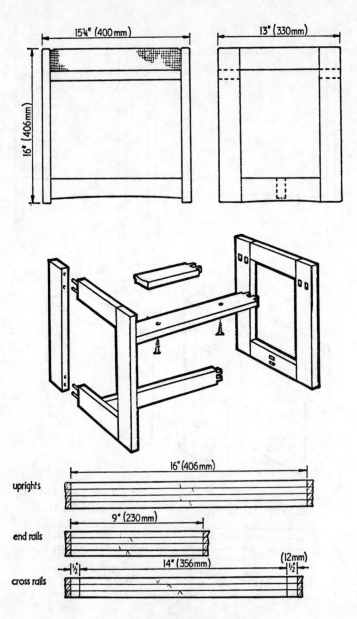

15¾" (400 mm)

13" (330mm)

16" (406mm)

16" (406mm)

uprights

9" (230 mm)

end rails

14" (356mm)

(12mm)

1½

1½

cross rails

Fig 120   Small upholstered stool

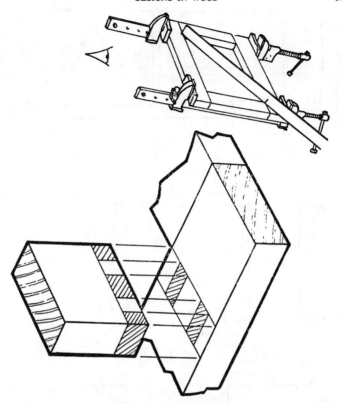

Fig 121 Small upholstered stool. Checking framework for squareness
and flatness. Marking out the joint

Work on the side frames first. Dowel the joints together,
clean up and polish the inside edges, then glue up. Take care
that the frames are identical in shape and size. Sight across
each frame for twist, check the diagonals for equal length, and
correct any discrepancy that is discovered before leaving the
frames for the glue to set. Mark out and cut the joints for the
cross rails after the side frames have been glued up.

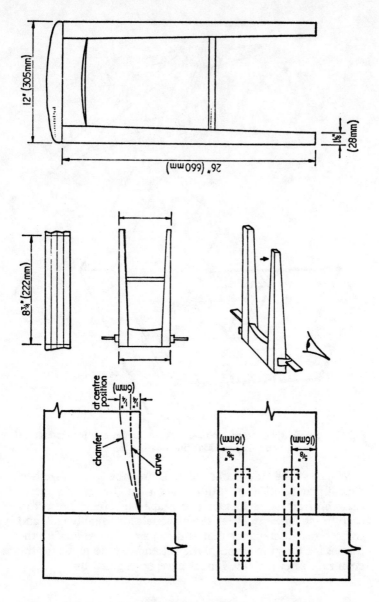

Fig 122 High stool

HIGH STOOL

Legs	4	$26\frac{1}{2}$in (680mm)	x	$1\frac{5}{8}$in (f) x (41mm)	$1\frac{5}{8}$in (f) (41mm)
Rails	4	$9\frac{1}{4}$in (240mm)	x	$2\frac{1}{2}$in (f) x (63mm)	$\frac{7}{8}$in (f) (22mm)

Kicking Rails of aluminium or stainless steel.

4ft   x $\frac{5}{8}$in diameter
1.200m   16mm

The legs are drilled for these and *araldite* will secure them in place.

This is a more difficult model to assemble than the small stool so take special care when checking for truth.

Material is required for the seat.

□ UPHOLSTERING THE TOP

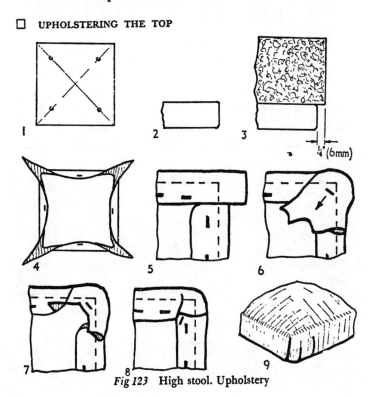

Fig 123 High stool. Upholstery

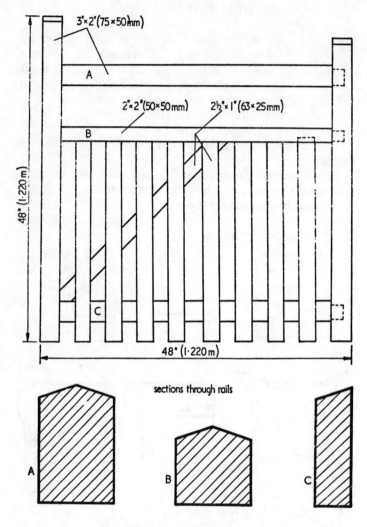

3″×2″ (75×50 mm)

A

2″×2″ (50×50 mm)   2½″×1″ (63×25 mm)

B

48″ (1·220 m)

C

48″ (1·220 m)

sections through rails

A   B   C

Fig 124 **Garden gate**

Covering: vinyl leathercloth with flexknit backing.

1 Cut the seat to size in $\frac{1}{2}$in plywood or $\frac{3}{4}$in blockboard. Drill four air escape holes.

2 Round off the sharp edges with a rasp or plane. This will prevent the top covering being cut through in use.

3 The 2in foam should be cut $\frac{1}{2}$in oversize all the way round. It can be worked with a bandsaw or with scissors. Remove the sharp corner of the foam with scissors or it will show as a line across the top covering. Glue the foam to the plywood to prevent it shifting.

4 Cut the cover oversize. Work the top upside down. Pull out the centre of each side in turn firmly and tack or staple with a trigger gun. Check that the profile of the seat is correct.

5 Tack from the centre of each side towards the corner. Replace any offending staples where the cover is not tensioned satisfactorily.

6 Pull the corner hard and tack across.

7 Cut off the surplus covering by making three cuts.

8 & 9 Tuck the surplus under and pull top down and staple. This may require some time to obtain the best results.

GARDEN GATE

When the brace is in the position shown in the illustration the hinges must be fitted to the left-hand stile. Bevelling the top surfaces of all members helps to deflect the rain and prevent early rotting of the timber. The pailings can be fitted in shallow bare-faced mortises in the centre rail and then secured to the brace and bottom rail with screws.

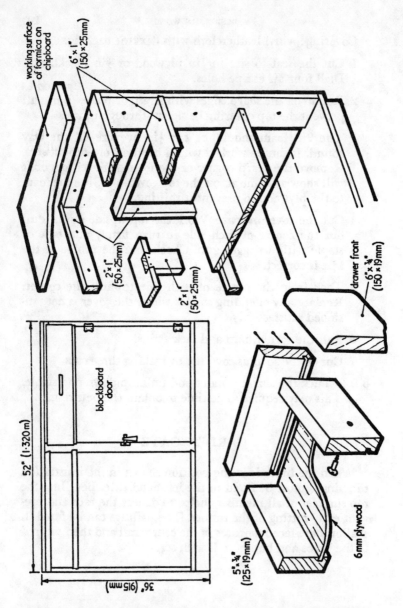

Fig 125 Built in furniture. A guide to the construction of a cupboard

BUILT-IN FURNITURE

One example of built-in furniture has pinewood shelving coated with clear polyurethane varnish which is supported by battens plugged to the wall. The shelves are spaced to suit the items they have to contain.

Units built into the kitchen are also very popular. Figure 125 suggests one method of tackling this work. This will provide shelf and cupboard space, a simply made drawer, and a plastic-covered working surface.

DINING CHAIR

☐ CUTTING LIST

Back legs	2	$31\frac{1}{2}$in (800mm)	x	4in (100mm)	x	$\frac{7}{8}$in (f) (22mm)
Front legs	2	$18\frac{1}{2}$in (470mm)	x	$1\frac{3}{4}$in (f) (45mm)	x	$\frac{7}{8}$in (f) (22mm)
Side seat rails	2	16in (410mm)	x	2in (f) (50mm)	x	$\frac{7}{8}$in (f) (22mm)
Front, back seat rails	2	18in (460mm)	x	2in (f) (50mm)	x	$\frac{7}{8}$in (f) (22mm)
Bottom rails	3	18in (460mm)	x	$1\frac{1}{4}$in (f) (32mm)	x	$\frac{7}{8}$in (f) (22mm)
Back rails	2	18in (460mm)	x	2in (f) (50mm)	x	2in (f) (50mm)

Materials for the seat are also required.

Consider the side frames first and make a start by planing the taper on the inside of the front legs. The bottom of the foot should finish $1\frac{1}{8}$in (29mm) by $\frac{7}{8}$in (22mm). Mark out the shaping on the back legs but shape only the inside surface of the back leg at this stage. If the whole of the shaping was done it would prove difficult to hold the back leg when cutting the joints.

Set out the wood for the side frames. Use a marking knife, sliding bevel and try square to mark the shoulder lines on the rails. Mark the mortise limit lines with pencil on the legs

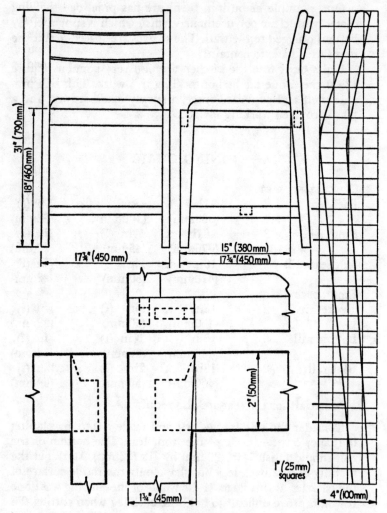

Fig 126 **Dining chair**

Gauge the four mortise and tenon joints on each frame. One joint will have a secret (sloping) haunch as illustrated, but the other three joints are straightforward stub mortise and tenon joints. Cut these joints then complete the shaping on the back legs. Remove most of the waste from the legs with a hand saw then place both legs together and clean them up with a spokeshave. This will ensure greater uniformity. If it is planned to make a set of these chairs a cardboard template for the back legs will prove helpful.

Clean up the inside surfaces, polish, and glue up the side frames before proceeding further.

Five rails are used to join the side frames together. These rails can be tenoned into the side frames. Alternatively, cut the rails accurately to length and dowel them in position. Take care to offset the joints on the ends of the back rails. The latter are next shaped to a smooth curve finishing each rail to $\frac{5}{8}$in (16mm) thick.

The seat is made from $\frac{1}{2}$in (12mm) plywood and is padded with foam. The covering material is wrapped over the foam and tacked underneath the plywood. Four wooden corner blocks are screwed inside the chair frame $\frac{1}{2}$in (12mm) below the top edge of the seat rails. These blocks support the seat and strengthen the chair.

MAKING AND FITTING A DRAWER

To make a drawer that works is one of the most difficult woodworking operations. The following is offered as a guide to the person who seeks this challenge.

A good quality drawer is held together by dovetail joints. A lap dovetail joint is used at the front of the drawer as this conceals the joint and gives a better appearance. Through dovetails are used at the back of the drawer. Tradition dictates that the bottom of the drawer is made from solid wood, though plywood does offer a good alternative. The grain of the bottom of the drawer must run from side to side of the drawer and never front to back. The bottom is fitted in a groove. This allows a solid timber bottom to expand out the back of the drawer, the drawer back being narrower than the sides and

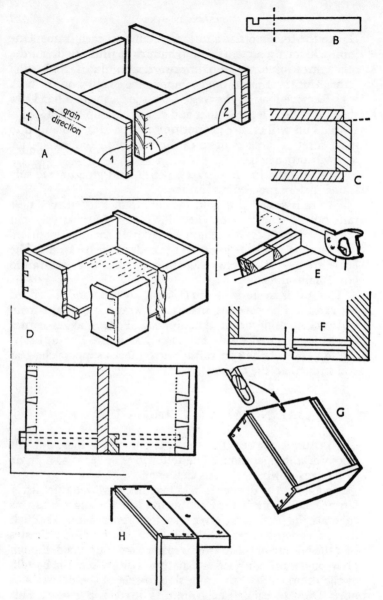

Fig 127 Making and fitting a drawer

allowing this to happen. Quite often the drawer sides are made from this material $\frac{1}{16}$in (18mm) thick. To increase the wear resistance of the drawer a slip of wood is glued to the side. This slip can carry the groove for the drawer bottom.

1 Select the timber for direction of grain. It is helpful when planing the sides of the drawer if the grain runs from the front of the drawer to the back. Quarter sawn oak is best for the side rails. Choose these out of stuff at least $\frac{5}{8}$in (16mm) too wide. Curly grain timber can be used for the drawer bottom. Mark the lower outside corners as shown.

2 Plane up the inside faces of the drawer using a trying plane.

3 Square the bottom edges of the side rails.

4 Plough a $\frac{1}{8}$in (3mm) groove in the drawer side and saw for the side slips. It is easier to groove a wide piece of wood and saw off the piece required than it is to plough a groove in a very small section of wood (fig 128b).

5 Plane a face edge on the drawer sides.

6 Gauge and plane the drawer sides to width so that they just fit inside the carcase.

7 Plane the bottom edge of the front piece square and to the shape of the carcase.

8 Plane one end of the front piece to fit the carcase and plane the other end likewise so that the front is a snug fit lengthwise.

9 Plane the front piece to width to fit the carcase. Make the top edge one shaving out of square so that the drawer front enters for only half its thickness (fig 127c).

10 Plough a groove on the inside of the front piece. This will receive the drawer bottom. Allow at least $\frac{1}{4}$in (6mm) underneath the bottom for drawer stops.

11 Plane the back rail to width (usually $\frac{1}{2}$in [13mm] narrower than the drawer sides) and to a tight fit lengthwise.

12 Gauge the front and back rails for length of pin. The side rails are at present thicker than they will finish so set the cutting gauge to the final thickness of the side rails.

13 Gauge for length of tail across the end grain of the front rail (usually $\frac{2}{3}$ thickness of the front rail).

14   Saw the sides to length (somewhat shorter than the depth of the carcase). Place these together in the vice and plane the ends square.

15   Gauge the length of tails around both pieces.

16   Mark out the tails. Allow for the groove in the front rail, and for the fact that the back rail is narrow (fig 127d).

17   Saw the tails together (fig 127e).

18   Separate the pieces and remove the waste from between the tails in the normal way.

19   Mark the pins from the tails using a scriber.

20   Cut the pins. This is straightforward with the through dovetail joint at the back of the drawer, but the lap dovetail on the drawer front is a little more difficult. Cramp the work flat on the edge of the bench and saw down the sides of the joint as far as possible. This will be an angle cut on the waste side of the lines. The rest of the waste has to be removed with a chisel. Work downwards across the grain then into the joint from the end. Make sure the chiselled surfaces are vertical then fit the joint.

21   Polish the inside surfaces of the drawer but avoid polish on the joints and where the slips are to be glued.

22   Glue up using a hammer and block of wood to close the joint. Use sash cramps just to squeeze out the excess glue. Check the diagonals to ensure the drawer is square, and check the drawer for wind (twist). Leave for the glue to dry.

23   Cut the drawer slips to length. Fit them, then glue and cramp them in place (fig 127f).

24   Plane the drawer bottom to remove any saw marks. It may be necessary to glue several pieces together to make one wide board. Check that the direction of grain will be across the drawer.

25   Rebate the ends of the drawer bottom to form a tongue that will fit the groove in the drawer slips. Slide the bottom in place and mark the front edge of the drawer. Plane this edge true then rebate so that the bottom fits into the groove on the front. Glue the drawer at the front corners and along the front edge of the drawer. Fit one or more slotted screws in the underside back (fig 127g).

26 Plane down the sides to the end grain of the front and back pieces. Use a trying plane and a planing block screwed to the bench top. Plane from the front of the drawer to the back.

27 Place the drawer in position and plane the front level with the carcase. A little *Ronuk* rubbed onto the drawer will make it work well.

CHILD'S DESK

☐ CUTTING LIST

Sides	2	20½in (520mm)	x	4in (100mm)	x	⅝in (f) (15mm)
Ends	2	16½in (420mm)	x	4in (100mm)	x	⅝in (f) (15mm)
Top	1	21in (f) (533mm)	x	17in (f) (430mm)	x	12mm plywood
Bottom	1	20¼in(f) (540mm)	x	16¼in(f) (412mm)	x	4mm plywood
Back	1	21½in (545mm)	x	1½in (f) (38mm)	x	⅝in (f) (15mm)
Legs	4	21½in (545mm)	x	2in (50mm)	x	1in (25mm)
Rails	2	9in (230mm)	x	2in (50mm)	x	1in (25mm)

Construction starts on this desk by making a framework with the corners joined by through dovetail joints. A plywood bottom that is attached to the framework with panel pins provides extra rigidity. The top should be sawn 4in (100mm) from the long edge and a piano hinge inserted along this cut. This will make an opening lid, the back portion being attached to the framework with screws.

The legs can be attached to the rails using either a secret (sloping) haunched mortise and tenon joint or a dowel joint. The shoulder line for the joint on the rail should be marked out to a slope of 1 in 14 using a sliding bevel. Attach the legs to the desk by screwing from the inside of the framework.

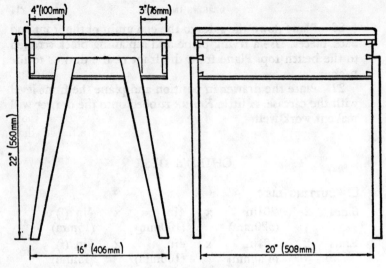

Fig 128 Child's desk

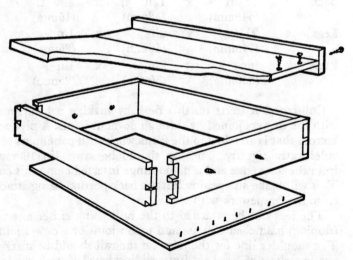

Fig 129 Child's desk. Exploded view

Appendix A

LIST OF HAND TOOLS RECOMMENDED

This list is given as a guide. It represents the tools that can form the nucleus of a kit.

Only the best tools should be bought. It is better to pay good money for tools now than discover later that your tools are inferior in quality. Always buy branded goods. Brands that can be recommended are Disston, Eclipse, Irwin USA, Marples, Millers Falls USA, Moore & Wright, Record, Ridgway, Stanley, Spear & Jackson, Woden.

The similarity in appearance between steel planes of different manufacture is very noticeable. The designer of the modern steel plane was Bailey, an American. He spent many years with Stanley Works USA. When the patent expired, planes of the Bailey design became manufactured by other firms. Some firms retain the original system of numbering the planes, eg 04, 05. Today the name Bailey can still be seen on the body casting of the planes produced by Stanley Works GB.

Crosscut handsaw   22in (560mm)   10ppi
(can be used for ripping, crosscutting and for cutting plywood)

Tenon saw   10in (250mm)   15ppi

Dovetail saw   8in (200mm)   18ppi

Coping saw and 10 blades

Firmer chisels $\frac{5}{8}$in (16mm), 1in (25mm)

Bevelled edge chisels $\frac{3}{16}$in (5mm), $\frac{1}{4}$in (6mm), $\frac{1}{2}$in (13mm)

Mortise chisels $\frac{1}{4}$in (6mm), $\frac{5}{16}$in (8mm)

Steel jack plane   no 05$\frac{1}{2}$ - 15in (380mm) x 2$\frac{3}{8}$in (60mm)

Steel smoothing plane   no 04   - 9$\frac{3}{4}$in (250mm) x 2in   (50mm)

Steel shoulder plane   no 041 - $\frac{5}{8}$in (16mm)

Spokeshave, flat, metal

Spokeshave, small round, wood

Marking knife (or small penknife)

Steel rule   12in (300mm)

'Pull-push' tape rule   6ft (2m)

Try square   6in (150mm)

Marking gauge

Mortise gauge, screw adjustment

Cutting gauge

Sliding bevel

Hand drill

Twist drills, high speed steel (HSS)
$\frac{1}{16}$in (2mm), $\frac{1}{8}$in (3mm)
$\frac{3}{16}$in (5mm), $\frac{1}{4}$in (6mm)

Round shank countersink bit

Brace and bits

Cabinet screwdriver   8in (200mm)

Mallet   5in (130mm)

Warrington hammer   14oz (400g)

Cork block

Medium oilstone   8in (200mm) x 2in (50mm) x 1in (25mm)

Appendix B

SOME SUPPLIERS

AMER MACHY & MOTOR CO INC
    22Howrd Manh ------------ **212 226-4577**
CELASCHI INC
    249WMerickRd VlyStrm ------- **LO 1-8697**
DELTA ROCKWELL TOOLS—
    BASS RUDOLF
    Sales, Parts, Service
    175Lafyet Manh --------- **212 226-4000**

Festo Woodworking Machines Inc
    10SintsinkDrE PtWash ---------**883-2671**
Joyce Research&Develpmt Corp
    249WMerikRd VlyStrm --------**LO 1-8697**
MITCHELL GEORGE M MACH CORP
    Delta, Dewalt, resto, Ramco, Holtz
    100Grand Manh ----------**212 226-6460**
Nut-House Mill&Hardware Supl Co Inc
    Rockwell, Skil, Delta, Black-Decker
    164 S OceanAv Ptchog---------**289-8220**
POWERMATIC WOODWORKING MACHINES—
      DISTRIBUTORS
    AMER MACHY & MOTOR CO INC
    22Howrd Manh ----------- **212 226-4577**

Reiner Machy Corp
    1655JerchoTpk NwHvdPk ------ **GE 7-8080**
SUPREME WOODWORKING MACHINERY
    CORP 200BrdhloRd Frmgdl----------**694-5005**
Tanner of Long Island Inc
    Rockwell, Skil, Delta, Black-Decker
    164 S OceanAv Ptchog---------**475-2090**
Vicens Woodcraft Ltd
    29LincolnAv RslynHts ----------**484-1476**
WEINIG MICHL K G WOODWORKING
    MACHY CORP
    249WMerikRd VlyStrm -------- **LO 1-8697**

General Index

The Complete Book
of Woodwork

Revised edition

Charles H. Hayward

Drake Publishers Inc. New York

ISBN 87749–665–X
Library of Congress Catalog Card Number 74–6079

This revised edition published in 1974 by
Drake Publishers Inc.
801 Second Avenue
New York, N.Y. 10017

© Charles H. Hayward 1959

Contents

Metrication

The changeover from Imperial to metric measurement has resulted in certain complications in the dimensions given in this book for both tools and designs. So far as tools are concerned it makes little difference because the exact length of a plane, saw, or whatever it may be does not affect its working. Generally we have given both metric and Imperial sizes but it will be realised that none of them will work out exactly. In the designs and their cutting lists we have kept to metric sizes as timber nowadays is nearly all sold to these dimensions. Those who prefer to work to Imperial sizes should use the following conversion table, or better still should use a flexible rule which has metric sizes at one edge and Imperial at the other. Remember, however, that the conversion will not work out exactly, but providing one keeps to one or the other throughout, there should not be any difficulty. Another useful detail to note is that in the timber trade 25mm. is taken as equalling 1in. Here again it is not exact, and in a large item there will be a marked divergence which should be allowed for.

Woodworkers' Conversion Tables

Imperial inches	Metric millimetres	Woodworkers' parlance (mm.)	Metric millimetres	Imperial inches	Woodworkers' parlance (in.)
$\frac{1}{32}$	8·0	1 bare	1	0·039	$\frac{1}{16}$ bare
$\frac{1}{16}$	1·6	$1\frac{1}{2}$	2	0·078	$\frac{1}{16}$ full
$\frac{1}{8}$	3·2	3 full	3	0·118	$\frac{1}{8}$ bare
$\frac{3}{16}$	4·8	5 bare	4	0·157	$\frac{5}{32}$
$\frac{1}{4}$	6·4	$6\frac{1}{2}$	5	0·196	$\frac{3}{16}$ full
$\frac{5}{16}$	7·9	8 bare	6	0·236	$\frac{1}{4}$ bare
$\frac{3}{8}$	9·5	$9\frac{1}{2}$	7	0·275	$\frac{1}{4}$ full
$\frac{7}{16}$	11·1	11 full	8	0·314	$\frac{5}{16}$
$\frac{1}{2}$	12·7	$12\frac{1}{2}$ full	9	0·354	$\frac{3}{8}$ bare
$\frac{9}{16}$	14·3	$14\frac{1}{2}$ bare	10	0·393	$\frac{3}{8}$ full
$\frac{5}{8}$	15·9	16 bare	20	0·787	$\frac{13}{16}$ bare
$\frac{11}{16}$	17·5	$17\frac{1}{2}$	30	1·181	$1\frac{3}{16}$
$\frac{3}{4}$	19·1	19 full	40	1·574	$1\frac{9}{16}$ full
$\frac{13}{16}$	20·6	$20\frac{1}{2}$	50	1·968	$1\frac{15}{16}$ full
$\frac{7}{8}$	22·2	22 full	60	2·362	$2\frac{3}{8}$ bare
$\frac{15}{16}$	23·8	24 bare	70	2·755	$2\frac{3}{4}$
1	25·4	$25\frac{1}{2}$	80	3·148	$3\frac{1}{8}$ full
2	50·8	51 bare	90	3·542	$3\frac{9}{16}$ bare
3	76·2	76 full	100	3·936	$3\frac{15}{16}$
4	101·4	$101\frac{1}{2}$	150	5·904	$5\frac{15}{16}$ bare
5	127·0	127	200	7·872	$7\frac{7}{8}$
6	152·4	$152\frac{1}{2}$	300	11·808	$11\frac{13}{16}$
7	177·5	178 bare	400	15·744	$15\frac{3}{4}$
8	203·2	203 full	500	19·680	$19\frac{11}{16}$ full
9	228·6	$228\frac{1}{2}$	600	23·616	$23\frac{5}{8}$ bare
10	254·0	254	700	27·552	$27\frac{9}{16}$
11	279·5	$279\frac{1}{2}$	800	31·488	$31\frac{1}{2}$
12	304·8	305 bare	900	35·424	$35\frac{7}{16}$
18	457·2	457 full	1,000	39·360	$39\frac{3}{8}$ bare
24	609·6	$609\frac{1}{2}$			
36	914·4	$914\frac{1}{2}$			

Introduction

Woodwork is a subject with many branches, each of which calls for a book in itself if it is to be dealt with adequately. Many people, however, need a general book which includes information on all the branches of woodwork which the home craftsman is likely to tackle. So this book was written. It does not pretend to cover any particular subject as fully as a book which specializes in that branch, but it does give all basic information, and in this sense it should be the best all-round book for the comparative beginner in the subject.

More people are doing woodwork as a hobby to-day than at any other period, and it is one of the most heartening signs of this age when the temptation to accept things ready-made is almost irresistible. Just as it is so much easier to listen to the music of radio or gramophone than to produce it yourself, so it is simpler to accept the product of the machine which in an effortless way turns out uniform items with a speed and regularity equalled only by its lack of individuality and feeling for the material.

If we have more leisure to-day than ever before, there is so much more temptation to do nothing useful with it. Radio, television, motoring, and the cinema all have their place in the scheme of things, but only too often they claim far more than their share of our spare time, and leave little to show for themselves. Thus it is, one hails this renaissance of handwork with relief, for through it comes the realization of what honesty of construction stands for, and an appreciation of the value of good design. And it is in this that the chief hope for the future lies.

Chapter one

Tools   The Kit

The selection of tools depends to an extent upon the type of work generally to be done, but there is a fundamental range which is always needed. The choice of individual items may vary slightly with the stature and the age of the user, but the list given on pages 11–17 makes a good representative kit, and we have marked with an asterisk the items the beginner should start with. As he progresses the necessity for other tools will become obvious. He can obtain them as the need makes itself felt.

Do not buy a 'complete box of tools'. If you do you will be accepting what someone else thinks you ought to have, and you will have to take the whole without being able to exercise any judgement on the individual items. Quite likely, too, you will pay for some items which you will never use, or which may be unsuitable for you. The best plan is to go to a reliable tool dealer and tell him what you want, explaining that you do not want 'cheap' tools (in fact they are not cheap in the long run). A good, sound tool should last you a lifetime (some last several lifetimes), and, though you pay more for it in the first place, it will easily repay its cost. It may easily happen that in buying a poor quality tool you may be handicapping yourself from the start. A plane or square which is inaccurate; a chisel or screwdriver which is soft; a stone which is liable to become hard; any of these may cause endless and quite unnecessary trouble in the future.

The choice of tools on pages 11–17 has been made on the assumption that the reader is a comparative beginner, and as such is not likely to be considering at present the installation of any machines. Those who have had some experience will know that much back-aching work can be saved by having a small machine, and we therefore give in Chapter VI some advice on the choice and installation of suitable machines. Those who propose to install a machine could modify the kit of hand tools in accordance with the operations the machine can tackle.

It pays in the long run to buy tools by a reputable maker. Faults in poor quality tools such as inaccuracy, second grade metal or bad design soon make themselves felt.

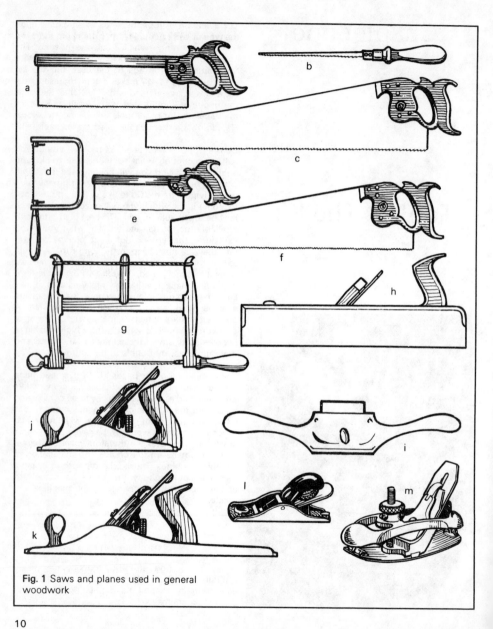

Fig. 1 Saws and planes used in general woodwork

Fig. 1 Special-purpose planes

Fundamental Kit of Tools

Items marked with an asterisk are what we suggest the beginner should start off with.

Saws (Fig. 1)

*(C) Cross-cut saw, 610 or 660mm. (24 or 26in.), teeth 8 or 9 points.

(F) Panel saw, 500mm. (20in.), teeth 10–12 points.

*(A) Tenon saw, 350 or 400mm. (14 or 16in.), teeth 12 or 14 points, brass or iron back.

(E) Dovetail saw, 200mm. (8in.), teeth 18–22 points, brass or iron back.
(If you wish to limit your kit you could substitute a 230 or 250mm. (9 or 10in.) backsaw with teeth about 16 points for the tenon saw and the dovetail saw. The two saws are the better choice, however.)

(G) Bow saw, 300mm. (12in.).

(D) Coping saw, 150mm. (6in.).

(B) Keyhole saw, about 280mm. (11in.).

Planes (Fig. 1)

*(H) Jack plane, wood, 400mm. (16in.), 50mm. (2in.) cutter.

*(J) Smoothing plane, adjustable metal, 228mm. (9in.), 50mm. (2in.) cutter.

(K) Fore plane, adjustable metal, 457mm. (18in.), 60mm. (2⅜in.) cutter.

(Q) Toothing plane, wood, 50mm. (2in.) cutter, medium teeth.

(L) Block plane, 42mm. (1⅝in.) cutter.

(M) Compass plane, 44mm. (1¾in.) cutter.

(R) Rebate plane, metal adjustable fillister, 38mm. (1½in.) cutter.

(P) Bullnose plane, 25mm. (1in.) cutter.

(N) Shoulder plane, 25mm. (1in.) or 31mm. (1¼in.) cutter.

(I) Scraper plane, 70mm. (2¾in.) blade.

(S) Plough plane, metal. Wide range available. Smallest works grooves, 4mm., 6mm., 12mm., also ⅛in., $\frac{3}{16}$in., and ¼in. Larger sizes up to 12·7mm. (⅛in. to $\frac{9}{16}$in.) Also the combination which works beads in addition. Get the best you can afford, but even the smallest works well.

(O) Router, metal adjustable.

(T) Moulding planes. Obtain only as required.

11

Chisels and Gouges (Fig. 2)

(A) Firmer chisels, *25mm. (1in), 13mm. ($\frac{1}{2}$in.) *6mm. ($\frac{1}{4}$in.), 3mm. ($\frac{1}{8}$in.).

(B) Bevelled-edge chisels, 31mm. (1$\frac{1}{4}$in.), *19mm. ($\frac{3}{4}$in.)

(C) Sash mortise chisels, 6mm. ($\frac{1}{4}$in.), *8mm. ($\frac{5}{16}$in.), 10mm. ($\frac{3}{8}$in.).

(F) Drawer lock chisel.

(D) Firmer gouges ⎫ Obtain only
(E) Scribing gouges ⎭ as needed. page 108.

Brace and Bits, etc. (Fig. 2)

(G) Ratchet brace, 200mm. or 250mm. (8in. or 10in.) sweep.

(O) Twist bits, *6mm. ($\frac{1}{4}$in.), *10mm. ($\frac{3}{8}$in), 12·5mm. ($\frac{1}{2}$in.), 19mm. ($\frac{3}{4}$in.)

*(J) Drill bits, 3mm. to 6mm. ($\frac{1}{8}$in. to $\frac{1}{4}$in.). (Used mainly for screw holes) Alternatively, engineer's drills can be used.

(K) Forstner bits. Obtain as needed.

(H, I) Countersinks, *snail and rose.

(M) Centre bits, 12·5mm. ($\frac{1}{2}$in.), *19mm. ($\frac{3}{4}$in.), 25mm. (1in.).

(L) Turnscrew bit.

(N) Expansion bit.

*(P) Bradawls. Birdcage maker's (square in section is preferable). Get two of varying sizes. Dowelling jig. Enables bits of various sizes to be used. Needs only one setting. See page 108.

Marking-out Tools (Fig. 2)

*(W) Try square, 300mm (12in), preferably engineer's type with sliding blade.

(Q) Try square, 600mm. (24in.), wood, home-made. Those having a steel roofing square will prefer this.

(X) Mitre square, 300mm. (12in.).

(Y) Adjustable or sliding bevel, 250mm. (10in.).

(Z) Straight-edges, 450mm. (18in.) and 910mm. (3ft.) wood, home-made.

*(T) Rule, metric, folding.

*(R) Gauge, cutting.

(R) Gauge, marking.

(S) Gauge, mortise.

(U) Dividers, 150mm. (6in.) with fine screw adjustment.

(V) Parallel strips.

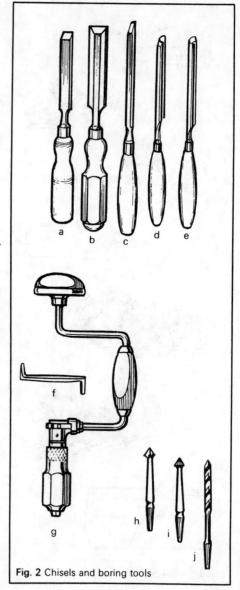

Fig. 2 Chisels and boring tools

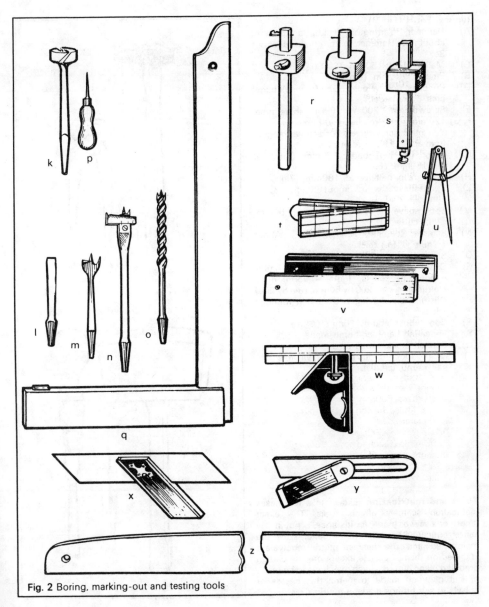

Fig. 2 Boring, marking-out and testing tools

13

General Tools (Fig. 3)

*(A)   Hammer, Warrington or London pattern, about 8oz. Hammer, pattern maker's, about 3oz.

*(C)   Mallet, about 150mm. (6in.) head.

*(B)   Pincers, 200mm. (8in.).

*(D)   Punches, hollow point. One for small panel pins, other larger.

 (E)   Screwdrivers, *200mm. (8in.), cabinet type.

*(F, G)   120mm. (5in.) ratchet, and fine. You need screwdrivers for screws ranging from about 12's to about 2's.

(I, J)   Wood file, half-round, 180mm. (7in.) rat tail; 150mm. (6in.).

 (H)   Wood rasp, half-round, 180mm. (7in.).

 (L)   Spokeshave, *wood, about 60mm. (2¼in.) cutter.

 (M)   Spokeshave, metal, round-face, 50mm. (2in.) cutter.

 (N)   Scraper, *cabinet, 125mm. (5in.). About 1·2mm. ($\frac{3}{64}$in.) thick.

 (O)   Shaped cabinet scraper.

*(K)   Oilstone, medium or fine grade, or combination fine-coarse, India, Carborundum, Unirundum, etc., 200 by 50mm. (8in by 2in.)

 (P)   Oilstone slip, having two varying rounded edges.

*(R)   Cork rubber, about 110mm. (4½in.)

 (S)   Veneering hammer, home-made.

 (Q)   Scratch-stock, home-made.

 (T)   Shaper tool. Various patterns available; flat, half-round, circular.

Tools and metrication. Except in a few cases metrication scarcely affects tools. The exact length of a saw or plane, for instance, is not in any sense critical. Generally the Imperial sizes are maintained and the nearest metric equivalent stamped on them. Possible exceptions are certain grooving plane cutters which may have to be made to suit plywood made to metric thicknesses or chisels to suit fittings made in metric sizes.

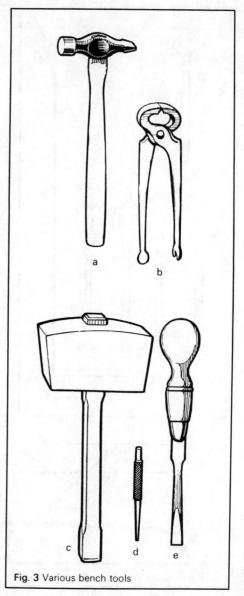

a   b
c   d   e

Fig. 3 Various bench tools

14

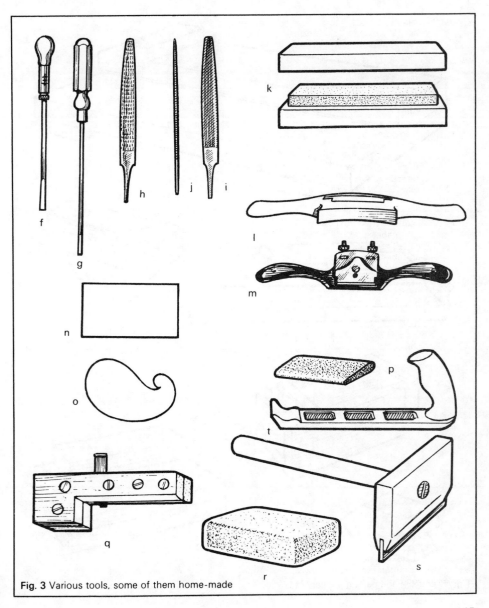

Fig. 3 Various tools, some of them home-made

15

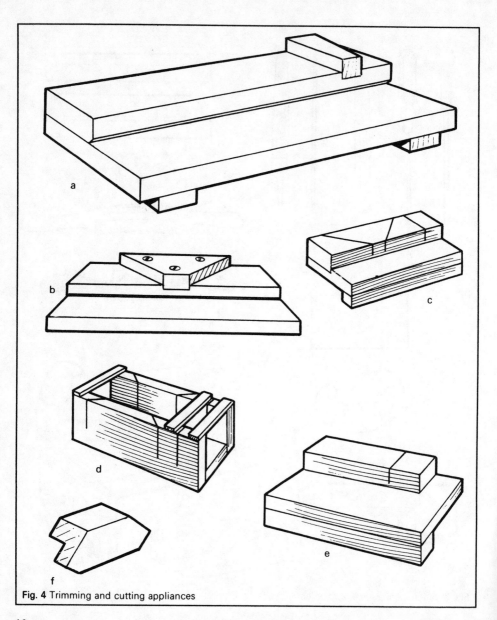

Fig. 4 Trimming and cutting appliances

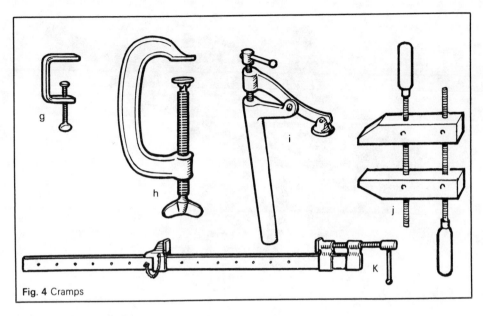

Fig. 4 Cramps

(A)   Shooting board, about *600mm. (2ft.) and 1·5m. (5ft.), home-made.
(B)   Mitre shooting board, about 450mm. (18in.)
*(C) Mitre block, about 220mm. (9in.), home-made.
(D)   Mitre box, for mouldings up to 100mm. (4in.) home-made.
*(E) Bench hook, about 180mm. (7in.), home-made.
(F)   Mitre template, home-made.

Cramps (Fig. 4)

(K)   Sash cramps, metal, pair about 600mm. (2ft.), pair about 1·2m (4ft.)
*(J) Handscrews, pair about 200mm. (8in.) More as needed.
(H)   G cramps. Alternatives to handscrews.
(G)   Thumbscrews, 80–100mm. (3–4in.) About 6 at least.
(I)   Bench holdfast.

Fig. 5 Small bench circular saw with tilting table, ripping fence and mitre gauge. (photo: courtesy of Parry and Sons (Tools) Ltd.)

As soon as possible after obtaining your tools make yourself a container of some sort for them. It may be a simple box, cupboard, or be built into the bench. Remember to allow for expansion. You will undoubtedly buy more tools later, and it is as well to allow for what you envisage as your eventual kit.

Try to arrange things so that edge tools do not come into contact with each other; chisels and saws in racks, planes in compartments, and so on. It will save you a lot of time in the long run in that you will avoid gashed edges, etc. It is possible to obtain a special paper known as V.P.I. (Vapour Phase Inhibitor) which prevents rust. A sheet of this in the tool box, and renewed from time to time, will save much trouble in this connection.

Circular saw. Of the many machines available to the home craftsman the circular saw is the most generally useful. Apart from ripping, cross-cutting, and mitreing it can be used for grooving, rebating, and in some cases for moulding. Essential features of the machine are rise-and-fall saw or table, ripping fence, mitre gauge, crown guard, and preferably a canting table or saw.

An alternative to the above is the basic lathe with various attachments such as circular saw, band saw, disc sander, belt sander, mortiser, planer with thicknessing attachment. One of the advantages of this lathe machine is the small space it occupies, an obvious benefit in the small workshop. Additionally it is less costly than buying several separate machines. Those who have the space, however, and are not worried by cost will find that machines designed to do one type of work are more effective than one machine which has to be designed to do several jobs.

Chapter two

How to Maintain and Use Tools

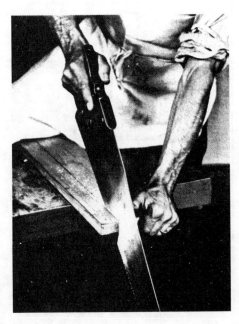

You can learn the chief points to note about using tools in this chapter, but, to quote an old adage, skill to do comes of doing.

Saws

Handsaw. This is used for cutting the larger pieces of wood. For instance, having marked out on a board the pieces you need, you cut them out with the handsaw. Choose a cross-cut saw as distinct from a rip-saw, because this can be used for cutting both with and across the grain. You can saw either with the wood laid on trestles or boxes, or on the bench, or held in the vice. It is just a matter of which is the most convenient.

Fig. 1 shows the method of sawing on trestles or boxes. Start the cut with the saw held at a low angle as in Fig. 2 because in this way you will be able to see whether the saw is in alignment with the line. This is most important because if you start wrong the saw will continue to go wrong, and in endeavouring to put it right you will probably err the other way. To start the cut hold the left hand over the end of the wood and raise the thumb so that the saw can bear against it as in Fig. 3. This steadies the blade and enables you to start it in the exact position. Once the cut has been started a short way the hand can be brought back and used to help steady the wood.

Move the saw up and down a few times so that the teeth find their way into the wood, and when a reasonable start has been made hold the saw so that it makes an angle about 45 deg. with the wood. It can then be worked in long, full, steady strokes. Forcing should never be necessary. If it cuts badly or slowly it needs sharpening. Apply light pressure on the down stroke to keep it up to its work. Note

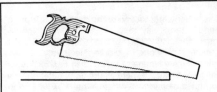

Fig. 2 (above) Start with the saw held at a low angle

Fig. 1 (left) Ripping a board with the handsaw

19

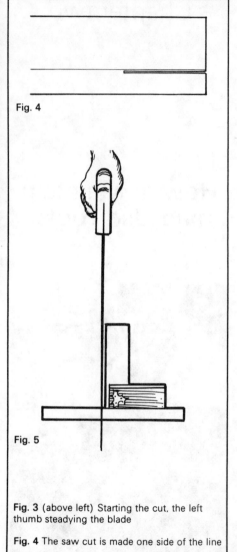

Fig. 4

Fig. 5

from Fig. 1 how the first finger of the right hand points along the blade. This is a great help in giving control.

Invariably the cut is made to one side of the line so that the plane can be used to trim the wood to the finished size. The idea is shown in Fig. 4. It is a help if the line is not hidden by the saw. Thus when practicable place the wood so that the saw cuts to the right of the line. Sometimes this cannot be done, but it is an advantage to have the line visible. Remember that the saw must always be on the waste side of the line.

It is clearly necessary to hold the saw upright. Undercutting may result in the wood being too small, and if the cut runs the other way a lot of unnecessary work in planing is involved. As a guide place a square of wood as in Fig. 5. You will not want to keep it there all the time, but it will give you an indication of whether the saw is upright. Try to get the feel of the position when it is upright, and look at your edge after sawing to see whether you err one way or the other. It is worth while taking trouble early on because it will save you a great deal of work in other operations.

Fig. 3 (above left) Starting the cut, the left thumb steadying the blade

Fig. 4 The saw cut is made one side of the line

Fig. 5 Guide to holding the saw upright

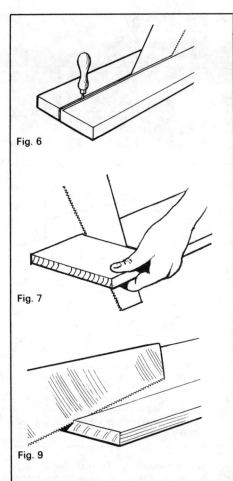

Fig. 6

Fig. 7

Fig. 9

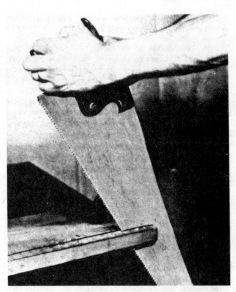

Fig. 6 Preventing the wood binding on the saw

Fig. 7 Supporting overhand on completion of cut

Fig. 8 (above right) Overhand ripping on the bench

Fig. 9 Starting the cut for the overhand rip

It sometimes happens when you have a long cut to make that the kerf will tend to close so that the wood binds on the saw. A bradawl stuck to the kerf as in Fig. 6 will keep it open and prevent binding.

When cross-cutting a board never arrange the wood so that the cut is between the trestles. It will only cause the wood to bend as the cut progresses, and at best will cause the saw to bind. At worst the wood will snap off. Instead arrange the wood so that the piece to be sawn off overhangs at one end. The start of the cut is much as has already been described, but as the cut reaches its completion the left hand should be brought over so that the wood is supported as in Fig. 7. Otherwise it is liable to splinter off, especially when the over-hanging piece is of any great size.

Another method of ripping is what is known as the overhand rip shown in Fig. 8. Many consider it less back-aching. The wood is cramped down on to the bench with the line to be sawn overhanging the edge. To start the cut a few strokes are made with the saw pointed upwards (Fig. 9). As soon as a short cut has been made the upright position is assumed, the saw grasped in both hands, and used

21

for its full stroke. In some ways it is easier to tell when the saw is being held upright.

When the cut has to be along the middle of the board and it is inconvenient to fix it to the bench, you can lay the board on trestles and use the overhand rip, sitting astride the wood.

Comparatively short cuts or cuts in short wood are generally best made with the wood held in the vice as in Fig. 10. Do not give it more projection than is essential as otherwise it will chatter. To an extent it depends upon the thickness, but 22mm. ($\frac{7}{8}$in.) stuff, say, should project about 200mm. (8in.). As the saw approaches the bench top the wood is raised in the vice. Remember to see that no tools are lying on the bench top, otherwise the saw may foul them.

The back saw is used for the general cutting up of smaller pieces, cutting joints and so on. It is a matter for discretion whether the tenon saw or the dovetail saw is used. Sometimes it is convenient to hold the wood in the vice; sometimes the bench hook is better; occasionally it is desirable to fix the wood to the bench with a cramp.

Exact sizes are not important in a bench hook. The dimensions given in Fig. 11 can be taken as a general guide. Note, however, that the lower strip which bears against the edge of the bench is held with a dowel at the end where the saw operates. This is because the saw eventually scores a rut across the wood with continual use, and a screw would be liable to be bared and so blunt the saw. Screws or nails can be used for fixing at the other end.

Fig. 12 shows the bench hook in use. Note how the ball of the left hand presses on to the edge of the wood being sawn, so keeping it up to the back of the hook. The lower edging of the bench hook prevents movement due to thrust from the saw, but unless the wood is kept up to the back it is liable to shift at the return stroke. The thumb of the left hand is used to steady the saw when the cut is started, as shown. Begin by raising the saw handle slightly so that the far corner is sawn first, and gradually lower it as the cut proceeds. For work of great accuracy, as when sawing the shoulders of a tenon, make a few strokes in this way, then start at the front corner. It is a matter of just bringing the saw level, so joining the two cuts.

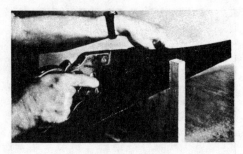

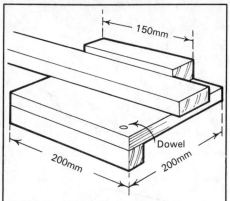

Fig. 10 (top) Using the handsaw, the wood held in a vice
Fig. 11 (above) The bench hook
Fig. 12 (opposite) The use of the bench hook when sawing. The left hand presses the wood hard up against the back of the hook to prevent it from moving backwards

Learning to cut square is of great importance. A useful help in this respect is to square the line round on to all four surfaces of a thick block. Cut down about 2mm. ($\frac{1}{8}$in.) on one surface, turn the wood once towards you so that this cut faces you and make a second cut also about 2mm. ($\frac{1}{8}$in.) deep on the surface now on top. Repeat this until you have sawn all four surfaces, then gradually deepen each cut in turn. In this way the saw tends to run into the cuts already made.

When an end must be sawn perfectly square, as

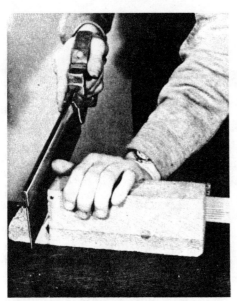

when dowelling or when sawing shoulders, it is a great help if the line is squared across with the chisel. By making a sloping cut against the line on the waste side a channel is formed in which the saw can run. This is shown in Fig. 4, page 107.

When the cut is being made with the wood held in the vice, make sure that the wood is level. Otherwise it will be awkward to saw to the line. On this score, when a cut has to be made at an angle it is a help to position the wood so that the cut is vertical. In this way it is only necessary to hold the saw upright. This idea is often useful when sawing dovetails, the wood being fixed at a slight angle so that the saw is used upright.

Never try to use the saw without supporting the wood in one of the ways mentioned. Wood which is not firmly held will shift about, making the sawing difficult, and may result in a buckled saw blade. If you turn to Fig. 13a and b you will see that a pivoted end support to the bench is suggested. This is excellent for holding wood whilst being sawn. Another and still simpler plan is to bore a 12·5mm. ($\frac{1}{2}$in.) hole through the bench top near the tail, and knock a length of dowel rod into it as at

(C). It can be tapped down flush when not in use. At all events avoid the bad practice of holding the wood against the bench stop when cutting right through. Eventually the saw scores a deep furrow, and when the stop is used for planing the wood is liable to tilt into the gash(see F).

For general sawing the bench hook is perfectly satisfactory, but when it is essential that the wood is held more rigidly you can use either the holdfast at (D) or the handscrew or cramp at (E). The former is extremely handy, but needs a fairly thick top to be effective as it relies upon the angularity of the post in the hole in the bench top to obtain its grip. If the top is thin you will have to thickness it on the underside locally. Of course, there must be clear space beneath. Some holdfasts have a metal socket for recessing into the bench top.

Saws for curves. For fairly large curves in, say, 22mm. ($\frac{7}{8}$in.) wood the most generally useful tool is the bow saw (see page 25). Its blade is held in tension by a tourniquet arrangement, and with its handles can be turned to cut in any direction. The advantage of the latter is that it enables a shape to be cut which is more or less parallel with an edge. It will be realized that when set square the saw can only cut in from an edge a distance equal to that of the blade from the cross bar. By turning the handles, however, the saw can cut along the wood parallel with the edge. It is important that the blade is not twisted.

Square sawing is clearly important, as otherwise a great deal of unnecessary cleaning up is involved —in fact it may easily happen that the wood is spoilt by being undercut. It is purely a matter of judgment and practice. The best plan is to test your work as you saw it, note whether you are tending to cut one way or the other, and endeavour to correct it in future cutting. You can tell within a little whether the blade is square with the work. Fig. 14 shows the bow saw in use.

When a cut is to be made internally in the wood, that is, not emerging at the edge, it is necessary to bore a hole in the wood big enough to allow the saw blade to be passed through. This is bored on the waste side of the line, of course. The blade is held by a rivet which is easily punched out.

Generally the wood is held in the vice and it is

23

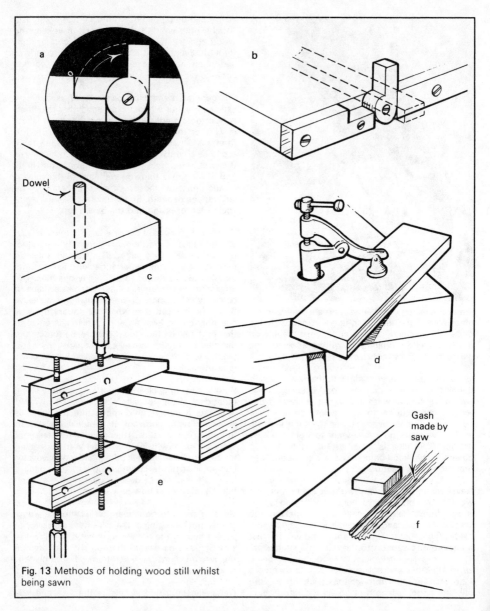

a

b

Dowel

c

d

e

Gash
made by
saw

f

Fig. 13 Methods of holding wood still whilst being sawn

advisable to keep it as low as possible to avoid vibration. This may necessitate raising the wood once or twice, but it makes the sawing much easier. Grasp the handle with both hands and work in long strokes, gradually turning the saw so that it follows the curve.

Another saw which has similar uses but is for smaller work is the coping saw (p. 10). In this case the wood is frequently horizontal, and is fixed so that it overhangs the bench top. Avoid too great an overhang as this will cause chatter. Here upright cutting is essential. For a start you can hold a small square near the blade as a guide, but soon you should be able to do without it. Tension in this case is secured by turning the handle.

Used in this way the teeth of the saw point towards the handle. Sometimes, however, it is more convenient to hold the wood upright in the vice, and in this case it is better to point the teeth away from the handle so that the rag from the saw is at the back of the wood. Really thin wood is cut with the fretsaw, and a special table with a V cut at the projecting end is used.

Sometimes an internal cut has to be made at a distance from the edge too far for the bow saw to reach. You then have to use the keyhole saw. It is not a very efficient tool, however, as the blade has to rely upon its stiffness to keep it from buckling. The rule then is to give the blade the minimum

Fig. 14 (left) How the bow saw is handled, wood held in a vice

Fig. 15 (above) Using the keyhole or pad saw

projection consistent with a reasonable stroke. Fortunately not many cuts of this kind occur in woodwork, and the chief use of the saw is in sawing the side of keyholes when fitting locks. You could, of course, use a bow saw if necessary, but it would involve taking out the rivet and threading the blade through the hole to make two short cuts. Fig. 15 shows the saw in use for a larger curve. Note that both hands grasp the handle.

Generally it is not advisable for the beginner to sharpen his own saws, as he will probably file the teeth unevenly, and a professional saw sharpener would charge more to put right the damage than the money saved. If you do decide to make the attempt, start on the saw with the largest teeth.

You will realize that, in addition to filing, the teeth have to be set—that is bent outwards alternately right and left. This is an essential feature of a saw in that it makes a kerf slightly wider than the thickness of its blade. Without it the saw would bind in the wood. The sharpener will give just the amount which experience has shown to be necessary. Excessive set is to be avoided since it means that you are removing wood unnecessarily (and so working harder than you need with no advantage).

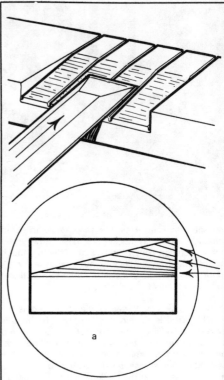

Chisels and Gouges

Apart from chisels made for special jobs, there are three general kinds: firmer, bevelled-edge, and mortise. Of these the first (A, Fig. 2, p. 12) is the bench tool for general purposes. It is robustly made so that it will stand up to the work involved in chopping dovetails and other joints, yet can if necessary be used for finer work such as paring. The latter, however, is better done with a lighter chisel kept specially for the job, the bevelled-edge chisel shown at (B, Fig. 2, p. 12). Mortising, which calls for heavy blows with the mallet, and for a certain amount of levering over, needs the specially made chisel (C, Fig. 2, p. 12). Two kinds are available, the heavy mortise chisel, and the lighter sash mortise which is strong enough for most work without being so cumbersome.

Paring. A typical operation, that of paring a groove, is shown in Fig. 18. The left hand can either be held as shown, or the fingers can be brought up over the top leaving the thumb below. In all cases, no matter what the operation, both

Fig. 16 (left) Cutting down the corner of wood with the chisel

Fig. 17 (above) Stages in chiselling the groove

hands are behind the cutting edge. In a job of this kind the sides of the groove are sawn first, and one or two intermediate, shallower cuts are made to break up the grain. The chisel is then taken in at a slight angle as in Fig. 17, the handle being struck either with the palm of the hand or the mallet. The waste is removed down to about the diagonal. Then, reversing the wood, work from the other side as at A. Finish off as in Fig. 18, using the chisel with a slicing action if possible. This not only eases the cut, but shows more clearly the high parts which need reducing.

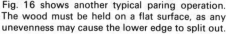

Fig. 16 shows another typical paring operation. The wood must be held on a flat surface, as any unevenness may cause the lower edge to split out.

Fig. 18 (left) Paring groove with bevelled-edge chisel
Fig. 19 (above) Chopping a mortise

Mortising. Fig. 19 shows a door stile being mortised, and there are several points to note. Firstly the worker stands at the end of the wood, because it is then obvious whether the chisel leans to the right or left (it is clearly important that the mortise is upright). Secondly the wood is cramped down over a solid part of the bench, generally the leg. Also a thumbscrew is put on at the end to prevent any tendency for the wood to split. It is usual to leave about 25mm. (1in.) of wood beyond the mortise to minimise this risk, but even so the thumbscrew is advisable. When several stiles are being mortised they can be cramped together side by side. To lighten the work much of the waste can be removed by boring a series of holes with a twist bit slightly narrower than the mortise width.

The first cut is made at about the centre of the mortise and is shallow only. The next, about 3mm. ($\frac{1}{8}$in.) from the first, is deeper, and so until within about 1mm. ($\frac{1}{16}$in.) of the end when much of the waste can be levered away. A slightly narrower

chisel is useful for this. Work up to the other end in the same way, levering away the waste as you proceed. The depth, of course, has already been decided, and it is useful to stick a piece of paper to the chisel as a depth guide. When the mortise has been cleared in this way the final cuts can be taken on the lines at each end. This cleans up the dubbed-over ends caused by the levering.

Drawer lock chisel. This, shown at (F, Fig. 2, p. 12) is intended for use in the restricted space of a drawer. It is also useful when chopping the recess into which the bolt shoots in the drawer rail. Fig. 21 shows how it can be struck with the side of the hammer. It will be realized that it would be practically impossible to chop down with the ordinary chisel.

Sharpening the chisel. This procedure is much the same as when sharpening a plane iron. The usual grinding angle is about 25 deg., whereas sharpening on the oilstone is in the region of 30

27

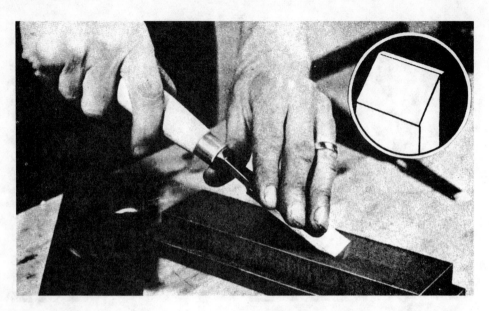

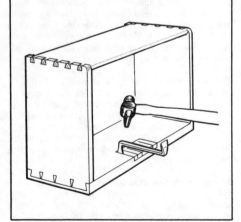

Fig. 20 (above) Sharpening the chisel on the oilstone

Fig. 21 (below) How the drawer lock chisel is used in a confined space

deg., except in the case of mortise chisels and those reserved for chopping which are better sharpened at nearer 35 deg. as this gives a stronger edge. Fig. 20 shows the sharpening operation. The burr is turned back on the stone (again as in the plane cutter), and it is vital that it is held flat as otherwise it will be impossible to pare with it properly. The burr is got rid of finally by stropping.

Gouges. These are not widely used, but are required sometimes for forming a hollow or recess. Carving tools are dealt with more fully in the chapter on carving. The firmer gouge has the bevel at the outside, and is for general work. To sharpen it hold it at right angles with the stone with the bevel flat. Raise the handle a trifle so that just the edge touches, and work back and forth with a rocking movement until a burr is turned up at the inside. To turn this back use the oilstone slip at the inside, keeping it flat. The curvature of the slip should be slightly quicker than that of the gouge.

Scribing gouges are bevelled inside, and must be sharpened with the slip. To turn back the burr hold the outside of the gouge flat on the stone and half revolve it, keeping it flat.

Tools for Boring

The brace. You can obtain either the simple brace or the ratchet brace. The latter is well worth its extra cost, partly because it enables you to work in a corner where a full revolution of the brace is impossible, and partly because it is an advantage to have the hand in a certain position when boring a large hole as it gives more purchase. For average purposes a 200mm. (8in.) sweep is about right.

It is fairly easy to tell when the brace leans to right or left, but more difficult to detect whether it bears away from or towards you. You can often make use of this fact when the verticality of a hole is more important in one direction than another. For instance when boring dowel holes in a rail it would clearly be fatal if the holes were to lean sideways. Consequently it is advisable to stand at the end of the wood as shown in Fig. 22.

Using the brace. Various aids can be had as a guide, one being the square placed alongside the bit. In the case of a hole being bored in the end of a post two straight strips can be cramped temporarily to the post on adjacent faces as a guide as in Fig. 23. Another plan is to ask an assistant to stand alongside to indicate whether the brace is vertical.

Sometimes it is advisable to hold the head on the left hand when boring, as it helps both in steadying the brace and in increasing the pressure. Sometimes it is more convenient to hold the wood in the vice, and the pressure is increased by pressing with the body behind the left hand. For holes, the accuracy of which is important, the method is not recommended as it is difficult to tell whether the brace is square with the wood.

When a hole has to be bored accurately at an angle a guide should be made as in Fig. 24. This is cramped to the wood and the bit passed through the hole.

Bits. For dowelling the twist bit is invariably used. Owing to its straight spiral shank it is not liable to wander with the grain if properly started, and it cuts cleanly. Furthermore, its screw point draws it into the wood without undue labour. It is rather delicate, however, both its thread and cutters being easily damaged if contact is made with a hidden nail. For dowel work an extra short bit is

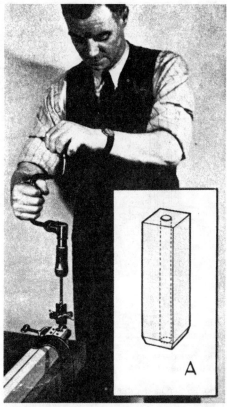

Fig. 22 Boring holes in stile preparatory to mortising

available. It is sometimes an advantage to use a morse drill. This, however, needs a jig as it is impossible to start the drill correctly in the right place otherwise.

For boring to a definite depth a stop is used. An adjustable metal type is available, but it is liable to mark the surface, and is especially awkward when the hole is being bored into an edge owing to the liability of the bearing surfaces to foul the edge of the wood. The simple devices in Fig. 25 are effective and make no mark that a single shaving will not remove. That at (A) is made specially for

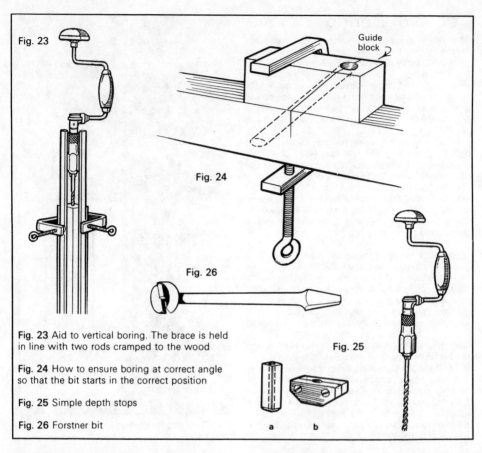

Fig. 23 Aid to vertical boring. The brace is held in line with two rods cramped to the wood

Fig. 24 How to ensure boring at correct angle so that the bit starts in the correct position

Fig. 25 Simple depth stops

Fig. 26 Forstner bit

the particular job in hand, whereas (B) is adjustable to any position along the spiral of the bit.

For shallow holes, or holes right through thin wood, the centre bit is used. For the latter purpose the hole should be taken in from one side until the point emerges just beneath, when the hole is completed from the other side. The centre bit with thread point has an advantage in that it pulls itself into the wood and saves the necessity for pressure. The expansion bit (N), Fig. 2, p. 13 is useful for larger holes. It saves having to keep a wide range of centre bits.

Screw holes are generally bored with the morse or the drill bit, (J, Fig. 2, p. 12). Two or three sizes are kept to suit the general size of screws being used. These drills can be obtained with square shank to fit the brace, though generally the plain round drill is held sufficiently tightly. Many men keep a small hand drill in which to use the smaller sizes of drills.

Half-twist bits with gimlet points are quick borers, and are useful for tough hardwoods. They should never be used on softwoods or near the edge, however, as they are liable to split the grain.

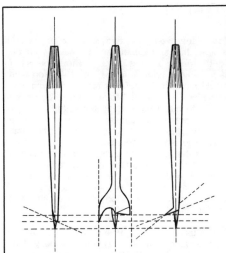

Fig. 27 (above) Details of the centre bit
Fig. 28 (below) Sharpening the cutters of the twist bit

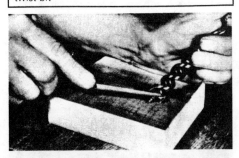

For screw work, the snail countersink at (H, Fig. 2, p. 12) gives a clean finish. Sometimes it is necessary to enlarge the countersinking in a brass fitting, and the rose countersink (I) is used for this. For the rapid driving of screws and when considerable purchase is needed the turnscrew bit is useful. It is essential that a strong downward pressure is maintained.

As mentioned above, the morse drill is used for the shank hole for screws. For the thread hole a convenient tool for small screws is the bradawl. When the normal round type is used the cutting edge should be at right angles with the grain. A most useful type, however, is the bird-cage maker's or square awl. It cuts well and is not liable to split the grain even when used near an edge. Furthermore it has a point rather than a square end. For the screw holes of small fittings the reciprocating drill with spiral stem is useful. When the hole has to be extra small a needle can be ground to a cutting edge and used, the eye being broken off.

Forstner bit. This (Fig. 26) is a clean-cutting bit which can be used for some jobs which would be impossible with other bits. Although it has a slightly projecting centre, it is guided by its circular rim. It is especially useful when a hole has to be bored deeply without penetrating right through. This would be impossible with a centre or twist bit since the centre point would project at the other side. To bore a hole in an exact position calls for care in that the centre point has the minimum projection and is concealed by the rim. When starting it is often an advantage to give it a couple of backward turns first so that its rim cuts the circle before the cutters begin to scoop out the waste. Some makes of bit are more satisfactory in use than others.

Sharpening bits. The centre bit has three chief parts, and they should project in the following order: centre point, nicker, and cutter as shown in Fig. 27. Use a fine file to sharpen, sticking the point of the bit into a block of wood to steady it. Note that the nicker edge runs at an angle (Fig. 27) so that it cuts rather than scratches. This is sharpened on the inside. It is important that the outside is not burred over. The cutter is sharpened on top. The edges of the centre point may need a slight rub. The latter is generally triangular in section.

Twist bits are sharpened similarly, but the screw point must not be touched. If possible use a small file with a safe edge. Sharpen the nickers on the inside only, and the cutters on the side farthest from the screw point, as shown in Fig. 28. If a burr is set up on the outside of the nickers the bit can be rubbed flat on the oilstone.

Occasionally the countersink calls for a rub up with a small rat-tail and flat file. For the Forstner bit grind a small three-cornered file until the serrations are removed, and use this as a three-cornered scraper on the inside only.

Chapter three

How to Maintain and Use Tools (continued)

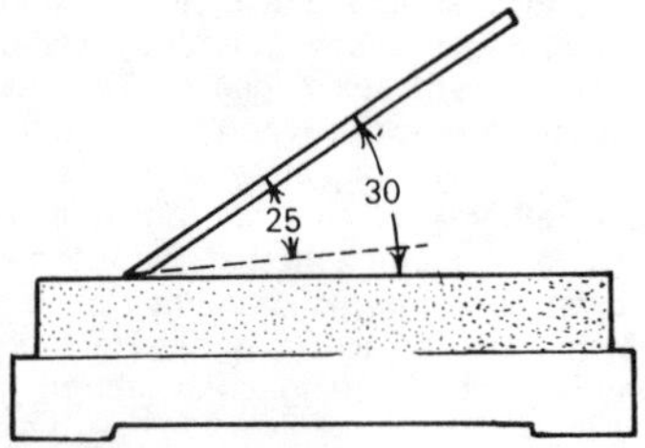

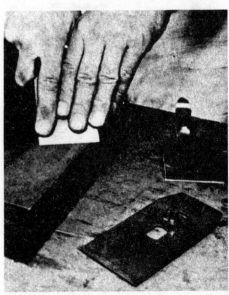

Fig. 1 (above) Grinding and sharpening angles

Fig. 2 (right) Plane cutter being sharpened on the oilstone

Planing

You plane wood for two reasons; to make it straight, flat, and square; and to make it smooth. For the former purpose the plane should be as long as possible in relation to the wood. A short plane would dip into the hollows too much, whereas a long plane is prevented from doing so by its own length. In the woodworking trades the craftsman uses either the fore plane or the jointer to make an edge straight or to make a joint. For the preliminary planing to remove saw marks or other roughness he uses the wood Jack plane. This is long enough not to dip into the surface, and, by setting it fairly coarse, it removes the roughness quickly. In this way the fore plane is reserved for accurate work, and thus keeps its edge longer and can always be set fine.

This is the ideal arrangement, but if you have not yet been able to get a trying or fore plane, you will have to use the Jack plane for jointing as well as for the rougher operations. Should this be the case you will find that your best plan when you have a number of similar pieces to prepare will be to set the plane slightly coarse and remove the roughness from them all. You can then re-set the plane (sharpening it if necessary) and make them all true.

The truing of wood enables all marking out to be done, and joints to be cut. It does not follow, however, that because wood is true that it is necessarily smooth. The grain of wood is liable to tear out if not planed in the right way, and a plane as set for truing is not adapted to deal with this. Consequently you have the smoothing plane which is of handy size for the work, and which is specially set to prevent the grain from tearing out. We shall see more about this under the heading of setting a plane.

Sharpening the plane. When you first buy a plane the cutter (or iron as it is generally termed) has been ground on a grindstone, but it is useless until it has been given a really fine edge on an oilstone. To save unnecessary work the grinding is done at a lower angle than that used on the oilstone. In this way only the extreme edge has to be rubbed. The idea is shown in Fig. 1.

To remove the cutter from a wood plane, hold the latter with the left hand so that the thumb passes into the escapement and bears on the back iron. Strike the front of the plane (on the striking button if it has one) and the wedge and cutter will slip out, but are prevented from dropping by the thumb. A wood smoothing plane is struck at the rear. In the case of a metal plane it is only necessary to raise the cam of the lever cap.

You will find that a back or cap iron is held to the cutter with a bolt. Holding the two on the bench and gripping the cutter at the unsharpened end release the bolt until it can slide along the groove in the cutter and out at the hole. There is no need to completely remove the bolt—in fact it is better not to do so as otherwise it may be lost in sawdust or shavings. Pour a few drops of oil on to the oilstone and place the cutter on it so that the ground bevel lies flat. Raise the hands a trifle so that only the extreme edge touches the stone, and you have the right angle. The latter is not critical, but if you aim at 30 deg. you will be about right. The grinding angle is 25 deg. (see Fig. 1).

Fig. 2 shows the sharpening operation. Hold the cutter so that it is skewed at a slight angle, and work it back and forth either straight or with an oval movement. Some prefer one, some the other. After a few rubs draw the thumb across the back. If it has been sharpened you will be able to detect a burr or roughness since the sharpening turns back the edge. When this appears reverse the cutter flat on the stone and rub it back and forth a few times to bend back the burr as shown in Fig. 3.

You need to get rid of this burr as otherwise it may be forced back on to the edge and blunt it. Draw the edge once or twice across a hardwood block as in Fig. 4. This will take it off but leave the edge rather rough. Put this right by giving a few rubs as in Fig. 2, and once again reverse flat as in Fig. 3. Finally strop it alternately on the bevel and on the back on a piece of leather dressed with oil and fine emery powder.

As you complete the sharpening look at the edge in the light. A keen edge cannot be seen, whereas

Fig. 3 Turning back burr on oilstone

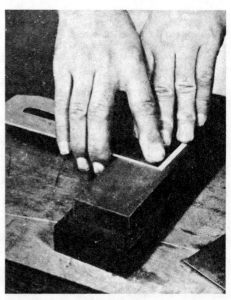

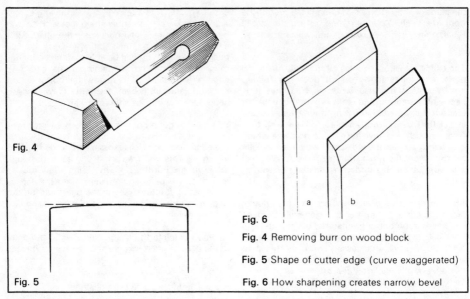

Fig. 4

Fig. 6

a   b

Fig. 4 Removing burr on wood block

Fig. 5 Shape of cutter edge (curve exaggerated)

Fig. 5

Fig. 6 How sharpening creates narrow bevel

a blunt one will reflect a thin line of light. In the same way any gashes will show as flecks of light. When you get used to it you will be able to tell by the appearance whether the edge is keen. The burr is an indication that the edge has been turned, but not reveal gashes.

For the fore plane and smoothing plane the edge should be slightly rounded as shown in exaggeration in Fig. 5, with the corners taken off. As the Jack plane has generally to take a heavier shaving the curvature can be slightly increased. After being sharpened several times the sharpened bevel will become wide as in Fig. 6, b, and it is time to have the cutter ground so that there is not so much metal to remove. Incidentally, some workers never have the cutter of a metal plane re-ground (unless it has been gashed) because it is quite thin and there is not much metal to rub away.

Setting. To set the plane place the back iron in position and turn the bolt until finger tight. The distance of the back iron from the edge depends on the work to be done. For the Jack plane which takes coarse shavings it might be about $1\frac{1}{2}$mm. ($\frac{1}{16}$in.) or more; for the fore plane which takes fine

shavings rather less. For the smoothing plane when set for cleaning up difficult wood with twisted grain it should be as close as it is possible to get it. When correct tighten the bolt right home.

All adjusting of the adjustable metal plane is by the screw and lateral lever. It is never struck with the hammer. Look along the sole as in Fig. 7, with a piece of white paper or light coloured wood beneath. The cutter should appear as a thin black line tapering to nothing at the sides. You can adjust the cutter until correct, using the rear screw to regulate the thickness of shaving, and the lever to give even projection at both sides.

In the case of the wood plane, place the cutter and back iron in the escapement, back iron uppermost, and hold in position with the thumb of the left hand. Place the wedge in position and lightly tap with the hammer. Take another look along the sole, and if there is insufficient projection tap the cutter out. If one corner sticks out strike the rear of the cutter at the side. When the cutter projects too much tap the striking button lightly. When all is in order knock the wedge home. There is no need to hammer it home really hard—you may distort the plane.

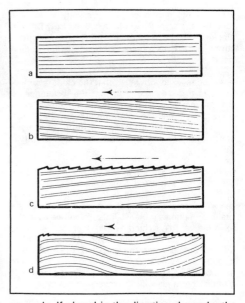

Fig. 7 (above) Sighting the cutter by looking along the sole
Fig. 8 (right) How grain affects direction of planing

Incidentally, the soles of all planes should be lubricated to assist working. With metal planes it is essential. A good plan is to keep a pad of cotton wool lightly soaked in linseed oil on a piece of wood and draw the plane across this occasionally, or rub a piece of candlegrease across the sole.

Use of the back iron. At this point perhaps we had better consider the purpose of the back iron. It is needed solely because of the tendency of some woods to tear out owing to the undulating grain, leaving little depressions in the surface known as tears (pronounced 'tares') which look unsightly. If the grain of the wood were always straight and parallel with the surface as in Fig. 8a there would be no tendency for the grain to tear out. As, however, a tree is never perfectly straight it is inevitable that the saw which cuts the boards will run across the grain in parts, and you get grain which either slopes or undulates. At (b), for example, the grain runs at

an angle. If planed in the direction shown by the arrow it would not tear out, but if turned the other way as at (c) it would inevitably tear as the plane was taken along it. First a split would start. It would run in the direction of the grain, that is downwards, but the raised shaving would be caught up by the cutter edge, wrenched up, and broken, and the same thing repeated over and over again until the end of the wood was reached. The trouble, you will observe, is that the cutter is not actually cutting most of the time because the split runs in front of it. It is only when the cutter edge catches up the split that it cuts and then the shaving is more or less wrenched up. If, therefore, you could break the shaving immediately it is raised it would lose its strength and the split would not develop. That is the purpose of the back iron, to break the shaving as soon as possible after it is raised.

The idea is shown in Fig. 9. The closer the back iron is to the cutting edge the sooner the shaving is broken, and the less liable it is to tear out the grain. Matters are helped, too, by having a small mouth to the plane. Fig. 10 shows how this restricts the lift of the shaving even when there is no back iron, causing it to break earlier than it would if the mouth were excessively wide. The fact that the smoothing plane is used only for thin shavings also helps in that the thin shaving is not so strong as a thick one and breaks earlier or just bends away.

It will be realized, however, that the close-set back iron has a disadvantage in that the resistance to the movement of the plane is increased. It is therefore a matter for compromise, the back iron being set farther back for medium or coarse shavings at cost of slightly increased liability to tear out.

In the case of the wood in Fig. 8c, the simplest plan would be to turn it the other way round as at (b), and it is always worth while looking at the edge of the wood before planing to see the direction of the grain. Sometimes it makes little difference as in the example at (d), which would tear out in parts whichever way the plane were taken. Another difficult case is when the grain runs in streaks side by side as in some varieties of mahogany. Alternate streaks will be smooth whilst the others tear out. If planing the other way the reverse happens.

Using the plane. When the surface of the wood is planed the wood is generally laid on the bench and the bench stop knocked up to prevent it from moving. There is one precaution to take, however. Bench tops are frequently not flat, and the weight of the plane and the pressure used will cause the wood to bend. This may not matter a lot when it is merely being smoothed, but it may upset the accuracy when it is being trued. In Fig. 11 at (a), for instance, owing to the hollowness of the top, the wood is bent down under the pressure, and in all probability the plane would cease to cut when in the middle of the wood. At (b) the bench top is round, and consequently the far end of the wood is raised when the plane is started, and the whole thing is shot forward. These two illustrations are exaggerated, but they show the idea.

Generally the best plan is to use a planing board which is perfectly flat, and put the wood on this. This board is any plain, true piece of wood which is rather longer than the wood to be planed. A couple of screws driven part-way in at the far end serve as a stop. They can be given projection to suit the work in hand. When these are undesirable in that they might mark the wood, they are withdrawn and

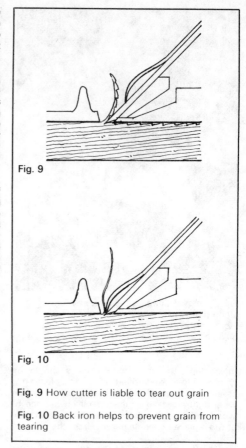

Fig. 9

Fig. 10

Fig. 9 How cutter is liable to tear out grain

Fig. 10 Back iron helps to prevent grain from tearing

replaced by a crosspiece screwed on as shown by the dotted lines at (c), Fig. 11. Even when the planing board is used or when the bench top is true, it is usually a help to put a shaving beneath the middle of the wood, especially when narrow stuff is being dealt with. Incidentally if a large piece of wood is liable to shift about the bench top whilst being planed you can help to steady it by chalking the bench top, or sprinkling it with plaster of Paris.

The usual trouble the beginner finds is that he is inclined to make the surface round, especially at the

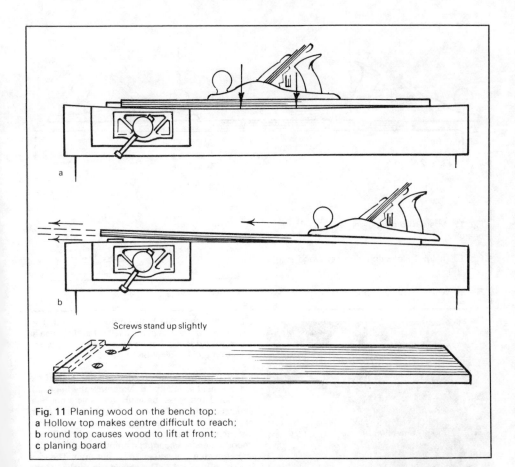

Fig. 11 Planing wood on the bench top:
a Hollow top makes centre difficult to reach;
b round top causes wood to lift at front;
c planing board

Screws stand up slightly

ends. To avoid this adopt the plan shown in Fig. 12. At the start of the stroke press well down at the front of the plane, and as the far end is reached transfer the pressure to the rear. After a while you will find that the process will be practically automatic.

Testing for wind. Nowadays most timber is bought ready planed, and requires little more than a skim to finish it after cutting to size, jointing, etc. When it is rough, however, it needs testing for truth, and this means that it must be straight in

length, flat in width, and free of wind (pronounced as when you wind a clock). The straight-edge is used to test the straightness, but the winding strips are necessary to test for winding. However, a quick test is to look across the surface as in Fig. 13. Any serious winding will be at once obvious. For a closer test use the winding strips. If the wood is true the top edge of the near strip will appear parallel with the inlaid line on the back one. Fig. 14 shows the strips in use.

To correct a surface which winds work the plane

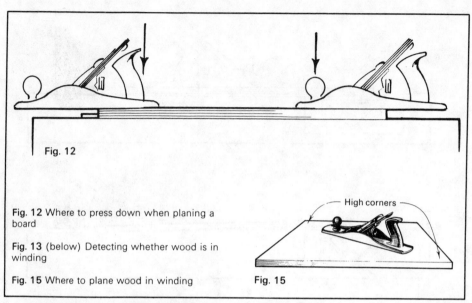

Fig. 12

Fig. 12 Where to press down when planing a board

Fig. 13 (below) Detecting whether wood is in winding

Fig. 15 Where to plane wood in winding

High corners

Fig. 15

diagonally from one high corner to the other as shown in Fig. 15. The plane itself is handy to use as a straight-edge. Laid at an angle across the wood it gives a quick indication of truth.

Edge planing. When an edge is being planed the plane is held as in Fig. 16. Note how the fingers of the left hand pass beneath the sole and bear against the side of the wood. They thus act as a sort of fence, so that the plane projects the same distance from the edge throughout the cut. This is important because correct manipulation enables an edge which is not square to be put right. The idea is shown in Fig. 17. The shaving is thicker at the middle of the plane than at the edges owing to the slight curvature of the cutting edge. When therefore an edge is out of square the plane is held so that it projects more on the high side. The sole is held flat on the edge, of course. Never attempt to rock the plane to correct an edge which is out of truth.

Sometimes an edge is square at one end and out of truth at the other; or out of truth at both ends but in opposite directions. Start the stroke with the plane towards the high side, and gradually shift the

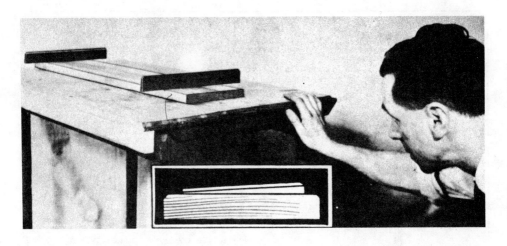

Fig. 14 (above) Testing a board for winding using the winding strips
Fig. 16 (below) Planing an edge

Fig. 17 (below) How thickness of shaving varies across the width

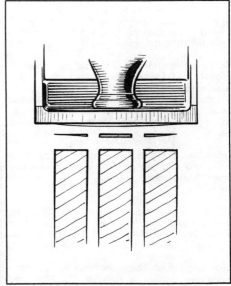

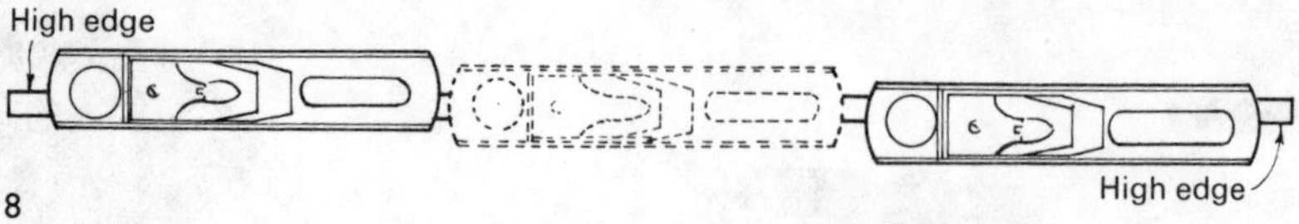

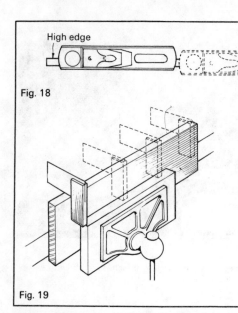

High edge

Fig. 18

High edge

Fig. 19

Fig. 18 Correcting edge out of square at one or both ends

Fig. 19 Testing edge for squareness using the square in several positions along the length

Fig. 20 (below) Planing an edge true on the shooting board

position of the fingers of the left hand on the sole so that the plane shifts to the other side as the end of the stroke is reached, as shown in Fig. 18. Fig. 19 shows how the edge is tested at various positions along the wood.

To test whether an edge is straight use a straight-edge. This, of course, is unnecessary when a joint is being planed because the two parts are tried together. A good working method of straightening an edge is to use the fore plane and remove shavings from the middle until the plane ceases to cut.

Follow with a shaving right through. A plane which has a true sole will plane an edge considerably longer than itself reasonably straight by this method.

The edges of wood about 12mm. ($\frac{1}{2}$in.) thick and over can be planed in the vice in this way. On thinner wood the plane would be liable to rock, and it is advisable to use the shooting board.

Shooting board. This is shown in Fig. 20 and is being used to plane an edge straight. The wood

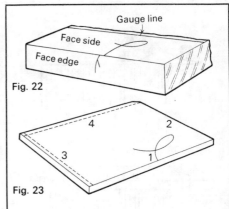

Fig. 22

Gauge line

Face side

Face edge

Fig. 23

4   2

3   1

Fig. 21 (left) Trimming end grain on shooting board

Fig. 22 Identification marks of face side and edge

Fig. 23 Order in which edges of panel are planed

lies on the upper platform, and the plane rests on its side and is moved along the lower platform. The side of the plane must, of course, be square with sole if it is to plane the wood square. Since the plane makes the edge straight by virtue of the accuracy of its own sole, the wood is held so that it overhangs the upper platform by about 3mm. ($\frac{1}{8}$in.). Shavings are removed from the middle of the wood until the plane ceases to cut, after which a couple of shavings are taken right through. In the case of a butt joint, the one piece is planed with the face side uppermost, and the other reversed. Then if the plane is slightly out of square the two angles cancel each other out.

The method of using the shooting board is rather different when the end of a piece of wood is being trimmed. In this case the plane is kept up to the edge of the upper platform, and the wood held against the stop with sufficient inward pressure to keep it up to the sole of the plane as in Fig. 21.

Sequence in planing. In all planing operations there is a sequence to be followed. One side is made true first and one edge made square with it. These are known as the face side and face edge respec-

tively. They are marked in pencil as in Fig. 22, and all subsequent marking made from one or other of them. For instance the try square has its butt resting against one of them, or the gauge is used with its fence bearing against either face side or face edge. There are exceptions to this rule, but it applies in most instances. When wood has been obtained machine planed it will already have been brought to an even thickness; otherwise the gauge will have to be set to the thickness required and both edges gauged from the face side. When the wood is wide the ends are gauged as well. The width will have to be gauged in any case as in Fig. 22.

When the edges of a wide board are to be planed they should be done in the order given in Fig. 23. This enables the rear corners to be taken off at an angle to prevent the grain from splitting out. The final trim at (4) takes out the chiselled corners. This method of taking off the corner to prevent splitting is shown in Fig. 24. (A) shows how the plain corner is liable to splinter out, whereas (B) shows the corner taken off. When the wood is not wide enough to permit this chiselling a block can be cramped on at the rear as at (C). Another plan is

41

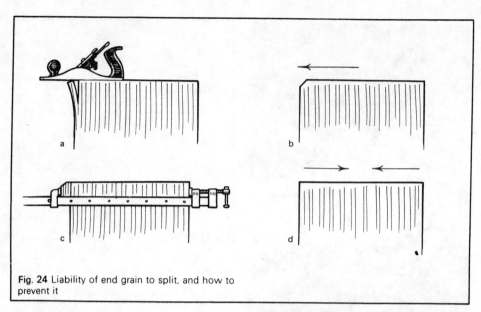

Fig. 24 Liability of end grain to split, and how to prevent it

to plane half-way in from each side as at (D). This applies equally when the wood is being trimmed on the shooting board.

Cleaning up. It will be seen that the wood Jack plane is used for the preliminary planing of rough timber, and the fore plane or its smaller counterpart, the panel plane, for truing it. At this stage all marking out, joint cutting and so on are carried out. Before the work can be assembled, however, certain parts require to be cleaned up finally, and the smoothing plane is used for this. The same plane is used for the cleaning up of table tops and similar parts, framed doors, and so on. Nowadays the adjustable metal plane is generally used. It is an extremely handy tool for bench work generally. Fig. 25 shows one of the older pattern metal smoothing planes in use in cleaning up a surface.

One other small plane which is extremely handy for trimming small parts is the block plane shown in section in Fig. 26. It is particularly handy for trimming the mitres of small mouldings and similar

Fig. 25 Cleaning up with the metal smoothing plane

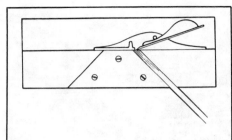

Fig. 26 Sectional view of block plane on mitre shooting board

parts because of the smallness of the mouth. The larger bench planes have the bevel of the cutter downwards so that, although the mouth itself may be small, there is an aperture behind it, and the end of a narrow piece may drop into this making accurate work impossible. The block plane has its bevel uppermost which necessarily reduces the aperture as shown in Fig. 26.

Planes for Special Purposes

Rebate plane. The most generally useful kind is the adjustable metal type which has a moving fence. It thus acts as a fillister plane. Once set, any number of rebates can be planed to the same size. A depth stop ensures that the plane ceases to cut when the required depth is reached. A spur is fitted to the right hand side, but this is used only when the plane is used across the grain. Its purpose is to cut across the grain so that it does not tear out. It is necessary to draw the plane backwards with a fair pressure a couple of times before using it in the normal manner. Otherwise the grain will not be cut through sufficiently. As the spur cuts quite deeply it is necessary to stop the rebate about a bare mm. short of the finished depth, and finish off with the spur taken out or reversed into a neutral position.

The wood rebate plane is preferred by some. It has no fence, and to start the plane the fingers of the left hand are curled beneath the sole to enable it

to be kept equidistant from the edge. Sometimes it is more convenient to fix a straight-edge to the wood to act as a guide. As no spurs are fitted it is essential that a saw cut is made first when cross grain is being worked. Otherwise the grain will inevitably tear out.

Fig. 27 shows a rebate being worked with a metal plane. Start at the far end of the wood and remove one or two short shavings. Then at each successive stroke bring the plane a little farther back until it takes a shaving along the whole length. In this way it is not so liable to drift from the edge. In any case, however, it is essential that a firm inward pressure is maintained. The cutter should stand a trifle proud at the side of the plane facing the wood— not more than the thickness of a piece of stout paper. Unless this is done the plane is liable to shift outwards a trifle at each stroke so resulting in a rebate which is not square.

Fig. 27 Working a rebate using the metal fillister plane

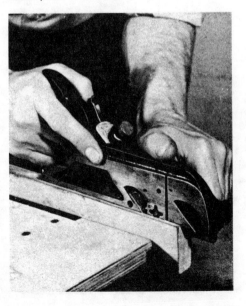

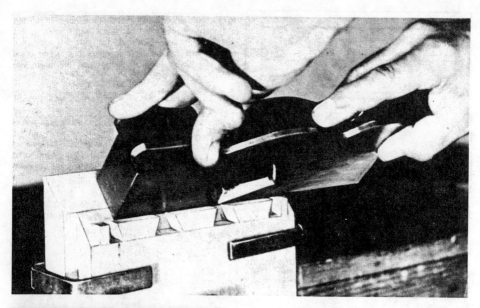

Fig. 28 (above) Typical use of the shoulder plane—it is especially useful for end grain
Fig. 29 (left) The bullnose plane in use

Shoulder plane. Although this is a special form of rebate plane, it is used for trimming rather than working a rebate. It is of special value for end grain. Thus wide shoulders can be trimmed with it, hence the name. The cutter has its bevel uppermost, and this means that it has close support practically up to the cutting edge. It is always set fine since its purpose is solely that of trimming. It is important that the edge of the cutter is sharpened square, because, although it is generally possible to knock the back of the cutter over slightly if not true, it causes the side of the cutter to protrude unevenly so that the plane does not bed down properly on its side. Fig. 28 shows a typical operation, that of trimming the mitred lap of a secret dovetail joint.

Bullnose plane. This again is another form of rebate plane, but the cutting edge is near the front of the plane so that it will work close up into a corner. Apart from this, however, it is an invaluable little tool for general work, and can often be used more conveniently than the shoulder plane. Fig. 29

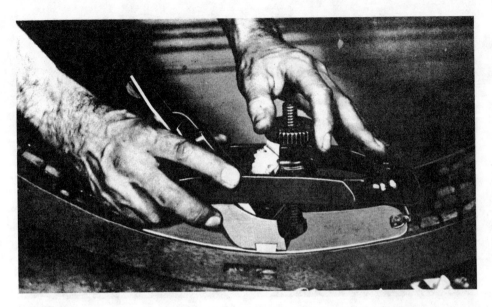

Fig. 31 (above) Planing a curved surface with the compass plane
Fig. 30 (right) The side rebate plane

shows it in use. A quite narrow type is also available.

Side rebate plane. This is not required often, but when it is wanted it is wanted badly. An example of its use is when it is necessary to widen grooves to hold polished or veneered shelves. Clearly the latter could not be planed in thickness. The side rebate plane is the only tool that can be used to widen the groove. It is shown in Fig. 30.

Compass plane. The metal type with flexible sole is shown in Fig. 31. It can be used for both concave and convex curves. Although provided with a back iron, the plane should be used *with* the grain as far as possible. Only curves which are struck from a circle can be planed. To set it hold the plane over the sawn wood and turn the adjusting screw till the sole takes up approximately to the shape. For concave shapes the sole should be of slightly quicker curvature, and rather flatter for convex shapes.

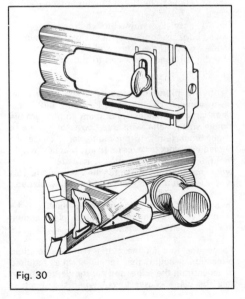

Fig. 30

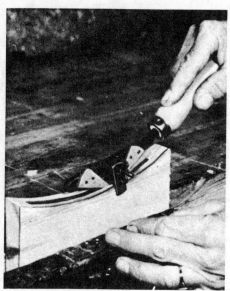

Fig. 32 (above) The Record plough plane (044C) in use

Fig. 33 (right) Working a groove around a curved edge using the Technikos plough. Two hands would normally be used on the tool but here the left hand is lowered to show details

Grooving plane or plough. There are a great many varieties of this, both in wood and metal. Metal grooving planes are of many forms from the simple small plane with three sizes of cutters to about 6mm. ($\frac{1}{4}$in.), to the multi-plane. These last named will work grooves up to any practical width, though for extra wide ones it is usual to use it twice, resetting the fence for the extra width. This is specially true when hardwood is being planed.

In addition to grooving this multi-plane can be used for rebating, though the fillister plane shown in Fig. 27 is more satisfactory for this work.

To set the tool fix the cutter with the required projection, secure the fence at the required distance from the edge, and set the depth stop so that the plane ceases to cut when the depth is

reached. Fig. 32 shows the Record plough plane No. 044C in use.

Whichever type of plane is used, it should be started at the far end of the wood and one or two short cuts taken. Then at each successive stroke it is brought a little further back until it can run right through. In this way the plough runs into a groove it has already worked, and any liability to drift from the edge is avoided. In any case a steady inward pressure must be maintained.

The above grooving tools are for straight work only. When a groove has to be worked around a curved edge the Technikos plough, Fig. 33, is invaluable. It has two opposed cutters and when a groove of odd width is needed the cutters can be staggered to give the required width. A narrow fence is incorporated to enable the tool to negotiate the curve, and a depth stop is provided. Grooves curved in either a horizontal or vertical direction can be cut.

Router plane. The metal type with adjustable cutter is used widely nowadays. It can be obtained with either open or closed mouth. The cutter is

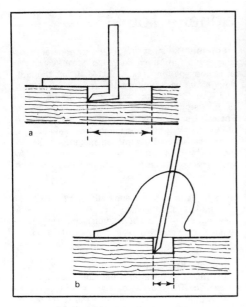

Fig. 34 (above) Section through (a) metal router and (b) wood router
Fig. 35 (right) The Stanley metal router plane in use

cranked and the cutting edge is almost horizontal so that it cuts easily. On the other hand it is liable to tear out woods with difficult grain. Furthermore it cannot work in a recess which is less than double the length of the cranked part of the cutter. This is made clear in Fig. 34. The tool in use is shown in Fig. 35. The old router or old woman's tooth still has its uses since it will work in a much more confined space (see Fig. 34.), and is not liable to tear out the grain since its action is more akin to scraping than cutting.

Moulding planes. These have only a limited use nowadays since most mouldings are machined. A small round plane is handy for working hollows, however. This has no fence and the angle at which

it is held is a matter for judgment. The fingers of the left hand pass beneath the sole and act as a sort of fence. To work a hollow at an edge a plain chamfer should be worked with the bench plane first.

Other types of moulding planes to work special mouldings have a fence, and this is held hard up against the edge of the wood. Many planes require to be held at an angle. You can tell this by the fence member which must be upright when the plane is in use.

Toothing plane. This, shown at (Q), Fig. 1, p. 11, is used to roughen the surface before veneering and on certain wide joints. Its cutter, which is practically vertical, has a series of grooves at the face which produce a saw-like cutting edge. Apart from giving a suitable key for the glue, it takes out inequalities left by the ordinary plane. It is shown in use on page 132.

Chapter four

How to Maintain and Use Tools (continued)

Fig. 1 Use of the cork rubber when using glasspaper

General Tools

Hammer. The most useful type for general indoor woodwork, furniture making, etc., is the Warrington or London pattern (see A, p. 14). It has the cross pene at the back which is handy for starting nails, and also for rubbing down inlay strings, etc. A useful weight (including the handle) is about 11oz. For extra small nails the pattern-maker's type of about 6oz. weight is invaluable. The claw hammer is of little value for furniture making. It is used mostly by carpenters for whom the claw for withdrawing nails is useful. An inclusive weight of 1lb. 11oz. is a good size.

Hold the hammer by the end of the shaft and so take advantage of the leverage it gives. Always look at the point of the actual object you are striking. Thus, when using a punch, look at the head of the punch, not at the nail which it is driving.

Punches. Sometimes known as nail sets, these are required to drive nails beneath the surface of the wood. The most generally useful type is the hollow point which is not so liable to start from the nail head, though for flooring brads and other cut nails a square punch is mostly used. Pincers are a necessity, and a fairly large pair is desirable. When using them always place a spare block of wood or a scraper beneath to avoid damaging the surface.

Mallet. An all-round useful size is the 180mm. (7in.) head which weighs in the region of 2½lb. Make sure that it has the tapered handle which fits the head with a wedge fit, so preventing it from flying off.

Screwdrivers. At least two are required, preferably three. The large one should be capable of driving 12 to 16 gauge screws, and be 250–300mm. (10–12in.) long. ((E), p. 14). For screws around the 8 gauge size a smaller driver is needed. The large one would not fit the slot, and would project at the sides.

The small screwdriver is needed for the screws you would use for small hinges, etc., say 4–6 gauge. An excellent type is the ratchet ((F), p. 15) which can be used with one hand whilst the other supports the door, or whatever it might be. It is only necessary to turn the hand back and forth without altering its position. The finger grip is also a great convenience since the first turn or two can be made with the thumb and finger, the rest of the hand remaining still and just exerting pressure. For the smallest screws the long thin electricians' screwdriver ((G), p. 15) is invaluable.

Veneer hammer. This is usually made at home. It is used to force out glue from beneath the veneer. It consists of a main stock with a handle let into it at right angles (see (S), p. 15). A strip of brass fits in a slot in the stock, the edge of this being straight and rounded over in section. Exact sizes are not important. The brass strip might be about 150—180mm. (6—7in.) long.

Cork rubber. Always use this when cleaning up a flat surface, Fig. 1. Its use prevents corners and edges from being dubbed over. Use it always in the direction of the grain in a straight line. Working across the grain or in a circular path causes scratches to show badly, and results in stain taking

unevenly in patches. Sometimes it cannot be avoided. In a quartered panel, for instance, it is impossible to follow the grain, and the only way is to avoid coarse paper and work along the length of the panel as in Fig. 2.

Another occasion calling for compromise is when a door framework is being cleaned up. First the rubber is taken across the shoulder as at (a), Fig. 3, when it will inevitably work across the grain. If, however, the rubber is afterwards taken parallel with shoulder (b) it will take out the scratches previously made.

To clean up mouldings it is necessary to make small wood rubbers shaped to a reverse of the section as in Fig. 4. Unless this is done the edge will be dubbed over. In any case it is the only way of exerting any degree of pressure.

Spokeshaves. Both wood and metal shaves are available. The latter is similar to a plane in both the setting and sharpening. As the cutter is rather short to handle it is a good plan to make a holder having a slot in it. It can then be handled much like a plane

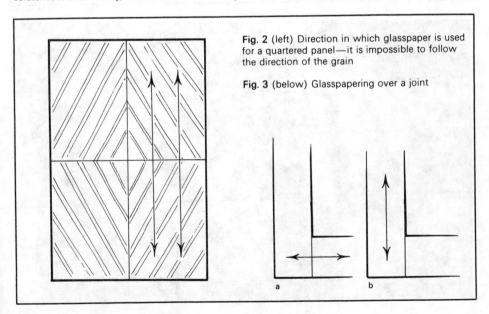

Fig. 2 (left) Direction in which glasspaper is used for a quartered panel—it is impossible to follow the direction of the grain

Fig. 3 (below) Glasspapering over a joint

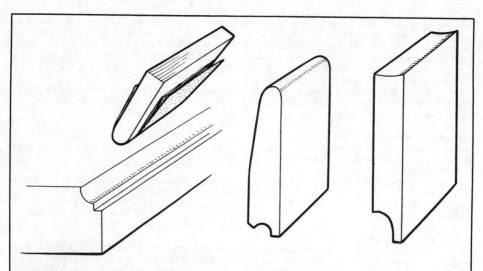

Fig. 4 Glasspaper rubbers used for cleaning mouldings

Fig. 5 (below) The round-faced metal spokeshave in use

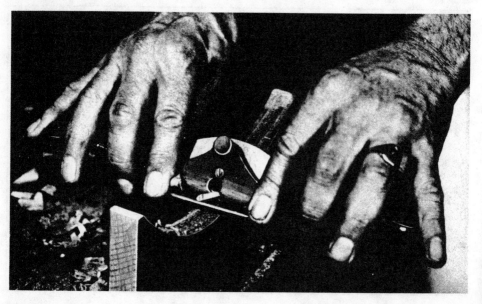

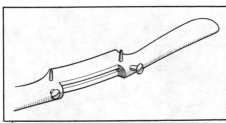

Fig. 6 (above left) Sharpening the cutter of the wood spokeshave

Fig. 7 (left) Loose cutter held with screws

Fig. 8 (above) Cleaning up a concave edge with the wood spokeshave

cutter. Fig. 5 shows the tool in use. To sharpen the wood type one way is to hold the cutter in the jaws of a handscrew or in the bench vice, and work an oilstone slip on the bevel. Another method is to use the edge of the oilstone as in Fig. 6. As a rule the tool works better if no attempt is made to remove the burr.

The cutter is held purely by the friction of the tangs, and these are tapped one way or the other to give the required setting. After prolonged use the tangs tend to become loose and liable to drop out. Round-head screws with the points nipped off can

be driven in as in Fig. 7. Fig. 8 shows the wood spokeshave in use.

Two chief points need to be watched when using the spokeshave; to work in the direction of the grain, and to keep the edge square. The former point is obvious from Fig. 9. Squareness of edge, however, comes only with practice, and the only plan is to test the work frequently and at various points.

Clearly the spokeshave cannot reach into the extreme corners, noted at (X), Fig. 9, and such

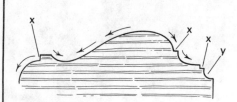

Fig. 9

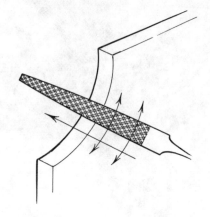

Fig. 10

Fig. 9 Direction in which spokeshave is used

Fig. 10 Compound action of the rasp or file over a shape

Fig. 11 (below) Cleaning the edge of abrasive material with the shaper

parts need rubbing with the file followed by the scraper, and finally glasspaper. In the same way a concave curve of small radius could not be reached by the spokeshave (Y). For this either a small half-round file or a rat-tail file would be needed.

File and rasp. The file is used with a sort of compound movement as shown in Fig. 10. As it is pushed forward it is partly revolved. In this way it takes out lumps and removes saw marks. In its turn it leaves file marks, of course, and these are removed by the scraper. When a lot of wood has to be removed it is quicker to begin with the rasp, the coarse face of which takes out inequalities quickly. It is followed by the file, which should be of rather quicker curvature than the curve being cleaned.

Shaper. This has similar uses to the rasp and file, and has the advantage that it is not liable to clog since there are open spaces between the cutting edges. The shaper is made in various patterns; flat, curved, and circular. Its chief value is in the rapid removal of unwanted wood, and for use on abrasive materials such as chipboard, etc. It is shown in use in Fig. 11.

Scraper. No matter how carefully a surface is planed, the plane is bound to leave some marks. Furthermore some woods tear up in parts no matter in which direction the plane is taken. The only way of taking out such blemishes is to use the scraper. A handy size is about 130mm. (5in.), the thickness being about 1·2mm ($\frac{3}{64}$in.). A thin scraper heats up quickly and becomes painful to use. A thick one is difficult to bend and is therefore tiring to use.

Fig. 12 shows it in use. It is pushed forward by the thumbs, the fingers at the ends bending it back slightly. In this way the edge is slightly curved, the centre part touching the wood. Note that it leans forward at an angle, the exact slope depending upon the way it is sharpened. Trial shows the most effective slope. Fine shavings should be removed, not mere dust.

The most awkward part of scraping is the start at the near edge, and the best way is to hold the scraper at a slight angle as in the plan view, Fig. 13. In this way part of the scraper is already lying on the wood, and there is no difficulty about starting the cut.

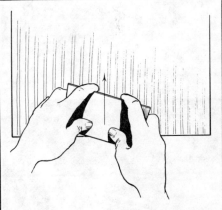

Fig. 12 (left) Cleaning up a surface with the cabinet scraper

Fig. 13 (above) How scraper is started at the end of wood

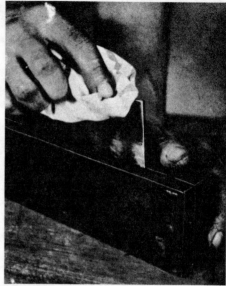

Fig. 14 (top left) Rubbing down the scraper edge with the file

Fig. 15 (above) Finishing the edge on the oilstone

Fig. 16 (middle left) Rubbing the sides on the oilstone

Fig. 17 (bottom left) Flattening the sides with the gouge or burnisher

Sharpening the scraper. To sharpen the scraper hold it in the vice and with a fine flat file make the edge straight and square, taking out any rounding-over that may have ocurred at the edges, see Fig. 14. To remove the file marks hold the scraper in a pad and work it on the oilstone, changing the direction of the movement so that wear on the stone is equalised. Some prefer to use the edge of the stone, working it between the case and its lid, as in Fig. 15. A slight burr will be set up at the edges, and this is removed by laying each side of the scraper on the stone and rubbing flat as in Fig. 16.

The edge is now ready to be turned. Hold the scraper flat on the bench about 5mm. ($\frac{1}{4}$in.) from

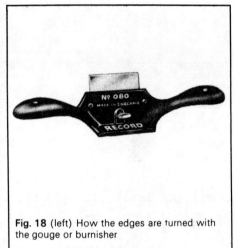

Fig. 18 (left) How the edges are turned with the gouge or burnisher

Fig. 19 (above) The scraper plane

the edge and draw a hard steel tool such as a gouge along it once or twice as in Fig. 17. Take care not to catch the fingers with the gouge. A special rounded sharpener known as a burnisher or ticketer is available. Bring the scraper forwards so that it overhangs the edge of the bench by about 5mm. ($\frac{1}{4}$in.). Wet the side of the gouge in the mouth and, holding it at a slight angle, draw it along the scraper, first in one direction, then the other, using strong pressure, as in Fig. 18. This should turn up a strong edge. Some prefer to hold the scraper upright, and draw the gouge upwards.

After being in use for a while the edges will become dull. They can be restored a few times by turning back as in Fig. 17 and re-turning as in Fig. 18. Eventually, however, this will fail to turn up a satisfactory edge, and it is necessary to use file and oilstone again.

For some purposes the scraper plane, Fig. 19, is useful, especially for woods with hard and soft grain. Whereas the ordinary steel scraper is liable to dig into the soft parts of the grain, the plane avoids this. The cutter of the tool is filed and honed at about 45 deg. and the edge turned up to hook

form with a burnisher. The cutter is held vertically in the vice and the burnisher held flat on the bevel and gradually brought up to within about 15 deg. of the horizontal in successive strokes. To set the cutter the plane is held on a flat board with the fixing screws entirely free. The cutter is dropped into its slot when it will fall to the wood by its own weight. The two fixing screws are then tightened and the rear adjusting screw fed forwards, thus bending the cutter slightly and giving it projection beyond the sole.

Oilstone and oilstone slips. Nowadays the manufactured stones such as the India, Carborundum, and Unirundum are widely used in preference to the natural stones, because of their consistent quality combined with rapid cutting. They can be obtained in three grades, coarse, medium and fine; also in combination form. For cabinet work the fine grade is recommended. Use a thin lubricating oil, and wipe clean after use. Make a container for it immediately as it is easily broken.

One or two oilstone slips are needed, and it is advisable to choose those of tapered section, as these give rounded edges of varying curvature.

Chapter five

How to Maintain and Use Tools (continued)

Rules, Gauges, Dividers, Square, Bevel, Parallel Strips

These are most important because accurate work is impossible unless the wood is set out correctly.

Rule. For general bench work the 1 metre (2ft. or 3ft.) rule is convenient, though there is a tendency to replace it with the flexible metal type, which has the advantage of opening up to a much greater length, yet taking up little space when closed. The type with combined metric and Imperial markings has advantages.

Always hold the rule so that the calibrations actually touch the wood. Thus in Fig. 1 the rule is on its edge and there is no doubt of the measurement as there might be if the rule were held flat. In the latter case the measurement would appear to vary according to whether the wood were seen from the right or left. This illustration is also of value

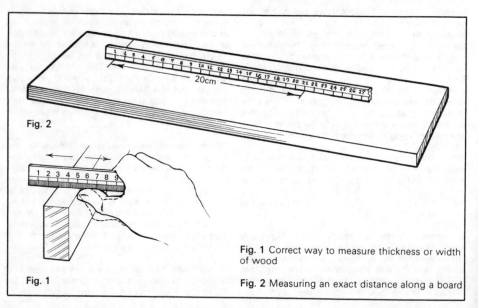

Fig. 1 Correct way to measure thickness or width of wood

Fig. 2 Measuring an exact distance along a board

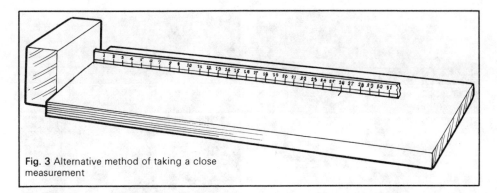

Fig. 3 Alternative method of taking a close measurement

in that it shows how the thickness (or width) of a piece of wood is measured. Note that measurement is not taken from the end of the rule, but from one of the calibrations. It is far easier to judge when a mark is level with the edge of the wood rather than the end of the rule. By rocking the thumb over one way or the other the rule can be made to slide the most minute distance, and the exact measurement can be noted with ease. In any case the thumb acts as a bearing in keeping the rule steady.

The same idea is followed in Fig. 2 when an exact distance is being marked. Instead of the end of the rule being placed on the mark, the first 1cm. (10mm.) calibration is used. Then in measuring the distance 10mm. is added. Thus, suppose the distance to be noted is 200mm., the mark is made opposite the 210mm. calibration on the rule. Another way is to place a block of wood exactly on the mark and put the end of the rule against this. The same idea can be followed when the distance has to be taken from the end of the wood as in Fig. 3. All these methods are used for close work. They are unnecessary for approximate measurements.

The rule can often be used for drawing a pencil line parallel with an edge as in Fig. 4. Although it does not give the close accuracy of a gauge line, it is quite suitable for, say, the marking of a board for ripping out. Sometimes the finger gauge method in Fig. 5 can be used for rough marking. Rather more accurate is the use of notched wood as in Fig. 6. This is specially useful when chamfering when a gauge mark would be unsightly.

One other occasional use for a rule is in marking a board of odd width into approximately equal parts. Thus, suppose a board say 142mm. wide has to be divided into five equal parts. Take the first figure above the width into which five will go easily. Clearly it is 150. Set one end of the rule at one edge of the board, and 150 at the other, the rule sloping at an angle. Mark the wood at 30, 60, 90, and 120mm. as shown in Fig. 7.

Gauges. The three chief kinds are, marking, cutting, and mortise. In addition there is the panel gauge which is similar to the marking gauge but is much bigger and has a pencil in place of a steel marker. It is used for marking wide boards.

Fig. 8 shows how the marking or cutting gauge is held. The first finger bears down on the top of the gauge, whilst the root of the same finger and the thumb push forward. The remaining three fingers press inwards towards the edge. This last is of great importance in that it is vital that the gauge does not drift outwards. This may easily happen, especially if the grain tends to run in that direction. Only marks *with* the grain or at *end* grain should be made with the marking gauge.

For cross grain the cutting gauge is necessary; the other would merely scratch. This tool has a knife rather than a marker. It is used in the same way but it is advisable to set the cutter at a *slight* angle as in Fig. 9 so that it tends to run *into* the wood. The fence, of course, prevents it from actually doing so; the great thing is to stop any tendency for it to run outwards.

57

Fig. 4 (above left) Drawing a pencil line parallel with an edge

Fig. 5 (above right) The finger-gauge method showing a line parallel with an edge

Fig. 6 (left) Use of a rebated slip for drawing a pencil line parallel with an edge

Fig. 7 (below) Dividing an odd measurement into equal parts

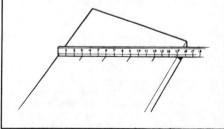

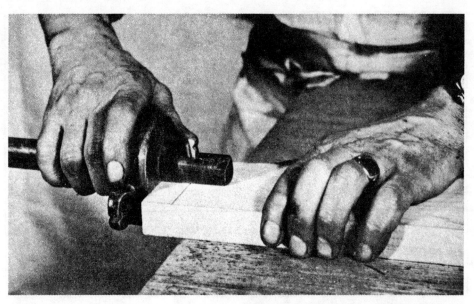

Fig. 8 (above) How either the cutting gauge or the marking gauge is held

Fig. 9 (below) Setting of cutting gauge. The cutter inclines at a slight angle so that it tends to draw the gauge inwards

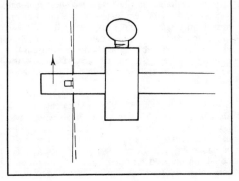

In addition to marking, the cutting gauge is used to cut right through thin wood. The cutter is given a fair projection, and a deep cut made from each side. Softer varieties of wood can be cut up to about 6mm. ($\frac{1}{4}$in.) thick in this way.

The gauge can either be set with the rule, or to the item for which it is needed. In the former case the end of the rule is held against the fence of the gauge and the latter adjusted until the cutter or marker is level with the required measurement. Final fine adjustment is made by tapping one end or the other of the stem on the bench. When a fitting such as a lock or hinge is being fitted the gauge is set to the fitting itself, the latter being placed on the fence and the marker set to the pin or whatever it may be. When dovetailing the gauge is held to the wood itself so that it can be set to its thickness.

The mortise gauge has two markers, one fixed and the other adjustable. The distance between them is regulated to the width of the chisel to be used in mortising, the latter being held to the gauge. The fence is set afterwards to whatever position is required. In the case of a mortise and tenon joint to

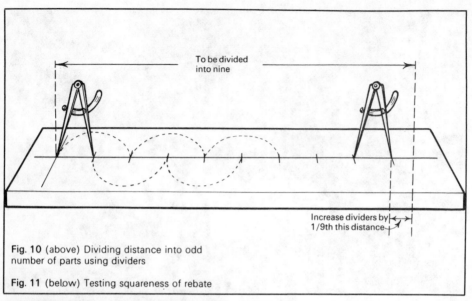

To be divided
into nine

Increase dividers by
1/9th this distance

Fig. 10 (above) Dividing distance into odd number of parts using dividers

Fig. 11 (below) Testing squareness of rebate

fit flush, the gauge is used from the face side of both pieces.

Dividers. These have various uses, from scribing a circle to dividing a distance into an odd number of parts. Fig. 10 shows how the latter is done. It is assumed that the distance has to be divided into nine equal parts. Set the dividers to what you think is one ninth, and step along as to the left. If badly out re-set until approximately right—some trial and error is inevitable. If nine steps are short increase the setting by what you estimate one ninth of the remaining distance, and step out again. This will bring the setting much nearer, and a second adjustment will put it right. If on stepping out the nine moves takes the point beyond the mark, the setting is decreased by one ninth of the distance over-run.

Square. The adjustable type of engineer's square shown at (W), p. 13, has many advantages. Apart from normal use in marking and testing, it can be used for rebate work as in Fig. 11, and as a set square in Fig. 12. The ordinary wood-metal square could not be used for either purpose. In any case this latter type of square is often inaccurate.

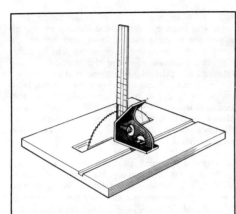

Fig. 12 Testing squareness of circular saw or any other item

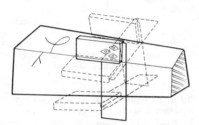

Fig. 13 Use of square from face side and edge

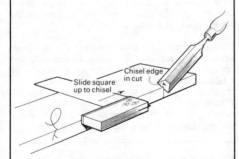

Chisel edge in cut

Slide square up to chisel

Fig. 14 Marking shoulder with chisel and try square

A rule to keep in mind is that the square should be used from either face side or face edge whenever possible. There are exceptions, but since these two have been made true and square with each other the desirability of working to them is obvious. Fig. 13 is an exaggerated example of the application of the rule. Lines such as might be required for the shoulders of a joint are to be marked round all four sides of a piece of wood. This particular piece is shown intentionally inaccurate, but if the butt of the square rests always against either face side or face edge the marks should meet.

When two or more pieces have to be marked alike it is an advantage to cramp them together and square the marks across all. They can then be separated and the mark squared round each independently. A typical example is in the rails or stiles of a door. For close accuracy always make a knife or chisel cut rather than a pencil line. The latter is for approximate or rough working only, or when the knife marks might appear as a blemish. As a typical example of marking with the square, take the rails of a door, the shoulders of which have to be marked. Cramp the rails together flush and, using the rule, make marks with a sharp pencil at the shoulder positions. Placing the knife or chisel on each mark in turn, square lines right across both rails. Separate the rails, and square the marks round each independently. To do this place the knife at the corner of the wood, its edge resting in the slight cut already made as in Fig. 14, and slide the square up to it. In this way the position is bound to be correct. Note that the chisel or knife should bear over to the right so that the bevel is about square with the edge. Otherwise the bevel may prevent the blade of the square from sliding to the correct position. This sliding up of the square to the knife is invariably more accurate than trying to position the square by eye only. For large work the wood square shown at (Q), p. 13, is necessary. It is usual for the craftsman to make his own.

Mitre square. This is needed for marking and testing 45 deg. mitres. There is no special point in its use, except that when mitre lines have to be squared on to all four surfaces, care has to be taken to position the square exactly, otherwise the lines may not meet owing to the angle.

Sliding bevel. This is used mainly for odd angles —for instance the rail shoulders of a stand with

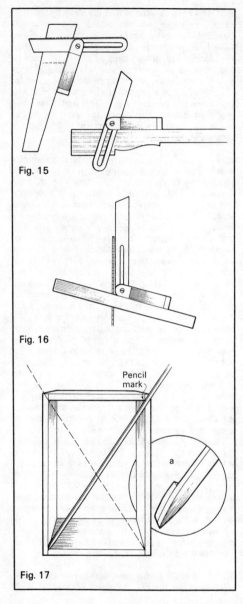

Fig. 15

Fig. 16

Pencil
mark

a

Fig. 17

legs set at an angle. The angle can be set by a protractor or by a drawing. For some work it is an advantage to have the blade set centrally in the stock as this gives the acute angle and its complementary obtuse one. Fig. 15 shows it in use when marking the joint of a stand with leg set at an angle. In the leg the bevel must be worked from inside the leg owing to the taper, whereas the rail, owing to its shaped edge, needs to be marked from above. On the other hand, in Fig. 16, which shows the table of a circular saw being set at an angle, the blade projects at one side only.

Straight-edge and parallel winding strips. Both of these are usually made by the worker himself. The former should be in well-seasoned straight-grained hardwood. A test for the working accuracy of the edge is to place it on a flat board and draw a line along the edge with a keen pencil. When reversed on to the other side it will align with the pencil line if true. It has many uses for marking out and testing generally, and can be of any convenient size. Many workers keep two; about 500mm. (20in.) and 1m. (3ft.) respectively. Incidentally the accepted scientific method of testing is to plane three straight edges, each of which should match up to the other two when tried in both directions, but this is scarcely necessary for the woodworker.

Parallel strips (winding strips) are used mostly to test whether a surface is free from winding, see Fig. 14, p. 39. Another use is in testing whether the four legs of a cabinet will stand square on the floor. If the strips are not long enough to reach across the legs they are placed on longer strips of wood, the edges of which are parallel.

Diagonal strip. When a large carcase has been assembled it may be misleading to test with the square since any curvature in the wood would give a false reading. It is therefore advisable to use the diagonal strip or squaring rod shown in Fig. 17. Placed across the job the diagonal length is noted with the pencil. When reversed into the opposite corners it will show the same length if true.

Fig. 15 Marking stand with splay legs, using sliding bevel
Fig. 16 Testing angle using sliding bevel
Fig. 17 Diagonal strip used to test squareness

Appliances

All of these can be made by the craftsman himself.

Shooting board. There are various ways of making this. The simplest is shown in Fig. 18. Exact sizes are not important, but those given can be taken as a general guide. Two are handy; a short one, say 600mm., (2ft. or 2ft. 6in.) for general trimming and short joints; and one from 1m. to 1·5m. (3ft. to 5ft.) for long joints in thin wood. Note the chamfered lower corner of the upper platform which forms a dust trap and avoids false working. The effective edge of the stop is at 90 deg. Its wedge formation ensures a tight fit. It can always be tapped in in the event of its becoming loose, and the projecting end levelled. If possible use quarter-cut wood throughout as this is not liable to warp.

The shooting board is used in two distinct ways. The first is in planing joints in thin wood, or in planing an edge straight and square. Its advantage for thin wood is that there is no liability for the plane to wobble. The operation is shown in Fig. 19. Note that the wood overhangs the upper platform by about 6mm. ($\frac{1}{4}$in.), and that the plane makes the edge true by virtue of the truth of its own sole. It does not run along the edge of the upper platform. The usual plan is to remove shavings from the middle until the plane ceases to cut, then take a couple of shavings right through. Generally this will automatically make the edge straight, though in the case of a joint the parts are tried together, or the edge tested with a straight-edge in the case of a single edge.

Theoretically the edge should be square, assuming the sole of the plane to be square with its side. In the case of a joint, however, it is always advisable to plane one piece with the face side uppermost, and the other with it downward. In this way any angularity in the one is cancelled by that in the other, and the parts go together in alignment.

The second use of the shooting board is in trimming the ends of wood square. In this case the wood is held tight up against the stop, and the plane is worked along the edge of the upper platform. The wood is pressed towards the plane and in this way is fed steadily out as planing proceeds. As the far

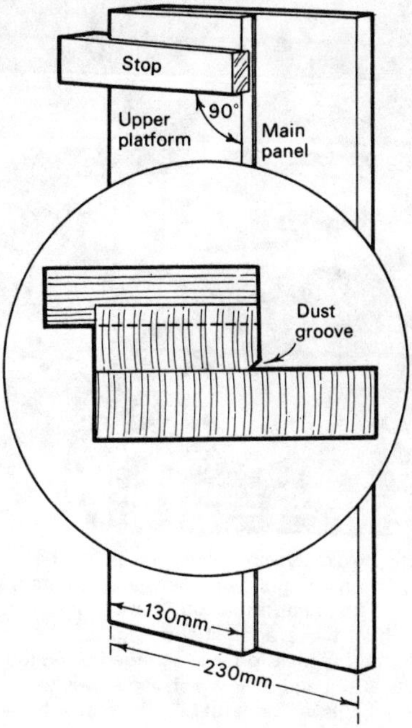

Fig. 18 Shooting board suitable for small work, the length need not be exact

corner is liable to splinter out, it is advisable to chisel it off. If this is impracticable owing to there being insufficient width the plane will either have to be taken halfway in from each edge, or a spare piece of wood with parallel edges placed behind it as in Fig. 20.

Mitre shooting board. This has similar uses to the normal shooting board but is for trimming mitres. It is shown on p. 16 at (B). The direction of the plane is reversed when the wood has to be placed on the far side of the stop.

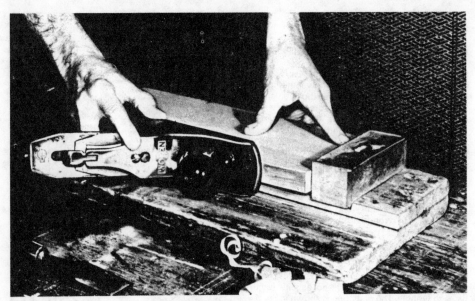

Bench hook. Used chiefly to hold the wood steady when being sawn, this is a useful item (see (E), p. 16). An important point about it is that the strip which bears against the edge of the bench should be dowelled on, not screwed or nailed—at any rate at the end over which the saw is used. The reason for this is that with continual use the wood is worn away by the saw and fixing screws or nails may ultimately become bared and foul the saw. Fig. 12, p. 23, shows how it is used, the wood being held firmly against the back of the bench hook.

Mitre block and box. These are needed for sawing mitres, the former for small mouldings. The only special point about the mitre block is that the wood must be kept firmly up against the stop, and whenever possible the saw should cut *into* the section not out of it. In other words the back of the moulding should be against the stop of the mitre block, so that any rag created by the saw occurs at the back where it does not matter. Fig. 21 shows the mitre block in use.

The same thing applies to the mitre box. Thus when cutting, say, a large cornice moulding it is advisable to place it upside down and saw towards the

Fig. 19 (above) Truing the edge of a board on the shooting board

Fig. 20 (below) Avoiding splintered corner when trimming end grain

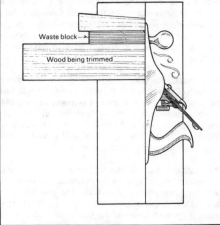

Waste block

Wood being trimmed

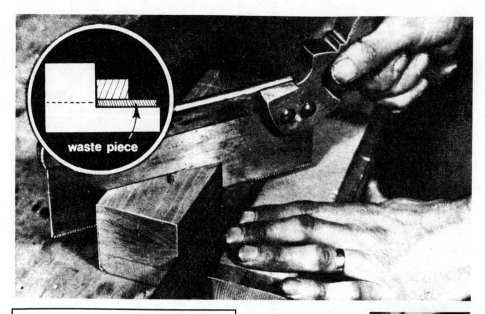

waste piece

Fig. 21 (above) Use of the mitre block. The waste piece (inset) avoids cutting into the base of the block
Fig. 22 (below) Pitched cornice moulding being mitred
Fig. 23 (right) Trimming moulding using mitre template. The thumb is normally on the chisel to steady it but to avoid hiding the blade is shown here at the side

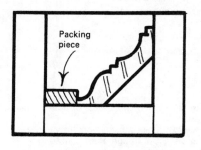

Packing piece

moulding as in Fig. 22. In this way the teeth cut into the section in both a horizontal and vertical direction. This illustration is also interesting in that it shows the way to deal with a pitched cornice moulding which has no backing. To form a true mitre the top and back faces of the moulding which are at right angles with each other must bear against the back and bottom of the mitre box, and, to ensure this, a packing piece is planed so that it fits exactly between the edge of the moulding and the side of the box. This makes the position definite. It does not matter if the saw cuts right through it.

Mitre template. Fig. 23 shows the use of this in cutting the mitre needed in a door frame having a moulding worked in the solid. It is placed over the moulding and its sloping end (at 45 deg.) used as a guide for the chisel. For small mouldings it can be held in position with the hand. On larger ones a thumbscrew can be tightened over it.

Cramps

These are used to pull the parts of joints together and to hold them whilst the glue sets, and also to hold the wood to the bench whilst being worked.

Sash cramps. For assembling a door frame or a butt joint these are a necessity. Length ranges from 600mm. (2ft.) upwards, and size should be selected to suit the average work done. Blocks should be placed beneath the cramp shoes to prevent damage to the surface.

Tests for both squareness and freedom from winding should be made as soon as possible after tightening the cramps. If the square reveals an inaccuracy as in Fig. 24 the position of the shoes should be shifted in the direction shown by the arrows. A winding test is made by looking across the work. Both near and far rails should appear parallel. If out as shown in exaggeration in Fig. 25 the cramps should again be adjusted in the direction of the arrows.

A point to remember is that cramps are necessarily heavy and may pull a framework out of truth by their weight and so give a false reading. They may also cause a framework to appear true when the weight of the cramps is pulling it down. The frame

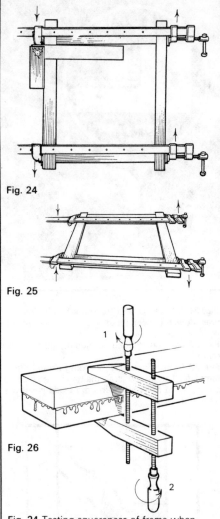

Fig. 24

Fig. 25

Fig. 26

Fig. 24 Testing squareness of frame when cramping
Fig. 25 Cramped framework in winding
Fig. 26 Order of tightening screws of handscrew

may spring into winding again after the cramps are removed.

When an extra large framework has to be assembled and the available cramps are not long enough, two can be held together by nuts and bolts passed through them. In this way the length can be adjusted to suit the job in hand. The two shoes are removed, enabling the screws to be tightened from either end.

G Cramps, handscrews, and thumbscrews. These are used chiefly when wood is joined in its thickness. Their application is fairly obvious. The handscrew is particularly useful. To use it open the jaws to the approximate size by grasping a handle in each hand and revolving the one about the other. Rapid adjustment can be made in this way. The inner screw is then tightened (1) Fig. 26 (see arrow), and lastly the outer screw, again in the direction of the arrow. This has the effect of levering the jaw on to the wood. When finally tightened the jaws should be approximately parallel.

The thumbscrew is just a small edition of the G cramp and is used for small work.

Bench holdfast. This (I, p. 17) is used to hold wood still on the bench whilst being worked. Its stem passes through a hole in the bench and it exerts its power by being levered over sideways. It is therefore effective only on a thick bench top. If the latter is thin it is necessary to thickness it locally. Some holdfasts have a metal socket for recessing into the bench top. When a hole is bored through the bench to receive it it is clearly necessary to avoid doing so over a drawer or cupboard.

Improvised cramps. These can always be made from lengths of wood with stops screwed on at the ends to act as shoes. Pairs of folding wedges are knocked in at one end to give the necessary pressure. For the light cramping of odd shapes springs can be used. These are simply old uphol-stery springs cut down and partly straightened out in the form of a C. They are specially useful in repair work in which moderate pressure only is required over surfaces of awkward shape.

Fig. 27 Testing squareness of a cramped-up framework

Chapter six

Light Machines for Woodwork

Although most home woodworkers follow hand methods, there is an increasing tendency to install a machine of one kind or another to cut out some of the more tedious and back-aching operations. The most obvious choice in this connection is a small saw since sawing is probably the most laborious task connected with woodwork. It is as well to point out at the outset, however, that there is a great advantage in having a basic machine to which various machine attachments can be added. This basic machine usually takes the form of a wood-turning lathe, for which circular saw, bandsaw, planer, sander, and mortising attachments are available. There is also the small universal machine which may include circular saw, planer, and borer, but is not a lathe.

As a general rule a machine which is designed for a single purpose is more satisfactory than one which has to be adapted to various uses, but taking into account the limitations of workshop space and the fact that it costs less, the single adaptable machine is generally the better proposition for home craftsmen than several separate machines. A typical machine is shown in Fig. 2, and the various attachments are detailed below the illustration. The use of the individual machines is much the same whatever the type or make, though slight variation in method of use or of sharpening may be needed in accordance with the particular type. The following general principles apply.

Circular Saw

For general woodwork this is the most useful type of saw to have because not only can ripping, cross-cutting, and mitreing be done on it, but rebating and grooving are also possible. An essential feature is a table which can be raised or lowered so that the depth of rebates and grooves can be adjusted. Preferably too it should be adjustable at an angle up to 45 deg. to enable wood to be cut at angles other than a right angle. In some machines the saw is adjustable rather than the table, and this has the advantage that, since the table remains flat, there is no tendency for the wood to slide sideways when bevel cuts are being made.

Fig. 1 Use of a light machine in the workshop

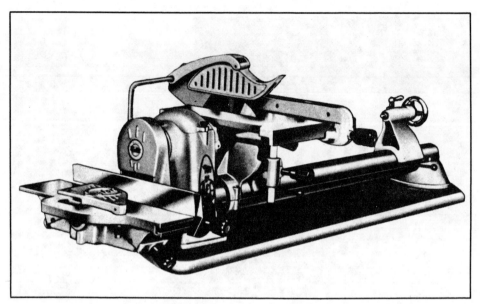

A fence is an obvious requirement so that wood can be ripped to width; also a grooved bench top so that the mitre gauge can be used for cross-cutting at right angles or any other angle. A riving knife is a necessity so that the wood does not tend to bind on the saw in the event of the kerf closing. Lastly an efficient guard should be fitted both above and below (though in many machines the lower casing acts as a guard beneath the top).

For general use either the combination saw (B), Fig. 3, or that with radial cross-teeth (A) should be fitted, as either can be used for both ripping and cross-cutting. Here a word of warning is necessary: keep the saw sharp. A dull saw will burn the wood, and an endeavour to force the wood may result in inaccurate work and possibly cause an accident. Saws with tungsten carbide tipped teeth (C) have the advantage that they remain sharp for a long period and can be used on hard or abrasive materials such as chipboard and other resin-assembled boards without losing their edge.

Ripping. When the timber already has a straight edge it is only necessary to set the fence to the required distance from the saw (the latter cutting

Fig. 2 (above) The Myford ML8 lathe showing circular saw and planer attachments. Other attachments are bandsaw, disc sander and mortiser
Fig. 3 (below) Types of saw teeth

a

b

c

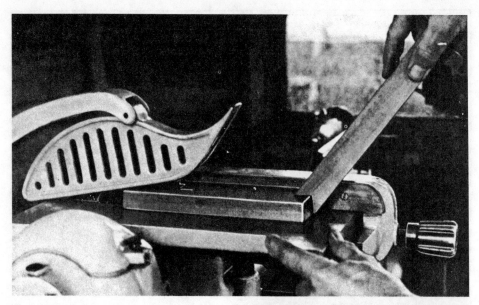

Fig. 4 (above) Use of pusher stick to avoid bringing fingers close to saw
Fig. 5 (right) Cross-cutting using the mitre gauge

on the waste side), and push the wood through, keeping the edge close up against it. For long boards it is a help to have someone at the back to take it off, pulling and supporting the boards as the cut nears completion. If this is not possible the wood can be cut half-way from one end, reversed, and the cut completed from the other end. In all cases avoid putting the fingers near the revolving saw and never have them between the saw and the fence where they might be trapped. The pusher stick shown in Fig. 4 should always be used to push the wood at the end of the cut.

If there is no straight edge to start off with, you can either plane it straight first (by machine or hand) and work from this, or you can draw in a pencil line with the straight-edge, and, standing behind the wood, pass the wood through without using the fence. All subsequent cuts can be made from this, using the fence as a guide.

70

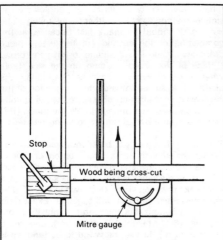

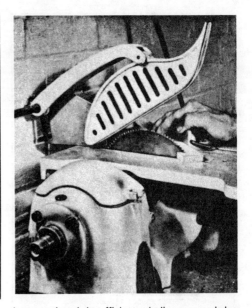

Fig. 6 (above) Cross-cutting to length
Fig. 7 (right) Cutting a mitre on the circular saw using the mitre gauge. The guard is shown raised to reveal the saw

Labels in Fig. 6: Stop; Wood being cross-cut; Mitre gauge

Cross cutting. Fig. 5 shows a typical operation. Note that both hands are kept to the side of the saw. When several pieces have to be cut all to the same length the method shown in Fig. 6 can be followed. A block of wood to act as a stop is fixed to near the front of the saw table with a G cramp. Its position is adjusted so that its distance from the saw equals the length of the pieces to be sawn. The wood is held against the mitre gauge and pressed up to the stop. The gauge is pushed up to the saw, and the process repeated until the required number of pieces has been sawn. Mitreing is done similarly to square cross-cutting, Fig. 7, and in the case of compound cuts the table is also tilted.

Grooving. Frequently on light machines it is necessary to pass the wood over the saw for as many times as may be needed to give the required width of groove. If a drunken saw is available this can be set to the width, though the bottom of the groove is not flat, but slightly curved. For most work, however, the curve is so slight as not to matter. Some saws can be fitted with a dado head which will cut grooves. Light machines, however, are frequently not made to take these, partly

because there is insufficient spindle room, and also because the cut would be too heavy.

The table (or saw) is first adjusted so that the saw projects by an amount equal to the required groove depth. The fence is positioned so that the cut is level with one side of the groove to be cut. If the fence reaches only to the saw, a lengthening piece must be screwed on so that the wood can bear against it until it is past the saw. After a trial cut all the parts are run through. The fence is shifted to cut to the other side of the groove, and again all the parts cut. For narrow grooves this second cut will probably give the required width, but third or even fourth runs may be needed. Remember in every case to keep the face side of the wood to the fence.

The pusher stick, Fig. 4, is needed for completing the cut, though the push block is sometimes an advantage, as shown in Fig. 8. It enables downward as well as inward pressure to be maintained.

Rebating. Narrow rebates can be worked by taking parallel cuts side by side as at (a), Fig. 9, the wood being passed through as many times as may be needed to give the rebate width. For a larger

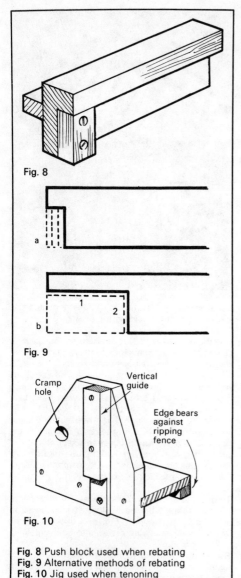

Fig. 8

a

Fig. 9

1
2
b

Cramp hole

Vertical guide

Edge bears against ripping fence

Fig. 10

Fig. 8 Push block used when rebating
Fig. 9 Alternative methods of rebating
Fig. 10 Jig used when tenoning

rebate, however, two cuts at right angles are the simpler method as at (b). Other things being equal cut No. 1 should be made first because, at the completion of the second cut the waste piece drops away, and it is desirable to have the broad surface of the wood bedding on the saw table where it is not liable to tilt over. Once again the pusher stick is used towards the completion of the cut. This is specially desirable since the riving knife cannot be used, and quite possibly the guard (this depends on the size of the wood being rebated).

Tenoning. It would not be economical in time to set up the saw to cut a single tenon or pair of tenons, but considerable saving in time occurs when a whole series is required. The simplest plan is to make the special device shown in Fig. 10. The parts are glued and screwed together. Exact sizes are not important, but the length might be about 150mm. (6in.), height 175mm. (7in.), and width 100mm. (4in.). In use the wood to be tenoned is held against the vertical guide with a thumbscrew, the latter being either passed through the cramp hole or fixed at the side according to the width of the wood being tenoned. The far edge bears against the ripping fence, the latter being positioned so that the saw cuts to the side of the gauge line. A lengthening piece must be screwed to the fence so that the device is supported throughout its cut. The height of table or saw is arranged so that the shoulder line is just reached. One cut is made at each tenon, the saw readjusted, and the other side of all the tenons cut. Fig. 11 shows the operation. It is usual to cut the shoulders by hand.

It will be realized that the over-all length of all tenons must be alike, otherwise the saw will over-cut some tenons, and under-cut others. This means that a different system must be followed as compared with that usually used for hand work. Exact over-all length including tenons must be fixed beforehand. Apart from actual cutting there is a further saving in time in that only one piece need be marked with the gauge.

Speed. The theoretical optimum speed of an 20cm, (8in.) circular saw is in the region of 4,500 r.p.m., but few small saws are designed for so high a rate. The more usual speed ranges from 1,500 to 2,500 r.p.m., and the saw should cut perfectly well if kept sharp. As a guide to the power required, the following are average.

Saw diam.	H.P. motor
(7in.)	$\frac{1}{3} - \frac{1}{2}$
(8in.)	$\frac{1}{2} - \frac{3}{4}$
(9in.)	$\frac{1}{2} - 1$

Band Saw

Next to the circular saw this is the most useful machine saw to have, Fig. 12. It can be used for straight cuts much as the circular saw is used, and also for curves for which the latter is useless. On the other hand, it will neither rebate nor groove, though tenons can be made on it.

Adjustment. There are several adjustments to be attended to on the bandsaw. First the table is usually made to tilt, and the correct angle should be tested with try square or protractor. The top wheel has a tensioning screw which is slackened off when the saw is not in use. When a new saw has to be fitted the locking device has usually to be un-screwed at the front of the table to enable the saw to be passed through the slot. The purpose of the device is to hold the table rigid.

Tracking is the first adjustment of the saw itself, and is accomplished by tilting the top wheel one way or the other. It should be carried out without guides or thrust wheel. Turn the wheel by hand and note whether the saw tends to keep central on the wheels or run to front or rear. If it is inclined to run towards the rear tilt the top of the wheel slightly forward at the top. Continue to adjust until it runs in the required position. It is advisable to vary this from time to time so that wear on the tyres can be equalized.

When satisfactory bring forward the thrust wheel so that it barely touches the back of the saw—it should turn only when the saw is being pressed against it in use. The guides may be blocks of metal or hardwood, and they are adjustable horizontally. They should be just short of touching the sides of the saw—not the teeth, of course. As a rule the upper guides form a complete unit with the thrust wheel, the whole being movable vertically. In use it should be set to clear the wood being sawn with just sufficient space above to enable the line to be followed.

Practical sawing. When possible avoid backing

Fig. 11 Cutting a tenon on the circular saw—the lower guard is shown removed to reveal saw
Fig. 12 (below) Bench bandsaw of the three-wheel type. Coronet Tool Company

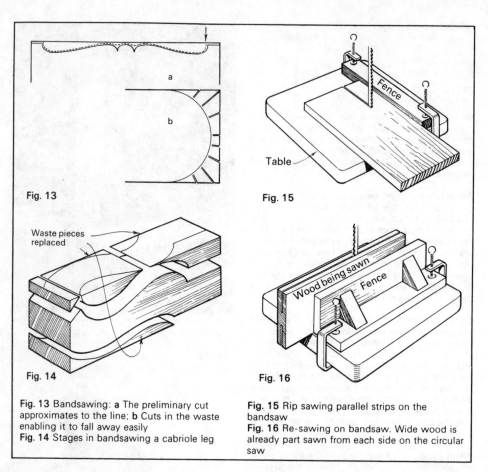

Fig. 13 Bandsawing: **a** The preliminary cut approximates to the line; **b** Cuts in the waste enabling it to fall away easily

Fig. 14 Stages in bandsawing a cabriole leg

Fig. 15 Rip sawing parallel strips on the bandsaw

Fig. 16 Re-sawing on bandsaw. Wide wood is already part sawn from each side on the circular saw

the wood from the saw. Sometimes it cannot be helped, when it should be done carefully and the path of the kerf followed. When a line is fairly intricate follow the main sweep first, ignoring the smaller detail. For instance, in Fig. 13 (a), the first cut would be shown by the dotted line. This would clear away the bulk of the waste without backing, and enable the acute corners to be cut afterwards. Note that the cut is made to the waste side of the line, allowing for later cleaning up. In the case of Fig. 13 (b), the preliminary cuts enable the waste to fall away when the acute curve is being sawn.

Some items call for sawing on two surfaces. For example, the shape of a cabriole leg is marked out on two adjacent faces, and saw cuts made at right angles, producing a square section ready for rounding. The shapes on one side having been cut, the waste parts are replaced as in Fig. 14 enabling the remaining cuts to be made. In some cases the lower waste is also replaced to act as a sort of supporting cradle. It is scarcely necessary in the present case because the back curve reaches practically to the bottom and there is no tendency for it to be unsteady.

When the saw is used for ripping straight cuts a fence is used. This may be a special adjustable item made for the table, or simply a straight piece of wood cramped to the table as in Fig. 15. Make sure that it is fixed parallel with the edge so that the saw is in alignment with the cut.

Sometimes it is useful to use the bandsaw for resawing—that is cutting a board in its thickness. It is a great help if preliminary saw cuts can be made on the circular saw as it lessens the work the bandsaw has to do. The operation is shown in Fig. 16 which shows the tall fence used to ensure that the wood is upright. Fig. 17 shows the bandsaw in use for tenoning.

Planer

Two kinds of machines come under this heading; the surface planer and the thicknesser. The latter, as the name suggests, is used to bring timber to an even thickness, but is not much used in the small home workshop because it is expensive. It is, however, possible to obtain a thicknessing attachment for most planers.

Parts of the surface planer. The diagram in Fig. 18 shows the chief parts. There is the main body in the centre of which the cutter block revolves. This block may have either two or three cutters. In front and to the rear of the cutter block are two tables which are adjustable along two inclined beds. Their height in relation to the cutters is thus adjustable. A fence is fitted to the front table, this being adjustable to any position and also free to cant to any angle. On many machines a rebating table (which is really a side extension of the front table) is fitted. Invariably, too, there is a guard which should be capable of extending right across the cutter block, and also be variable in height.

Sharpening and setting. Although ground, the cutters of a new machine require to be honed on an oilstone to give a fine edge. A simple jig is shown in Fig. 19, and variations can be worked out to suit the individual cutters. The device enables the correct angle to be maintained. When regrinding is needed it is necessary to mount the cutters upon a special carrier which runs back and forth across the

Fig. 17 (above) Sawing a tenon on the bandsaw
Fig. 18 (below) Diagram showing chief parts of the planer

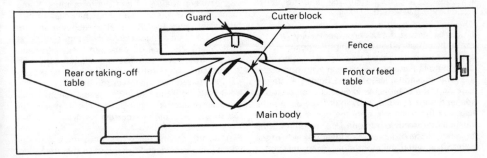

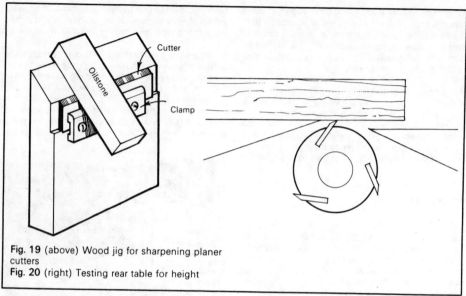

Fig. 19 (above) Wood jig for sharpening planer cutters

Fig. 20 (right) Testing rear table for height

face of the grinding wheel, thus ensuring even grinding.

The cutters are held in the block in various ways, some with wedge pieces held by bolts, or by a separate cap again bolted. As a rule there is some means of adjustment for height—either an adjustment screw at each end or a hole at the rear which enables the cutter to be tapped. Turn the bolts finger tight only when placing the cutters in the block and carry out all adjustment before finally tightening. When there is no adjustment the cutters must all be ground and honed to exactly the same extent.

In use the rear table must be exactly level with the tips of the cutters when in the highest position, and once set is never moved for normal planing until sharpening is required again. Deal with one cutter at a time. Place a piece of wood having a straight edge on the rear table, as in Fig. 20, towards one side and turn the block by hand, adjusting the height of the rear table until the cutter just barely touches the wood. When one side is correct bring the wood to the other edge and test this side of the cutter. The latter will probably need raising or

lowering, and this should be done until both sides just touch the wood, no more. From this point on the rear table must not be moved (the front table is set well down below the level).

Now deal with the second cutter, adjusting this until both sides of this also just touch the wood. When all is in order tighten the fixing bolts and make a second test. The thickness of the cut is fixed by the height of the front table. To ascertain this hold the straight wood on the back table as before. The thickness of the cut will be equal to the gap between the wood and the front table. Some machines have a scale showing thickness of cut, but this requires adjustment after each sharpening. To do this set a gauge to exactly 3mm. ($\frac{1}{8}$in.) and mark along the edge of a straight piece of wood. Set the front table to what is obviously less than 3mm. ($\frac{1}{8}$in.), and, setting the machine in action, pass the wood part way over the block. Lower the front table until the gauge line is just reached and set the pointer to the 3mm. ($\frac{1}{8}$in.) mark. All thicknesses will then be correct to this.

Surfacing. Set the fence to slightly more than the width of the wood, and the guard so that the wood

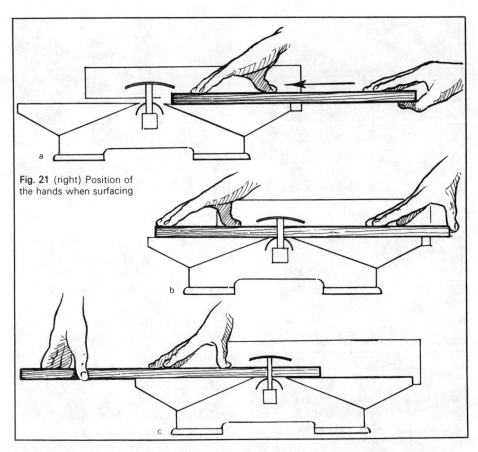

Fig. 21 (right) Position of the hands when surfacing

will pass beneath with comfortable clearance. The front table is also adjusted to the required thickness of cut. Push the wood forward with the right hand and press steadily down with the left on the front table. As the wood passes over the block withdraw the left hand so that it does not approach near to the block. When a reasonable length has passed beyond the block take the left hand over to the wood on the rear table and again press down. As the end of the wood approaches the block take also the right hand over to the rear table where it assists in both pressing down and moving the wood. Done in this way neither hand is ever immediately over the revolving block. Fig. 21, 22.

When a short piece has to be planed it is advisable to use a pusher block as given in Fig. 23. At the start of the cut the wood is fed with the hands in the usual way, but once the rear end is fairly on the table the pusher block is used. When practicable put the hollow side of the wood down on to the table as it is easier to get it straight. If this cannot be done it is necessary to take shavings from the middle first before passing the wood right across.

Edging. This is a similar operation, but the wood

77

Fig. 22 Surfacing on the planer

Fig. 23 Use of the pusher block when surfacing

Fig. 24 Use of thicknessing attachment to bring wood to constant thickness

Fig. 25 The planer set up for rebating

must be held firmly up against the fence so that the edge is planed square. If the guard is of telescopic form it is usual to set it low over the block and leave just sufficient gap between its end and the fence for the wood to pass through. In the case of extra wide wood it is as well to increase the height of the fence by screwing a wood fence to it. This gives an increased bearing surface against which the wood can bear. As a fair amount of pressure is required in all planing operations it is as well to wipe over the surface of the tables and the fence with a lightly oiled rag. One last word. Examine the wood and

pass it through in the direction in which it is less likely to tear out the grain.

Thicknessing attachment. This is attached to an ordinary surface planer as in Fig. 24, and is used after one surface of the wood has been planed true. The main pillar of the attachment is secured to the front table, the thicknessing plate thus rising or falling with it. The rear table is set as for normal planing and the distance between it and the thicknessing plate equals the finished thickness of the wood after planing. If much wood has to be removed pass the wood through twice, the machine being reset for the second pass.

Rebating. Many machines are provided with a rebating table which is a lateral extension of the front table. This supports the wood as it passes through. The rear table is unaltered, that is it remains level with the tops of the cutters. The front table is lowered to the rebate depth, and the fence brought over so that it leaves exposed a length of cutter equal to that of the rebate width. Normally the wood can be passed through in a single operation, but if the rebate is large or the wood extra hard it is as well to set it to half the depth first and pass the wood through twice. At the start of the cut feed the work slowly; otherwise the cutters may snatch the wood and jolt it backwards. Fig. 25 shows the rebating process.

Fig. 26 (left) Stopped chamfer being worked on planer
Fig. 27 (below) Working tapered legs

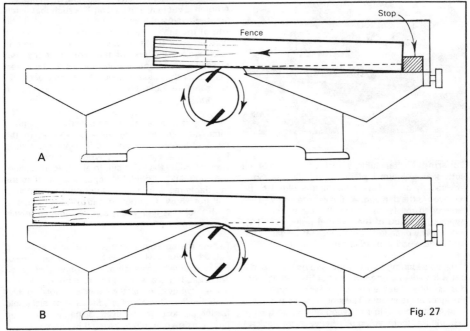

Fig. 27

Bevelling and Chamfering. When these run right through the procedure is much as in normal edging except that the fence is set over at the required angle.

Stopped chamfers are different, and it is necessary for both tables to be exactly level with each other, the cutter block standing up by an amount equal to the chamfer depth. A wood facing is fixed to the metal fence, and stop blocks are screwed to this so that the chamfer begins and ends in the required positions. The wood is held firmly against the near stop and the far end slowly lowered on to the revolving block. The cutters tend to grab as this happens, but the rear block prevents it from being knocked back, and once it lies on the table all grab ceases. The wood is fed forward until the front stop is reached. Fig. 26 shows wood being stop-chamfered.

Tapering. The rear table is level with the top of the cutters as in normal planing, and the front one lowered by an amount equal to the wood to be removed at the thin end. A stop is fixed either to the table or to the fence so that the cutters begin to operate just short of the required point as at (A), Fig. 27. The near end of the wood rests against the stop. The wood is pushed forward as at (B).

If the entire length of the wood is to be tapered, the cut will have to be started short of the end because it is essential that the end of the wood drops on to the lip of the rear table. The stop fixed so that there is at least 6mm. (¼in.) of wood resting on the lip. Without this there would be a heavy throw back.

Sanders

There are two chief kinds of sanders used in the home workshop; disc and belt. The former of these is shown in Fig. 28, its chief use being to trim wood rather than to smooth it. For instance it is invaluable for trimming mitres after sawing, or for cleaning up squared ends of wood. Another use is in cleaning the shaped edges of wood when the curvature is convex. Clearly the table must be at right angles to the disc, and the groove along its surface must be parallel with it. The mitre gauge is used as a guide for the wood, and this is slid back and forth so that wear on the abrasive is equalized. Only the down-coming side of the disc is used, as otherwise the wood is liable to be lifted.

Perhaps the chief way in which the disc sander saves time is when a number of pieces have to be trimmed all to the same length. One end of all the pieces is first made square by holding it against the mitre gauge. A jig is then made as shown in Fig. 29. A notch is cut in it, and its length is such that when pressed against the end of the work it touches the end of the table when the far end of the work is hard up against the sanding disc. In use the jig is held against the end of the work and the two pressed forward until the jig touches the table and the sander thus ceases to cut. For large pieces it is advisable to hold the jig to the work with a cramp.

Mitreing is done in much the same way as square trimming, but with the mitre gauge set to the required angle. If necessary a jig similar to that in Fig. 29 can be made, but with its notch cut to accommodate the mitre cut. In all cases the face of the moulding should be uppermost so that the inevitable rag is formed on the underside where it will not show. Compound mitres which slope in both thickness and width can be trimmed readily on the sander.

Renew the abrasive paper as soon as it ceases to cut, otherwise it will merely burn the wood. One of the cold tube glues such as Seccotine gives good adhesion. Place over a flat board, if necessary with a weight above, so that the paper is in close contact with the disc. One of the special sanding discs sold for the purpose can be used, or garnet paper can be stuck down. Avoid allowing it to become damp.

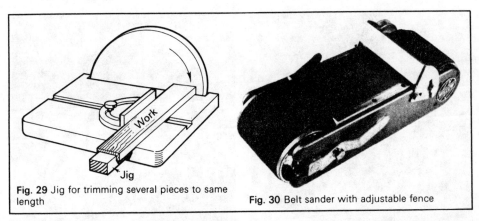

Fig. 29 Jig for trimming several pieces to same length

Fig. 30 Belt sander with adjustable fence

Belt sander. This type can be used for trimming much as the disc sander is used, but it has two advantages; the movement is in a straight line so that it can be used for cleaning up polished work for which the disc sander would be quite un-suitable; and the drums around which it passes enable concave shapes to be smoothed. Fig. 30 shows a belt sander.

Nearly all belt sanders are provided with a stop of some sort, and in the better models an adjustable table is fitted. When this is not provided it is usual to build up one, the details being adapted to suit the individual machine. It should include a table which can be set to various angles so that mitres, etc., can be trimmed. A tracking device is invariably included which ensures that the glasspaper remains on the drums.

Powered Hand Tools

Just as the lathe is the basis of a series of attach-ments for sawing, planing, sanding, etc., so the electric drill is the basic powered tool for which saw, sanding disc and grindstone can be obtained, although of course individual portable machines are available.

The drill gun itself will generally take drills up to 6mm. ($\frac{1}{4}$in.) (larger and heavier drills go up to 12mm. ($\frac{1}{2}$in.) but their use in woodwork is limited). The usual metal-worker's morse drills can,

of course, be used, but it is necessary to pop all holes with a centre punch, as morse drills have no centre point, but an edge. Special twist bits with round shanks can be obtained, but if there is any difficulty the square end can always be sawn from the ordinary twist bit intended for use in the brace. Many of these twist bits have a screw centre and, owing to the speed of the drill, are inclined to grab into the wood and when the hole is large the machine may stall. It will generally be more satisfactory if the screw is filed into the form of a square pyramid, as the drill can then be fed into the wood at whatever speed is required. For holes which must be dead upright it is advisable to use a drill stand which enables the drill to be lowered into the wood. There are two advantages; the hole is perfectly square or at whatever angle is desired, and the hole can be stopped at any depth without the necessity of individual testing.

Slik bits, Fig. 31, used with the electric drill bore clean holes. They are interchangeable on a common shaft and work with a scraping rather than a cutting action. The edges are ground at a low angle which has the advantage of avoiding digging in. They are ground on a small wheel.

A small circular saw attachment is shown in Fig. 32. It is provided with a depth gauge and adjustable fence, and both square cuts and cuts at an angle can be made. The advantage of the tool is in work in which it is more convenient to take the machine to the wood rather than vice versa.

81

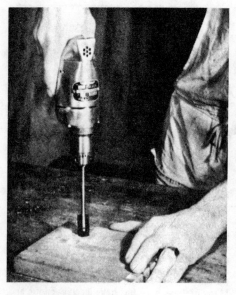

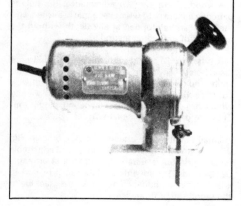

Fig. 31 (above left) The slikbit used in the electric drill
Fig. 32 (above right) Portable saw attachment
Fig. 33 (below) The portable jig saw. Photo: courtesy Black and Decker Ltd.

Jigsaw. This is used for cutting curves and has the advantage that it can be used for interior cuts. It is shown in Fig. 33. It is at its best for wood 12mm. ($\frac{1}{2}$in.) thick and under, but can be used for the occasional cutting of thicker stuff. It can be used in one of two ways, the choice depending upon the job. For a large panel the saw can be taken to the wood, but small items are best done in reverse. The saw is fixed reverse way up on the bench or in the vice, and the wood passed across it.

Sanders. Of the various types of portable sanders the orbital (Fig. 34) is the most generally useful for flat surfaces. It can be obtained as an individual machine or as an attachment for the electric drill. It does not rotate in the ordinary sense, and perhaps the simplest way of describing the action is to imagine a series of pencil dots on the surface of the pad each of which moves round in a tiny circle somewhere in the region of 2–3mm.

High speed electric router. For such work as recessing, grooving, rebating and moulding, etc., this machine has great advantages. It is somewhat expensive, however, and for this reason, plus the fact that it may be difficult to fit a suppressor to it,

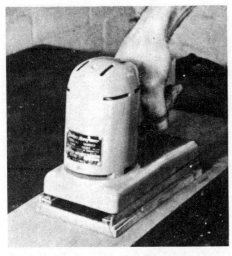

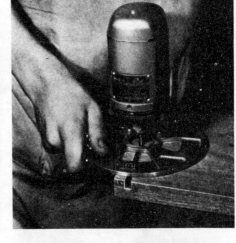

Fig. 34 (above) The orbital sander in use
Fig. 35 (top right) Cutting a groove with the portable high-speed electric router
Fig. 36 (middle right) Working a rebate with the Arcoy rebater—the rebate is formed by two cuts at right angles with each other
Fig. 37 (bottom right) Cutting dovetails with the Arcoy dovetailer—the variable pitch comb is shown

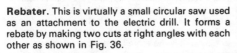

is not often found in the home craftsman's workshop. It will however perform many operations which would be difficult or impossible by other means. It is shown working a groove in Fig. 35.

Rebater. This is virtually a small circular saw used as an attachment to the electric drill. It forms a rebate by making two cuts at right angles with each other as shown in Fig. 36.

Dovetailer. This is an effective machine for cutting lap-dovetails. It cuts both tails and pins in one operation. Apart from the standard equipment there is a variable pitch device, Fig. 37, which enables dovetails to be spaced on wood of varying widths without part of a dovetail being exposed at one end. There is also an attachment for cutting slot dovetails.

Chapter seven

Construction

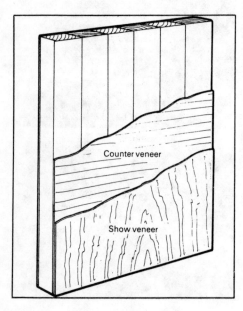

Counter veneer

Show veneer

There is a growing tendency today to use man-made materials rather than solid wood. This is largely because it is almost impossible to obtain many of the more attractive hardwoods in the solid. Consequently veneer has to be used over a groundwork of plywood, laminboard, or chipboard, the edges being lipped with strips of solid wood or veneered. Only such parts as legs, narrow rails, and items to be turned, shaped or carved are made in the solid. Since such manufactured materials are free from liability to shrink there is considerably more freedom in methods of construction than was possible when only solid wood was used. On the other hand each of these materials has its own peculiarities that have to be allowed for in construction, especially in the types of joints to be used.

Items such as doors and drawer parts are frequently made in these modern materials, either ready-veneered boards being used or veneer being laid over the basic panel later. Thus flush doors are popular, these needing only to be lipped or provided with wide edgings suitable to receive hinge and lock screws, etc. On the other hand panelled doors are still preferred for some jobs and have their advantages in some circumstances, though even here panels are frequently in plywood. Traditional methods of construction in solid wood still require to be known, especially by those to whom reproduction furniture appeals.

A point to be kept in mind is that some modern materials require the use of machines if they are to be used effectively. An example of this is chipboard which needs to be cut dead to size on the circular saw because it is difficult and sometimes even impossible to trim the edges really cleanly. The plane removes only dust and in any case loses its edge quickly owing to the abrasive nature of the bonding adhesive. A cut with the handsaw leaves only the roughest of edges and trimming is essential. It is therefore far more satisfactory to use the circular saw which, on a reliable machine, makes a straight cut perfectly square and with a clean finish. The use of a saw with tungsten-tipped teeth avoids the rapid dulling of the teeth.

Fig. 1 Strips glued together side by side and veneered

Another point in this connection is in the use of boards which are ready-veneered on both sides. The use of the handsaw would almost certainly cause the veneer to splinter away at the back, and when only hand methods are possible it is necessary to make the cut well on the waste side so that any splitting out can be planed out later. Better still the cuts are made on the circular saw, the saw itself being given the minimum projection above the board so that the oncoming teeth cut more nearly in alignment with the board rather than striking downwards when they would be more liable to split out the veneer on the underside. Sharp teeth are essential. In really important cases it is advisable to cut through the veneer on the underside first with the cutting gauge (or chisel and straight-edge) so that the grain of the veneer is severed. There is no difficulty about trimming plywood or laminboard with the plane.

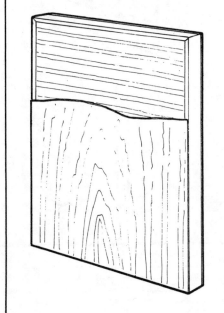

Fig. 2 Laminated or plywood door, edged and veneered

Flush Doors

These are generally in accordance with modern ideas of design, and have become practicable largely owing to the introduction of materials such as plywood and laminated board which are available in wide panels and are free from shrinkage.

Jointed and veneered door. In smaller sizes the method in Fig. 1 can be followed, this being the original way of making such doors, and still used to an extent. Straight-grained, dry, reliable wood is used, strips about 50mm. (2in.) wide being glued together with the heart side alternately front and back. Both sides are levelled and laid with a plain veneer, the grain of which runs crosswise. Over these counter veneers the face show veneers are laid. It is important that veneers of equal thickness are laid on both sides. Sometimes the counter veneer is omitted, but the result is not so reliable.

Lamin board or multi-ply. This is shown in Fig. 2. Whichever substance is used, the veneers should have their grain at right angles with that of the outer surface. In the best way counter veneers are used as in Fig. 1, but frequently this is omitted. Both sides should have the same treatment. To conceal the layers at the edges a lipping is needed, and in many cases this is added before veneering as this gives an unbroken effect at both front and back. If, however, the panel is liable to be subjected to much wear at the edges it is better to veneer first. The edging then affords protection, and it is so narrow that it does not show up unduly.

Methods of arranging the edging are shown at (a), (b), and (c), Fig. 3. The simplest, that at (a), is about 5 or 6mm. ($\frac{3}{16}$ or $\frac{1}{4}$in.) thick and is glued round, the corners being mitred. The veneer is taken right over it. A stronger method is that at (b) and is widely used in the trade. As, however, the edging section is rather awkward to make by hand methods owing to the two rebates having to be of exactly the same depth, the edging at (c) may be preferred. Here only a groove is needed, and the rebates on the ply which form the tongue are more easily worked because there is a much larger area to grip. The rebates could be marked out with cutting gauge and worked independently from each side.

85

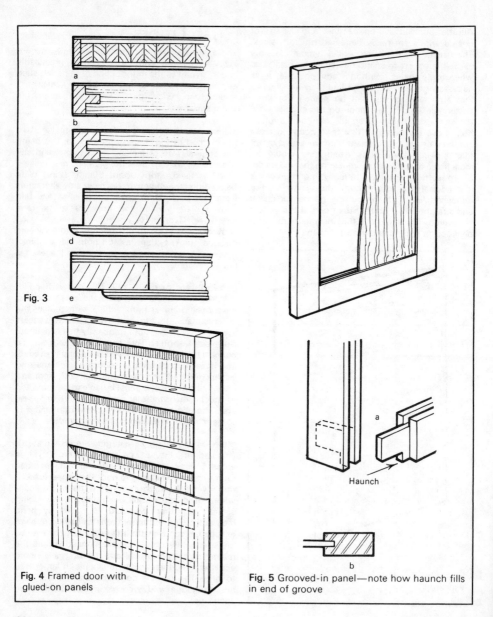

Fig. 3

Fig. 4 Framed door with glued-on panels

Fig. 5 Grooved-in panel—note how haunch fills in end of groove

Haunch

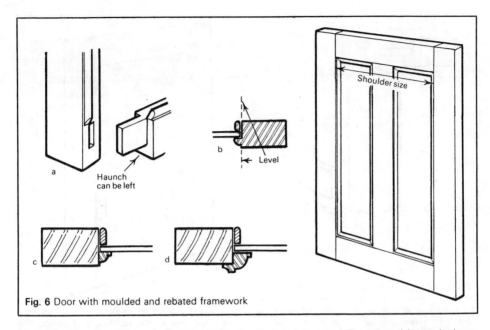

Fig. 6 Door with moulded and rebated framework

Framed and covered door. The method in Fig. 4 is frequently used, especially for painted work. In the best way both sides are covered with ply, though the back one is often omitted. Intermediate cross-rails are desirable to stop any tendency for the panels to sink in locally. When both sides are covered complications are sometimes caused owing to the air necessarily trapped between the panels not being equalized with that of the surrounding atmosphere. To get over this a series of holes can be drilled through all rails as shown. The front ply can either finish flush with the framing at the edges, or it can be made to project as at (d), Fig. 3. The latter is useful in that it forms a rebate and helps to keep out dust. Alternatively the set-in panel at (e), Fig. 3, can be used.

Framed doors. These consist of a main framework put together with mortise and tenon joints, and one or more panels fitted either into grooves or rebates. The idea is that the framework provides the strength, the panel being simply a filling-in piece. If of solid wood it is free to move in its grooves or rebates as shrinkage or swelling occurs.

Grooved-in panel. The grooved-in type is shown in Fig. 5. It is used chiefly for painted doors in which there is no difficulty about the application of the finish since the brush is used. It is undesirable for a polished finish in that it is difficult to work the rubber into the internal edges and corners. The panel should preferably be of plywood, laminboard, or hardboard depending upon the particular job.

Note that grooving automatically cuts away the tenon at the inside; consequently the mortise must be set in at the inside correspondingly. Another point is that a haunch is left at the outside of the tenon as at (a) to fill in the groove which necessarily runs right through in the upright.

Moulded and rebated door. For cabinet work with polished finish this is widely used since the panel can be polished separately and fitted afterwards. The front edges are moulded in the solid in the best work, as at (b), Fig. 6, (as distinct from an applied moulding), and an essential feature is that the bottom of the moulding is level with the rebate as shown. This is because

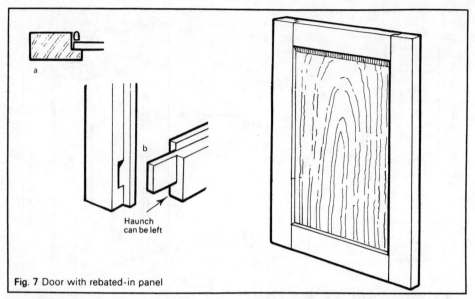

Fig. 7 Door with rebated-in panel

the moulding is cut away locally opposite the joint, and this produces a flat surface for the shoulders of the tenon.

When setting out notice that the shoulder length is taken up to the rebate, not to the edge of the stiles. This seems obvious enough after moulding and rebate have been worked, but it is not so clear beforehand when the wood is still square-edged. It makes a stronger job if a haunch is cut at the bottom as suggested in (a).

For cheaper work the moulding is applied separately (c), Fig. 6, being mitred round. It is quicker to make because only a plain square-edged frame is needed, and the moulding can be obtained ready-made. A more legitimate use is when a bolection moulding is required as at (d). This could not easily be worked in the solid.

Rebated panel. When the panel is to be rebated in and there is no moulding, the joint at (b), Fig. 7 is used. This calls for long- and short-shoulders to the tenon, the back shoulder being longer than the front one by the rebate depth. Here again a haunch can be allowed with advantage. In all these examples the joints are marked out and cut first. This is followed by the rebating or grooving, the moulding being worked last. Any mitreing (as in (b), Fig. 6) is the final process and is carried out during the fitting.

Making a framed door. Fig. 8 shows the general procedure. Details would be adapted in accordance with the particular kind of door being made. In the example given at (a) the framework is moulded and rebated, and the joint used would be that shown on p. 104, at d. Having planed stiles and rails true, mark out the rebate and moulding depth with the gauge (the two are equal). Holding a stile against the cupboard carcase (b) mark with pencil the door height, adding about $1\frac{1}{2}$mm. ($\frac{1}{16}$in.) to allow for trimming and fitting. To mark the shoulder size of the rails place the two stiles at the bottom of the carcase and lay the rail on them as at (c). Transfer the line of the rebate, again adding about $1\frac{1}{2}$mm.

To ensure both stiles being alike they should be cramped together temporarily as at (d) and the marks squared across both. Note that in addition to the over-all width it is necessary to square in the

88

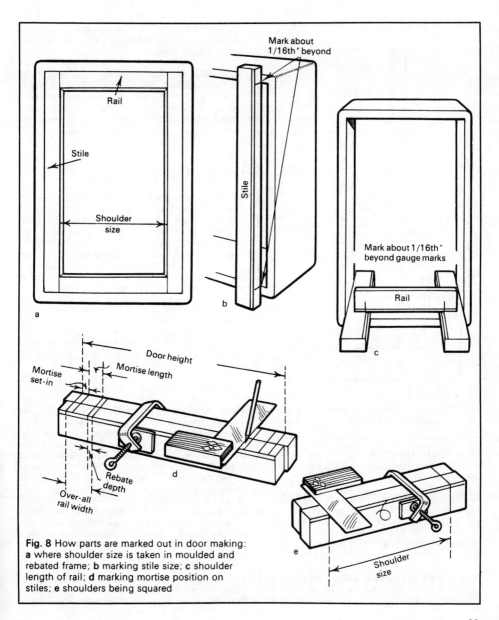

Fig. 8 How parts are marked out in door making:
a where shoulder size is taken in moulded and
rebated frame; **b** marking stile size; **c** shoulder
length of rail; **d** marking mortise position on
stiles; **e** shoulders being squared

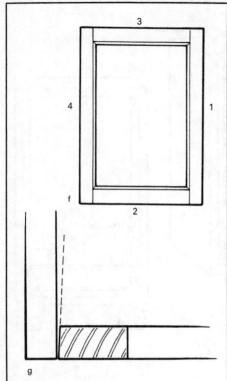

Fig. 8 f order in which door edges are trimmed; **g** how closing edge slopes

rebate depth and the mortise set-in at the end. The two latter lines give the mortise length. All marks should be put in with pencil.

A similar procedure is followed for the rails, but the marking knife or chisel is used (e). Afterwards the parts are separated and the marks squared all round each rail independently. The butt of the square should be against face side or face edge in every case.

Cutting the joints follows, after which the rebates are worked, and lastly the mouldings. The shoulders should not be sawn until the last two

processes have been completed. The mitreing of the moulding is described at (f), page 16, done with the mitre template.

After assembling level the joints and fit the door in the order shown at (f). If, after planing the No. 1 edge to fit the cupboard, the door is appreciably too wide, plane the surplus equally from both edges. Otherwise they will not balance. The same thing applies to the top and bottom edges.

Large Doors

Ledged and braced door. The simplest form of door is the kind one might make for a shed. It consists of tongued and grooved boards, usually 22mm. ($\frac{7}{8}$in.) or less for a light door, with ledges or cross pieces of heavier stuff—say 32mm. ($1\frac{1}{4}$in.) — nailed across. To prevent sagging diagonal braces are added as in Fig. 9, these fitting into notches cut into the ledges. It is unlikely that the width can be made up by an exact number of boards, and the procedure is to go beyond the width and reduce the two outer boards so that the effect is balanced Remember that the outer tongue and groove have to be removed from these outer boards in any case. It may occasionally happen that very narrow strips are left at the outside, and it is then advisable to reduce the width of all the boards, re-grooving them where necessary; or, better still, choose a width of board which is more convenient.

Prepare the ledges, remembering to set them in where necessary to clear the door jamb. Bevel or chamfer the edges as shown. Ledges are usually inside, but for outside work the lower edges should be left square and a drip groove worked. It is convenient to cut the notches to receive the braces before fixing as it is merely a matter of sawing across the grain and chiselling the sloping notches. Nail all three ledges to one stile as in Fig. 10, test for squareness, and turn the whole over. With straight-edge and pencil mark the positions, and nail the boards, punching in the heads. In this way the nails pass through the thinner wood to the thicker.

Once again reverse the door and cut the braces to make a close fit in their grooves. Nail on finally from the other side, pencil lines being drawn in as

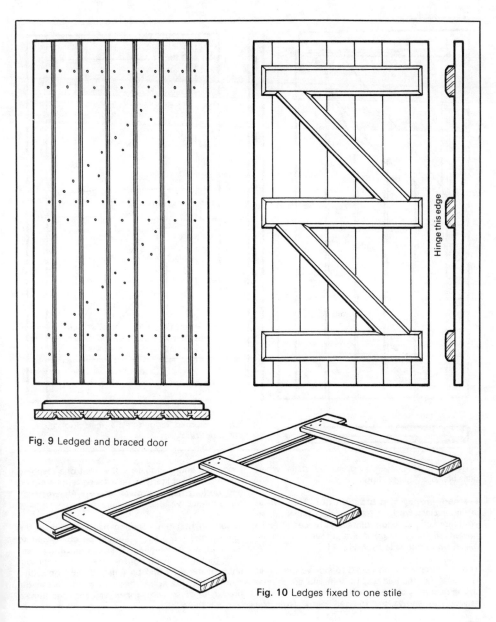

Fig. 9 Ledged and braced door

Hinge this edge

Fig. 10 Ledges fixed to one stile

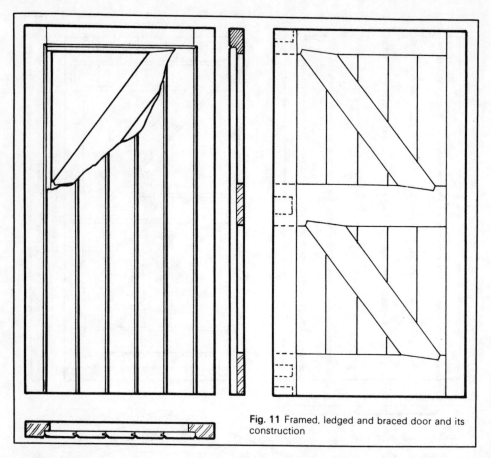

Fig. 11 Framed, ledged and braced door and its construction

a guide. In all cases stagger the nails when possible to avoid splitting.

Framed, ledged and braced door. This is used in better class work. A framework is put together with mortise and tenon joints, and braces fitted to prevent sagging. Tongued and grooved boards are nailed on to one side as in Fig. 11.

Top rail and stiles are rebated to receive the T and G boards, but the mid and bottom rails are thinner by the thickness of the boards and have bare-faced tenons. (a) shows the top rail joints. Note the long- and short-shoulders, the front one reaching down to the rebate. The bare-faced tenons of mid and bottom rails are given at (b). All are taken through and wedged from outside.

Assuming that the boarding has a V joint at the tongue, the main frame should be chamfered to agree before assembling. That of the top rail runs right through, but that of the stiles should run out short of the joint and be finished with a mason's mitre cut in the solid after gluing up. Cut in the braces, and fix with a nail at each end driven through the edge.

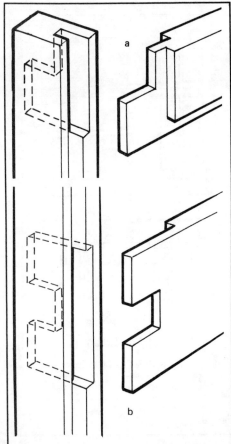

Fig. 11 **a** mortise and tenon joint at top; **b** barefaced tenon of mid-rail

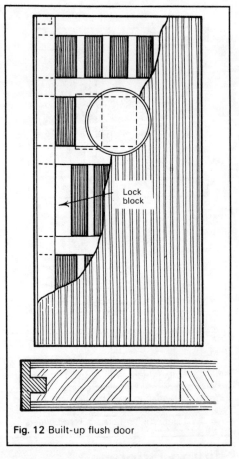

Fig. 12 Built-up flush door

The T and G boarding should be even as far as possible. Any reduction that may be needed should be taken equally from the outside boards. Nail in position, and punch in all heads.

Flush door. These are of many kinds. An attractive pattern with or without glass panel is shown in Fig. 12. A main framework is put together with mortise and tenon joints and a veneered plywood panel glued on at each side. To prevent sinking between the rails a number of slats are inserted. Also a lock block is set in to enable a mortise lock to be cut in, and uprights to enable the circular window to be cut. Tongued edges are added finally, partly to give a neat finish, and also to protect the veneer edges.

It is essential that the door frame is entirely free from winding; also that the whole is kept completely flat when the panels are being pressed. Otherwise any winding will be perpetuated.

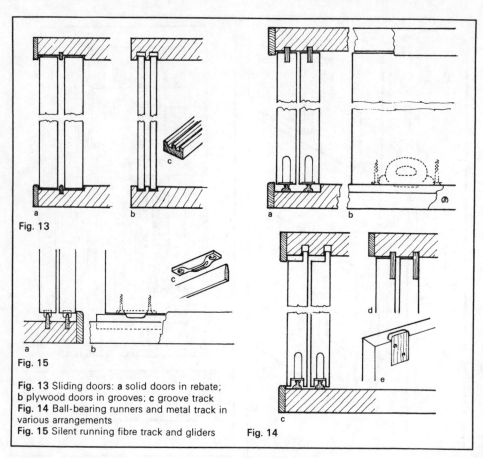

Fig. 13

Fig. 15

Fig. 13 Sliding doors: **a** solid doors in rebate; **b** plywood doors in grooves; **c** groove track
Fig. 14 Ball-bearing runners and metal track in various arrangements
Fig. 15 Silent running fibre track and gliders

Fig. 14

Sliding Doors

There are many ways of arranging these.

Solid wood doors. A simple method for wood doors is given in Fig. 13 at (a). There is a rebate wide enough to take both doors with a separating bead between. It is successful up to a point, but the bearing surfaces are wide, and there is consequently considerable friction. Furthermore the wear takes place on the surface and edge of the door itself, and an unsightly wear mark is eventually

formed. The use of candlegrease as a lubricant is a help in reducing friction.

The separating bead is inserted when the doors are being put in position. Make it a tight fit and use only one or two dabs of glue so that removal is not unduly difficult. If preferred the top bead can be glued in permanently beforehand. The lower one can be in two lengths with a short spliced joint. One piece only is glued in permanently. This allows the door to be passed in and slid along, after which the remaining piece is tapped in with two dabs of glue to hold it.

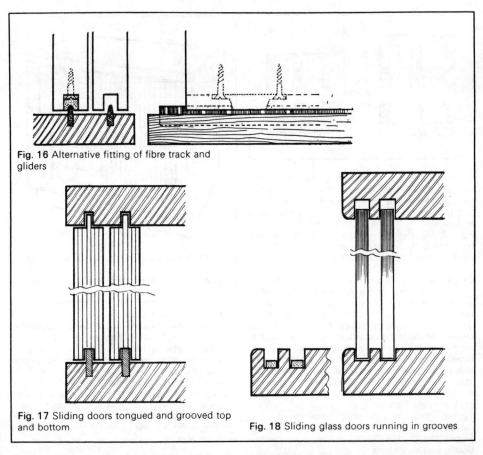

Fig. 16 Alternative fitting of fibre track and gliders

Fig. 17 Sliding doors tongued and grooved top and bottom

Fig. 18 Sliding glass doors running in grooves

Lighter doors in plywood can be arranged as at (b). The top grooves are double the depth of those at the bottom so that the doors can be raised and pulled forwards to remove them. Alternatively the special grooved section at (c) can be inserted in a rebate.

Special tracks and runners. For heavy doors the ball-bearing runner and track in Fig. 14 is often used. The runners are let into the underside of the door as at (a) and (b), and the track is screwed to a rebate in the cupboard bottom. When a facing-fillet can be fixed the arrangement as shown is

satisfactory. Otherwise it is necessary to groove the underside of the door so that it fits right over the track as at (c). At the top are simple wood tongues. A simple alternative is that shown at (d) and (e). Pieces of hardwood are let into the backs of the doors and fixed with screws. They slide in grooves as shown and can be screwed in after the doors are in position. In this way the doors can be released easily.

A specially successful fitting is the fibre track and gliders in Fig. 15. The fibre track is let into grooves worked in the cupboard bottom, and when a

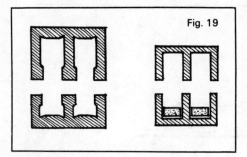

Fig. 19

covering bead can be used the gliders are merely recessed into the underside of the door. A better method, however, is to work grooves in the door so that the latter fits closely down to the cupboard bottom as in Fig. 16. An alternative is the scheme in Fig. 17, often used for multi-ply doors. The top tongues are slipped in first and the bottom beads again arranged in separate lengths.

Glass doors. A simple method is given in Fig. 18 in which grooves to give a free fit are worked in top and bottom. It will be noted that the top grooves are extra deep to allow the doors to be lifted up and dropped into the bottom ones. This allows for the removal of the doors at any time. Rather sweeter running is obtained by placing strips of fibre in the bottom grooves as shown to the left. Tempered Masonite does very well for the purpose. An alternative is to glue strips of felt along the grooves, though this does not wear so well.

Special metal and fibre channelling is also available as in Fig. 19. In both of these a large groove is worked in top and bottom to receive the channelling as a whole.

One last word with regard to any scheme which has projecting beads at the bottom is that it is a good plan to stop both beads about 50mm. (2in.) short at one end so that the bottom can be dusted out easily.

Tambours

A tambour consists of a series of narrow strips of wood glued down on to a canvas backing. The

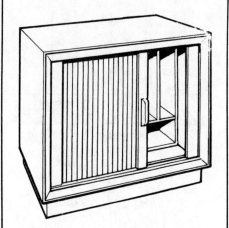

Fig. 19 (left) Examples of fibre tracks

Fig. 20 (above) Small cabinet with tambour front

ends fit in grooves worked in the cabinet, Fig. 20 and it can travel around any curve of reasonable radius. Generally only convex curves can be negotiated (the canvas fitting on the inner side) because the joints can open as the tambour passes around the bend. Some tambours, particularly those fitted to the older type of writing desk, have wires passing through them to hold them together in place of canvas. This makes it simple to use a tambour which can bend either way since the pivoting point is in the middle of the wood in line with the wire.

Various sections. Some sections of tambours are given in Fig. 21. The simplest is that at (a). In this particular case the surface is veneered but solid strips could be used. For the latter a common practice is to use alternate strips of light and dark wood. When veneer is used as at (a), the grain is often taken cross-wise, and a single sheet of veneer is used so that the grain is continuous. In making such a tambour the work is prepared in a width sufficient for all the strips to be cut, two or more pieces being jointed together. It is then veneered, and the whole cut into strips afterwards, each being numbered so that it can be replaced in

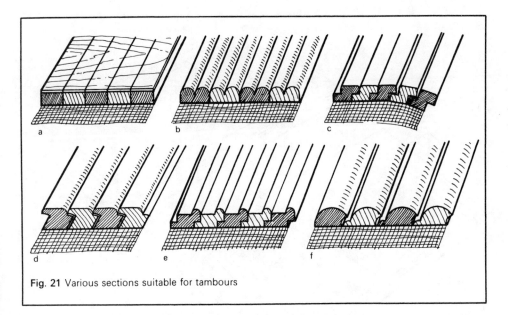

Fig. 21 Various sections suitable for tambours

the same order and so preserve the continuity of grain. To avoid casting both sides can be veneered.

When a bead section is required the strips can be prepared to form single beads each, unless they are extra narrow, in which case they can be formed in two to each strip as at (b). It will be realised that in both this section and that at (a) the joints necessarily open as the tambour passes around a curve. As a rule this does not matter because it is generally concealed around the curve. Where this cannot be arranged an overlapping section is advisable as shown at (c).

A rather neater section is that at (d), in which the small curved portion is struck from a centre in line with the canvas backing. The two parts thus fit neatly within each other. It is, however, an awkward section to work by hand. (e) is simply a variation of (c), whilst (f) has the advantage that it can bend in either direction.

Assembling a tambour. It is necessary to make an assembly board on which the parts can be put together as shown in Fig. 22. This has edging pieces nailed down on three sides, the thickness of

the strips being rather less than of the tambour pieces. The last named must be all of exactly the same thickness, and the edges should be planed perfectly square, and straight. Before placing in position rub a piece of candlegrease along the edges to prevent any glue which may penetrate from adhering. They are assembled side by side and the fourth edging piece passed on at the end. This should be lightly tightened with a cramp then nailed, thus bringing all the pieces close together. To prevent any tendency for the pieces to be lifted up by the pressure hold a batten across the face of the tambour pieces until the nails have been driven into the edging piece. In any case only light pressure is needed.

For the backing use a good quality piece of fine canvas. Stretch it as far as possible by drawing it back and forth over the rounded edge of a straight bar of wood. Fix it to one end of the board with a few tacks, and fold it back clear. Glue the tambour pieces, draw the canvas right across to the far end, and fix down with one or two tacks. Smooth out any creases in the canvas, and fix down a top board with cramps, (Fig. 23). A sheet of paper prevents any glue which may have squeezed

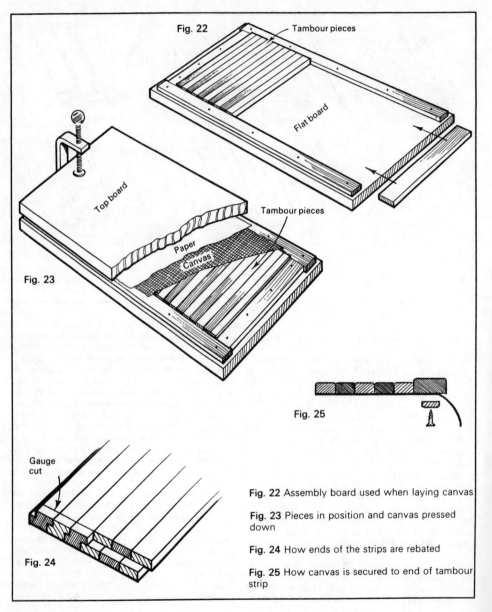

Fig. 22

Tambour pieces

Flat board

Top board

Tambour pieces

Paper

Canvas

Fig. 23

Fig. 25

Gauge cut

Fig. 24

Fig. 22 Assembly board used when laying canvas

Fig. 23 Pieces in position and canvas pressed down

Fig. 24 How ends of the strips are rebated

Fig. 25 How canvas is secured to end of tambour strip

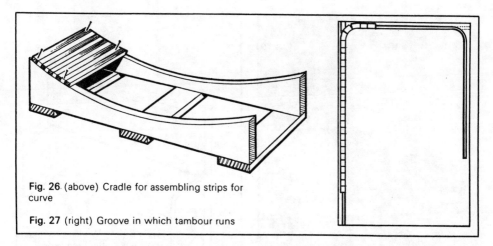

Fig. 26 (above) Cradle for assembling strips for curve

Fig. 27 (right) Groove in which tambour runs

through from sticking to the board. Often it is not necessary to use the top board, the canvas being just smoothed down by hand. Make sure that all creases are got rid of.

Fitting. Allow ample time for the glue to set and try the movement, making sure that every joint opens. The ends are then trimmed so that they enter the groove. Sometimes the groove is narrower than the thickness of the tambour pieces, a rebate being worked at the front of the tambour as in Fig. 24 to form a shoulder. The advantage is that the groove is entirely hidden by the shoulder even after considerable wear. It is specially useful for moulded tambour pieces as otherwise the groove would be visible in the recesses. To work the rebate cut the face of the tambour with the cutting gauge and use the shoulder or bullnose plane.

When the tambour is fitted to a bow shape which is visible it is usual to have the members in the form of beads and to glue up flat. The slight opening at the curve scarcely shows. If, however, the flat section ((a), Fig. 21) is required it is desirable to fit on a cradle which has the same curvature as the job as shown in Fig. 26. The pieces are cut about 38mm. (1½in.) over length and are placed face downwards on the cradle. When the joints are shot the shooting board should be arranged so that the edge is a trifle out of square thus ensuring a close

joint when the parts are in the curve. The first strip has a couple of nails driven half way in, about half a dozen strips laid in and pushed tightly home, and another piece nailed. You can turn the cradle upside down to see that there are close joints on the face side.

As a rule the end member is made extra large as this enables a handle to be fixed to it. The canvas is glued about half way across it and 50 or 75mm. (2 or 3in.) free end left as in Fig. 25. This is taken around a fillet or bead and the latter screwed at the back so locking the canvas. Alternatively the bead is screwed straight down over the canvas.

Tambour grooves. The groove in which the tambour works has usually to be cut in with the chisel. The router can be used to finish off to even depth, and for the straight portions a fence can be fixed to enable it to be used as a plough. Do not have the curves too sharp. As a rule it is necessary to cut the groove rather fuller at the curves to enable the tambour to pass easily. There must of course be a place (generally at the rear) where the tambour can be started (see Fig. 27). This can be blocked up after the tambour is in position or a stop can be fitted. Sometimes it is practicable to make a separate lining for the cabinet in which the grooves can be worked. The Technikos plough is useful for working the groove, especially round flat curves. The tool is shown in use in Fig. 28.

99

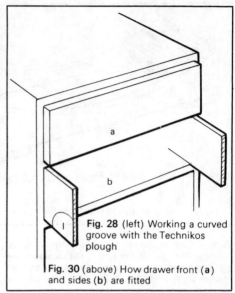

Fig. 28 (left) Working a curved groove with the Technikos plough

Fig. 30 (above) How drawer front (**a**) and sides (**b**) are fitted

The tambour should not be finally fitted until both it and the cabinet have been polished because it would be impossible to polish cleanly. In fact, in the case of a moulded tambour the individual members should be polished—or at least bodied up before the canvas backing is glued on. Otherwise it would be impossible to reach the quirks with the rubber. When the whole thing has been fitted and the working tried, the ends of the tambour should be lubricated with candlegrease. This will both ease the running and make it silent.

Drawer Making

In the best way drawers are dovetailed, and the joints are still cut by hand in good cabinet work. Fig. 29 shows the setting out for the usual form of drawer at (A). The lapped dovetails at the front have the pins running almost to a point, this giving a very neat appearance. Note that, since the bottom fits in a groove worked in the front it is necessary for this groove to be contained within the bottom dovetail (see dotted lines). Otherwise a gap would appear at the sides. The sides are not grooved since an applied grooved moulding is used (see sections (B) and (C)). At the back the bottom fits beneath the square lower edge of the back.

In the case of a small shallow drawer in which the utmost interior depth is required, the bottom fits flush with the lower edges of the sides and rests in rebates. This necessitates a small square member being cut at the bottom as at (D), Fig. 29. Sometimes the drawer sides have to be set in from the ends, in which case the slotted dovetail at (F) is used. This is stopped at the top. At (A) the bottom is shown projecting at the rear. This is needed only when solid wood is used, its purpose being to enable the bottom to be pushed forward in the event of shrinkage. If it is of plywood or hardboard it can finish level.

Making a drawer. Plane the drawer front to make a close fit in the opening ((A), Fig. 30). It helps to make it slightly tapered—no more than the thickness of a thin shaving. Plane the bottom edge first, and trim one end to align with the opening. Mark the length, trim to fit, and plane the top edge lastly. The back is treated similarly but the width is less owing to its resting on the drawer bottom, and

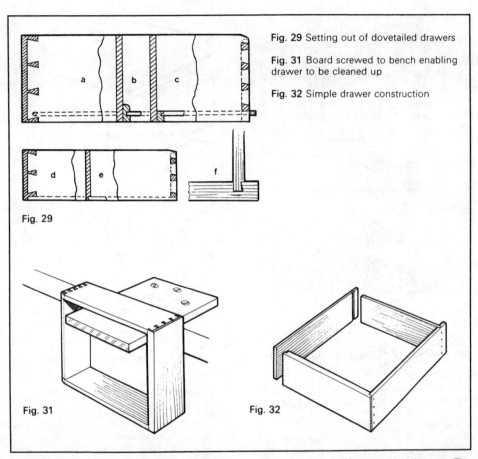

Fig. 29 Setting out of dovetailed drawers

Fig. 31 Board screwed to bench enabling drawer to be cleaned up

Fig. 32 Simple drawer construction

Fig. 29

Fig. 31

Fig. 32

the set-down from the top. Trim the bottom edges of the sides, plane the ends square, making both alike, and plane the top edge until a fairly tight fit is secured ((b), Fig. 30). Dovetailing follows (see p. 114), and, after assembling, the drawer is fitted before the bottom is added. A convenient way of planing without danger of racking is shown in Fig. 31. Candlegrease rubbed cold over the bearing surfaces is a good lubricant, but should not be used until after polishing.

For a quick and cheap alternative the construction in Fig. 32 can be followed. A lapped joint is cut at the front, and a simple groove at the rear. The whole is assembled with glue and nails, the last named being driven in askew so that they slope towards each other dovetail fashion.

Window Frames

It is seldom that the home craftsman needs to make a house window, but he often requires one for a garden shed or garage. A light double frame casement window is given in Fig. 33.

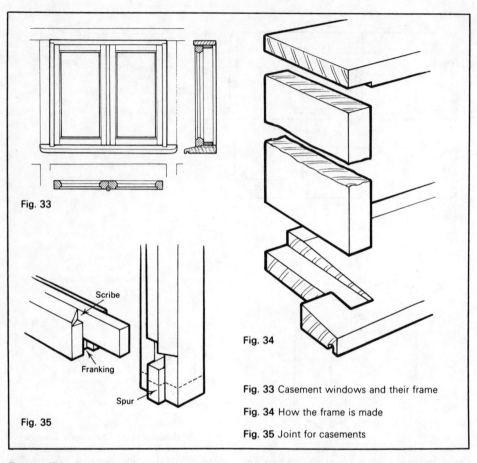

Fig. 33

Scribe

Franking

Spur

Fig. 35

Fig. 34

Fig. 33 Casement windows and their frame

Fig. 34 How the frame is made

Fig. 35 Joint for casements

Frame. This is made as shown in Fig. 34. Uprights and top have a simple rebated joint. At the bottom the uprights fit into a sill which is planed at its top outer surface to give a slope. Under the front edge is a drip groove. A simple checking is to cut to receive the upright, and it is advisable to do this before working the chamfer because this enables the router to be used.

Casements. A standard section is used for this. The joint shown at Fig. 35 is used, and it will be noticed that in place of the cabinet maker's haunch is a franking. The mortise width is made equal to the width of the centre square. Wedged through-tenons are used, and the chamfer is scribed rather than mitred. Note how the chamfer is cut away locally opposite the mortises, enabling equal shoulders to be used on the tenon. The centre closing bead should fit in a rebate as in Fig. 33, and this necessitates each frame being rebated. It is necessary to bevel the bottom edges to align with the sloping sill.

Chapter eight

Joints

The number of joints used in woodwork is little short of staggering when their variations in detail and size are taken into account. One need only bother with the relatively few basic joints, however, and we give these on the following pages. Their application will be found in the designs for things to make.

Mortise and tenon joints. The chief kinds are shown in Figs. 1 and 2. Generally the tenon is as near as possible one third the thickness of the wood, and it is a case of selecting a chisel for mortising which is the nearest to this size. Thus for 19mm. ($\frac{3}{4}$in.) stuff a 6mm. ($\frac{1}{4}$in.) chisel is used; for 22mm. ($\frac{7}{8}$in.) and 25mm. (1in.) wood an 8mm. ($\frac{5}{16}$in.) size is suitable.

A simple stub-tenon joint and the method of cutting is given in Figs. 1, 3 and 4. At the outset it should be realized that when several corresponding joints are to be cut, as in, say, a door, all tenons would be marked out at the same time, the shoulder marks being squared across all. This is explained more fully on p. 88, where door construction is dealt with. Here, however, we give the procedure in a single joint for clearness.

Square the rail width in pencil across the edge of the stile as at (b), Fig. 3, noting that the whole thing is invariably set in from the end of the wood leaving a waste piece as it lessens any liability for wood to split (a). A third line is put in to give the mortise length. Now set the pins of the mortise gauge to the width of the chisel being used, (c), and fix the fence so that the pins are as near as possible central on the edge of the wood (in the case of rebated frames the mortise is generally level with the corner of the rebate). Mark the wood (c) with the fence bearing against the face side of the wood.

Much of the waste can be removed by boring, using a bit slightly smaller than the mortise width. This is shown more clearly on page 27. The mortising is shown at (d), Fig. 3. The wood is cramped over a solid part of the bench, and a thumbscrew put on at the end with a waste piece of wood beneath the screw. This reduces any liability for the wood to split. Make the first cut at about the middle, and cut in a little way only. Shift the chisel a little way along and chop down again, this time a little deeper, and so work

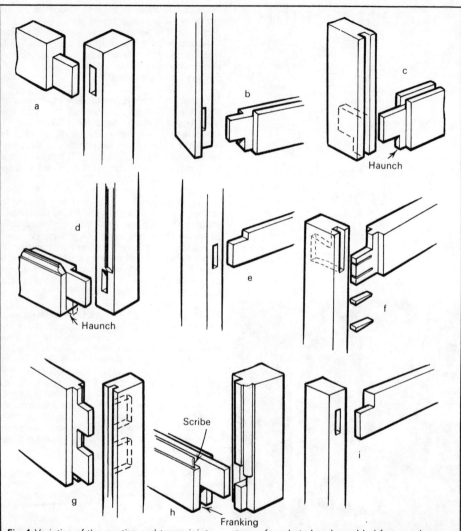

Fig. 1 Varieties of the mortise and tenon joint: **a** stub mortise and tenon (a haunch could be added as at **c**); **b** mortise and tenon for rebated frame, note long and short shoulders; **c** mortise and tenon for grooved frame; **d** mortise and tenon for rebated and moulded frame; **e** barefaced mortise and tenon; **f** wedged-through-mortise and tenon; **g** double mortise and tenon; **h** mortise and tenon for window frame; **i** barefaced mortise and tenon

Labels in figure: Haunch; Haunch; Haunch; Scribe; Franking

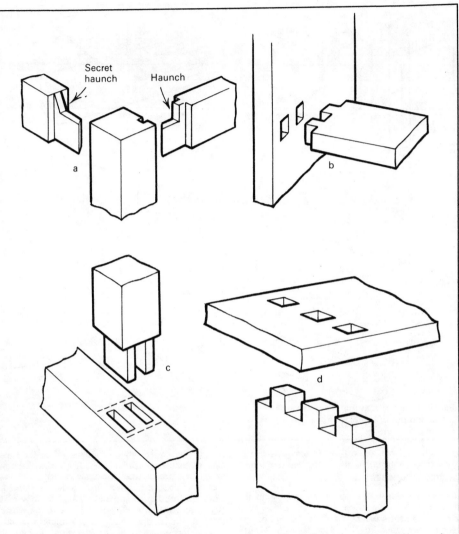

Fig. 2 Further examples of mortise and tenon joints: **a** mortise and tenon for leg and rails, alternative haunches are given—tenons are cut at an angle at ends to meet in thickness of wood; **b** twin tenons for drawer rails; **c** twin tenons for heavy framing; **d** pinned joint for carcase partitions, etc.

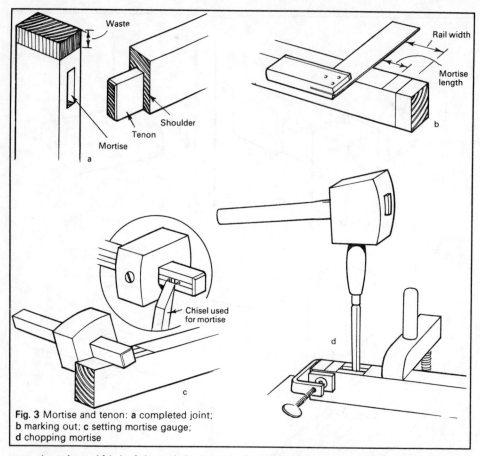

Fig. 3 Mortise and tenon: **a** completed joint; **b** marking out; **c** setting mortise gauge; **d** chopping mortise

up to about 1mm. ($\frac{1}{18}$in.) of the end. A piece of paper stuck to the chisel shows the depth to which the chisel is taken.

Reverse the chisel and repeat the process in the other direction. Levering over the chisel will remove the centre waste. Finally cut down on the pencil lines, keeping the chisel upright. These final cuts take out the dubbed-over ends caused by the levering-over with the chisel.

The tenon shoulders should be squared round with the chisel or a knife as at (a), Fig. 4. Hold the

butt of the square always against either the face side or face edge of the wood. Mark the tenon with the mortise gauge, again used from the face side. End and both edges should be marked. Hold the wood at an angle in the vice as shown at (b) when sawing, and place the saw to the waste side of the gauge line. To complete the cut reverse the wood as at (c), this time upright. A properly cut tenon should fit as it is with no further attention.

To enable the shoulders to be sawn make a sloping cut with the chisel on the waste side as shown

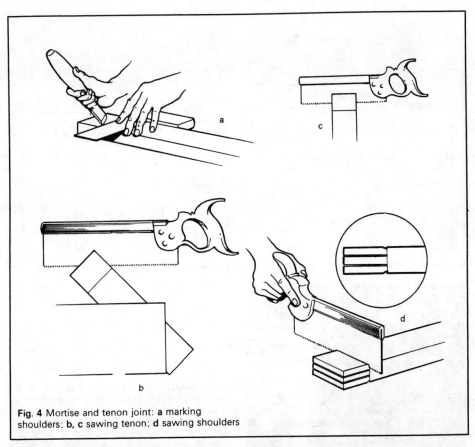

Fig. 4 Mortise and tenon joint: **a** marking shoulders; **b, c** sawing tenon; **d** sawing shoulders

inset at (d). This provides a channel in which the saw can run. Lastly mark the amount to be cut away at the side of the tenon and cut. It is advisable to put a thumbscrew on the wood at the mortise end to prevent splitting when the joint is being fitted. In some cases a haunch is left on the tenon as in Fig. 1C.

Dowelled joints. Although these have a perfectly legitimate place in some work, they are often used as a quick substitute for the mortise and tenon joint for some types of framework as in Fig. 5B. Chairmakers frequently use dowels for joining seat rails to the legs. Although there are various ways of marking out the joint the method chiefly used today employs a special proprietary dowel guide. The only marking out required with this tool is a centre line, the dowels being spaced equally at each side. Apart from a saving in time in marking out, the bit is guided by the sleeves fitted to the guide, and the holes are therefore perfectly true. Several sizes of sleeves are available to suit different sizes of bits. The tool is shown at D and E.

A groove should be formed along the length of all

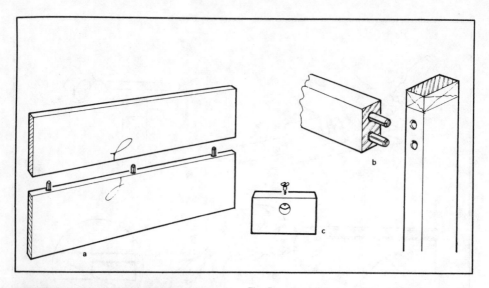

Fig. 5 a edge joint strengthened with dowels; **b** framing joint; **c** appliance for grooving dowels; (left) The Record dowelling jig (below left) The Woden dowelling jig

dowels to enable surplus glue to escape when the dowels are knocked in. Without it the wood would be liable to split out. A simple means of forming this groove is the appliance at Fig. 5C. A hole slightly larger than the dowel size is bored in a piece of hardwood and a screw driven in at the edge so that the point protrudes at the hole. The dowel rod is pushed through the hole whilst in a long length, the screw point forming the groove.

Another detail is that it is advisable to lightly countersink the bored holes as glue is awkward to remove cleanly after the dowels have been inserted in the one piece. It helps, too, if the ends of the dowels are lightly chamfered as it enables them to be started easily in the holes. A special dowel sharpener for the brace is available.

Halved joints. These are used in the construction

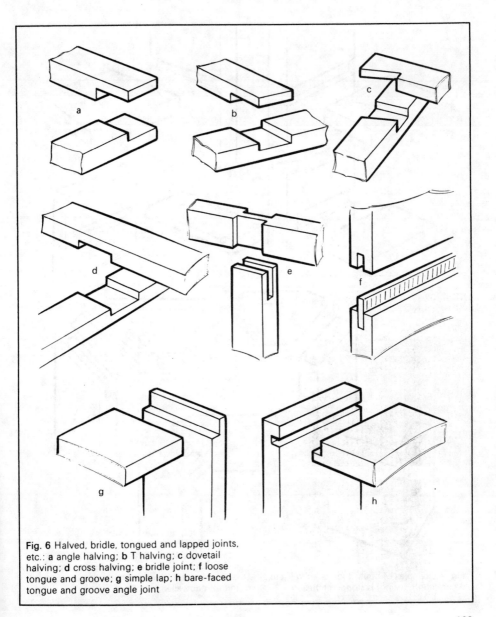

Fig. 6 Halved, bridle, tongued and lapped joints, etc.: **a** angle halving; **b** T halving; **c** dovetail halving; **d** cross halving; **e** bridle joint; **f** loose tongue and groove; **g** simple lap; **h** bare-faced tongue and groove angle joint

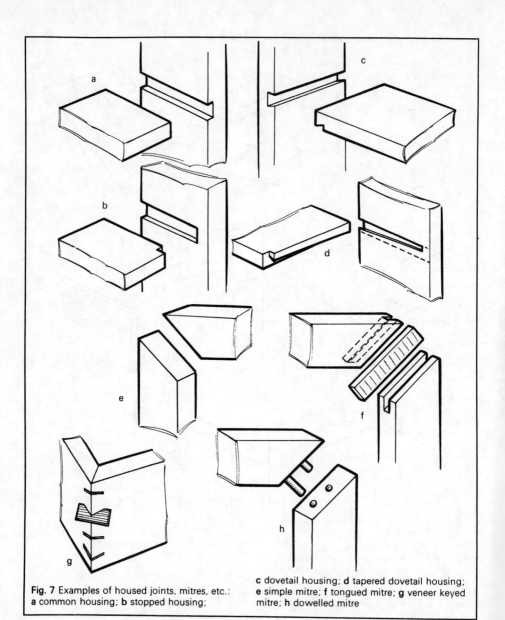

Fig. 7 Examples of housed joints, mitres, etc.:
a common housing; **b** stopped housing;
c dovetail housing; **d** tapered dovetail housing;
e simple mitre; **f** tongued mitre; **g** veneer keyed
mitre; **h** dowelled mitre

of frames, etc., often as a simple substitute for the mortise and tenon. Their chief value is when the material is too thin for the mortise and tenon to be cut. The positions in which the joints are used are obvious from Fig. 6 (a, b, c and d). A centre line is marked with the gauge from the face side in a, b and c, and a saw cut made immediately to the waste side of the line. The shoulder line is squared across with chisel or knife, and a sloping groove cut similarly to that of the tenon, (d) Fig. 4. When the joint has to withstand any strain (as in the loose seat of a chair, for instance), it should be screwed as well as glued. In the case of the cross-halving (d) the parts should be just hand tight. Too tight a fit may cause distortion.

The bridle joint (e) is handy when a sideboard, table, or similar piece has three legs at the front. The top rail can be in a single length and the centre leg bridled into it.

The grooved joint (f) with loose tongue is used for strong joints required when boards are glued side by side—table tops, carcase ends, etc. The lapped joint (g) is often used as a simple alternative to the lapped dovetail. It requires to be both glued and nailed. (h) is used similarly, but is not very satisfactory owing to the short grain at the end which is liable to split away.

Housed joints. The simple housing (a), Fig. 7, is used chiefly for shelves, partitions, etc. When its front appearance is an objection the joint is stopped as at (b). In the case of (a) the groove is simple to cut. Two lines are squared across the wood with knife or chisel, sloping grooves chiselled on the waste side, and the tenon saw worked in these. The bulk of the waste is chiselled away, and the depth made even with the router.

It is not quite so simple with the stopped groove. The method is to chop a recess immediately against the stop as in Fig. 8. This enables the saw to be worked back and forth in short strokes until the depth is reached. The removal of the waste is with chisel and router as before.

For a stronger joint the dovetail housing at (c) can be used. This can be cut right through as shown, or it can be stopped similarly to (b). As a guide to holding the saw at the correct angle a

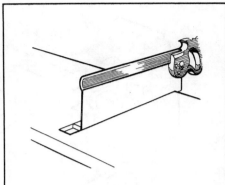

Fig. 8 How sides of stopped groove are sawn

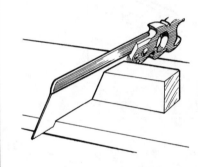

Fig. 9 Guide for sawing dovetail groove

block of wood can be fixed to the side of the line as in Fig. 9, being either cramped or nailed down.

Just as easy to cut and certainly simpler to fit is the tapered and shouldered dovetail housing at (d). Its advantage is that the joint is quite slack until pushed right home. This makes it much easier to tell just where the joint may need easing.

Mitred joints. The simple mitre is given at (e), Fig. 7. It is cut on the mitre block or box according

111

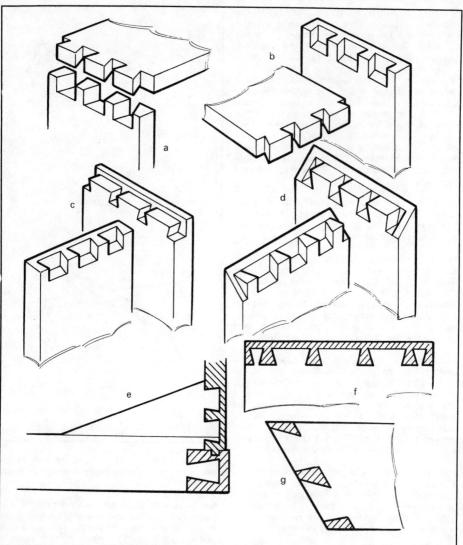

Fig. 10 Various types of dovetail joints: **a** through dovetail; **b** lapped dovetail; **c** double-lapped dovetail; **d** mitre secret dovetail; **f** lapped dovetail for carcase—note narrow end dovetails to prevent corners from curling away; **g** angle dovetails

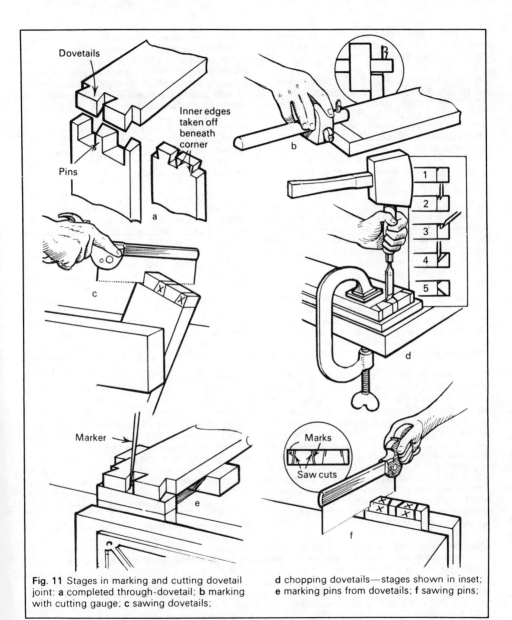

Fig. 11 Stages in marking and cutting dovetail joint: **a** completed through-dovetail; **b** marking with cutting gauge; **c** sawing dovetails; **d** chopping dovetails—stages shown in inset; **e** marking pins from dovetails; **f** sawing pins;

to its size. Small mitres can often be glued up straightway from the saw but larger ones need trimming on the mitre shooting board, (b), p. 16.

Various ways of strengthening mitres are given at (f), (g), and (h). The first and last are used chiefly for frames, whereas (g) is handy for strengthening a small mitred box to be veneered. Saw cuts are made across the mitre, and slips of veneer glued in, these being levelled after the glue has set.

Dovetails. These make the strongest joint for such structures as boxes, etc. When the appearance of the dovetail does not matter the through dovetail (a) Fig. 10, is the simplest and strongest. The lapped dovetail (b) is used when one side must be plain, as in carcase sides, drawer fronts, etc. At (c) the joint is concealed on both sides except for a thin line of end grain formed by the lap. At (d) it is entirely hidden.

The application of the lapped dovetail to the joining of a top rail to a cabinet side with corner post is shown at (e). (f) is for a wide carcase where the narrow end dovetails prevent any tendency for the wood to curl away at the corners. When one piece slopes at an angle the arrangement at (g) is followed.

The method of cutting the through dovetail is given in Fig. 11. The thickness of the wood is gauged across as at (b). When the thickness of the two varies, the thickness of the one is gauged on to the other. Do not cut in deeply as the mark has later to be planed away. Pencil in the dovetail positions. In an important position they are measured and marked with a template. The slope is 10mm. ($\frac{1}{2}$in.) in 60mm. (3in.) as shown in Fig. 12. Place the wood in the vice at an angle so that the saw can be held upright and cut down as at (c). Put crosses on the waste pieces. Much of the latter can be cut away with the coping saw at about 1mm. from the line.

Chop away the waste as at (d). Make a sloping cut up to the gauge line (1), and chop down about 1mm. ($\frac{1}{16}$in.) from the line (2). Make a sloping cut at (3) so that the actual corner is not removed. Repeat the process right on the gauge line, (4), and finally turn over the work from the other side (5).

Place the part with the pins in the vice, and lay the dovetailed piece on it in position as at (e). A waste piece at the back will support it in the correct position. Run a marker around the dovetails as shown, and cut as at (f). The saw should be held just to the waste side of the mark, this giving a comfortable hand-tight fit. Note the crosses which denote the waste pieces. It makes it obvious which parts are to be removed. The chopping is much the same as for the dovetails. Before assembling the inner edges of the dovetails are lightly chiselled away as at (a) so that they start together easily.

The lapped dovetail is cut similarly, but the pins can only be chopped from the one side. In the mitre dovetail the pins must be cut first as otherwise it is impossible to mark the one from the other.

Carcase joints. When solid wood is used for a carcase such as a cupboard the lapped dovetail shown at (a), Fig. 13, is used for work for which it is desired to conceal the joints. It is assumed that a separate top is used which covers the dovetails at the top. At the sides the lap of the dovetails conceals the joint. An alternative sometimes used at the top is the use of rails at front and back with angle braces glued on at the inner edges, as at (b). If there is no objection to the joints showing, ordinary through dovetails can be cut as at (c), in which case they need to be nicely spaced and neatly cut. In the case of a carcase in which there is no separate top and in which the joints have to be concealed the double-lapped dovetail at (d) is used. In this the only indication of the joint is the thin line of end grain showing at the side. The joint at (e) is sometimes used for a cheap job and is a simple lap, the parts being glued and nailed together, though sometimes a dovetailed bracket such as that shown in Fig. 17 can be added, at the inner angle.

Man-made materials. These include plywood, blockboard, and chipboard, and special forms of construction are invariably necessary when they are used. In one sense they have an advantage in that they are free from the shrinkage and swelling that is a feature of solid wood. On the other hand their construction often means that normal joints cannot be used. For multi-ply and blockboard the method in Fig. 14 is useful. Rails

114

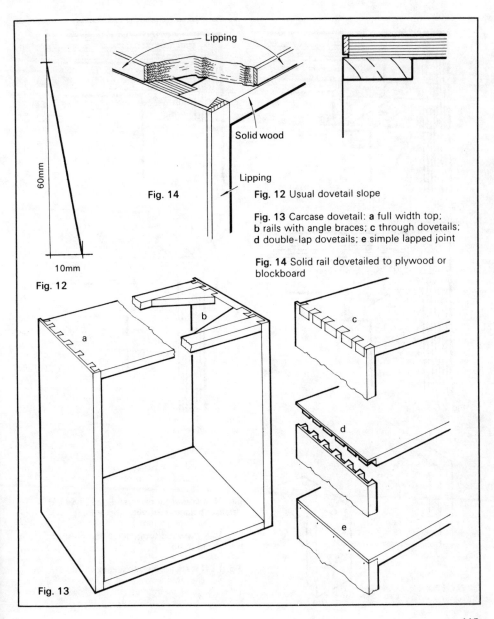

Lipping

Solid wood

Lipping

Fig. 14

Fig. 12 Usual dovetail slope

Fig. 13 Carcase dovetail: **a** full width top;
b rails with angle braces; **c** through dovetails;
d double-lap dovetails; **e** simple lapped joint

Fig. 14 Solid rail dovetailed to plywood or
blockboard

60mm

10mm

Fig. 12

Fig. 13

a

b

c

d

e

115

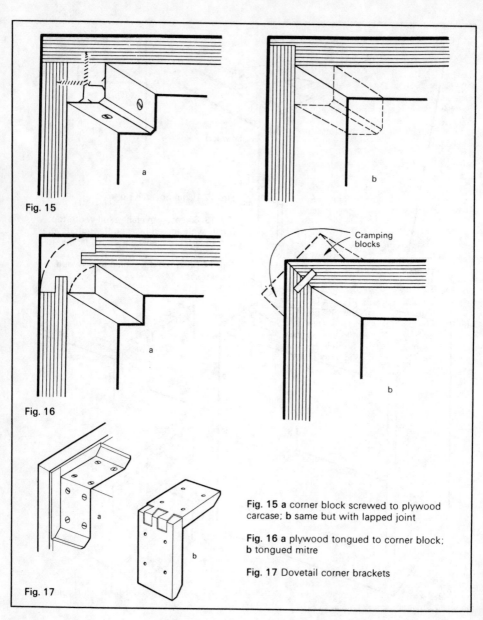

Fig. 15

Fig. 16

Cramping blocks

Fig. 17

Fig. 15 a corner block screwed to plywood carcase; **b** same but with lapped joint

Fig. 16 a plywood tongued to corner block; **b** tongued mitre

Fig. 17 Dovetail corner brackets

at the top are used at front and back and possibly in the middle, these being dovetailed in. This can be done successfully if somewhat coarse dovetails are used. The front edges of the ends are lipped; also the edges of the top which is fixed with screws driven upwards through the rails. It gives an attractive appearance if a narrow rebate is worked round the underside of the top.

Another method also suitable for either multi-ply or blockboard is either of those in Fig. 15. At (a) the parts are merely butted together and strengthened with blocks glued and screwed in the angle. A rather neater method is (b) in which the top is rebated so that only a thin line of plywood shows at the end. The glue block is fitted as in the previous case as shown by the dotted lines.

Sometimes the design allows a double-grooved block to be used, the top and side being tongued into it as at (a) Fig. 16. If preferred the rounded corner effect can be given (dotted lines). A neater effect is the mitred and grooved joint at (b), Fig. 16. The grooves, however, are awkward to work by hand as the short grain of the plywood is liable to crumble under the plough. If a circular saw or high-speed router is available, however, it makes a strong joint. Triangular blocks can be glued on temporarily as shown by the dotted lines to enable cramps to be applied when assembling.

The use of screwed brackets is sometimes an advantage for a mitred, butted or rebated joint as shown in Fig. 17. These can be glued and screwed at front and back as at (a). They are dovetailed together, and when making the dovetails, it is an advantage to set the gauge bare of the thickness so that when the parts are assembled the end grain of both pieces stands in slightly as at (b), Fig. 17. Unless this is done the wood, being liable to shrink slightly in its thickness, may eventually leave the ends of the pins and dovetails slightly projecting, causing a loose joint. In some pieces of furniture this bracket method can be used for solid wood such as the rebated joint at (e), Fig. 13.

Coarse dovetails can sometimes be used for blockboard as at (a), Fig. 18. It does, however, depend to an extent on the grain direction of the material. Pelleted screws can also be used for

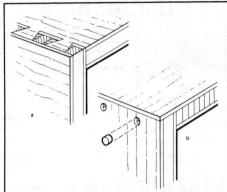

Fig. 18 Joints for blockboard a coarse dovetails; b lapped and screwed

Fig. 19 Bolted knock-down fittings

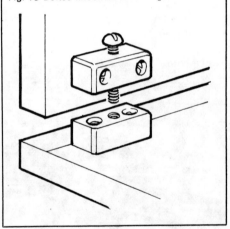

blockboard as at (b). Note however that it is only practicable when the core of the rebated piece runs crosswise as shown. Otherwise the screws enter end grain where they have poor hold.

In the case of some veneered chipboards the only really practicable method is the use of special bolted fittings shown in Fig. 19. The fittings, in two pieces, are screwed in the angle of the joining parts. Bolts draw the parts tightly together.

117

Chapter nine

Metal Fittings, etc.

Locks

There are many kinds of locks made for special purposes. Fig. 1 shows those most commonly used. (a), (b), (c), (d), (e), (f) and (g) are furniture locks; (h), (i) and (j) are for house doors.

Kinds of locks. (a) is the straight cupboard lock which is screwed to the inside of the door and is not let in. Mostly these locks shoot both right and left, and can so be used for doors opening right or left. The cut lock at (b) is much neater, but requires recessing into the wood. As the bolt shoots in one direction only the lock must be ordered R or L. To tell which you need, face the door from the outside. If the lock is on the left you need a L.H. lock. Thus the lock shown is L.H.

Similar in form is the drawer lock at (f). This has to be let into the drawer front. The box lock (g) is also let into the wood, but in addition is a plate which needs recessing into and screwing to the lid.

The lock at (d) is known as the link-plate lock, and is used for a door which closes over the face of the cabinet. It is recessed into the back of the door, and the link-plate into the front edge of the cabinet. The link passes through a slot in the lock, the bolt passing through it. Since the bolt shoots right or left it can be used at either side. For a sliding wood door the lock at (e) is used. The lock at (n) is used for glass sliding doors. It is held with a thumb screw to the leading edge of the rear glass. The detachable lock is slid on to this bar and prevents either door from being moved. (1) and (m) are two forms of ball catches, and (k) is a mortise bolt for a room door.

Of locks for house doors the simplest and cheapest is the rim lock at (h). It is simply screwed on, though there is sometimes a project-ing plate which need to be recessed into the edge. (i) shows the Yale pattern latch in which the cutting-in is reduced to a minimum. The mortise lock at (j) requires to be set right into the edge of the door.

Fixing a cut door lock. This is widely used on furniture. The stages of fixing are given in Figs. 2–7. Square across the surface and edge of the

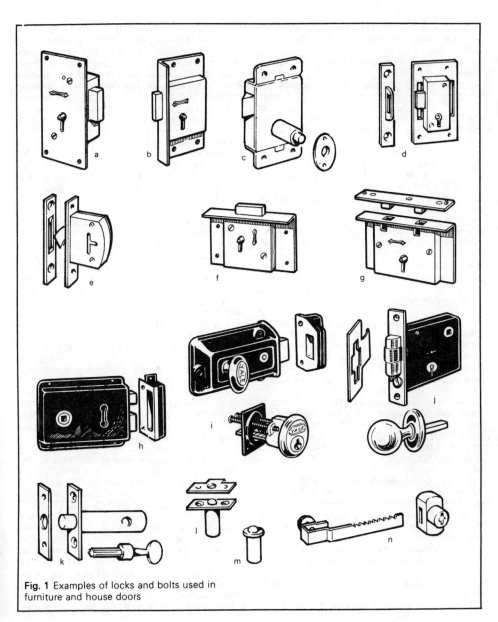

Fig. 1 Examples of locks and bolts used in furniture and house doors

door a centre line. Set the gauge to the distance of the pin from the outer plate as in Fig. 2, and mark across the pencil line. This gives the keyhole position, and a bit is selected which will give a close fit to the rounded portion of the escutcheon. A hole is bored right through the door and the escutcheon laid in position as in Fig. 3. A slight tap with the hammer will give an indentation of the shape, the sides of which can be sawn with the keyhole saw. A narrow chisel will remove the waste.

Place the lock with the pin level with the pencil line, and mark the door in line with the body of the lock as in Fig. 4. Set a gauge to the thickness of the body including the plate, and mark the edge of the door. This gives the position and extent of the wood to be cut away. Make a series of saw cuts across the grain down to as far as they can be taken as in Fig. 5. The door should be held down on the bench with handscrews. Remove the waste with the chisel as shown, and chop down at the ends and back. The latter needs to be done carefully to avoid splitting along the grain. Once again ease away the waste.

Place the lock in position, making sure that the pin is level with its hole, and mark round the ends of the plate with a marking knife. It is of little use marking the sides of the plate as at this stage the lock cannot be pushed right home. The simplest way of marking these sides is to use the gauge in conjunction with a waste piece of wood with parallel sides. Set the gauge as shown in Fig. 6. Then, holding the waste piece right over the lock recess (this waste piece must be longer than the lock) mark the door edge. The back plate is marked similarly. Fig. 7 shows the completed recess.

Screw on the lock and try the action with the key. To find the position of the recess to be cut to take the bolt, shoot out the latter and smear its surface with thin paint, or, say, the dirty oil from the oilstone. Shoot the bolt back and close the door. Now turn the key as far as it will go. This will leave a mark on the cupboard side which can be chopped out with a small chisel.

Drawer locks are fitted similarly, but the keyhole is the other way round. It may also be necessary to use the special drawer-lock chisel (p. 12) when the space is restricted. In the case of a box lock (g), Fig. 1, the link plate also has to be attached. To find its position place it on the lock and turn the key. Bring down the lid and thump it. There is generally a small spike at the back of the plate which will be driven into the lid. Turn the lock, and raise the lid, the plate being lifted with it. Mark round its edge and chop the recess to receive it, finally screwing it in position.

Mortise lock. Assuming that you are fixing the lock to a framed door, the vertical position will be decided by the main centre horizontal rail. The tenons of this rail run right through and there is a fair distance between them. The lock should be let in here, as shown in Fig. 8.

Marking the position. Wedge open the door and, holding the lock in the position shown in Fig. 9, mark lines across the edge level with the top and bottom of the body of the lock. The lock should extend equally into both tenons. Now turn the lock into the position it will occupy, and, keeping the body level with the marks made just at the edge, mark the position of the spindle hold and keyhole as in Fig. 10, using a pointed scriber. Mark all round the holes. Work from the inside of the door because the edge is frequently planed at a slight angle to allow it to clear easily. The holes cannot be bored directly over these marks because they do not allow for the face plate. The bit must therefore be started farther in by a distance equal to the thickness of this plate. The usual sizes are 9mm. ($\frac{3}{8}$in.) for the keyhole and 16mm. ($\frac{5}{8}$in.) for the spindle. When the point of the bit just emerges finish the hole by boring from the reverse side.

The mortise. Turning now to the edge again, draw in a pencil line exactly down the centre (see Fig. 10), using the rule and finger as a gauge. With a twist bit of the same size as the thickness of the body of the lock bore a hole on the centre line so that it is just inside the top horizontal line. A lath of wood cramped to the door as in Fig. 11 will enable you to judge whether the bit is being held square. A series of holes is bored right along the mortise, and it is desirable to bore them as close together as possible so that the subsequent chopping out is minimized. To enable this to be done, knock a plug of wood into the first hole before you bore

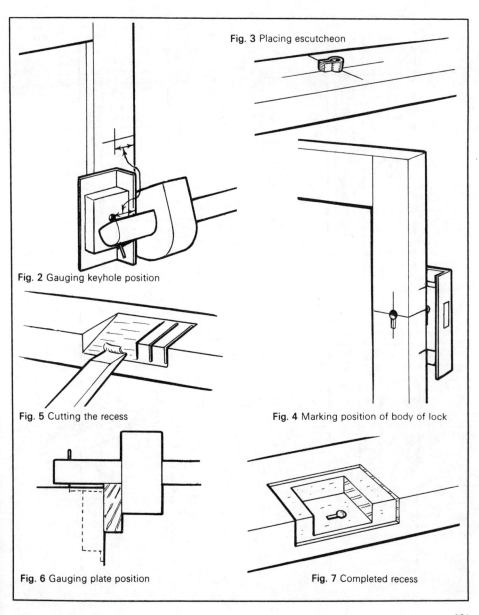

Fig. 3 Placing escutcheon

Fig. 2 Gauging keyhole position

Fig. 5 Cutting the recess

Fig. 4 Marking position of body of lock

Fig. 6 Gauging plate position

Fig. 7 Completed recess

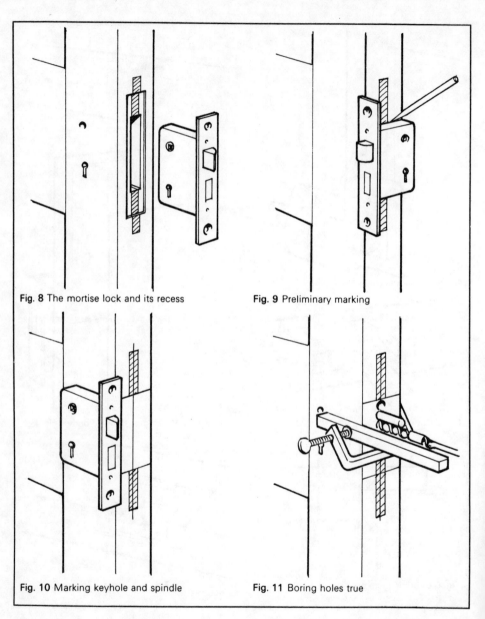

Fig. 8 The mortise lock and its recess

Fig. 9 Preliminary marking

Fig. 10 Marking keyhole and spindle

Fig. 11 Boring holes true

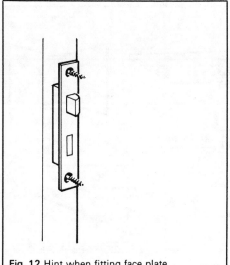

Fig. 12 Hint when fitting face plate

outer one being held with metal screws. This should always be removed during re-painting.

Fitting the striking plate. To fix the striking plate, nearly close the door and scribe a line where both bolts occur. Square this across the door rebate. Now open the door, shoot out the bolts and put a film of the dirty black oil from the oilstone on the faces. Shoot the bolts, close the door tightly, and open the bolts as far as they will go so that they leave a mark on the jamb. This gives the position for the striking plate which can now be placed level with the top of the marks and a line scribed round. Always work to the top, because this allows for subsequent dropping of the door. Screw on the plate and mortise the holes. You will probably find that part of the plate projects at the front. This should be bent over, partly to enable the latch to close more easily, and also because a projecting corner is liable to catch the clothing of anyone passing.

Hinges

the second. Remove it and put it into the second before boring the third, and so on. This will enable you to start each hole right up against the previous one without danger of the wood crumbling away and making the bit run out of true. A piece of paper stuck to the bit will mark the depth to which each hole should be taken.

Chop out the mortise with the chisel. The professional carpenter has a swan-necked chisel for finishing, this enabling the cross grain of the tenons to be cut in the corners, but it is not essential. You can now finish the keyhole with pad saw or with the chisel. A waste block in the mortise will prevent the wood from splitting.

The face plate. The face plate has now to be fitted. The lock is put in position and a line scribed round. As it may be awkward to withdraw the lock when it is pushed right home a useful hint is to put a couple of screws in the plate the reverse way round as in Fig. 12. These give you something to grip when you want to withdraw the lock. Test to see that the spindle hole and keyhole coincide with those bored, and screw up. Incidentally, some locks have two face plates, the

Kinds of hinges. Some of the more generally used hinges are shown in Fig. 13. Of these the butt (a) is the kind mostly used in furniture making, windows, and internal doors, etc. It is intended to be recessed into the wood, and its comparatively narrow shape makes it suitable for the edges of doors. The back flap (b) is let in similarly but is wider, and is used for bureau falls, flap table tops, etc., where there is plenty of width. For the special kind of flap table having what is known as the rule joint, the fixed edge rounded and the flap edge hollowed, the table top hinge (c) is used. Note that the screw holes are countersunk on the side opposite to the knuckle, and that one flap is longer than the other to bridge across the hollow.

The ornamental hinge (d), sometimes known as the butterfly hinge, is screwed straight to the surface without being let in. For narrow edges the strap hinge at (e) is used. The acorn hinge, (f), is used when for some reason the hinge has to project well beyond the face of the door. The acorn ends have an ornamental effect. When the pivoting point has to be at the outer corner of a door which closes over the face of a cabinet the lift-off hinge, (g), is used. This enables the door to

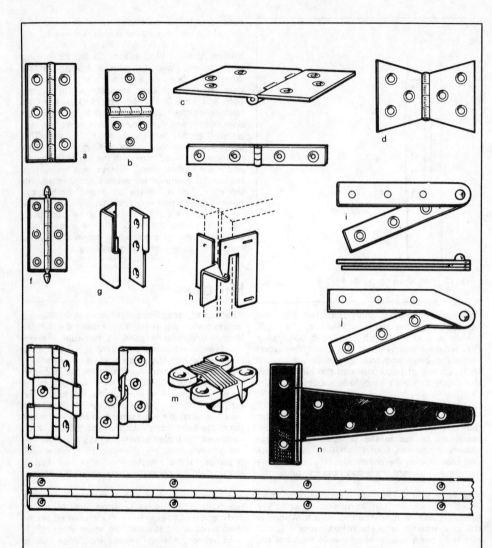

Fig. 13 Common types of hinges for various purposes: **a** plain butt hinge; **b** back flap hinge; **c** table top hinge; **d** butterfly hinge; **e** strap hinge; **f** acorn hinge; **g** lift-off cabinet hinge; **h** pivot hinge; **i** centre hinge; **j** cranked centre hinge; **k** reversible screen hinge; **l** rising butt hinge; **m** soss hinge; **n** cross-garnet hinge; **o** strip hinge

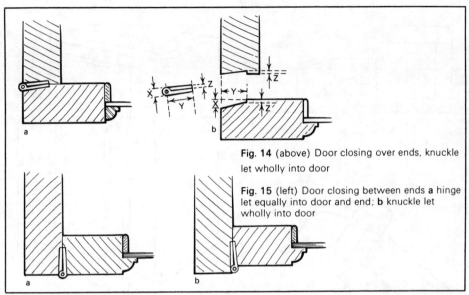

Fig. 14 (above) Door closing over ends, knuckle let wholly into door

Fig. 15 (left) Door closing between ends **a** hinge let equally into door and end; **b** knuckle let wholly into door

open without projecting sideways. That at (h) has a similar effect.

The centre hinge, (i), fitted at top and bottom edges, is generally used when the pivoting points of butts would not be practicable. The cranked type (j) brings the centre to yet another position. For such items as screens the reversible hinge at (k) is used. The centres of the knuckles equal the thickness of the wood. If the latter is more than this the hinge will bind. Rising butts, (l), are used for a room door which has to clear a centre carpet. They are made R and L hand. To tell which is required stand outside the door. If the hinges are to the right then the RH hinges are required, and vice versa. The soss hinge at (m) is let into the joining edges of, say, a table top and is completely hidden on the surface. The leaf can move through 180 deg. The cross garnet hinge (n) is for large external doors of the ledged and braced type. The strip hinge (o), sometimes known as the piano hinge, is used for wide falls.

Position of butt hinges. These can be fitted in various ways, according to the position and detail of the door. At (a), Fig. 14, the door closes over the face of the cupboard. If preferred the hinge could be let equally into the door and cupboard. Usually, however, the method shown at (a) is followed because a bead is generally worked along the edge of the door to give a neat finish, and the knuckle of the hinge lines up with this. The knuckle is let into the door in its entirety, but to make the appearance as neat as possible and relieve the screws of the entire strain it is usual to cut sloping recesses in the cupboard edge. Note that only the opening edge is let in; at the knuckle side the wood is uncut. (b) shows how the sizes taken from the hinge are marked on door and cupboard.

When a door is contained between the sides of the cupboard either of the methods in Fig. 15 can be used. At (a) the door is flush at the front with the cupboard ends, and the butt is let equally into door and cupboard. At (b) the door is recessed and the butt knuckle is let entirely into the door, though sloping recesses for the flange only are cut in the cupboard. To enable this door to swing through 180 deg., the centre of the knuckle is brought forward so that it is midway between the surface of the door face and the outer edge of the cupboard.

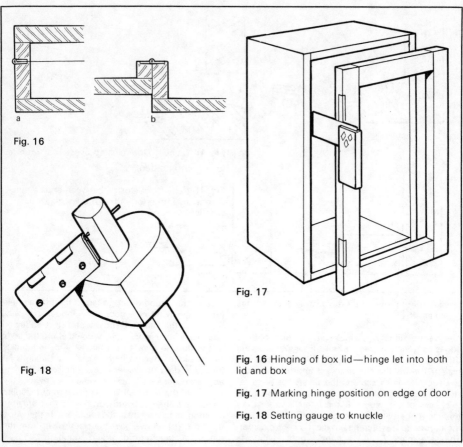

Fig. 16

Fig. 17

Fig. 18

Fig. 16 Hinging of box lid—hinge let into both lid and box

Fig. 17 Marking hinge position on edge of door

Fig. 18 Setting gauge to knuckle

Boxes are hinged similarly to doors, but as a rule the butts are let equally in lid and box as shown in Fig. 16, which shows the opening movement.

Rising butts. These, (l), Fig. 13, are used for room doors, their function being to raise the door clear of a centre carpet. They are made in sizes corresponding with ordinary butts, and can therefore be used to replace ordinary butts. One point to note is that they are right- and left-hand and the correct hand must be ordered. A framework intended for rising butts has its top rebate at an angle to allow for the slope. When the rebate is square, as when

simple butts are used, it is invariably necessary to take off the corner of the door when rising butts are fitted. This does not show when the door is closed because the rebate hides the corner. The hinges should be oiled periodically to give easy movement.

Hinging a door. Decide on the position of the hinges and square in across the edge as at Fig. 17. There is no rule about this but its own distance from the end is a general guide. To mark the width and depth set the gauge to the hinge itself as in Fig. 18. Do not over-run past the pencil lines. Saw

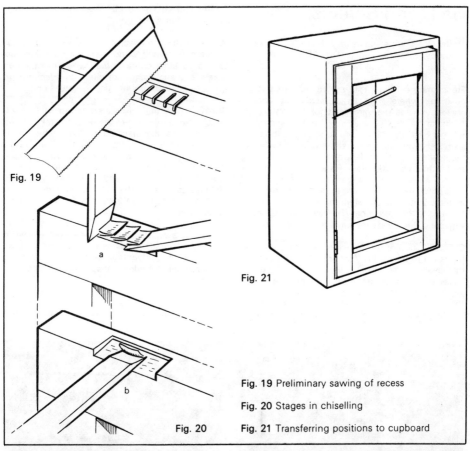

Fig. 19

a

b

Fig. 20

Fig. 21

Fig. 19 Preliminary sawing of recess

Fig. 20 Stages in chiselling

Fig. 21 Transferring positions to cupboard

across down to just short of the diagonal as in Fig. 19, the intermediate cuts serving to break up the grain thus preventing a split from developing. With a keen chisel cut in the ends (a), Fig. 20, and waste away the wood to be removed. Finally pare the recess flat as at (b). Fix the butts with two screws each only.

Placing the door in position, transfer the butt positions to the cupboard as in Fig. 21, and mark and cut the recesses similarly. Fix with a single screw to each hinge, and try the movement. Carry out any adjustment before adding the remaining

screws. The closing edge of the door needs to be taken off at a slight angle at the inside, otherwise it will tend to bind as it is opened.

Reversible screen hinges. These, (k), Fig. 13 enable a screen to open in both directions. They have knuckles at both edges, and it is important that the thickness of the wood equals the distance between the pins. If the wood is thicker than this the screen will bind as it opens. If it is thinner there will be a gap down the joint as it opens. This is the lesser evil of the two, but in the case of a draught screen it means that it is not wholly effective.

Nails and Screws

Nails. Of the wide variety of nails made for special purposes, those shown in Fig. 22 are the most useful for general woodwork.

French nails (a) have a strong grip, and are used in positions where their large heads are not an objection. Thus they are used for carpentry, etc. A similar nail having a smaller head is known as the lost head (b). Not being so strong, but having a smaller head and not so liable to split the wood is the oval wire nail, (c). It is driven in with the long oval in line with the grain. Panel pins (e) are the general nails for cabinet work as they are thin and have small heads. They are thus not so unsightly, and are not liable to split the wood. A smaller variation is the veneer pin (f). Apart from its use in veneering it is handy for small mouldings, etc.

Cut nails (d) are for carpentry generally. Similar but rather heavier is the floor brad. Both kinds have the advantage of not being liable to split the grain. Tacks (g) are used generally for upholstery. The improved tack has a rather larger head. Clout nails (h) are used to a limited extent in upholstery for webbing, but are more generally used for fixing roofing felt, etc. The cut clasp nail (i) is an extremely strong carpentry nail.

Whatever the nail used, always endeavour to nail from the thin wood to the thick. It is an advantage, too, to dovetail the nails; that is, to drive them in askew at a slight angle in alternate directions. In the case of outdoor work use galvanized nails.

Screws. The main types are given in Fig. 23, which also shows where the length is taken from. The gauge is the diameter of the shank and is regardless of length. Thus a No. 8 50mm. (2in.) screw has the same diameter as a No. 8 75mm. (3in.) screw. The clearance hole should be an easy fit as shown in Fig. 23e, and the thread hole should be bored to the diameter of the central rod without the thread. It is purely the hold of the thread which gives the grip.

Phillips screws, (d), Fig. 23, are mostly used in industry. There is a cross recess in the head rather than a slot, the advantage being that there is no danger of the screwdriver slipping out and causing a scratch.

Nailing the mitred corners of a picture frame.

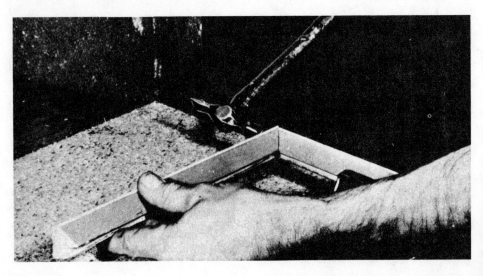

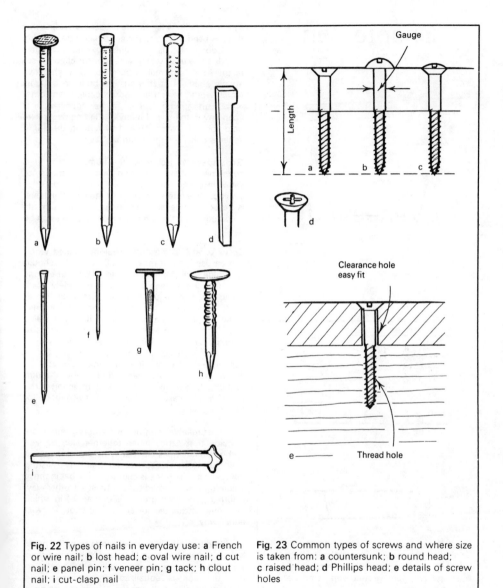

Fig. 22 Types of nails in everyday use: **a** French or wire nail; **b** lost head; **c** oval wire nail; **d** cut nail; **e** panel pin; **f** veneer pin; **g** tack; **h** clout nail; **i** cut-clasp nail

Fig. 23 Common types of screws and where size is taken from: **a** countersunk; **b** round head; **c** raised head; **d** Phillips head; **e** details of screw holes

Chapter ten

Veneering

This is an entirely legitimate process providing that it is not used merely to cover up bad workmanship and poor materials. It enables certain decorative woods to be used which would be unreliable if cut in the solid, and makes possible many attractive effects such as quartering and built-up patterns which would be entirely impracticable in any other way. Furthermore it has to be accepted that economy in the use of many of the fine decorative hardwoods is essential, and by cutting them into veneers there is a minimum of waste.

Groundwork. So far as the home craftsman is concerned, there are two main methods of veneering; caul and hammer. When a press is available this offers the simplest means. Whichever is used, however, the groundwork and its preparation are the same. Various materials can be used.

Solid wood. Almost any straight-grained wood can be used, but it must be reliable and it should hold glue well. Mahogany is excellent but expensive. Obeche, Parana pine, etc., are widely used. Baltic pine, too, is used, but it must be as free of knots as possible, any small, unavoidable ones being chopped out and the holes filled in. It is also necessary to give softwood a coat of glue size after preparation before the glue proper is used otherwise it soaks up more than its share. Oak is sometimes used, but it is not ideal because its coarse grain is liable eventually to show through to the surface owing to the glue contracting in the pores. In any case it is not the best of woods for holding glue.

The most reliable form of solid wood groundwork is made from strips glued together side by side with the heart sides alternately up and down as at (a), Fig. 1, the reason being that any twisting tendency in one piece is countered by that in those adjoining which would tend to twist the other way. Another good solid ground is that at (b) in which the wood is quarter-cut and is not liable to twist either way.

It will be realized that veneer tends to pull a panel hollow as it dries out, and for this reason it is always wise to veneer the ground-work on both sides so that the pull is equalized. By taking certain precautions this pull can be minimized or even eliminated altogether, but it is always safer to

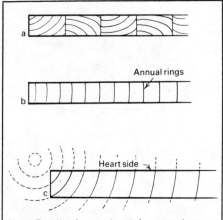

Fig. 1 Details of groundwork for veneering: a solid ground made from solid strips with heart sides alternately up and down; b quarter cut board making good groundwork; c how to tell heart side of wood

veneer both sides, especially for such parts as doors which have no stiffening framework. When single side veneering is unavoidable it is advisable to lay the veneer on the heart side of the wood, (c), Fig. 1. The reason is that the pull of the veneer is opposed to the natural twisting tendency of the wood.

Plywood. This makes a good groundwork if of reliable make; the cheaper tea-chest variety is useless. Gaboon ply is specially suitable. The veneer should always be laid with its grain at right angles with that of the outer layer of the ply. The edges are sometimes a problem. Veneer does not hold really well on the end grain, and generally the only plan is to fit an edging as in Fig. 2. That at (a) is the usual trade method but, as the section is rather awkward to work with hand tools, that at (b) is simpler. The tongue on the ply is more easily worked as there is more wood to grip. (c) is altogether simpler, being just glued and pinned. It would not be used in first-class work.

A point to note in all these edgings is that if veneered first the edging affords considerable protection to the veneer which is always vulnerable at the edge. On the other hand the edging necessarily shows on the surface.

Laminboard, blockboard. These make good, reliable grounds. The former is the better since the narrow strips used in the core are less liable to movement. The notes about the direction of the grain given about plywood apply equally. The edgings in Fig. 2 can also be used.

Chipboard. This has come in for increasing use as a groundwork—much of it in fact can be obtained ready veneered. For panels and supported parts it is satisfactory, but it is not recommended for flush doors which have no stiffening framework. As an edging that at (a), Fig. 2, is the most suitable, with (c) as a cheaper alternative. (b) is unsuitable.

Hardboard. There are many varieties of these, some being more suitable than others. None is as durable as the materials already mentioned, and they would only be used for cheap work or less important parts.

Preparation of groundwork. As the veneer must be in close contact with the surface of the groundwork it is obvious that any inequality in the latter will show through the veneer. Solid wood if used must be planed dead true. Plywood and laminboard are already true enough. To roughen the surface so giving a key to the glue, and to take out marks left by the plane, a toothing plane, Fig. 3, is used, this being worked in all directions; along the grain, across, and diagonally. If the ground is softwood it should be given a coat of glue size and allowed to dry out. The inevitable roughness is removed by rubbing with coarse glasspaper held on a rubber.

Handling veneer. Most veneer nowadays is knife cut as it is produced with practically no waste. Occasionally saw cut veneer is found, and it is always thicker, and shows the marks of the circular saw on which it was cut. These marks on the side to be glued must be removed with a toothing plane, the veneer being held down on a flat board. The most convenient way of cutting knife-cut veneer is to place it on a flat board, press a batten with a straight edge on it, and cut with keen knife or chisel as in Fig. 4. The batten is essential as otherwise the veneer may cockle and split. When several strips of equal width have to be

Fig. 2 Edgings for multi-ply and laminated boards

131

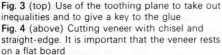

Fig. 3 (top) Use of the toothing plane to take out inequalities and to give a key to the glue

Fig. 4 (above) Cutting veneer with chisel and straight-edge. It is important that the veneer rests on a flat board

Fig. 5 (top) Cutting parallel strips with cutting gauge. The batten pressed down over the veneer prevents it from cockling

Fig. 6 (above) Trimming veneer on the shooting board. A batten prevents cockling

cut the cutting gauge may be used as in Fig. 5. Here again the veneer rests on a flat board, the edge overhanging about 3mm. ($\frac{1}{8}$in.), and a batten is pressed across it to stiffen it. A single cut will generally sever it, but thick veneer may need cutting from both sides. Saw-cut veneer has usually to be cut with a fine-toothed saw, the veneer held on a flat board and the saw drawn across it.

Sometimes it is necessary to trim the edge of the veneer, for example, when jointing. It is done on the shooting board, the veneer overhanging the upper platform by about 3mm. ($\frac{1}{8}$in.), and a batten is pressed down to prevent cockling. This is shown in Fig. 6.

Resin adhesive. This is described fully on page 163. It is widely used in the trade for veneering, and it is well adapted for use when presses are available. When there is no press the only plan is to

use cauls. The hammer method (see under hammer veneering) is impracticable because the adhesive has not the tacky nature of animal glue and the veneer is liable to lift before adhesion takes place. To cheapen the cost the glue is often extended with rye flour. Resin is specially suitable for surfaces liable to wear as in the case of a table top, particularly as the adhesive is largely resistant to heat and damp. One advantage it has over animal glue is that it is used cold. There is thus ample time for assembling. Generally it is sufficient if the adhesive is applied to the groundwork only, but of course care must be taken that the joint is not glue-starved. In the trade a glue spreader is used which gives an even coat, but for home use the brush will have to be used, this being followed by a strip of wood with straight edge which will even the application. If a piece of work is wanted quickly, advantage can be taken of the fact that the resin sets rapidly with heat by using a heated caul. It needs rapid, deft handling, however, so that all the cramps are in position before setting takes place. For details of the method of applying cauls see page 134 where animal glue is dealt with.

P.V.A. glue. This is used similarly to resin glue but the even spread of glue is still more important because the glue tends to congeal quickly on exposure to air. The glue can be heat cured but this is not advisable unless a press is available because of the tendency to set rapidly before adjustment can take place. With some woods there may be a tendency to penetration.

Impact adhesives. These are useful on occasion, and a special type for veneering is marketed, being rather thinner and more easily spread than the normally-used type. It is scarcely suitable for really large areas because it might be difficult to obtain an even spread, free from lumpiness. The adhesive is applied to both groundwork and veneer, and a rather better result is obtained if two coats are given. The two are allowed to dry and the veneer is then pressed down when the bond is immediate. In fact care in positioning the veneer is essential because the two glued surfaces grab when brought into contact and it is almost impossible to shift the veneer when once in position. Many men use the slip-sheet method, a piece of flat brown paper being placed between veneer and groundwork and gradually withdrawn. The paper does not adhere as the impact glue on the one surface sticks only to that on the other surface after initial setting has taken place.

Another occasion on which impact adhesive is useful is when a small curved surface has to be veneered. It might be awkward to make a shaped caul, and if hammer veneering were used the veneer might be liable to spring up. With impact adhesive the grip is immediate. A further advantage of impact adhesive is that it is not liable to pull the groundwork hollow since there is no water used. Thus there is no swelling followed later by shrinkage, the cause of distortion when other adhesives are used.

Animal (Scotch) glue. The chief way in which the method of using this differs from other adhesives is that heat is necessary. Thus when a caul is used the latter must be thoroughly heated so that the glue is reliquified and can thus be pressed out all round. The same applies when a press is

used. Another feature is that it is the only adhesive for which the hammer method of veneering can be used. The glue is prepared in a proper glue kettle (see page 163) and both groundwork and veneer coated. It does not matter if the glue chills because heat is applied later. There are jobs for which Scotch glue has its advantages over other adhesives. Thus when veneering a shaped edge the tacky nature of the glue enables the glue to be pressed down with a hammer without danger of its springing up. The application of a shaped caul might be difficult or impossible. Scotch glue is still widely used in the antique trade for repair work. The hammer method of laying is dealt with later.

Caul veneering. In this method the veneer is pressed down with a flat board of wood known as a caul. If any jointing in the veneer is needed this is done before laying. In a simple joint the edges are planed, the parts put together on a flat board, and a piece of gummed tape put over the joint. A pattern, other than the simplest kind, would need a drawing on which the veneer could be assembled.

The caul is a flat panel of wood slightly larger than the groundwork, and is cramped down over the veneer with a sheet of newspaper interposed to prevent squeezed-out glue causing it to adhere. For a small panel the cramps can be applied all round, but for a larger one it is necessary to use pairs of cross bearers with slightly curved edges as in Fig. 7. The idea is to drive the glue from the centre outwards, the curve ensuring that the pressure is felt in the centre first. Since the curvature in the pairs of bearers is opposed the work remains flat. Note too the order in which the battens are applied, the centre ones again being fitted first to drive the glue outwards. When both sides are being veneered, the operation is simultaneous, two cauls being used, one each side.

In the case of animal glue it is necessary to heat the caul because the glue has to be reliquified to enable it to be pressed out. The heating must be thorough, not merely on the surface, as the whole operation must be gone about speedily so that pressure is applied before the glue chills. When the veneer has to be positioned exactly as in the case of a built-up pattern, centre lines are drawn on both veneer and groundwork and these lines

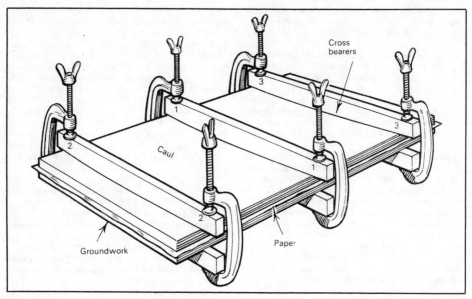

Fig. 7 (above) How caul is cramped down in caul veneering

Fig. 8 (below) How the veneer hammer is used

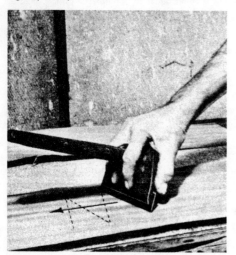

made to coincide. To prevent the veneer from floating out of position a couple of fine veneer pins should be driven in in unnoticeable positions.

Hammer veneering. This method is used with Scotch glue only. The special tool shown at s, page 15, is used. It has a strip of brass about $1\frac{1}{2}$mm. ($\frac{1}{16}$in.) thick let into the edge, and it is used to press out the surplus glue. The groundwork being prepared and the veneer cut to size, both are covered with glue and the veneer placed in position and smoothed down. The Scotch glue must be free of lumps. If a light wood is being used a little flake white powder should be added to the glue as this prevents dark glue lines from showing.

For a job of any size lightly damp about one half with a swab, and pass a warm flat iron across it to liquefy the glue. Use only a minimum of dampness, and do not have the iron hotter than is essential. Work the veneering hammer with a zig-zag movement from the centre towards the end as in Fig. 8, and try to avoid stretching the veneer in its width. Most veneers will go down easily, but woods with tricky grain may be inclined to lift, and quite a lot of patience may be needed. It is some-

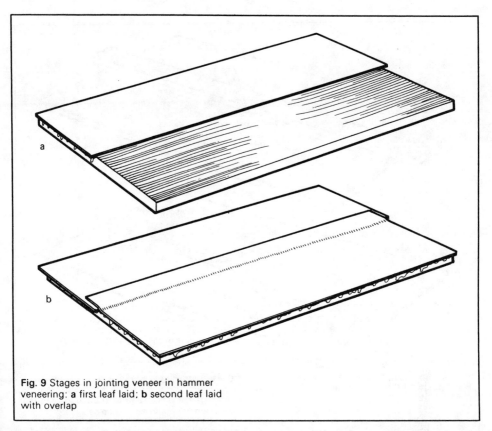

Fig. 9 Stages in jointing veneer in hammer veneering: **a** first leaf laid; **b** second leaf laid with overlap

times a help to place a block of metal (say an iron smoothing plane) on a part which is inclined to lift, as the cold metal will make the glue set more rapidly and hold the veneer. In extreme cases it may be necessary to cramp a wood block over the part with a piece of newspaper beneath to prevent it from adhering. To test whether the veneer is down tap it with the finger nails. A bubble (as it is called) will be apparent from the hollow feeling it gives.

One half being down correctly deal with the other in the same way. Any traces of glue on the surface should be wiped off with the damp swab straight away, but use as little moisture as possible because

it is chiefly this which causes the pull.

Jointing. This may be necessary simply because the veneer is not wide enough, or it may be needed in a halved panel in which two consecutive leaves of veneer are put down side by side, the grain matching. In this latter case the joint line must be drawn in pencil on the groundwork, and care taken in positioning the veneer to make sure that the grain is balanced.

For width jointing one piece of veneer is laid as at (a), Fig. 9. The next is laid similarly, overlapping the first as at (b). A straight-edge is laid along the overlap (in line with the pencil mark, if there is

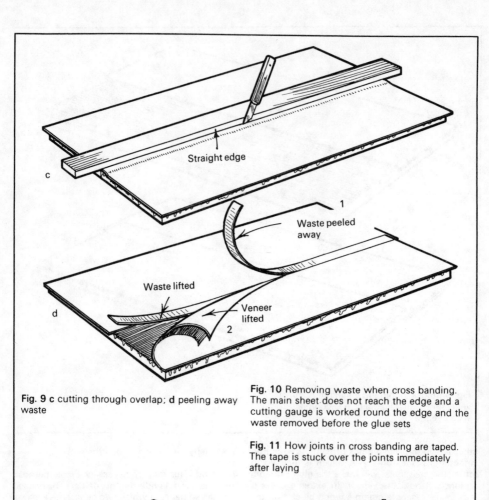

Straight edge

c

1

Waste peeled away

Waste lifted

Veneer lifted

d

2

Fig. 9 c cutting through overlap; **d** peeling away waste

Fig. 10 Removing waste when cross banding. The main sheet does not reach the edge and a cutting gauge is worked round the edge and the waste removed before the glue sets

Fig. 11 How joints in cross banding are taped. The tape is stuck over the joints immediately after laying

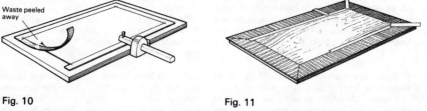

Waste peeled away

Fig. 10

Fig. 11

one), and a keen knife or chisel drawn along it as at (c). If the panel is large it is advisable to fix the straight-edge down with thumb-screws.

The one strip of waste can be peeled away straight away. The other is removed by lifting the veneer (d), so revealing it. It is necessary to replace the veneer at once and rub it down with the hammer. A piece of gummed tape stuck over the joint will prevent it from opening as the glue dries out. Some men prefer to shoot the joint in the veneer before laying and put the parts together with gummed tape, but some tricky veneers are liable to distort with the moisture and heat and may form either gaps in the joint or cause cockling.

Crossbanding. A detail sometimes needed in veneering is the crossbanding of a panel, especially in reproduction work. To do this the main panel is veneered normally except that the veneer is cut short all round. Immediately after laying a cutting gauge set to the banding width is run all round as in Fig. 10, and the waste peeled away.

The crossbanding is cut in cross-grain strips a trifle wider than the banding. The edge is trimmed on the shooting board and the strips cut with the cutting gauge (Fig. 5). In a panel of any great size it will be necessary to joint the strips, and this is done on the job itself, Fig. 11. Mitres are cut with a wide chisel and trimmed if necessary on the shooting board. The veneer is rubbed down with the cross-pene of the hammer, and pieces of gummed tape are stuck over the joints to prevent opening as the glue dries out.

Cleaning up. Leave the work for as long as possible before cleaning up. Any gummed tape on the surface should be lightly damped and peeled off, but avoid water as far as possible. Clean up the surface with a scraper. Often it is a help to hold the scraper at an angle so that it has a slicing cut. This is specially necessary on a crossbanded part as otherwise the grain may tear up. When satisfactory go over the whole with glasspaper wrapped around a cork rubber, first *Fine* 2, the No. 1. In the case of woods with intricate grain such as burr walnut, use only the finest glasspaper and use the rubber with a circular movement. This is necessary because the wood has no definite grain direction. Those who have an orbital sander will find it ideal for such work.

Fig. 12 Assembling cross banding around a sheet of veneer ready to be put down

Chapter eleven

Wood Carving

To get good results in wood carving it is essential that the tools are really sharp and are sharpened in the right way. The method is different from that used in ordinary woodworking chisels in which the bevel is on one side only. Carving gouges have the main bevel at the outside, but a second bevel is formed inside, and this with repeated sharpening eventually becomes about one quarter or one third the length of the other.

There are several reasons for the inside bevel. One is that when the tool is used with the hollow side downwards it gives it a tendency to lift as the cut is made. Without it the tool would tend to run into the wood. Another point is that the inside bevel widens the clearance of the tool so that it passes through a deep cut more easily. Lastly it considerably strengthens the edge.

Main sharpening is done with the oilstone and oilstone slips, but a leather strop dressed with a fine abrasive is used to give a still finer edge and to keep it in condition. The carver keeps these strops handy, and rubs up the tools frequently. The guiding principle is little and often.

Range of tools. The chief kinds of tools are shown in Fig. 1, and of these the straight gouge (a) is used for all general carving. The curved gouges (b) are for removing the waste when hollowing, say, a bowl. Similar in form but for much more acute hollows is the front bench gouge (c). The back bench gouge (d) has not many uses, and should not be obtained until actually required.

There are two kinds of straight chisel, square (e) and corner (f). They are used mostly for setting in, the corner type being useful for reaching into acute corners. For the cleaning up of recessed backgrounds the spoon bit (g) is invaluable. In addition to the square type the L and R corners are needed, again for acute corners.

The V or parting tool (h) is used chiefly for outlining, lettering, and sometimes for leaf detail. It

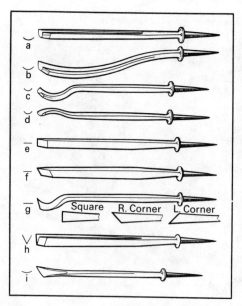

Fig. 1 Chief forms of gouges used in carving: a straight gouge: b curved gouge; c front bent gouge; d back bent gouge; e chisel; f corner chisel; g bent chisel; h V tool; i spade gouge

Fig. 2 (top) Sharpening the main bevel of the gouge on the oilstone—it is given a twisting movement so that the whole of the edge is sharpened

Fig. 4 (above) How gouge is stropped after sharpening on the oilstone

Fig. 3 (right) How inside of gouge is rubbed with the oilstone slip

can be obtained with either 90 deg. or 60 deg. angle. Spade gouges are available in almost all the above forms, but it will be seen that the tool splays out at the ends and is of lighter form. It is used chiefly for finishing off delicate carving.

All the tools are obtainable in varying degrees of curvature and in several widths. It can be rather confusing, but the rule is that all tools of a certain number have the same degree of curvature in relation to their width. As an example, the No 9 straight gouge is a half-round curve, whatever its width. Thus the 6mm. ($\frac{1}{4}$in.) No. 9 would be one half of a circle struck from a 3mm. ($\frac{1}{8}$in.) radius. The lower the number the flatter the curve. Straight gouges run in numbers from 3 to 11. Curved and bent gouges, chisels, etc. have other numbers.

Sharpening the tools

Gouges. The main outer bevel is sharpened on the oilstone, the tool being held at right angles with the stone and turned with a twisting movement as it is moved back and forth as in Fig. 2. Now use an oilstone slip of curvature that approximates to the inside or is a trifle quicker, and rub it along the inside at a slight angle much as in Fig. 3. It takes many sharpenings to get the gouge into first-class working order, but it helps after the initial outer rubbing to sharpen chiefly inside.

Stropping follows, and for this a piece of soft leather is dressed with a mixture of oil and the finest crocus powder. The fine grade preparation sold for grinding in motor car valves can also be used. Place the leather on a flat board and draw the bevel of the gouge flat along it, as in Fig. 4, rocking it so that every part of the edge is stropped, and drawing it back slightly so that the edge is drawn away, not into the leather. For the inside either a piece of leather can be wrapped round the finger or bent on itself, as Fig. 5 shows, or the leather can be glued to a rounded rubber.

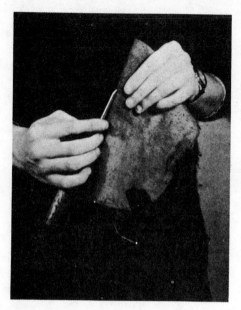

Fig. 5 Stropping the inside of the gouge

Chisels are sharpened in much the same way except that they are kept flat, not rocked. The bevels are equal on both sides. The V tool sometimes causes difficulty. Each outer bevel is rubbed on the stone, and a V shaped oilstone slip used at the inside, this being at an angle much as when the gouge is sharpened. When the slip becomes worn it frequently fails to reach into the corner, and instead of being sharp the angle becomes a slight hollow. This results in a point being formed, and will necessitate taking off the outer extreme corner.

Bench. The bench at which carving is done should be sturdy with a fairly thick top so that there is a solid feeling when the mallet is used. To hold the wood various methods can be used. Sometimes the ordinary joiners' G cramps are suitable, but it is always an advantage to avoid projecting parts. For this reason the carver's screw, Fig. 6, is useful, especially when the wood is fairly thick and when a hole in the back does not matter. The pointed

screw end is driven into the wood and tightened by using the wing nut as a spanner. The end of the screw is passed through a hole in the bench and the nut tightened from beneath. When the wood is thin the method in Fig. 7 can be followed. Round-head screws are passed through dogs or little pieces of hardwood or metal into the bench. The outer ends of the dogs rest on waste blocks of about the same thickness as the work, and so hold the work firm. Some metal dogs are cranked and have saw-like ends.

Lighting is important and should be from one direction only so that the undulations of the surface can be seen easily. An all-round light eliminates the shadows caused by the varied surfaces and so robs the carving of form. For daylight a window at the back of the bench is ideal. At night time a single electric lamp which can be raised or lowered at will is the most satisfactory. It should have a shade so that the work itself is illuminated without glare to the eyes.

Using the Tools

When using the tools for the general run of work the right hand provides the forward pressure, whilst the left hand guides the tool and exercises a certain restraining effect, so preventing the tool from overshooting. Note also that the wrist and ball of the hand rest firmly on the work or the bench so steadying the tool, as shown in Fig. 8. We speak here of right and left hand, but in fact the good carver is ambidextrous and can vary the hands at will, this enabling awkward parts to be reached without having to shift the work.

Sometimes the mallet is used, especially for some setting-in operations, and the best type of mallet is round in form. This enables the tool to be struck with any part of it, it being unnecessary to turn the mallet to bring the right face into use.

The tools should be laid out in a row at the back of the bench, blades towards the carver. This enables the carver to grasp any tool with the hand in the position it will be held, so saving much unnecessary handling. A common practice is to have all the handles different, either in form, kind of wood, or in colour, so that the right tool is quickly recognisable. In an elaborate piece of work there

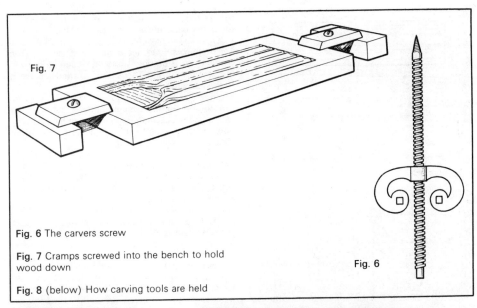

Fig. 7

Fig. 6 The carvers screw

Fig. 7 Cramps screwed into the bench to hold wood down

Fig. 8 (below) How carving tools are held

Fig. 6

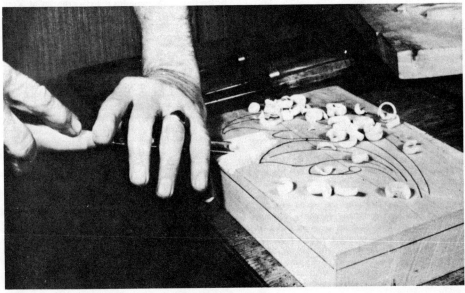

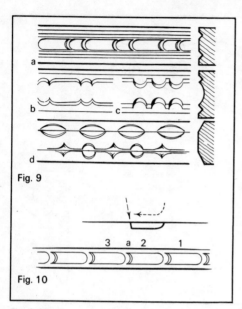

Fig. 9

Fig. 10

Fig. 9 Simple gouge cuts in a moulded section

Fig. 10 How gouge cuts are made and order of the work

may be as many as thirty or forty tools in a row, and much time is saved if the right tool can be spotted quickly. Sometimes a carver puts a ring of colour on the handle as a help. Handles are mostly octagonal as this prevents their rolling sideways on to the floor.

Carving may be divided into three main groups:

Incised work, in which the design is cut into the wood, generally with the V tool. The cut-away part forms the design.

Modelled work. Here the groundwork is recessed leaving the design standing up, and a certain amount of modelling is carried out. Thus the form of a leaf may be made to undulate, or one detail, such as a ribbon, made to appear to pass over another.

Carving in the round. The most difficult, all sides

being carved, without any background. The human form, animals, etc., are examples of this.

The same general rules apply to all carving. The whole thing is brought up to one stage before any further work is done. These stages, varied according to the job, are:

Setting-in. Here the main outline is cut in, either with a gouge cut on the waste side, or by chopping down with gouges to suit the curves. Often both are used as explained later.

Bosting in. In this stage the bulk of the unwanted wood is removed, leaving main chunks where the detail will later be cut. The main undulations are worked without any attempt at detail.

Modelling. Here the detail takes shape, the form being worked, and the final surface chiselled.

In all carving, wood must always be cut, not scraped, torn, split, or levered away. The surface, too, must be left straight from the tool. Glasspaper spoils it, and it is this that makes the work exacting. No attempt is made to remove all the facets formed by the tool, and it is probably in this that the work of the skilled man shows most to advantage. In his work the tool marks are purposeful and crisp, and their direction helps the flow of the design.

Sometimes the background can be given a special texture by the use of a punch, but this must not be made an excuse for bad work with the gouge. Its purpose is solely to show up the design itself by giving the background a completely different appearance. Punches can either be bought ready made, or they can be made from a 150mm (6in.) nail filed off square, and with indentations filed in the end.

Gouge cuts. The best way of describing the process is to take actual examples, and for a start the simple gouge cuts in Fig. 9 are good practice. At (a) is a flat moulding formed with V cuts at each side. A gouge rather narrower than the centre member is used to make a series of downward stabs at the points (a), Fig. 10. Hold the gouge at a slight angle as shown by the dotted arrow in the section, and use the mallet. There is an advantage in making all the downward cuts first. The heavy work is rather hard on the tools, and, once this is done, it enables

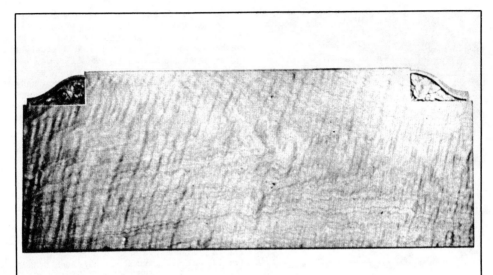

Fig. 11 Bed head with decorative carved corners

the edge to be kept in good condition for the following process, that of scooping out the waste. Furthermore the downward chopping may cause the short grain occasioned by the adjoining cut to split out, though this difficulty can be avoided by making the cuts in the order shown in Fig. 10.

Note that to preserve the parallel sides of the cuts the gouge must be taken downwards and the handle rapidly lowered as shown by the dotted line, Fig. 10. As a rule a single cut is made first to remove the bulk of the waste, and a second cut to finish cleanly to size. This work is mostly done by eye, apart from the initial stepping of the stabs, though pencil lines can be put in as a guide. They will have to be scraped out locally afterwards.

At (b), Fig. 9, a hollow section is worked first, and the position of the members either stepped in with dividers or marked from a slip of paper. A gouge is used to cut downwards each side of the indentation, this being held at an angle so that the edge finishes in line with the outer sloping side of the V. The cuts must meet. A flat gouge can be used in line with the side of the V to cut away small waste pieces.

A similar process is followed at (c), the gouge being used to cut the semi-circle. Again it is held at an angle so that the edge finishes in line with the outer slope of the V. This enables the little waste pieces to be cut out cleanly with a flat gouge or chisel. Some may find a skew chisel easier to use for this.

At (d) are similar devices worked at the corner of a chamfer. In both cases downward stabs are made, and the waste eased away with a flat gouge afterwards.

Modelled designs. In Fig. 11 are shown decorative corners carved at the top of a bed head, but the general idea could be used in other places. The designs could be varied, and alternatives are given in Figs. 12 and 13. The design could be drawn in on paper and transferred to the wood with carbon paper, or if preferred it could be drawn straight on to the wood from a preliminary sketch. The procedure is similar in both examples. The main shapes are outlined approximately with a V tool, and then set in with gouges which follow the final shape. This enables the background to be recessed, the waste being removed with narrower

143

gouges or chisels, and finished with the spoon bit. It is for work of this kind that the R and L corner tools are invaluable. Care should be taken to make all the recesses even in depth. The slight modelling of the leaves and flowers follows. Where one leaf passes over the other, the curve should appear natural, not abruptly sloped at each side. Finally the background can be punched, though some prefer to omit this detail. Its advantage however is that it gives distinct texture which throws up the detail clearly.

Fig. 14 shows a swag partly completed. To the right is shown the background set back and the detail partly outlined. As the carving progresses the inner outlines are necessarily cut away, but it is as well to put them in because they show the places to be left full and those to be cut away. In

Fig. 12 (top left) Enlarged view of an alternative design for the bedhead in Fig. 11
Fig. 13 (middle left) Another alternative
Fig. 14 (below) A decorative swag carved in the solid in mahogany. The right hand side shows the early stage in carving

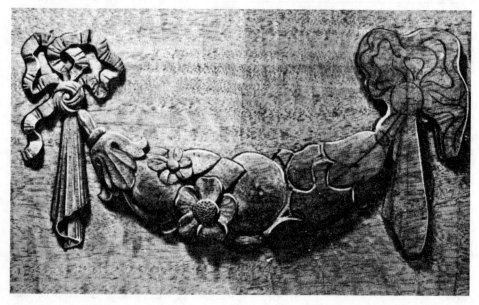

Fig. 15 (above) Carved detail cut in thin wood fretted to shape and stuck to a backboard

Figs. 16, 17, 18 show stages in carving a candelabrum

any case they are easily cut in afresh as the work proceeds.

Another piece of carved detail is that in Fig. 15. In this case it is intended to be applied rather than cut in the solid, and the wood is fretted to the outline and stuck down on to a flat board with newspaper interposed to enable it to be lifted away on completion. It will be realised that without this backing it would be difficult to grip the wood, and in any case the carving would be fragile. The swag given in Fig. 14 could be cut and applied in the same way.

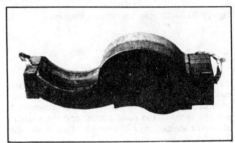

Fig. 16

Figs. 16, 17, and 18 are given as they show stages in carving the arm of a candelabrum. Other items would pass through similar stages. In Fig. 16 the shape has been fretted out and the detail pencilled in. The next stage shows the work partly bosted in, that is the main form is roughly carved. In Fig. 18 the modelling is largely completed.

Fig. 17

Mouldings are frequently carved, especially in reproduction work. It is advisable to make a stencil in oiled paper or thin foil showing one or more complete repeat details. The shapes of the leaves etc. should be cut in the stencil with the same gouges used for the actual carving. It may in fact be a matter of adapting the actual detail to the curve of the gouges available. Work of this kind should be done with as few cuts as possible. For

Fig. 18

Fig. 19 Repeat detail carved in a moulding

instance in Fig. 19 the curve of the large leaves could be stabbed in with a single gouge. The lower ends separated by the darts are then deepened, also the sides of the darts cut in, and the triangle of wood between cut away with a chisel in a single chip. This is not only to save time. It also gives a clean crisp quality to the work. The modelling of the darts can also be done in two cuts, each sloping towards the leaves. At the top the small circular recesses are formed by revolving a small half-round gouge. If the latter is given a lateral flick after cutting the circle it will usually snap off the boss, leaving a clean finish. If not it may be necessary to make a punch from a French nail of suitable size, filing the end flat. Do not use this as a substitute for proper carving, however.

Chapter twelve

Turning

Wood turning is a big subject, and it is impossible in a single chapter to do more than outline one or two basic operations. For fuller details the reader should study a handbook on the subject.

It may be roughly divided into two classes: between-centres turning and face-plate turning. The former is used for all long items such as lamp columns, spindles, etc., and face-plate work for wide, shallow items, such as bowls, platters and so on. The actual turning operation is of two kinds: cutting and scraping. Each has its purposes and is essential for certain classes of work, though in some cases the methods are interchangeable. Cutting is generally much quicker than scraping, and is therefore often used for the preliminary roughing, even when scraping is necessary to finish off with. It is also essential for most softwoods, which cannot be scraped cleanly. On the other hand, it is difficult to cut many really hard woods, as the tool edge is lost too quickly.

Between centres turning. The prong chuck is used at the driving end and the ring centre at the tailstock. The wood should be centred reasonably accurately by eye and then revolved by hand to see whether one corner stands out more than the others. This is easily tested by seeing whether the corners are the same distance from the tool rest. Incidentally, the wood at the tailstock end should be given a spot of oil to lubricate it. When running is satisfactory tighten the tailstock screw up hard then slacken off slightly. Too much pressure may bow the wood, causing excessive friction and consequent heating.

Gouge work. With a fairly large gouge run from end to end until all flats are taken out. Fig. 1 shows the operation. If working to an exact size set a pair of calipers to about 2mm. ($\frac{1}{16}$in.) full of the required diameter, and continue turning with the gouge until the calipers will just slip over, as in Fig. 2. Using the gouge will not produce an entirely flat, smooth surface, but large irregularities should be avoided.

Using the chisel. The long-cornered chisel is now substituted; this should be 30–40mm.

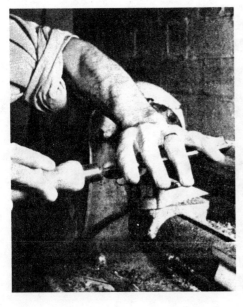

Fig. 1 Preliminary rough turning using the large gouge

(1¼–1½in.) wide. Hold it as shown in Fig. 3, using only the portion between the heel and the centre. The long point is never used for this work—if it should slip down it will dig into the wood with disastrous results. The chisel will enable a perfectly smooth and straight surface to be obtained. It cannot be started at the end, but must be placed in about 25mm. (1in.) and moved slowly along and right off at the other end. It can then be reversed and the process repeated in the other direction. Again test with the calipers until down to size. It will quickly be realised that the gouge removes the wood far more quickly than the chisel and it is for this reason that the wood should be brought down as close as possible to finished size with the gouge before the chisel is substituted.

The chisel is a tricky tool to use until mastery has been obtained. The secret is largely in letting the bevel of the tool rub the work. Unless this happens

Fig. 2 (left) Testing diameter with calipers

Fig. 3 (below) Using the long cornered chisel to smooth the cylinder

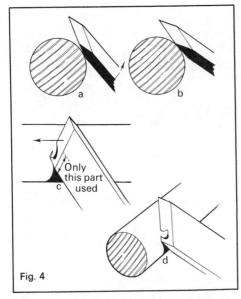

Only
this part
used

Fig. 4

the edge is liable to be carried in by the revolving wood so that the long corner digs in. The best way is to hold the tool so that only the bevel is on the wood as at Fig. 4a, they raise the handle until the edge begins to cut. The position is then maintained.

The chisel can be held in either of the two ways shown in Figs. 3 and 5. Fig. 5 is of special value when thin material is being turned. It supports the wood at the back, since the fingers bear lightly against it, so preventing bouncing of the wood and a trouble known as ribbing, which is a sort of spiral set up in the surface. Note that in both cases the edge of the chisel is at an angle to the wood, so that it has a slicing action.

Turning hollows. For the general run of hollows a small gouge is used, the edge being sharpened as in Fig. 6. The tool is taken in from each side of the hollow. Unless this is done it will leave a rough

Fig. 4 Using the chisel: **a** preliminary position; **b** handle raised to bring edge to wood; **c** and **d** side movement of chisel

Fig. 5 (below) Alternative way of holding chisel

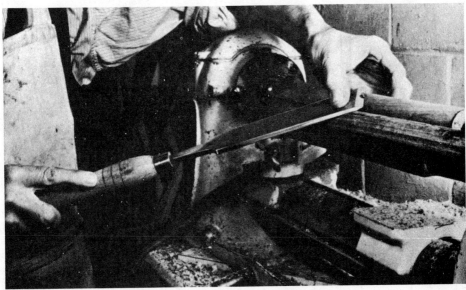

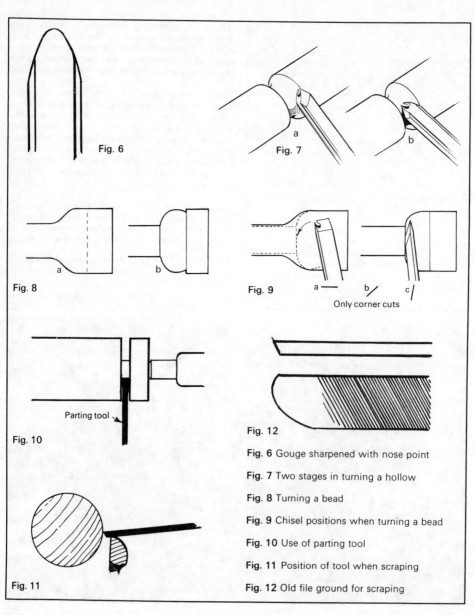

Fig. 6 Gouge sharpened with nose point

Fig. 7 Two stages in turning a hollow

Fig. 8 Turning a bead

Fig. 9 Chisel positions when turning a bead

Fig. 10 Use of parting tool

Fig. 11 Position of tool when scraping

Fig. 12 Old file ground for scraping

Fig. 6

Fig. 7

a

b

Fig. 8

a

b

Fig. 9

a

b

c

Only corner cuts

Parting tool

Fig. 10

Fig. 11

Fig. 12

finish. Dealing first with the right hand side of the hollow hold the gouge on its side, the bevel more or less at right angles to the wood, and by a combined movement move the handle to the right raising it at the same time and twisting it over so that it is on its back. The idea is shown in Fig. 7. In practice, the hollow is not taken down to full depth in one cut. What happens is that a cut is made as described at one side and the waste removed by a second cut from the other side. The hollow is then completed by further cuts from each side. The tricky part is in the initial entry of the tool, because it is liable to start over to the side and gash the wood, the reason being that, until a slight start has been made, the bevel has nothing to rub on. Once slightly into the wood the bevel prevents all side movement by rubbing on the wood.

The answer is in starting boldly because only a slight penetration is enough to give the bevel support. Equally important is starting with the gouge on its side so that the bevel is about at right angles with the wood, and straightway moving the handle to the side so that the bevel is pressed against the cut in the wood. The cut is in fact made by swivelling the handle rather than by pushing the tool forwards.

To turn beads and similar round parts the point of the square chisel is used. The work can be lightened by removing much of the waste first with the gouge. For instance, in Fig. 8 much of the preliminary wasting away can be done with the gouge as at (a), before finishing with the chisel. Remember that not only is the gouge an easier tool to use but it also removes wood more quickly.

Fig. 9 shows how the corner of the tool starts at the top of the bead and is turned over as it progresses down the curve. Only the point of the tool is used, and it is held at an angle as shown, passing from position (a) to (b), and on to (c). It is usual to use a square sharpened chisel so that each side of the bead can be formed without changing the tool.

Parting can be done either with a special parting tool or with the ordinary skew chisel. The latter gives a generally cleaner finish, but requires a greater length of wood in which to operate. Fig. 10 shows the parting tool. Note that it is slightly wider at the end so that it clears itself as it is pressed into the wood.

Scraping. Whereas chisels and gouges cut the wood, taking thick shavings like a coarsely set plane, scraping tools only scrape, removing little more than dust. Most softwoods cannot be scraped successfully but many hardwoods respond well, and in fact in some cases scraping is the only way. The tool is held as in Fig. 11 from which it will be seen that it droops slightly towards the wood. The idea is that if it should dig into the revolving wood it will immediately disengage, whereas if it were pointed upwards the movement would tend to draw it farther into the wood.

Sets of scraping tools can be bought, but usually they are ground from old files. These do perfectly well and can be ground to whatever section is needed. Fig. 12 shows how the serrations are ground away at an angle on the surface, and the edge ground at about 80deg. After a while one collects a number of such tools. When grinding always do the surface first and the edge last, as the latter sets up a burr which helps the cut. Some woods, such as elm and oak, scrape best with the tool direct from the grinding wheel. Others need the edge to be finished on the oilstone.

For boring holes through standards, etc., a special boring tool is used.

Face-plate turning. Items such as bowls are generally fixed to the face plate with screws, and it is as well to place a waste piece between the two, as this enables the turning to be completed without danger of the tool touching the face plate. Fig. 13 shows the idea. If the entire work is to be done in a single chucking the bottom of the wood must be planed flat so that it beds snugly on to the waste piece. The screws pass through the back plate and waste piece and engage only in the work (Fig. 13). Their length must be carefully calculated so that they do not project into the inside of the bowl. This must also be considered when boring the holes, because such holes would appear as a blemish.

Deal with the outside first, using a 6mm., ($\frac{1}{4}$in.) or 9mm. ($\frac{3}{8}$in.) gouge. Hold it so that it cuts, not merely scrapes, and let the bevel of the tool rub the wood, so that any tendency to dig in is

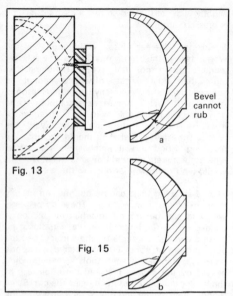

Fig. 13

Bevel cannot rub

a

Fig. 15

b

avoided. Fig. 14 shows the method. The inside can be dealt with in the same way to remove the bulk of the waste, but here it is vital to let the bevel rub. A point to remember here is that the angle of bevel affects the work. In fact, a long, thin bevel cannot be used for the inside, as it is impossible to let it rub as shown at (a) Fig. 15. Note how the less-acute bevel at (b) does enable it to rub.

To finish off cleanly the wood must be scraped as in Fig. 16. Again note that the tool is drooped slightly towards the point so that if it should dig in it will at once be thrown clear. Generally two tools are needed; a slightly curved one for the bottom (a), Fig. 17, and one of more acute curve, (b). Work the flat one across the bottom as far into the sides as it will go, then substitute the tool with the quicker curve. Work the tool sideways as this enables the sweetness of the curve to be judged. Fig. 17 shows the operation.

Get the shape right before using glasspaper and take out any tears. These last named can be troublesome to get rid of in a bowl which has the grain running crosswise as in Fig. 18. The

Fig. 13 Wood mounted on face-plate for bowl turning

Fig. 14 (top) Shaping outside of bowl using gouge

Fig. 15 Inside of bowl turned with gouge

Fig. 16 (above) Scraping inside of bowl

parts marked (a) and (b) have necessarily to be worked against the grain. The answer is sharp tools and a fine cut. Any attempt to make a heavy cut will cause the grain to tear out. If possible, mount a grindstone on the other side of the headstock and rub up the tool on it frequently.

Finally, smooth with glasspaper, Middle 2 first, followed by No. 1½, and finally flour grade. A good finish can be obtained by the use of Speedaneez. The work is run at its slowest speed, and the rubber moved slowly across the surface. Leave for a few minutes, and repeat the process so that a medium gloss is built up. Allow as long as possible to harden, and polish with wax. With some wax polishes it is necessary to leave to harden after application before polishing; others can be polished straight away. The advantage of the preliminary french polish is that it builds up a foundation gloss, and helps to keep out dirt when the item is in use.

An attractive bowl with handles is shown in Fig. 19. In making this a wide rim has to be turned, the section of which approximates to that of the handles. The plan shape of the handles is then marked out on the top, and the unwanted part of the rim sawn away with the coping saw, and the surface cleaned up with file and spokeshave. Afterwards the scrolled effect is cut in with carving tools.

Fig. 17 Scrapers used for inside of bowl

Fig. 18 Parts of bowl liable to be rough

Fig. 19 (below) Turned bowl with carved handles

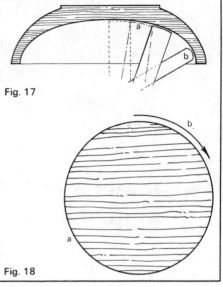

Fig. 17

Fig. 18

Chapter thirteen

Timber and Materials

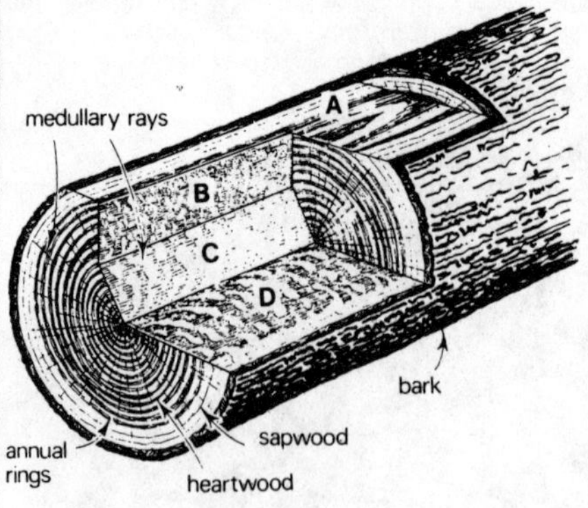
A
medullary rays
B
C
D
bark
sapwood
annual rings
heartwood

Oak log showing how figure is produced by different methods of cutting. **a** reveals no figure; **b** shows small figure; **c** and **d** show full figure

The range of timbers runs into thousands, and here we can deal with only the relatively few in common use.

To make a broad distinction timbers may be divided up under two headings: hardwoods and softwoods, the former referring to deciduous broad-leaved trees which shed their leaves in winter, and the latter to coniferous trees which have needle-pointed leaves. The terms are purely of convenience and frequently bear little reference to actual hardness. The hardest of the softwoods are heavier and harder than the lightest of the hardwoods.

Hardwoods. For general cabinet-making oak is widely used. English oak when suitable boards are available has a fine figure, but frequently it is unreliable owing to bad seasoning and is liable to shakes and warping. An excellent alternative is Japanese oak, which, properly seasoned, is sound, well-figured, works well, and is available in good sizeable boards. Slavonic oak also is used, and is a fine timber.

Often oak is available only in squares of 37, 50, 62, and 75mm. ($1\frac{1}{2}$, 2, $2\frac{1}{2}$, and 3in.), suitable only for legs, etc., but when wider pieces are needed for such parts as rails these squares can be sawn through when a circular saw is available and jointed together to give greater width.

American oak is not often seen nowadays, presumably owing to exchange difficulties, but when it is found it is in fine standard boards. There are two kinds; red and white, the latter being invariably of better quality.

Much of the attractiveness of oak is due to the figure derived from the rays which radiate from the heart. A board cut parallel with these exhibits the largest figure and makes the most reliable wood. The more the board departs from the parallel the smaller the figure until the rays pass through it at right angles and appear only as minute specks on the surface.

Silky oak, occasionally available, which derives from Australia is not a true oak at all, but gets its name from the pronounced figure it has. It works well and is quite suitable for cabinet making as it is capable of good finish and polishes well.

As a substitute for oak, chestnut is sometimes used. It has no figure derived from the medullary rays, but resembles plain oak closely in both grain and colour. Beech is often available in squares and is thus suitable for turned legs, etc. It has a good figure, though smaller than oak. Owing to the shortage of walnut it is often used for turned parts, the rest of the job being walnut veneered.

Mahogany is an excellent cabinet wood, though the finer wide boards are becoming difficult to obtain. Practically the only true American mahogany available is the Honduras kind; Cuban is almost unobtainable. African mahogany is frequently used, and, although it has not the same fine figure, is considerably cheaper. It varies widely in reliability and quality.

Sapele is sometimes referred to as a mahogany, and has something of the colour and marking of true mahogany. Its chief characteristic is the stripy roe figuring consisting of narrow stripes of light and dark wood. Both rauli and niangon have something of the general appearance of mahogany, but boards vary enormously. Some are entirely plain, whilst others have a most attractive figure. There are many substitutes for mahogany, of which gaboon is quite common. It is not a true mahogany, but is a useful secondary hardwood for drawer sides, cabinet backs, etc. It is often used in the manufacture of multi-ply.

Walnut is a fine cabinet wood, but is generally difficult to obtain. Both English and French walnut are occasionally seen but stocks of the plainer American or black walnut are seldom available. Australian walnut makes a good cabinet wood, many of the boards being finely figured.

There are many other imported hardwoods, supplies of which fluctuate. Of these there is rauli from Chile, a lightish-brown timber somewhat like beech but without ray markings. Mansonia has somewhat the colour of walnut and is a useful cabinet wood. Afara from Nigeria has a light straw colour and is sometimes available. Afrormosia has a brownish yellow shade with interlocked grain which needs care in planing. All these woods vary considerably in quality and the best plan is to consult a text book for their characteristics, or to see whether the timber merchant has any information to offer.

Teak has become popular as a furniture wood and can be obtained in a good range of thicknesses and widths. It is not a good gluing wood owing to its greasy nature but the use of a degreaser helps. One of the modern P.V.A. adhesives with resin additives are the most successful.

Softwoods. Of the softwoods the chief timber for carpentry is the red Baltic pine. Quality varies widely, the chief drawback of the poorer grades being the presence of knots, but better boards can be reasonably free from larger knots. It is used widely for structural timber—roofs, flooring, doors, etc., but needs care in selection when used for joists, rafters, and similar purposes, as knots in bad positions can reduce the strength enormously. For back frames, concealed rails, etc., it is frequently used in furniture making, though the poorer grades should be avoided.

Yellow or white pine from North America is a delightful wood, but it is most difficult to obtain. If once-used timber is available it is excellent for veneer grounds, etc. Parana pine (South America) is in good supply and is a first-rate timber, often entirely free from knots, and is useful, though it often twists in drying and splits easily.

When Western red cedar can be obtained it makes an excellent joinery timber, wide, long boards free from knots being available. It is suitable for indoor and for outdoor use. For the latter no preservative is needed, and it is often used for roofing for this reason.

Plywood. Qualities vary enormously. The cheap tea chest is useless for work of quality; the layers have probably not been properly dried out, the gluing may be faulty, and there are most likely blemishes, such as gaps in the middle layer or even overlaps. A properly made ply by a reliable manufacturer, however, is quite sound and can be used for the carcase of a veneered job. Fuller information on this appears in the chapter on veneering. Thinner plies have three layers, the centre one often being thicker than the others and known as stout heart. When more than three layers are used it is termed multi-ply. Various woods are used in the manufacture—birch, alder,

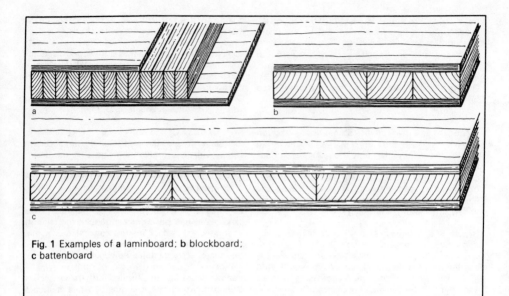

Fig. 1 Examples of **a** laminboard; **b** blockboard;
c battenboard

ash, pine, and gaboon. The latter when made up as multi-ply makes a good ground for veneered flush doors.

Laminated board, etc. These are built up as shown in Fig. 1, there being an inner core with thinner outer layers, the grain at right angles. Of the three kinds shown the laminated board is the least liable to move.

Chipboard. This is largely made from specially prepared chips bound with resin glue and highly compressed. It is frequently used for partitions, backs, furniture parts, but is unsuitable for outdoor use. In the best way the board is attached to a framework, but when used structurally as distinct from a filling, it should have a substantial lipping around the edges, this being tongued in. Apart

from strengthening it, it provides a suitable surface in which hinge recesses, etc., can be cut.

Veneering is quite successful, both sides being covered. Some chipboards are made by the extruded process and are faced on both sides with thick veneer. These boards are generally reliable, but deep grooves which penetrate right through the veneers should be avoided because they are liable to snap through.

Wallboards. These cover a tremendously wide range, from really hard, compressed boards suitable for a caravan covering etc., to softboards intended mainly for insulation. The better and medium qualities are frequently used for backs, drawer bottoms, and for panelling generally which is to be painted.

Chapter fourteen

Wood Finishing

A wide range of material is available nowadays, and the choice depends on whether the item is to be used out-of-doors or inside, the wear it will have, the kind of wood it is made of, and personal preference. Some of the older materials have fallen by the wayside but others still remain popular for some work.

Paint

To give best results at least three coats should be applied; priming, undercoat, and finishing coat. It is advisable to obtain all three from the same manufacturer, as this ensures that they are safe to use together.

Priming. Having cleaned up the wood go over any knots with painter's knotting. Leave for half an hour and give a second application. Really bad knots should be cut out and plugged. Any nails should be punched in. Rub smooth with glasspaper, and give the coat of priming. This is usually of a grey or pink colour, though for a white or cream paint it is frequently white. It should be comparatively thin, and should be applied evenly, and brushed well into the wood. Work in the direction of the grain to finish off. Brush the paint into cracks, etc. Leave for 12–24 hours to harden.

Undercoating. All nail holes, cracks, etc., should be filled with putty, or one of the proprietary stoppings. This is pressed well in and the surface made smooth by drawing the flat of the knife across it. Incidentally, in the case of glazed windows, etc., the rebates should have a coat of priming before putty is used. Otherwise it will fail to adhere properly.

Rub down any roughness or unevenness with wet-dry glasspaper used over a cork rubber, damping the surface beforehand so that all dust is kept down. Any nibs or runs that may have formed should be smoothed, though they should be avoided altogether as far as possible.

The undercoating invariably approximates in colour to the finishing coat, though there is usually a slight difference so that it is easy to see which parts have been covered. The application is similar to that of the priming coat. Work well into

157

awkward places first, avoiding the filling in of detail, and laying-off with long, even strokes in the direction of the grain. Again leave for 24 hours to harden.

Finishing coat. Once again rub down with abrasive paper as before, and brush away any dust. As gloss paints have the property of flowing out and eliminating brush marks no more re-crossing is necessary than that needed to give an even coat—in fact prolonged working is inadvisable because an initial set takes place early. Work towards edges as far as possible so that fat edges and runs are avoided. If there are any runs at adjoining edges work them out straight away.

All paint should be well stirred before use, and if a skin has formed on the surface cut it round with a knife and remove it. Oil paint which has stood for some time should be strained through old silk before use. Brushes which are to stand overnight for use next day can be placed in a jar of water. When finished with altogether they should be cleaned with turps, and finally in warm soapy water.

Furniture Finishes

Polyurethane Lacquer. This is based on synthetic resin and is generally known as P.U. lacquer. It is usually of the catalyst type, the lacquer remaining in good usable condition for an almost unlimited time if kept sealed. Only when the catalyst is mixed with it does hardening begin. As a rule a third container is supplied with the pack, this containing thinners which can also be used for brush cleaning. As a rule at least two coats are required for a good finish, and generally the best results are obtained by thinning out the lacquer and applying extra coats rather than using one thick coat. When hard the surface can be lightly smoothed with flour glasspaper or the finest grade steel wool. It can be brought to a brilliant gloss by burnishing with a fine abrasive cream after the lacquer is fully cured. The lacquer is brush-applied and does not call for great skill other than careful brush work. It may be necessary to use a grain filler if the wood is open-grained and this is used before the application of the lacquer. It is advisable to use the filler supplied by

the maker of the lacquer as other makes may not be compatible.

Cellulose. This is another finish frequently used today. According to type it can be either brush- or spray-applied, the latter preferably. When the brush is used it calls for a deft touch when a second coat is applied because the latter tends to soften that previously applied. In some cases the work can be left as it is from the brush or spray, but a more brilliant effect can be obtained from what is known as 'pulling over'. A pad is made from cotton wool covered with wash leather, the face brought to a smooth surface free from all creases. It is dampened with a special 'pull-over' liquid which has a mild solvent action on the cellulose, and is rubbed over the surface first with a circular movement and afterwards with straight strokes in the direction of the grain. This not only takes out inequalities in the cellulose but also has the effect of forcing the cellulose into the open grain. If this is too bright for taste it can be dulled down by rubbing over the surface with steel wool lubricated with wax polish.

Teak oil. The present-day use of teak as a furniture wood, plus the liking for a semi-gloss finish, has led to the popularity of teak oil as a finish. Apart from teak it can also be used on other hardwoods. It gives a soft lustrous finish and is one of the simplest finishes to apply. It has merely to be rubbed on with a rag. New woods need several applications, but a dull shine is gradually built up. Teak oil largely replaces the older oil polish in which linseed oil with terebene driers was used. It dries more quickly and gives better adhesion.

French polish. Although not used as widely as formerly this is still preferred by some workers, especially in the antique restoration trade. It is capable of giving a most attractive finish but has the drawback of not being resistant to heat, water, spirit, and other markings. Furthermore it calls for a considerable degree of skill if a really clean finish is to be obtained. For home use most workers prefer the more modern and simpler finishes.

To describe the stages briefly the wood is stained (if required), the grain filled in (again if required), and the polishing proper begun, this consisting of four stages; fadding, colouring, (if needed), bodying, and finishing. French polish is made in various types; garnet, a dark brown shade; button, a yellowish colour; orange, a medium polish; white, a creamy shade; and transparent, an almost colourless liquid. The light polishes are for light woods, and the garnet to deepen the colour of wood. Orange is the most generally used.

A polishing rubber is made as in Fig. 1, and the polish applied to the cotton wool pad, the covering cloth having been removed. In the preliminary fadding stage the rubber is moved along the work in straight strokes as at (a), Fig. 2, the rubber being fairly generously charged with polish. This is followed by the bodying process in which a good body of polish is built up. In this the polish is applied with a circular movement as at (b), Fig. 2, followed by the figure-of-eight (c), this being varied by an oval movement (d).

Finally straight strokes are used. A spot of linseed oil on the rubber face is necessary to lubricate the rubber, but no more than is essential should be used. Several applications with drying intervals are necessary.

The work can be finished by stiffing or spiriting off. In the former the rubber is charged with half-polish and half-spirit and is glided on to the surface in straight strokes along the length of the grain as at (f). Lightness of touch is essential.

For the spiriting off method a fresh rubber is made, and the cotton wool pad given a couple of drops of spirit only. Apply to the surface in large circles or figures-of-eight, changing gradually to straight strokes. As the rubber dries out the pressure can be increased until it acts as a burnisher in removing the oil. The face of the rubber will become greasy as the oil is lifted and the cover should be changed to a fresh face.

Wax polish. This is simple to use, and can be renewed at any time. If an oil stain has previously been used it is essential that it is first fixed with at least two coats of French polish. Otherwise it may be lifted unevenly in patches. In any case it is a good plan to body up the wood, using white french polish for a job to be in natural colour or lacquer. It not only helps to keep out dirt, but it builds up a preliminary shine.

You can use any good proprietary wax polish, or you can make your own from beeswax shredded into turps. Best American turps is the most satisfactory but a good grade substitute (white spirit) is cheaper and may have to be used. The absorbing process is quickened by heating the mixture in a can of hot water (do not use a naked flame). To harden the polish add a small proportion of rosin whilst molten and stir in well. When cold the polish should be the consistency of butter in summer time.

Apply freely with a brush (boot brush type) and leave to harden for 12–24 hours. Polish with a similar brush and finish with a rubber. No shine can be built up until the turps has evaporated.

Table top polish. This finish is considerably more resistant to heat, water, and spirit marking than ordinary French polish. It is applied in practically the same way but no oil is used.

Varnish. This is not widely used nowadays having been largely replaced by finishes based on cellulose and catalysed lacquers. There are many varieties of these, many of them setting to an extremely hard surface which is resistant to heat, spirit and water marking. However, varnish is still used to an extent, the two kinds being oil varnish, sometimes used over paint or on bare wood to be exposed to the atmosphere, and spirit varnish which includes the various french polishes, and is not so durable for outside work and is more generally used for finishing indoor items either by themselves or in combination with french polishing. It is sometimes known as transparent lacquer.

Stains. Although the tendency nowadays is to use wood in its natural colour, stains are still preferred in some circumstances. It should be realized at the outset, however, that some modern finishes are not compatible with all stains as a reaction may set in, causing various troubles. The instructions supplied with the finishes should therefore be consulted. There are many proprietary stains, water, oil, and spirit based, which are available in a wide range of shades. Apart from this however there are certain materials which are invaluable for darkening, lightening, or colouring woods.

For oak a most useful basic stain is made from

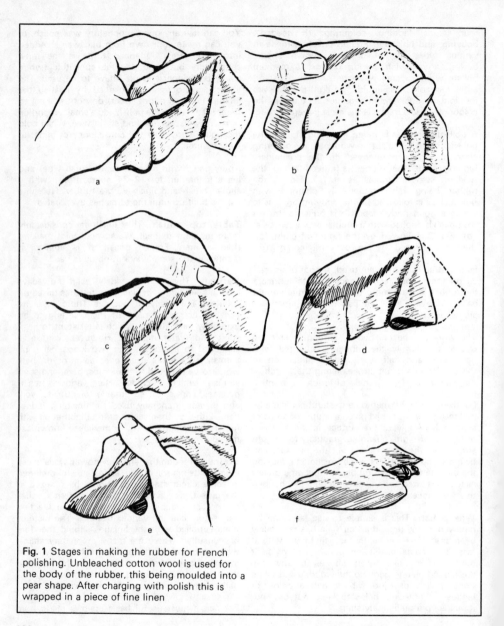

Fig. 1 Stages in making the rubber for French polishing. Unbleached cotton wool is used for the body of the rubber, this being moulded into a pear shape. After charging with polish this is wrapped in a piece of fine linen

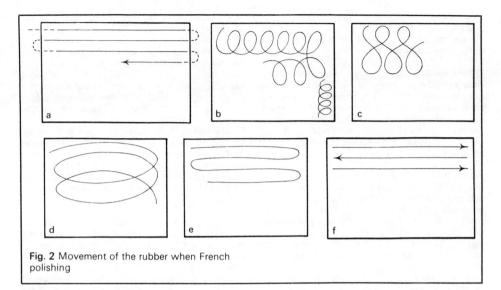

Fig. 2 Movement of the rubber when French polishing

vandyke crystals dissolved in warm water, the quantity depending on the depth of colour required. Stir thoroughly and strain through muslin. The usual plan is to make a concentrated solution and dilute as required. Immediately before use add a little ·880 ammonia as this helps to drive it into the grain.

Mahogany crystals can also be obtained, these giving a much redder shade. The two can be mixed together (after making up separately) to obtain any special shade. Another material useful for warming up is eosin powder which, dissolved in water, gives a bright red stain. It is seldom used as a stain by itself but is handy for adding to others. Be careful not to overdo its use.

To darken mahogany bichromate of potash is generally used. The crystals are steeped in water which becomes bright orange in colour. Its effect on the wood is chemical, however, and turns the mahogany a brown shade, the depth depending on the strength. It is widely used in the reproduction trade. It can also be used on oak which it turns a slightly greenish brown. By adding it to vandyke crystals and ammonia a variety of shades can be obtained.

Sulphate of iron, or green copperas, dissolved in water will turn oak a bluish grey tone (avoid using it too strong or you will end with a bright Air Force blue colour). It is sometimes used to make mahogany match up to walnut. As its effect becomes noticeable chiefly when it dries out it should be used with care. It should be practically water-clear, and the effect should be tried on spare wood and allowed to dry out. Sycamore is often treated with it to turn it a grey colour.

Ammonia has a darkening effect on oak. In the best way the liquid is not applied to the wood, but the latter is exposed to its fumes. The whole is placed in an air-tight container, all glue and grease being removed from the surface, and all doors, drawers, etc., opened. The liquid is poured into a couple of saucers, and the container sealed. If an inspection glass is not practicable, a hole should be bored and a piece of the same oak inserted. The time taken may range for ten minutes to several hours in accordance with the depth of colour required, and the size of the container. As some varieties of oak are more readily affected than others, the same kind should be used in any one job.

Take care not to bend over the fumes as they are powerful, and may have unpleasant results. Do not directly handle ammonia as it can be painful to the fingers and turn them yellow.

Oil stains. These are usually bought ready made. They have the advantage of not raising the grain, but are not so transparent as water stains, and their effect is different in that they leave a dark deposit in the open grain. After drying they should be given two coats of french polish before any wax polish is applied, as otherwise the stain may be lifted unevenly in patches.

Spirit stains. These again do not raise the grain, but, owing to the rapid evaporation, they require deft and confident handling. On larger surfaces it is difficult to keep the edge alive. They are obtained ready made, or in powder form mixing with spirit.

Aniline dyes. Owing to the colours being bright and somewhat unorthodox from the woodwork angle, the anilines should be used with care. Frequently they are used to add to other stains for toning purposes. Generally the most useful are vandyke brown, a somewhat cold brown used chiefly for oak, black for ebonising, and Bismarck brown, a powerful red used chiefly to tone brown stains. A wide range of colours is available, green, blue, yellow, etc., and they can often be used in finishing toys, etc.

Aniline dye is in powder form and can be obtained soluble in either water or oil. The former can be dissolved in either water or spirits, and if a binder is necessary add a little glue size to the water, or white French polish to the spirits. This spirit-soluble type is often useful to add to french polish to make colour polish. Oil-soluble aniline is dissolved in turps substitute, and in the event of a binder being required a little gold size can be added.

Application of stain. Either a brush or a rag can be used. In all cases keep the edge alive to avoid unsightly joining marks, and finish off along the grain. Before water stain is used the surface of the wood should be damped with warm water, allowed to dry, and glasspapered flat.

Then when stain is applied the grain will not rise unduly. As end grain soaks up the stain more readily and is inclined to turn darker in consequence, the stain should be diluted for these parts. When it has dried go over the surface twice with french polish. This serves to fix the stain.

Filler. Oak is usually polished just as it is, but hardwoods such as mahogany and walnut generally have the grain filled. Various proprietary paste fillers are available. Fillers can be obtained natural (grey) or in various tones to suit the wood. In any case it can always be toned with an oil stain. If too thick, thin out with turpentine. Keep the lid well pressed down as the filler will otherwise harden. It can be applied with a brush or rag, but the latter is used after the initial set has taken place to force the filler into the grain. It is applied across the grain.

For softwoods the usual plan is to use glue size. This can be ordinary glue thinned down until it no longer feels tacky. Thick size remains on the surface, whilst a thin size soaks into the grain and seals the pores. When thoroughly dry it is glasspapered smooth, and the work is ready for polishing. Incidentally, the size cannot be applied over work which has been oil stained. In this case the paste filler must be used.

Chapter fifteen

Adhesives

There is a wide range of adhesives available to the woodworker today. The modern types have largely ousted the older animal or Scotch glue because they are more convenient in use and in most cases are more damp resistant. On the other hand they are generally more expensive. Scotch glue is still widely used in the antique repair trade, and providing that the item is not exposed to damp is an excellent glue if properly used.

Synthetic resin. The UF (*urea formaldehyde*) is widely used in the trade and almost exclusively in the home workshop. It is used cold, is highly damp resistant and is non-staining. Various types are available. One is of syrup form with separate water-like hardener and having only a limited shelf life. More convenient for the small user is the powder form requiring only to be mixed with water when it becomes the same adhesive as the syrup form. Its shelf life is considerably longer. Another powder form of adhesive has the hardener already incorporated and again requires only to be mixed with water. It is an extremely strong, all-round adhesive.

PVA (*polyvinyl acetate*) is a white emulsion ready for use as it is. Several makes are available many of them having resin additives. It is used cold as a general adhesive and has good strength though its resistance to damp is low. It is free from staining though some brands are liable to turn brown on contact with certain woods such as oak.

Casein. This is not used so much as formerly, but is a strong glue in powder form for mixing with water. One drawback is its liability to stain some hardwoods such as oak, mahogany, walnut, etc. It has good damp resistance.

Epoxy resin. This is used mainly for bonding metal to wood. It is in two parts which have to be mixed before setting begins. It has limited use in the woodworking shop, being expensive. For special jobs it is useful and is highly damp resistant.

Animal glue *(Scotch).* A general-purpose strong glue, though it has no damp resistance and cannot be used for outdoor work. It needs to be used hot which entails joints being heated before assembly. Proprietary makes are available which require no heat except in winter time. Animal glue is non-staining and is the only glue that can be used for veneering by the hammer method.

It is obtained in pearl or cake form, the latter requiring to be broken up in sacking. It is placed in the container of a glue kettle, covered with water, and left overnight. The kettle is then heated and the glue stirred. When hot it should run freely from the brush without lumpiness yet without breaking up into drops. Never heat the glue directly over a flame, and avoid boiling it.

Impact. The chief use of this is in fixing plastic laminates to timber, though it can be used in some instances for special veneering jobs. It is applied to both joining parts, allowed to stand a short while and the two brought together when the grip is immediate. It is useful in some repair work of awkward shapes which would be difficult to cramp. It cannot be used for framing joints of any kind because the grab is immediate and such joints as tenons or dovetails could not be pushed home.

Chapter sixteen

Designs

Tea Trolley with Loose Tray

This is a handy item that could be used in the garden as well as in the house. The loose tray enables items to be carried from the kitchen, and is an advantage when steps have to be negotiated. The tray could also be used independently of the trolley. Practically any sound hardwood could be used for the framework though it should match up if possible with the plywood tray. Alternatively the tray could be covered with plastic laminate.

It will be seen that the legs are tapered both upwards from the shelf slats, and downwards to the bottom. The inner edges from shelf to top, however, are parallel. Apart from appearance, this has the advantage that the shoulders of the rails are square. A simple fixing for the slats is shown in Fig. 2, two thin rails being notched to the legs and the slats sandwiched between.

The legs are shaped and mortised at the top for the

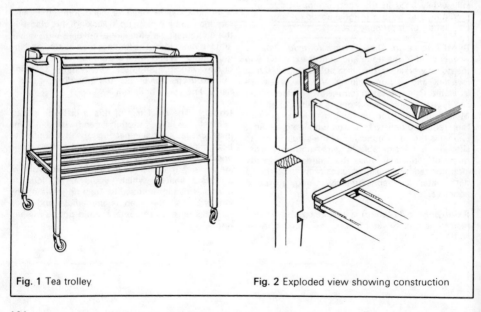

Fig. 1 Tea trolley   **Fig. 2** Exploded view showing construction

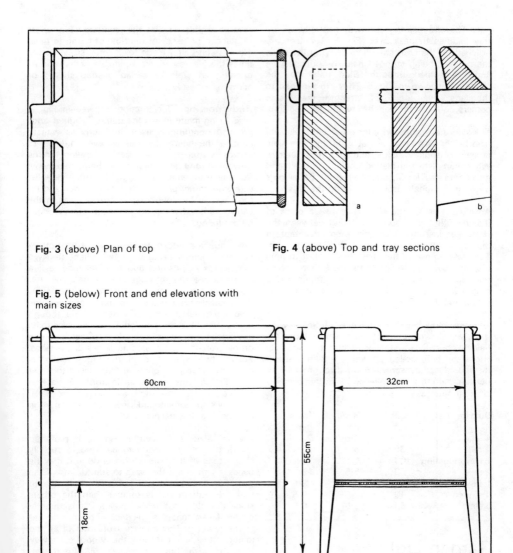

Fig. 3 (above) Plan of top

Fig. 4 (above) Top and tray sections

Fig. 5 (below) Front and end elevations with main sizes

60cm

32cm

55cm

18cm

a

b

rails. The end rails are cut away centrally for the tray handles to pass over, Fig. 5. The legs are notched for the twin stretchers carrying the slats, the notches being stopped near the outside face and not carried through. Side rails may be shaped as shown in Fig. 5. They are tenoned to the legs. For additional strength the inside corners could be braced below the tray bottom.

The slats have rounded edges and ends and are held by the two stretchers at each end, the slats projecting slightly. Glue and pin from below. When complete the slatted shelf is housed and glued into the legs, and good stout panel pins driven in diagonally from below into the legs.

An alternative for the shelf is to use a piece of 9·5mm. (⅜in.) plywood, this fitting between the stretchers. In some ways this is an advantage in that cups, glasses, etc. are not liable to fall off. The real purpose of the shelf, however, it to hold a spare tray. It is advisable to use 9·5mm. (⅜in.) thick plywood for the tray, the edges being rounded. If solid wood is used it should be sound and dry.

The rim mouldings are bevelled from a wide piece and sawn down. If the bevelled faces are held temporarily together with pins the opposite edges can be bevelled off with the plane. Attach the mouldings by screwing up through the tray bottom, mitring the corners and slightly rounding off from outside.

Cutting list	Long	Wide	Thick
	cm.	cm.	mm.
4 legs	58	4·5	22
2 rails	36	6	22
1 tray moulding	100	6	22
2 rails	60	5·5	19
1 tray	66	42	9·5
4 stretchers	40	2·5	6·5
5 slats	63	5·5	6·5

Garden Lights

The light can either be made single as in Fig. 1, or a two-frame light can be arranged as in Fig. 2. Sizes can be adapted within a little, but it is wise to keep to the 308mm. (12⅛in.) between the rebates as this enables the standard 12in. width of glass to be used. At the time of going to press glass is still being made to imperial sizes. Sometimes the glasses are arranged two or three to an opening, in which case an overlap should be allowed.

Body portion. Construction is given in Fig. 2, sizes being made to suit the frame. Tongued-and-grooved boarding is used, and it is as well to arrange the height so that an even number of boards is used front and back, allowing for the unwanted tongues or grooves to be planed away. Put the front and back together independently, screwing corner posts flush with the ends and (in the case of the double light) cross pieces in the centre. It is advisable to paint all joining edges before fixing.

The ends are added to these, the two bottom complete boards being fixed first. Place the two top boards in position above them, mark a line across with a straight-edge to give the slope, and cut away the unwanted parts. Screw the sides through the posts at the back, and add the guide pieces. The last named stiffen the whole, though centre uprights can be added if there appears to be any weakness. It is advisable to cut draining grooves along the top sloping edges of the sides. For the two-light frame an inverted T section is made by nailing or screwing two pieces together as in Fig. 2. Notches are cut in front and back to receive it. Punch in all nails as the work proceeds. The holes are not stopped, however, until after the priming coat has been given.

Frame. Sizes are given in Fig. 3. If preferred standard section timber can be used, especially in the case of the bars. If this is done it may be necessary to adapt the sizes to suit. Joints of the main frame are given in Fig. 4, and it will be seen that the bottom rail is thinner than the others since the glass has to lie over it. Consequently a bare-faced tenon is needed. A haunch is cut at the lower end as shown. Note that in all the joints mitres are cut and the wood cut away locally opposite the mortise level with the rebate. The advantage of this is that it enables level shoulders to be cut. In all cases the tenons are taken right through and are wedged from outside.

Fig. 5 shows how the bars are joined to the frame.

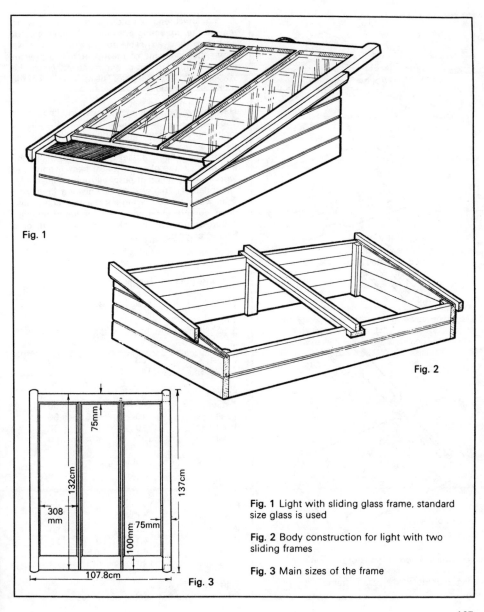

Fig. 1

Fig. 2

Fig. 3

Fig. 1 Light with sliding glass frame, standard size glass is used

Fig. 2 Body construction for light with two sliding frames

Fig. 3 Main sizes of the frame

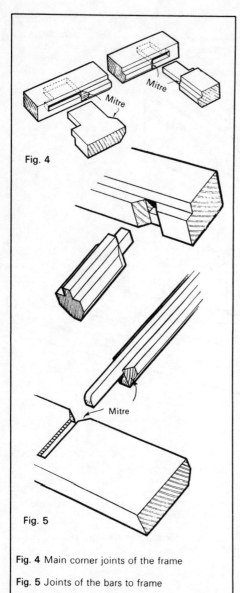

Fig. 4

Fig. 5

Mitre

Mitre

Mitre

Mitre

Fig. 4 Main corner joints of the frame

Fig. 5 Joints of the bars to frame

At the lower end a notch is cut in the rail to receive the projecting portion, and mitres are cut as before. It is advisable to work a drip groove along the underside of the upper rail to prevent moisture from running down inside. Assemble the whole thing with resin glue. The main tenons of the frame are wedged from outside.

Having levelled the joints go over any knots with knotting. Give the whole a coat of priming including all rebates, and when dry fill in all nail holes, cracks, etc., with putty and carry on with the glazing. Thumb a fillet of putty into the rebate and press in the glass so that it beds evenly, and work an even filling of putty all round. Finish with an undercoat followed by a finishing coat, and keep well painted, paying special attention to end grain, corners, etc. It increases the life of the light if it rests upon a row of bricks all round, or a fillet of cement.

Cutting lists Single light

Body	Long cm.	Wide cm.	Thick mm.	
6 pieces	107	15	22	T & G
8 pieces	137	15	22	,,
2 posts	64	5	50	,,
2 posts	33	5	50	,,
2 guides	140	10	23	,,

Frame				
2 stiles	140	7·5	50	,,
1 rail	110	7·5	50	,,
1 rail	110	10	38	,,
2 bars	137	4·4	50	,,

Double light

Body				
6 pieces	220	15	22	T & G
8 pieces	137	15	22	,,
2 posts	64	5	50	,,
2 posts	33	5	50	,,
2 guides	140	10	22	,,
1 T piece	140	7·5	22	,,
1 T piece	140	5·5	22	,,

Frames
As single light but double quantities.

Bench

Essential requirements of a bench are that it is rigid, has a top which is straight and as thick as possible and which can be completely flush when necessary, and is provided with strong vice and planing stop. Size is largely decided by the space available, but the rule is to make it as large as the workshop will allow.

Details. In the bench in Fig. 1 rigidity is ensured by the wide top front rail (apron rail) which is notched over the legs. The top is dependent upon the material available, but assuming that only 25mm. (1in.) stuff is used its freedom from bending is again helped by the wide front rail. If a thicker top is available it would certainly be better, and the sizes in Fig. 2 could be adapted accordingly.

A well is provided, as this enables everyday tools to be kept on top without fouling wide wood placed on the bench. In addition is a wide shelf for larger tools and appliances, and a tool rack at the back. The bench stop is a block of wood which can be tapped in flush. To help in cutting wood at the rear end of the bench an end stop is provided, this again folding down flush. To support long work when held in the vice a series of 12·5mm. (½in.) holes is bored in the right hand leg, a dowel placed in one of these affording a useful resting place.

Framework. For the legs 75mm. by 50mm. (3in. by 2in.) stuff is used. Hardwood such as beech, birch or ash is preferable, but softwood is frequently used with success. Square to section and mark out the joints. The back legs are shorter than those at the front to allow for the tool well, and the top end rails are notched accordingly (Fig. 2).

Side rails are tenoned in, those at the top being haunched as in Fig. 2. Bottom and back rails are also tenoned, and to avoid weakening the wood unduly the bottom rails are staggered, those at

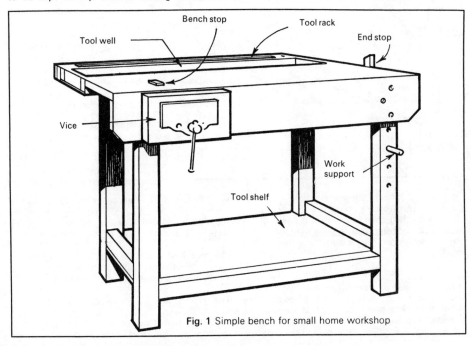

Fig. 1 Simple bench for small home workshop

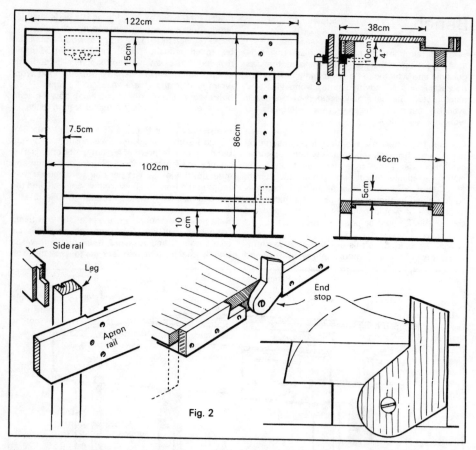

Fig. 2

front and back being immediately below those at the ends. Top front or apron rail (Fig. 2) is not tenoned but is grooved to fit over the face of the legs. A close-fitting joint is essential here as the chief function of this wide rail is to prevent racking.

Glue the two end frames together independently. It is a good plan to draw-bore them. This not only saves having many cramps, but helps to keep the joints tight. The peg hole is bored through the mortise, the tenon cramped in position, and marked by passing the bit into the hole. The parts are

separated and the tenon bored about $1\frac{1}{2}$mm. ($\frac{1}{16}$in.) near the shoulder. The pegs should be slightly pointed to enable them to enter easily. The parts are glued when assembling, of course.

The glue having set the front and back rails are added, these again being preferably draw-bored. Finally glue and screw on the apron rail.

Top. If possible use a hardwood such as beech for this. A thickness of 22mm. ($\frac{7}{8}$in.) the minimum; if possible it should be 50mm. (2in.), in which case the top end and back rails would be cut and positioned to suit. Fix it with screws driven downwards into the front rail, recessing the screws and plugging the holes. At the sides pocket screwing is the simplest method, but the holes should be generous in size to allow for possible movement caused by shrinkage.

The tool tray is like a simple shallow box with edgings nailed or screwed together with a plywood bottom screwed beneath. It is screwed in position, and a tool rack added at the back, this being simply a batten screwed at the back with three distance pieces interposed to enable tools to pass through.

Stops. To receive the bench stop a rectangular hole is cut through the top. The stop itself (of hardwood) is made a tight friction fit in the hole. Fig. 2 shows how the pivoted end stop can be added. It is shaped so that it folds down flush when not in use. Hardwood should be used for it, and an edging should be screwed to the end of the bench as shown. It is not an essential feature and can be omitted if preferred, the bench hook being used for all cross cutting.

Vice. This will certainly require a packing block beneath the top, the thickness depending upon the casting of the vice and the thickness of the top. Quite possibly too the apron rail will have to be recessed to take it, and slots may have to be cut—certainly holes to receive the screw and guide bars will be needed. It is impossible to give exact details since the vice casting varies in different makes. A strong rigid fixing is essential, and the face of the vice must be in line with the edge of the bench. In some cases it may be better to fix the casting to the back of the apron rail rather than in front. A wood check is screwed to the movable jaw.

The addition of a tool shelf completes the bench. It is screwed beneath the side rails, and fillets are added inside front and back rails to support it as in the side section in Fig. 2.

Cutting list

	Long	Wide	Thick
	cm.	mm.	mm.
2 legs	86	75	50
2 legs	84	75	50
1 apron rail	123	160	25
1 rail	102	75	50
2 rails	102	50	50
2 rails	46	—	50 sq.
2 rails	46	100	50
1 top	123	390	25
1 shelf	103	370	12·5 ply
1 well bottom	123	160	6·5 ply
1 well rail	123	30	22
1 well rail	123	50	25
2 well rails	12	50	25
1 tool rack	123	60	12·5

Coffee Table

This is a simple item to make, consisting of a plywood top with two screwed-on rails beneath into which the legs are tenoned. If preferred the top could have a facing of plastic laminate either in colour or in natural wood finish. Its light weight enables the table to be lifted easily to the chair side.

Cut out the top first. It is in 12·5mm. ($\frac{1}{2}$in.) plywood and should preferably be veneered both sides so that it does not tend to pull hollow. If, however, plastic laminate is used there is no bother providing it is put down with contact adhesive. In the latter case two coats of adhesive are advisable on the plywood to give good adhesion. First, however, cut out the top to shape. The curves can be marked out with a lath bent to shape, a pencil being drawn around the edge. A chamfer is worked around the underside as shown in the section in Fig. 1, and the upper corner is rounded. When plastic laminate is to be used the ideal way of cutting is on the bandsaw fitted with a metal-cutting saw. The edge can afterwards be trimmed to a sweet curve, and the lower chamfer worked. Finally the upper corner is rounded.

The two rails are chamfered on their outer edges and ends, and through mortises chopped to take the legs. As the last named slope, the mortises must be cut at a corresponding angle. They must also be wider at the top than at the bottom to allow the wedges to be effective. Fig 3 shows the tenon cut at the top of the leg. Note that the shoulders must be at an angle to give the slope. The ends of the tenon are parallel with the outer line of the leg.

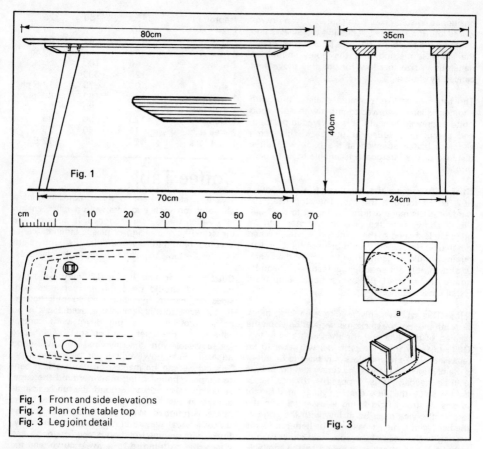

Fig. 1 Front and side elevations
Fig. 2 Plan of the table top
Fig. 3 Leg joint detail

Fig. 3 shows at A the section shape of the legs. Having cut the joints taper the legs from top to bottom in both width and thickness. In width all the taper takes place at the inside. The same thing applies to the thickness. The rounded oval section is now planed as at A Fig. 3. It is advisable to work all four legs progressively, passing from one to the other in stages. Thus tapered chamfers should be worked first on all followed by the rounding over.

Finally glue the legs to the rails, testing for the correct angle and driving in the wedges. When one leg has been glued the others can be tested against it. Lastly the rails are glued and screwed beneath the top. An excellent finish for all wood parts is plastic lacquer diluted to half strength followed by wax polish.

Cutting list

	Long cm.	*Wide* cm.	*Thick* mm.
1 top	81	36	12·5
2 rails	67	6·5	25
4 legs	41	4·5	32

172

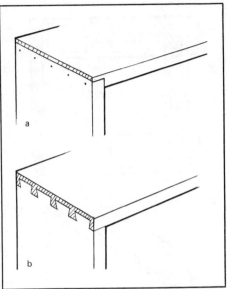

Fig. 1 (left) Room divider with good display space

Fig. 3 (above) Alternative construction of boxes

Room Divider

This would look well with solid parts of mansonia and Australian walnut veneers, or African mahogany solid members and Honduras mahogany veneers. Veneered parts have a groundwork of blockboard, and it should be noted that the grain of the outer layers of this should be at right angles with that of the facing veneers.

Cabinet construction. The various parts of the three boxes should be cut to size and veneered on their inner faces. They are then trimmed and the corner joints cut. For a simple job the plain rebated joint can be cut as at (a), Fig. 3. For a better job lap-dovetails can be cut (b). These illustrations show solid wood being used and this may be preferred. For blockboard the dovetails should be fairly large as otherwise the grain is liable to crumble. In the case of the bottom box a centre division is fitted, and this should be housed in. After assembling the carcases the outer surfaces should be veneered. When the glue has set the overhanging veneer should be trimmed, and the front lippings added.

The fronts of the bottom box could either take the form of doors hinged at the sides, or they could be falls hinged at the bottom and fitted with stays to limit the movement. Both sides are veneered, and at the front the veneer should be about 10mm. bare

173

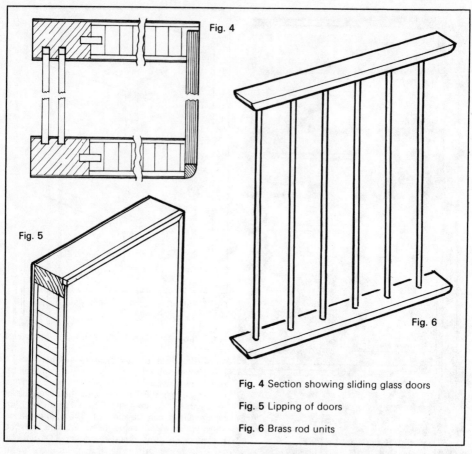

Fig. 4 Section showing sliding glass doors

Fig. 5 Lipping of doors

Fig. 6 Brass rod units

all round. This enables a cutting gauge to be worked round the edges for cross-banding. The waste veneer should be trimmed away before the glue hardens.

In the case of the middle box which has sliding glass doors it is necessary to work grooves near the front edges, and it should be noted that those at the top are double the depth of those at the bottom as shown in Fig. 4, this enabling the doors to be passed upwards and dropped into the bottom grooves. Note that when block-board is used it is

necessary to tongue on facings of solid wood as block board does not lend itself to grooving. Fig. 4 also shows alternative ways of fixing the plywood backs. At the top is a rebate, but a simpler alternative is that at the bottom where the plywood back is fixed straight on and a quarter-round mould added all round.

Stand. This is a separate construction. It is put together with mortise and tenon joints. The legs are tapered, and if the tapering is taken right through as in Fig. 2 the shoulders of the rails must

174

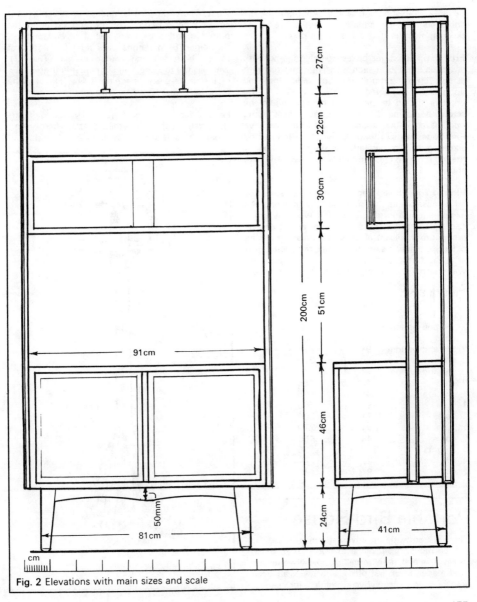

Fig. 2 Elevations with main sizes and scale

175

be at a corresponding angle. Alternatively the shoulders can be square, in which case the tapering must be started below the rails.

Fitting up. The three boxes are held together with two main uprights at each side. They are fixed with screws driven through the box sides into the uprights. Having bored the holes in the boxes, the uprights should be held with cramps whilst the screws are being driven in. It looks neat if the uprights are either chamfered all round or have their edges pencil rounded. The stand is fixed by screwing up from beneath into the bottom box. In the top box two brass rod units are fixed. They are shown in Fig. 6.

Finish. The whole thing should be dismantled as far as possible as this simplifies the finishing. An excellent finish is plastic coating which is brush applied. Several coats are needed, and it can be brought to a brilliant gloss with burnishing cream, or it can be given a semi-matt finish by rubbing over with the finest grade steel wool lubricated with wax polish. Alternatively french polish can be used.

Cutting list

		Long		Wide	Thick
		cm.	mm.	mm.	mm.
2	top and bottom	91	5	235	19
2	ends	27	5	235	19
2	top and bottom	91	5	325	19
2	ends	30	5	325	19
2	top and bottom	91	5	465	19
2	ends	46	5	465	19
1	division	44	–	465	19
1	back	91	–	460	6·5
1	back	91	–	300	6·5
1	back	91	–	270	6·5
2	doors	44	–	450	19
4	uprights	177	–	55	25
4	legs	27	–	—	63 sq.
2	rails	81	–	55	25
2	rails	41	–	55	25

Portable Bird House

There is frequently an advantage in a house that can be moved from place to place. That shown in Fig. 1 is preferably in oak or possibly chestnut. Well made in the first place, and given an occasional coat of preservative, it will last for years.

Post. The main post is made from a 5cm. (2in.) square, and is 147cm. (58in.) long, including the tenons at both ends. Plane it straight, and mark out the joints. Both tenons pass right through, that at the bottom being square in plan (Fig. 3), whereas the top one is in alignment with the grain of the cross-piece in which it fits (Fig. 4). The taper starts just above the struts.

For the feet use 7·5cm. (3in.) by 25mm. (1in.) stuff, halving them together. Blocks 10cm. (4in.) square are screwed on beneath at the ends. Cut

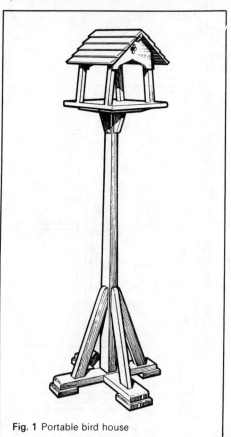

Fig. 1 Portable bird house

the mortise right through the halving, splaying out in one direction beneath so that wedges can be knocked in. The struts are also tenoned to the feet, but join the post itself with a form of sloping notch joint as in Fig. 3. Assemble the whole thing in one operation, fixing the struts on the post, and adding the base. Resin glue, which is water resistant, can be used, but it is advisable to peg the top strut joints.

At the top fit the cross-piece, enlarging the mortise at the top so that there is room for expansion when the wedges are knocked in. Fig. 4 shows how the brackets fit in sloping notches. If cut as shown they can be added after the cross-piece is in position.

House. This is made up complete in itself. Notches are cut in the edges of the floor to receive the uprights which are screwed in. Remember that the inner surfaces must be at a slight angle. Shallow notches at the top receive the gables. The top slope is not cut until later, when it is made to agree with the gable slope. A halved joint is used where the ridge joins the gables. Details

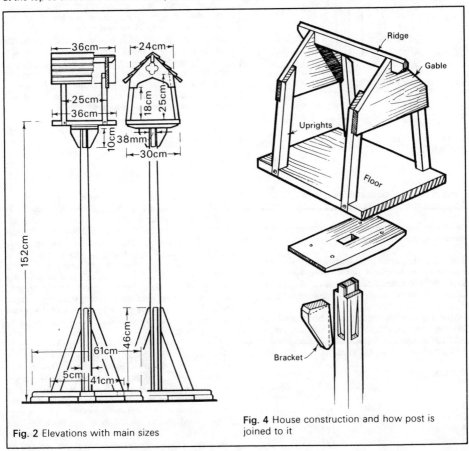

Fig. 2 Elevations with main sizes

Fig. 4 House construction and how post is joined to it

177

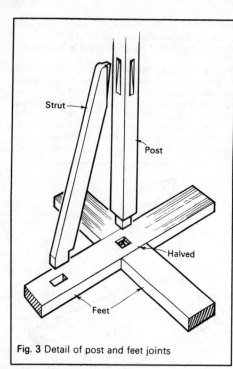

Strut

Post

Halved

Feet

Fig. 3 Detail of post and feet joints

1 table	37	310	25
4 brackets	12	90	25
1 cross piece	31	170	25
4 uprights	32	—	25 sq.
2 gables	26	190	12·5
1 ridge	37	60	20
10 weather boards	37	75	12·5

Jardiniere

Indoor plants have become extremely popular, and this has brought about a revival of the jardiniere, though in revised form to suit modern taste. That shown in Fig. 1 will hold five to six pot plants in the main container at the top, and several on the bottom rack. The sloping sides of the box are the natural outcome of the shape of the usual earthenware pots, but if any special or unusual pots have to be accommodated the size or shape should be altered accordingly.

The box is made up as a separate unit, the legs being fixed to it with screws. Cross-rails tie each pair of end legs together, and the slats which form the rack stiffen the whole. Note that the splay of the legs is desirable to give stability.

Box. This is put together with simple grooved joints. Those who have a machine router will find it a simple matter to work the stopped grooves. Otherwise they will have to be cut by hand methods. A circular saw could be used to partly cut them from the bottoms or open end, but it would have to be stopped well short of the top stop and finished by hand. Theoretically the groove should be cut slightly out of right angles, since both sides and ends slope, forming a compound angle, but the slope is slight and the angle can scarcely be measured. It can therefore be at right angles.

The tongue is easily cut either on the router, the circular saw or with the tenon saw. The tongue is bare-faced, and the first cut should be made across the grain. Use a fine-toothed saw. The thickness of the tongue should be gauged at the end, but the cut should not be made at this stage, because when the moulding of the main surface is carried out the shoulders may otherwise be damaged. Lastly, the bottom edges are rebated to

of the shaping and decorative holes in the last named appear in Fig. 2.

Put the parts together with resin glue, screwing or nailing where required. Screws through the cross-piece hold it in position. For the roofing use either plain tapered boarding or the rebated kind.

Assuming that the house is to be natural colour, give a coat of clear preservative and leave to weather naturally. If preferred, a combined stain and preservative can be used.

Cutting list

	Long	Wide	Thick
	cm.	mm.	mm.
1 post	150	—	50 sq.
2 feet	62	90	25
4 struts	55	60	25
4 blocks	11	110	25

up with glasspaper wrapped around a block. Begin with Middle 2 grade and finish with No. 1½ or No. 1.

The ends are shaped at the top, this being cut on either the bandsaw or the jigsaw, or by hand with the coping saw. It is cleaned up afterwards with a file, followed by scraper and glasspaper held around a rubber.

It will be seen from Fig. 1 that an inlaid panel is fitted at the front. This is not essential, and can be omitted if preferred. Alternatively, it can be a plain panel with a face veneer of an attractive wood. It is fitted in a recess cut at the front.

When assembling wood blocks should be placed beneath the cramp shoes, with paper beneath to prevent damage to the surface. If not enough cramps are available, cord will have to be tied around and tightened tourniquet fashion. In this case corner blocks are essential. The bottom is screwed in finally.

Stand. Legs are prepared first in square-edged form and are tapered. Stub rails are fitted at the top with the rather special mortise-and-tenon joint shown in Fig. 4. Note that the back edge of each leg is taken off at an angle at the top, this enabling square shoulders to be cut on the stub rails. As the leg has to be planed to an oval section, it is necessary to plane the sides of the rail towards the bottom. The simplest way is to fit the joint whilst the wood is still square-edged and to plane the leg to the oval section. When the joint is put together dry, a sharp pencil can be run around at the shoulder showing clearly the extent to which the rail has to be planed away.

After cleaning up, the legs can be fixed with screws driven downwards through the bottom. By planing the top edge of the rail and leg the latter can be set at any required slope. Short cross-rails are fitted at the ends, and the simplest construction is to cut small flats in the legs in which mortises can be cut. Shoulder length is obtained by direct measurement.

The woodwork is completed by the addition of the bottom slats, which are fixed with brass screws fitted into screw cups. As they must bed down flat, the top edge of the end cross rails must be at a slight angle, and this, of course, must be done

Fig. 1 Jardiniere in African mahogany

receive the bottom. The rebate will of course have to be stopped on the ends, and this again calls for the use of the router or chopping out by hand methods. The only other alternative is to take the rebate right through and fill in the ends after assembling.

Moulded surface. This takes the form of a stepped effect rather like the appearance of a venetian blind. There are various ways in which it can be worked, but, whichever way it is done, the main idea is first to cut a series of narrow grooves nearly down to the full depth and work the sloping grooves afterwards. The idea is shown in Figs. 2 and 3. The preliminary grooves are worked either on the circular saw, the router, or with the hand plough.

Lastly, the sloping surface is worked with the rebate plane. Finally, the surfaces are scraped to get rid of tears in the grain, and finally it is cleaned

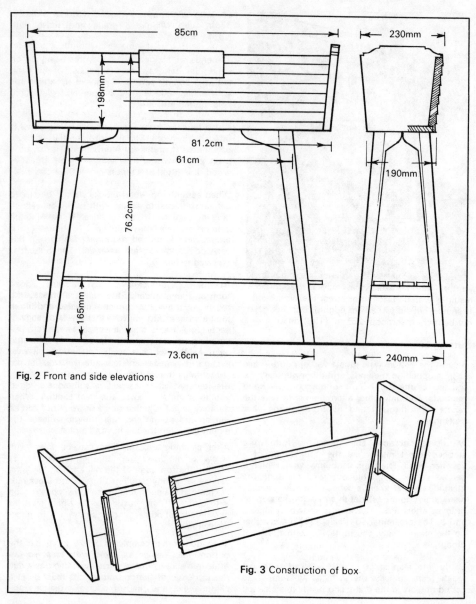

Fig. 2 Front and side elevations

Fig. 3 Construction of box

85cm

230mm

198mm

81.2cm

61cm

190mm

76.2cm

165mm

73.6cm

240mm

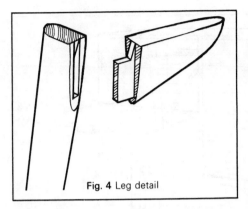

Fig. 4 Leg detail

before the tenons are glued into their mortises. The ends of the slats are cut off at an angle, so that when the four are screwed down they end in a curve.

A desirable addition to the interior is a metal liner, so that any moisture that may leak out as a result of watering does not affect the woodwork. It should have a turned-up edging, but this need not be more than about 25mm. (1in.) deep.

Cutting list

	Long		Wide	Thick
	cm.	mm.	mm.	mm.
2 sides	85	0	205	19
2 ends	—	232	232	19
1 bottom	81	2	190	12
4 legs	58	5	55	32
4 stub rails	16	5	55	32
2 rails	22	8	32	25
4 slats	77	5	38	10

Commodious Sideboard in Teak or Mahogany

This has been designed to enable veneered chipboard to be used for the main structure. The advantage of this material is that it is readily available, faced with either teak or mahogany veneer, whereas solid wood in suitable thicknesses

is more difficult. The only solid parts in fact are the legs and narrow rails. Sizes can be adjusted to suit individual requirements, though the standard sizes of the material should be kept in mind.

Ideally chipboard should be worked with machine tools, especially if tungsten steel cutters are fitted. This enables parts to be cut off dead to size and with complete accuracy so that only a rub with glasspaper is needed to finish off. Furthermore rebates and grooves, etc. can be easily worked. With purely hand methods it is rather more difficult, though it can be done. First the veneer has to be cut through on both sides with chisel or knife, and the saw cut made immediately to the waste side. It is then a matter of trimming with shaper or plane right down to the line. Chipboard is not a pleasant material to plane because only dust can be removed, not shavings, and the edge of the cutter is soon blunted owing to the abrasive nature of the resin adhesive with which the particles are assembled.

Ordinary joints such as dovetails, mortises and tenons, etc. are scarcely practicable, and it is simpler to use butt joints with dowels as shown in Fig. 3. For this it is an economy in the long run to make a dowelling jig, either for marking out the positions or actually to guide the bit or drill. An alternative is to use the special 'Conti join' fittings made for the purpose. These are screwed inside the carcase and hold the parts together with bolts. The only point to note in this case is that for such parts as drawers, etc. there must be clearance for the fittings, and it will probably mean setting down the drawers accordingly.

The main edges of the chipboard are veneered, but where saw cuts have been made it is necessary to veneer afresh. This is usually best done after the joints have been made. For such parts as drawer sides and backs 9·5mm. (⅜in.) plywood is used, though the fronts are in veneered chipboard.

Main carcase. Cut out all the parts for the main carcase first. Note that although the top rests upon the ends, the bottom is contained between them. Since the back fits against fillets set in from

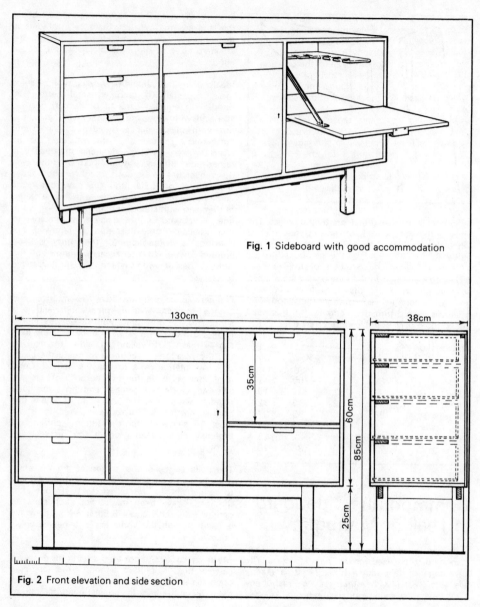

Fig. 1 Sideboard with good accommodation

130cm

38cm

35cm

60cm

85cm

25cm

Fig. 2 Front elevation and side section

the back edges, the ends and top are of the same width. The bottom, divisions, and shelf, however, are narrower by the thickness of the back because the back is fixed directly to their back edges. It will be found convenient to mark the positions of the drawer runners, shelves, etc. before assembling the whole thing—in fact the runners could be glued and screwed in position at this stage.

When gluing up, cramp the two inner divisions to the bottom, slipping in the centre drawer rail whilst doing so. If there is a shortage of cramps the work can be then left for the glue to set, providing that the whole is tested for truth. The main ends are now added, the drawer rails to the left and the shelf to the right being put in at the same time, and the work again set aside. Finally the top is glued down. It will be seen from Fig. 3 that square fillets are fixed inside the top corners, these being glued and screwed. They add considerably to the strength. They are set in at the front by the thickness of the chipboard drawer fronts and flap. The addition of the plywood

back screwed to fillets glued and pinned to the top and ends completes the main carcase.

Stand. At this stage the stand can be made. Solid wood is used throughout. The rails are tenoned to the legs, and there are two intermediate cross rails either dowelled or slot-dovetailed in. Glue the front and back rails to their legs and put aside for the glue to set before adding the end and intermediate rails. Pocket screws are used to fix the stand beneath the main carcase.

Drawers, etc. The most suitable construction is shown in Fig. 4. The plywood sides are fitted into rebates in the fronts. If these rebates are taken right across it is necessary to glue in blocks at the top corners because the sides stand down by the thickness of the drawer rails. It makes a neater job, however, if the rebates are stopped as at A, but it takes rather longer to cut the rebates. At the back through dovetails are used in the best way, though some may prefer the simpler alternative of the grooved joint at B.

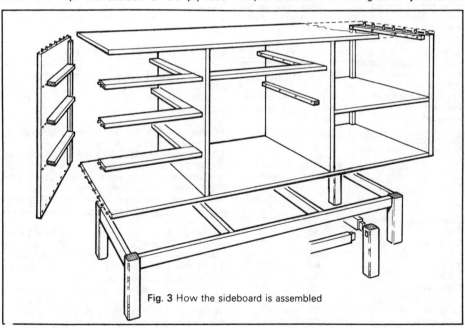

Fig. 3 How the sideboard is assembled

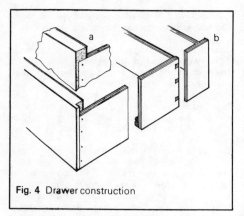

Fig. 4 Drawer construction

The bottom fits in a groove in the front, and in grooved drawer bottom moulding at the sides.

It will probably be necessary to joint two pieces of veneered chipboard for the main door. If the joining edges are veneered the veneer should preferably be removed first. When a close joint has been made four or five dowels should be used to strengthen it. A strip hinge is used to the left and fillets fixed beneath the drawer rail above and to the side of the partition to act as a stop.

For either mahogany or teak plastic coating can be used, or for a dull finish teak oil may be preferred.

Cutting list

	Long cm.	Wide cm.	Thick mm.
			Veneered chipboard
1 top	131	38	17
1 bottom	128	38	17
2 ends	61	38	17
2 divisions	58	38	17
1 shelf	45	38	17
1 door	47	47	17
1 flap	47	36	17
1 drawer front	36	12	17
1 drawer front	36	15	17
1 drawer front	36	17	17
1 drawer front	36	18	17
1 drawer front	46	12	17
1 drawer front	46	22	17
			Ply
1 back	130	60	6·5
1 back	36	10	9·5
1 back	36	13	9·5
1 back	36	15	9·5
1 back	36	16	9·5
1 back	46	10	9·5
1 back	46	20	9·5
2 sides	36	12	9·5
2 sides	36	15	9·5
2 sides	36	17	9·5
2 sides	36	18	9·5
2 sides	36	12	9·5
2 sides	36	22	9·5
4 drawer bottoms	35	35	5
2 drawer bottoms	45	35	5
			Solid
3 rails	36	5·5	22
1 rail	46	5·5	22
4 legs	27	5 sq.	—
2 rails	107	5·5	22
2 rails	35	5·5	22
2 rails	31	5·5	22

Garden Workshop

The shed in Fig. 1 is made in sections to be bolted together. The sizes are given in Fig. 2, but these could be adapted within a little to suit any special requirements.

Framework. For the main framework 50mm. by 38mm. (2in. by 1½in.) stuff is used, though 50mm. (2in.) squares would make a more rigid structure. Cut off the various members to length, and fit the uprights into the horizontals with notched joints. This is stronger than plain butted joints since the notches resist side thrust. Test for squareness with a diagonal rod, and fit the sloping struts.

Covering. The boarding should be from 16mm. (⅝in.) to 22mm. (⅞in.) thick. For thin stuff the rebated joint shown in Fig. 4 is effective. Thicker boards should be tongued and grooved. Cut off the boards full to allow a plane to be run along after fixing. The boarding of the short gable ends finishes flush at the ends, but that of the long sections projects by an amount equal to the thickness of the framing (see enlarged section in

Fig. 2). The fixing of the boarding to finish flush is obvious, but for the long sides it is advisable to have an odd piece of framing material handy to use as a guide for the projection at the end. Nail to the framework and punch the nails in straight away.

At the window openings the boarding at the sides finishes at the middle of the upright framework member (see Fig. 4). This enables the square fillet (B) to be nailed in afterwards. At top and bottom of the window opening the boarding finishes flush, and it may be necessary to trim the boards back locally. At the bottom a sill with sloping edge and drip groove is cut in and nailed on (Fig. 4), and at top a similar member is fixed. Finally the fillets (A) are nailed all round to make the windows weatherproof. They are set back by the thickness of the window frames.

At the door aperture the boarding finishes at the middle of the uprights similarly to the windows. This allows finishing fillets to be nailed on. To make the door weather-proof fillets are nailed around the opening. The boarding of the door stands in front of the bottom rail of the framework.

Floor. The side frames having been put together the floor should be made. Tongued and grooved 19mm. (¾in.) or 22mm. (⅞in.) boards are desirable. They are nailed down on to four joists at least 50mm. (2in.) square in section. It would make a stronger job to have 75mm. (3in.) by 50mm. (2in.) stuff. If a concrete base is to be laid the floor can rest directly on it. Otherwise a number of brick piers should be used to keep the timber away from the ground. Every joist should be supported at both ends, and preferably at the centre also.

Dig holes for the bricks and consolidate by tamping. Make all as level as possible, using a long straight-edge and spirit level. Lay the floor in position, and erect the sides. Later it may be necessary to carry out some adjustment of the level, and a convenient method is to make pairs of folding wedges in oak and drive these between the joists and bricks at any point where the floor sags. If you stoop down level with the floor and look along, any sag will be at once obvious.

Erecting. Put two adjacent sections together, knock in a couple of temporary nails, and bore two holes right through to receive the bolts. These

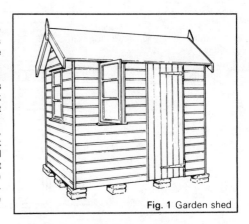

Fig. 1 Garden shed

should be 8mm. (₅⁄₁₆in.) or 9½mm. (⅜in.) round-heads with square shoulders. Oil the threads, and put washers beneath the nuts.

When all four sections are together the top boarding end of the long sides can be bevelled to align with the slope of the ends. Note also that blocks (X) in Fig. 2 are nailed in on the sloping ends. They serve to strengthen the gable end. The outer corners of the shed are filled with fillets nailed in. Fix them to one side or the other, not both.

Roof. One section of this is shown in Fig. 3. It consists of a series of 16mm. (⅝in.) tongued boards nailed to two purlins. Cut all the boards to length and nail the whole together. The ridge edge is planed at an angle so that a mitre is formed when the two sections are in position. To receive the upper purlin a notch has to be cut in both gable ends. This is essential because, apart from making a close fit, the notch serves to hold the purlin rigidly. The two roof sections should just drop into position.

To hold the roof down screws can be driven upwards through the sloping framing rails of the gable ends into the purlins. Two battens are also fixed to the lower side of the roof with screws driven from the outside. These battens should be level with the inside of the framework. Screws driven through them into the latter hold the roof firmly. When it is not intended that the shed shall

185

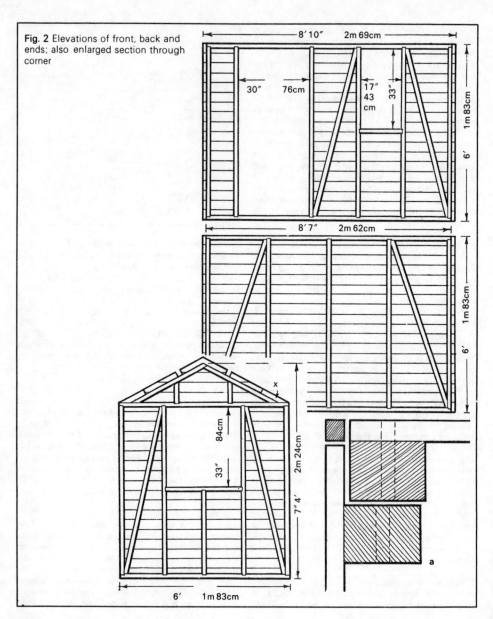

Fig. 2 Elevations of front, back and ends; also enlarged section through corner

186

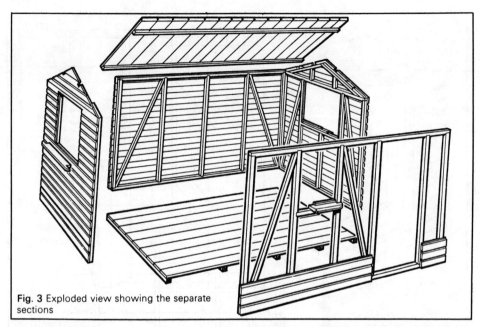

Fig. 3 Exploded view showing the separate sections

ever be dismantled the whole roof can be nailed down.

Three strips of roofing felt run along the length. Allow overlap for it to be turned under all round, and fix the two lower strips first. Hold in position temporarily with a couple of tacks each, and lay the centre strip which will lie right over the apex and overlap those below by several inches. Tack along the bottom edge using galvanised roofing nails.

The addition of barge boards nailed on at the ends completes the roof.

Windows. These are best made from standard sash material put together with the usual wedged mortise and tenon joint as in Fig. 5. The double windows can both be hinged, or one can be made a close fit and nailed in position. The centre join is made weather-proof by rebating the joining edges and inserting a bead in the moving frame. The glass is puttied in, but the rebate must be primed before the putty is applied.

Door. In the simplest way this can be the simple ledged and braced type shown in Fig. 5. Note that the ledges stand in at the edges so that they clear the framework.

Painting. Three coats of paint are needed, priming, undercoat, and gloss coat. The former should be given before any of the nail holes, etc., are filled with putty. The first step, however, is to go over all knots with two coats of knotting with a drying period of at least half an hour between.

Cutting list

The covering boards will have to be varied in accordance with the width of material available.

	Long Metres cm.		Wide mm.	Thick mm.
Gable ends				
12 uprights, struts	1	83	50	38
4 horizontals	1	88	50	38
2 uprights	—	97	50	38

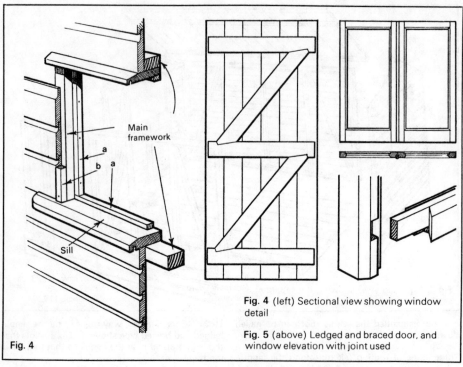

Fig. 4 (left) Sectional view showing window detail

Fig. 5 (above) Ledged and braced door, and window elevation with joint used

Fig. 4

4 roof rails	–	97	50	38
4 uprights	–	31	50	38
2 window rails	–	86	50	38

Long sides

15 uprights, struts	1	83	50	38
4 horizontals	2	70	50	38
1 window rail	–	48	50	38

About 150 metre run of 100mm. (sight) by 16mm. to 22mm. T & G Boarding for covering all four sides. This should be in lengths which will cut economically into 2·70 metres and 1·83 metres lengths.

Door

6 pieces	1	86	150 (sight)	22
3 ledges	–	76	100	22
2 braces	1	10	100	22

Windows

4 sills, drips	–	92	120	22
2 sills, drips	–	56	120	22
8 stiles	–	92 sash mould		
8 rails	–	46 sash mould		

Floor

9 boards	2	70	200	22
5 joists	1	83	50 or 75	50

Roof

32 pieces	1	10	180	16
4 purlins	2	80	50	38

Lengths allow for cutting. Widths and thicknesses are nominal. If the board widths vary the metre run will have to be corrected accordingly.

188

Index